PERFORMANCE AND RELIGION
IN EARLY MODERN ENGLAND

ReFormations: Medieval and Early Modern

SERIES EDITORS: DAVID AERS, SARA BECKWITH, AND JAMES SIMPSON

RECENT TITLES IN THE SERIES

The English Martyr from Reformation to Revolution (2012)
Alice Dailey

Transforming Work: Early Modern Pastoral and Late Medieval Poetry (2013)
Katherine C. Little

Writing Faith and Telling Tales: Literature, Politics, and Religion in the Work of Thomas More (2013)
Thomas Betteridge

Unwritten Verities: The Making of England's Vernacular Legal Culture, 1463–1549 (2015)
Sebastian Sobecki

Mysticism and Reform, 1400–1750 (2015)
Sara S. Poor and Nigel Smith, eds.

The Civic Cycles: Artisan Drama and Identity in Premodern England (2015)
Nicole R. Rice and Margaret Aziza Pappano

Tropologies: Ethics and Invention in England, c. 1350–1600 (2016)
Ryan McDermott

Volition's Face: Personification and the Will in Renaissance Literature (2017)
Andrew Escobedo

Shadow and Substance: Eucharistic Controversy and English Drama across the Reformation Divide (2017)
Jay Zysk

Queen of Heaven: The Assumption and Coronation of the Virgin in Early Modern English Writing (2018)
Lilla Grindlay

PERFORMANCE AND RELIGION

in Early Modern England

Stage, Cathedral, Wagon, Street

MATTHEW J. SMITH

University of Notre Dame Press
Notre Dame, Indiana

University of Notre Dame Press
Notre Dame, Indiana 46556
undpress.nd.edu
All Rights Reserved

Copyright © 2019 by University of Notre Dame

Published in the United States of America

Names: Smith, Matthew J., 1983- author.
Title: Performance and religion in early modern England : stage, cathedral, wagon, street / Matthew J. Smith.
Description: Notre Dame, Indiana : University of Notre Dame Press, 2018. | Series: Reformations: medieval and early modern | Includes bibliographical references and index. |
Identifiers: LCCN 2018043817 (print) | LCCN 2018050418 (ebook) | ISBN 9780268104672 (pdf) | ISBN 9780268104689 (epub) | ISBN 9780268104658 (hardback : alk. paper) | ISBN 9780268104665 (pbk. : alk. paper)
Subjects: LCSH: English drama—Early modern and Elizabethan, 1500–1600—History and criticism. | Christian drama, English—England—History and criticism. | Mysteries and miracle-plays, English—History and criticism. | Liturgy and drama—England. | Rites and ceremonies in literature. | Religion in literature. | Theater—England—History—16th century.
Classification: LCC PR658.R43 (ebook) | LCC PR658.R43 S65 2018 (print) | DD 822/.309—dc23
LC record available at https://lccn.loc.gov/2018043817

∞ *This paper meets the requirements of ANSI/NISO Z39.48-1992 (Permanence of Paper).*

for Ashley

CONTENTS

List of Illustrations ix
Acknowledgments xi

Prelude 1

Chapter One
Early Modern Theatricality across the Reformation 13

Chapter Two
The Real Presence/Absence of God in the Chester Cycle Plays 52

Chapter Three
Henry V and the Ceremonies of Theater 114

Chapter Four
God's Idioms: Sermon Belief in Donne's London 155

Chapter Five
Performing Religion in Early Modern Ballads 192

Chapter Six
The Devils among Us: Intertheatricality in *Doctor Faustus* and Its Afterlives 253

Postlude: Ending with a Jig 308

Notes 322
Bibliography 351
Index 376

ILLUSTRATIONS

Figure 2.1. Bakers at work, in *Ordinary of the Company of Bakers in the city of York*, ca. 1600 — 77

Figure 2.2. *Cena Domini* and *Manna Datur Filiis Israel*, in *Speculum Humanae Salvationis*, 1375–1400 — 79

Figure 2.3. Feast of Corpus Christi, in *Missale ad vsum insignis ecclesie Sarisburiensis*, 1555 — 89

Figure 4.1. Wenceslaus Hollar, *Interior of Old St. Pauls*, 1656 — 162

Figure 4.2. *St. Paul's Cathedral Precinct*, copperplate map of London, 1559 — 163

Figure 4.3. Wire frame image of the acoustic model, Paul's Churchyard, the Cross Yard — 165

Figure 4.4. John Gipkyn, *Old St Paul's (sermon at St Paul's Cross)*, 1616 — 168

Figure 5.1. Ballad, "The Heartie Confession of a Christian," 1593 — 216

Figure 5.2. "The order for the buryal *of the dead*," in *The boke of common praier*, 1573 — 220

Figure 5.3. *The Holy Gospel of Iesus Christ according to Iohn*, Geneva Bible, 1602 — 222

Figure 5.4. Ballad, "A Song of Syon of the Beauty of Bethell," 1642 — 224

Figure 5.5. Ballad, "The Dying Tears of a Penitent Sinner," 1678–80 — 229

FIGURE 5.6. Ballad, "Great Brittains Arlarm to Drowsie Sinners in Destress," 1672–96 — 237

FIGURE 5.7. Ballad, "Some Fyne Gloues," 1560–70 — 249

FIGURE 6.1. Master of the Holy Kinship, *Mass of St. Gregory*, 1486 — 255

FIGURE 6.2. Ballad, "The Judgment of God shewed upon one John Faustus," 1686–88 — 270

FIGURE 6.3. Ballad, "The Just Judgment of GOD shew'd upon Dr. John Faustus," 1640 — 271

FIGURE 6.4. Ballad, "The Judgment of God shewed upon one John Faustus," 1686–88 — 272

FIGURE 7.1. Ballad, "Frauncis new Iigge," 1617 — 312

ACKNOWLEDGMENTS

As I write these words to the people who have helped me create this book, I think first of those who have contributed over many years to my learning so as to make academic study possible and desirable for me in the first place. I want foremost to acknowledge my parents, Richard and Janice, for their support and steering from what has seemed to me time immemorial.

I'm eager also to recognize certain teachers whose words, wiles, and gambits I remember well and often repurpose for my own students—David Albertson, Virginia Doland, Deborah Harkness, Joseph Henderson, Cynthia Herrup, Tony Kemp, Clare Costley King'oo, Aaron Kleist, Greg Kneidel, Jeffrey Lehman, Robert Llizo, Marc Malandra, Ed McCann, Todd Pickett, Tom Recchio, John Mark Reynolds, Mary Robertson, David Rollo, Meg Russett, Fred Sanders, Melissa Schubert, Greg Semenza, Paul Spears, and Dan Yim. This book covers numerous types of performance, each with its own history, archive, and body of criticism; and consequently, these different genres and events are tied in my mind to distinct individuals I've named. I wonder now if this breadth has been a blessing or a curse, but, at any rate, the book now exists as a mnemonic index of my many wonderful teachers.

I am grateful to Heather James and Rebecca Lemon for their invaluable notes and guidance, especially during the earliest years of this project. I am proud, moreover, of the singular influence that Bruce Smith has had on my intellectual habits and proclivities. Whatever small portion of creativity and interdisciplinarity made its way into this book is gleaned from his advice and encouragement.

Many other literary scholars have helped me to think more carefully about the ideas in this study, and surely their influence has been more encouraging and constructive for me than they realize. Sometimes such help has come through friendship, correspondence, collaboration, translation assistance, or reading; other times it has come by way of disagreement, critique, or simply an insightful post-talk question. I would like to thank Sarah Beckwith, Rebecca Cantor, Roger Clegg, Kevin Curran, Ramon Elinevsky, Lori Anne Ferrell, Gavin Fort, Patricia Fumerton, Lowell Gallagher, Penelope Geng, Diane Glancy, Jim Kearney, John Kennedy, James Knapp, Kent Lehnhof, Naomi Liebler, Larry Manley, Meghan Davis Mercer, Christopher Perreira, Debora Shuger, Patricia Taylor, and Thomas Ward. A particularly wonderful and unexpected blessing in these early years of my career has come in the friendship, collaboration, and mentorship of Julia Reinhard Lupton. Her intellectual generosity has been unparalleled.

I thank my colleagues and friends at Azusa Pacific University and especially in the Department of English. I'm particularly indebted to Mark Eaton and Caleb Spencer, my friends and coeditors, for their continual audience and confidence in me. So much rests on keen and dependable conversation. I'm grateful as well to my deans, Jennifer Walsh and David Weeks, and to the institution as a whole for research support. My students at APU have been a source of inspiration, and I want to thank Jeremy Byrum, John Eliot Reasoner, and Emma Lee for their help with formatting.

Research for this project was made possible and enhanced by the financial support of several institutions, including a research grant from the Renaissance Society of America, a graduate research grant at the Huntington Library, a Francis Bacon Fellowship in Renaissance Studies at the Huntington Library, and the J. Leeds Barroll Prize from the Shakespeare Association of America. The Huntington Library, its Early Modern Studies Institute, and the Renaissance Literature seminar—organized by Heather James and Heidi Brayman Hackel—in particular have provided vital intellectual community. I'd be remiss without also recognizing the outstanding resource of the Early Broadside Ballad Archive at the University of California Santa Barbara, without which this book would have taken much longer to write. And the captions accompanying my illustrations acknowledge the help of the museums and libraries who have provided images.

An earlier and shorter version of chapter 3 was published in *Studies in English Literature* as "The Experience of Ceremony in

Henry V" (2014); and a version of chapter 4 was published in *English Literary Renaissance* by that chapter's same title (2016).

This book would not have been possible without the sort of support that only family can provide. For helping to make my life smoother, sustainable, and richer, I want to acknowledge the Berrys, the Honorés, my brother Ryan and his family, and my friends in Colorado. My unending gratitude goes to my wife and children. This book was written with the regular interruptions of my children playing outside the office door—and I don't regret the ten times out of ten that I've set down my book to accept their invitation. Cecily, Ambrose, and Richard, thank you for opening my eyes. Finally, I dedicate this book to my wife, Ashley, its *sine qua non*.

PRELUDE

Of the theatrical events performed in early modern England, commercial plays of the sort written by William Shakespeare, Ben Jonson, Thomas Middleton, and others have enjoyed by far the most literary historical attention, but they appear as just one pattern in the fabric of a greater performance culture. Plays existed not only alongside but also within and as containers for numerous other performance types, including cycle and miracle plays, masques, jigs, ballads, state processions, interludes, church liturgies, seasonal games, town wait songs, royal entertainments, and sermons. Deciding to view these different kinds of performance together potentially decenters commercial drama from its privileged place in depictions of the early modern theatrical climate, not because commercial plays diminish in historical significance but because they come to appear as less exclusive of other performance types with which they share environmental, dramaturgical, and occasional conditions. The various events of early modern English theatrical culture shared performance spaces, existed in common festival occasions, and, importantly, encountered a performance-going public that was practiced at viewing, participating in, demanding from, and even reproducing the events they attended.

In *Performance and Religion in Early Modern England*, I offer a wide view of early modern performance culture in England through thick descriptions of individual performances' environments, occasions, early reception histories, shared dramaturgical practices, and audience responses. My goal is to arrive at a both broader and denser definition of early modern theatricality itself—at once an abstract idea as well as a practical grid of presentational strategies and habits of audience engagement across performance genres. What I find in this study of plays, cycle drama, liturgy, state ceremony, sermons, ballads, and jigs is not only a cohesive performance culture that understood itself collectively but also a network of events that made nuanced performative use of this self-understanding. Early modern performance types constantly invoked one another in order to conjure a sense of mutuality and even responsibility among a performance-going public. A given event could use the environment and audience at hand to induce dramatic themes in the present moment, performatively repeated by the audience and carried into the social event around them.

A key reflection that becomes clear in a comparative approach to performances during and after the Protestant Reformation is that the theatrical is intertwined with the religious. This is apparent even in a quick scan of the performance types that existed. Some evolved from Christian festivals, while others continued to serve explicitly spiritual ends; and many crossed the Reformation divide. In the decades that followed the Reformation in England the psychological and material conditions of theatrical engagement developed within a religious society increasingly sensitive to the power of media over the emotions and faith. It is debatable as to how much the Reformation changed the role of visual and physical media in devotion, but what is certain is that reform movements drew attention to these media's theological and somatic complexities. Producers, performers, and audience members knew about the power of the theatrical to shape realities beyond their fictional and represented content; and accordingly performances took advantage of the "drama of performative utterance" created by a religious society that was conscious of continuities, losses, and promises involved in redefining its practices of devotion and theatrical signification.[1] The emergence of new forms of stage play, street performance, and liturgy coincided with experimentation with old and new theatrical strategies, as the "gap between language and the body afforded the playwright a new reach, cogency, and mobility in the uses of embodied signs."[2] In many ways, I will argue, various performance events continued to look to religious forms like ritual, festival, and Christian community as foundational resources for influencing the lives of their audiences. And it is largely through religion that early modern theater went beyond representation and attempted to create and augment reality. Even genres that might be located closer to the secular end of the spectrum of performance contexts faced their audiences—like a character's aside—and called them to action in the space and time of their events to participate in theatrical making, spiritual edification, and the formation of community.

Recent years' scholarship on early English drama has moved toward the comparative, and it is no surprise that much of this work presents religion as the dramaturgical and social glue that holds different kinds of performance together. In addition to overtly dramatic forms like masques, the performance types that scholars perhaps most frequently connect to the commercial stage are miracle and cycle theater. Recent books by Sarah Beckwith, Lawrence Clopper, Helen Cooper, Beatrice Groves, and Kurt Schreyer have argued that the sharing of practices between medieval and early modern theater is fueled by mutual notions of theatrical power and its foundations in religious and festival culture.[3] Schreyer's term for this relationship across the Reformation period is *synchronic diachrony*, characterized by Shakespeare's use of medieval dramatic conventions such as particular sound effects, stage spaces, and props to enable new performances to take advantage of the traditional perceptual habits of audiences while simultaneously and often by the same mechanism creating new interpretations.[4] Groves similarly styles Shakespeare's plays as under the influence of medieval aesthetic sensibilities, creating a "culture ripe for the most verbally sophisticated and visually affective dramaturgy."[5] Such studies on the lasting theatrical intersections between medieval and Renaissance drama consistently succeed in tempering assumptions about early modern novelty in theater history, and yet the scope of this work is out of balance with how little has been done to connect such medieval heritages to other early modern genres, or even to playwrights besides Shakespeare.

I believe that a clue as to why we have witnessed an increase in comparative approaches and yet why these studies still tend to be limited to comparing only two performance types is provided by Lawrence Clopper: "When we attempt to construct a history of the 'theater,' we put the theater at the center of the discussion and force the documents to operate within that arena. When we look for the emergence of drama from the liturgy—the problem of origins— we not only evoke an evolutionary model but may ignore how medieval writers imagined the liturgy to relate to the *theatrum*."[6] Clopper conveys the difficulty in attempting to discern the throughlines of the late medieval and early modern entertainment world as they might appear before us organically, as it were. Defining theatricality is intrinsically tendentious, first, because historical performances do not typically announce the extent and nature of their own theatrical manifestations, and, second, because many of the most direct characterizations of theatricality come in the forms of antitheatrical statements. The Elizabethan jig, for example, is frequently criticized by antitheatricalists for being bawdy; but should we understand the polemical source to make this trait of bawdiness more or less descriptive of jig theatricality? And while the proliferation of work on early drama is moving toward a broader approach to defining the theatrical climate through various and often competing forms, in practice many of these studies find a kind of historical closure with the commercial play and Shakespeare in particular. In this way, writing a history of performance is like writing a self-fulfilling prophecy: perhaps expanding the scope of the theatrical into diverse manifestations of *theatrum* at one end of the Reformation period will present new theatrical forms and insights at the other.

Indeed, few full-length studies have looked comparatively at other performance types, but what has been examined is challenging and insightful. Several scholars have investigated connections between plays and performed prayers within plays. Ramie Targoff, Joseph Sterrett, Daniel Swift, and Timothy Rosendale have explicated the theatrical inspiration that prayer offered playwrights for representing affect, character depth, and a common spoken form of devotion.[7] Branching outside the playhouse to the church (and back again), Jeffrey Knapp has written on how the rapid growth of commercial theater in Elizabethan England interacted with sermon culture.[8] He explores the personnel intersections between plays and sermons, noting especially the presence of chorister boy players, clergy playwrights, and clergy players, and describes the stage as a place of spiritual community. Moreover, Christopher Marsh, Bruce Smith, and Patricia Fumerton have traced some of the performative and cultural interchanges between ballads and other performance types, suggesting that ballads were powerful intertheatrical tools because of their mobility, "lyrical intensity," and "power to colonize oral culture."[9] And rounding out this incomplete list of comparative performance studies is research on the intratheatrical activities that existed alongside and within plays. Scholars including Andrew Gurr, Tiffany Stern, David Wiles, Robert Weimann, and Douglas Bruster have elucidated the importance of the music, dances, games, and clowning that filled the play event.[10] I suggest that what emerges in these pairings of plays and sermons, cycle drama and stage practice, character and prayer, is a coherent though varied glimpse of early modern theatricality that is not reducible to print, polemics, or authors but manifests most visibly in the ideas about performance itself that such events deployed.

Coinciding with such comparative work are recent studies on the physical conditions of early modern performance, especially in plays. And because of the rich medieval and theological heritage of Renaissance theater, the materiality of drama and the materiality of religion are often studied together. This focus on the material approaches primarily from two historical angles. Scholars like Jennifer Waldron, Margaret Owens, Katharine Eisaman Maus, Katharine Craik, Tanya Pollard, Ken Jackson, and Jay Zysk have shown how theater took advantage of the new representational categories provided by the Protestant Reformation's repositioning of the human body vis-à-vis sensual desire, the embodiment of inward spiritual states, and the question of human versus divine agency.[11] Conversely, scholars including Michael O'Connell, Elizabeth Williamson, Jane Hwang

Degenhardt, Kristen Poole, Erika Lin, and others have explored how the physical components of performance channel the Reformation's heightened sensitivity toward potentially conflicted objects, sights, spaces, and icons.[12]

The picture of performance culture that I'm outlining shows early modern theatricality appearing among the overlapping dimensions of the intertheatrical, the religious, and the material. And I want to argue that such attention to the variegated objects, spaces, and conditions through which audiences attended to performances amounts to a historical phenomenology of theater. As Smith describes it, historical phenomenology is an "erotics of reading" that "recognizes the embodiedness of historical subjects and attends to the materiality of the evidence they have left behind at the same time that it acknowledges the embodiedness of the investigator in the face of that evidence."[13] And as I've summarized elsewhere, "What this approach especially adopts from the philosophies of Edmund Husserl, Merleau-Ponty, and others . . . is a suspicion of abstracting and concluding too quickly about what a thing is, a text is, a symbol is."[14] In an introductory essay entitled "The Turn to Religion in Early Modern English Studies," Ken Jackson and Arthur Marotti argue that the recent turn to religion in early modern studies "is prefigured by a turn to religion in the French Continental philosophy that informs it," and I would suggest that many of the theatrical conjunctions among a performance event, its performance-going public, and the religious culture of post-Reformation England are observable through slowed-down attention to "the intentional object as intended."[15] As I discuss in chapter 1, a fuller description of early modern theatricality recognizes a habit of performances to subject themselves and their narrative themes overtly to the specific environmental, social, and sensory conditions of an audience member's encounter, while at the same time drawing attention to the singularity of each individual perspective. The result is a dialectical exercise familiar to phenomenological reflection. Namely, many early modern performances instigate a kind of reflection, a call to acknowledge the perspective of another by taking inventory of one's own point of view as individual, yet active within the historical frame of such individuality. Aspects of the phenomenological tradition can help us to approximate a performative self-consciousness that is more than the sum of its parts and that is certainly more than the theatrical overlaps between two genres only. Such an approach can, in fact, help us to become more fully comparative by honing, with each additional genre under consideration, the distinct engagements with spiritual community and performative self-reflexivity that characterize the theatrical milieu of the period and region.

Theatricality thus exists in the intentional spaces between and across venues, kinds, and the Reformation divide. Studying theatricality means investigating the content not just of performances but of historical audiences' activities of attending to them. In ballad performances, these activities might take the form of the labor of theatrical production or the exchange of goods or payment, or they might involve a self-conscious transition from liturgical participation to dramatic spectatorship. Alternatively, theatricality at one of London's higher-profile sermons often meant constant confrontation with distractions and the repetitive practices of note-taking. And the especially provocative theatricality of postlude jigs demanded the capaciousness and flexibility of audience expectations, as the potentially horrifying final act of a play concluded only to give way to the re-entrance of the clown, who conducted a bawdy and comedic farce.

Performance and Religion in Early Modern England rethinks the strategies of early modern theatricality and, in so doing, expands our view of the mutuality of performance culture in the contexts of religion. At the heart of my argument is the opinion that early modern theatrical and religious practices are fully comprehended only by comparison to one another and through a comparative study of multiple performance types, allowing us to triangulate the through-lines of broader performance culture and the habits of its audiences. My focus is on what performances looked, sounded, felt, and even tasted like, on the environmental and perceptual conditions that performances discovered and deployed to shape audience attention. It is my contention not only that the social and physical conditions through which performances appeared before audiences had direct influence on the reception of their religious material but also that performances created spaces where audiences could both imaginatively comprehend and immediately enact their social, festive, ethical, and religious overtures.

THE ORGANIZATION OF chapters is chronological, with the caveat that the chapter on ballads covers roughly one hundred years of publication. Similarly, the final body chapter on *Doctor Faustus* is essentially an attempt to theorize the reception both of play audiences and of the audiences of the Faustus-affiliated ballads that evolved throughout the seventeenth century, so it is situated last.

Chapter 1 offers three performance vignettes—boy bishop festivities, Elizabeth I's coronation progress, and a scene from *Twelfth Night*—that represent historically distinct sites for examining theatricality across the Reformation period. These three scenes also serve as bearing points for the chapter's description of the phenomenology of early modern theater, which I define with reference to modern theories of performativity in language and culture. Such awareness of the performative mode, I suggest, is not anachronistic but results largely from the heightened media consciousness that developed throughout the Reformation period. I conclude by revisiting an Elizabethan debate over sacraments and ceremonialism and by translating its vocabulary of mediation to that of performance culture broadly, represented in this chapter by readings of Augustine and Shakespeare.

In chapter 2, I explore how the Chester Whitsun cycle echoes and departs from the theology of perception found in the medieval Feast of Corpus Christi and from the sacrament that it celebrates. Dramatic conflict in the cycle is inaugurated by a theatrical event that Elizabethan commercial theater came to assume as a precondition of dramatic action: namely, the disappearance of God. As a result, the plays in the cycle, and especially the central episode of *The Last Supper*, speak to the transition from medieval to early modern drama. The sudden disappearance of God in the opening *Fall of Lucifer* seems initially to foreshadow the artificial and histrionic aspects of the ensuing cycle, but the play redirects audience attention to the perceptual activities of sight and touch to reframe the theatrical within a theology of the sign, here performatively manifest in the physical materials and social body at hand.

In chapter 3, I explore in depth the ways that Shakespeare invites comparison of theatrical, religious, and political "ceremony" in *Henry V*. Many scholars of religion and drama have been drawn to *Henry V* for its abundant Christian rhetoric and sacramental imagery, often depicting King Henry as a champion of a specific doctrinal position. I argue that Shakespeare uses ceremony—a combination of the religious, political, and dramaturgical—as a device for enacting what we might call Henry's conversion to the theatrical, not to be confused with Henry's theatrical conversion. This chapter challenges the traditional bifurcated reading of Henry as either a Machiavellian pragmatist or a Protestant idealist by treating Henry's struggle with ceremonialism as a cipher for interpreting the play's presentation of character, in the end depicting Henry's political rhetoric as a defense of the ritual impact of theater.

Chapter 4 brings the previous two chapters' insights on theatrical environment and immanence to bear on the prominence of the sacred Word in early seventeenth-century England. Because of the frequency with which he preached both indoors and outdoors at London's preeminent preaching venue, St. Paul's Cathedral, John Donne's sermons provide an ideal focus for describing the environmental conditions that sermon-goers navigated and also for consolidating the prolific practical literature for how to manage distracting sermon spaces in order to profitably receive the Word of God. I fundamentally reconceive audience belief in a sermon context: Donne perceives the phatic, ephemeral, and idiomatic qualities of his environment, uses them rhetorically to warn his audience of distraction, and then performatively endows his auditors' perceptual responses with the quality of faith.

If chapter 4 examines how the relatively fixed environments of sermons were, in fact, diffuse, then chapter 5 shifts focus to how the relatively unrestricted performance spaces of ballads could become surprisingly tight-knit. This chapter challenges the critical habit of not taking the *godliness* of godly ballads seriously. I argue that their myriad ulterior performance conditions, such as their environments, popular reputation, and excessive conventionality, motivated an emerging form of "street devotion" fundamental to early modern performance culture. I speculate about the potential transformations from textual broadside to theatrical performance, and I suggest that godly ballads in performance convey an imperative for the audience to pause in recognition of the social conditions around them, attending to the hawker's poverty, the street's sensory distractions, and the sense of intentional time created by the ballad event itself.

In chapter 6, I suggest that the enduring question of whether Marlowe's *Doctor Faustus* is primarily a moral cautionary tale or a subversive celebration of intellectual curiosity can be enhanced by theorizing its broader cultural reception among audiences in the theater, alehouse, and street. It is a culminating chapter insofar as it applies the first-person reception of festival, cycle drama, stage plays, ceremony, sermons, and ballads to one of the Elizabethan period's most sensational religious plays. It looks in depth at the stage-devil infestation of the playhouse and how this reputation for devilry affected the play's afterlives in balladry and Faustus lore, ultimately demonstrating how theatrical culture consisted of collaborative acts between theatrical spectacles and their audiences.

Finally in the postlude I "end with a jig." The jigs that immediately followed the final acts of plays in the early modern period remain a largely enigmatic performance type, but the reasons often cited for their problematic tonal abruptness, bawdiness, and derivativeness are also the reasons that I repurpose to argue for jigs' remarkable performative capabilities. The jig is perhaps at the furthest remove from the explicitly sacred contexts of the boy bishop festivities and biblical plays with which I begin this book, but for the same reason they are exemplary in their insistence on the mutuality of theatrical experience across performance culture and across the Reformation.

Among these performance types, the following chapters demonstrate that attending to an early modern theatrical event entailed the unconcealed exchanging of dramatic and ambient information among one's mind, emotions, body, and social environment and that performers and audiences turned to religious habits of perception in order to manage this exchange. In each of the performances that I examine there is a certain stripping away of illusion and an admission of theatrical strategy, where the audience are asked to attend to their own role as spectators, and, as I will argue, this process of stripping away and regenerating theatrical facades speaks to the power of performance both before and after the Reformation.

This gesture or dialectic of theatrical divesting and re-creation is the central performative move represented in these performances. For instance, as I will discuss, the Chester cycle plays concede part of the mechanism for producing dramatic meaning to the audience through the narrative disappearance of God, a dramatic move endued with greater interpretive power by virtue of increasing pressure from the London church against biblical drama. Likewise, *Henry V* magnifies its audience's potential suspicion about Henry's Machiavellian qualities by tapping into the ceremonialism controversy and an increasingly popular sensitivity toward religious and political mediation. Chapter 4's exploration of Donne's sermons examines the physical as well as auditory evolution of the post-Reformational emphasis on the preached "Word" of God and shows how distractions in the sermon environment were not merely obstacles to fight against but in fact constituted a spiritual battleground where the prize was salvation. Godly ballads effect their self-effacement by exploiting their own conventions and cheap and popular verse performances, reproducing in broadsides and performance spaces many characteristically Protestant themes of popular piety, such as prophecy, moral warnings for youth, and deathbed reflections. And yet despite this blatantly predictable representation of Protestant piety, godly ballads take advantage of their improvisational performance conditions to invite audiences to answer the call to Christian devotion even in the moment of performance. Finally, as is corroborated in its ballad afterlives, *Doctor Faustus* presents the act of spectatorship itself as what is at stake in Faustus's tragic decline. Marlowe grounds the question of theatricality in trans-Reformational figures of the medieval dramatic tradition—devils, angels, and the Seven Deadly Sins.

Throughout, I use the term *trans-Reformational* to indicate a paradox of theatrical practice in the Reformation period. There is much theatrical continuity across the Reformation, and this continuity with the past draws upon the social and spiritual power of medieval festival. But I want to recognize that such continuity coexisted, even in a singular scene or moment, with the peculiar social sensitivities often associated with the Reformation's effects on aesthetics, the tension between words and images. Early modern performers and audiences were more than sophisticated enough to see and harness the thematic possibilities presented by a past that was, and cannot be, yet still is.

Chapter One

EARLY MODERN THEATRICALITY ACROSS THE REFORMATION

Three Vignettes

I begin with three brief performance scenes: the boy bishop festival, Elizabeth I's coronation procession, and Shakespeare's *Twelfth Night*. These vignettes represent several corners of the field of early modern performance culture. The boy bishop festivities, also known as the *episcopus puerorum*, were locally organized community celebrations that punctuated the Christmas season's theme of social subversion. While they involved many different forms of performance, including plays, liturgical offices, visitations, and sermons, they existed in house, as it were, produced by and for a relatively small community. Boy bishop festivities were explicitly religious performance events. By contrast—and occurring not long after the *episcopus puerorum* was phased out in England—Elizabeth's coronation progress through London was primarily political in its aims, and its scope was enormous. Despite being sponsored by her regime, the event was staged and performed by multiple parties as well as by the queen herself, creating an atmosphere that juxtaposed a central political theme with copiousness of spectacle and the dispersal of perception across time and space. *Twelfth Night* contrasts with both of the previous performances by its later date and commercial setting, but I've chosen the play because it invokes aspects of the theatricality found in these earlier events. Its first recorded performance was in house at Middle Temple and had the feeling of an intimate festival occasion; and yet it also enjoyed tremendous success with commercial audiences.

In these three vignettes, we see numerous integrated performance types—liturgy, sermon, visitation, dance, procession, pageant, allegory, speech, indoor hall play, school revel, Christmas festival, and love lyric. I offer these scenes as cumulative illustrations of the inter-theatricality of early modern performance culture and also as introductory examples of the central performative move that I will describe in this chapter and that recurs in different forms throughout this book: a dialectical exchange between theatrical self-exposure and an audience response that performs and sometimes reproduces the drama's themes in ordinary life.

Episcopus Puerorum

The boy bishop festivities that were celebrated throughout England and on the Continent in the medieval and early modern periods were inherently intertheatrical. As is apparent even in the brief description that follows, the occasion's various performances and especially the capstone event of the chorister's sermon constituted an interactive spectacle that utilized its performative capabilities to integrate its different modes of festival, sermon, liturgy, and play. That is, the performance event acknowledged and made dramatic use of its own theatrical constraints by blurring the lines between which elements were mimetic expressions of saturnalia and which made real demands on the audience by way of devotion and ritual.

The boy bishop practices flourished in the Middle Ages and continued in England's cathedrals, parish churches, colleges, and grammar schools into the sixteenth century. They were generally associated with several other religious festivals of social inversion between Christmas and Lent. Most prominently, during the Feast of the Holy Innocents, on December 28, the bishop would vacate his ceremonial place in the liturgy and instate the elected boy (typically a chorister), who wore the bishop's vestments and miter and who carried his crosier. On the eve of Holy Innocents, known as Childermas Eve, multiple choristers attending the boy bishop would process and sing an antiphon drawn from scriptural passages relevant to Herod's slaughter of the innocents; the boy bishop would offer a blessing to his canons and assistants both gesturally and through a dramatized call and response.[1] While the boy would not celebrate an entire liturgy or administer the sacrament, he would direct some significant liturgical action and deliver a sermon. Three boy bishop sermons survive from the fifteenth and sixteenth centuries, including one written by Erasmus.[2] The ceremony and sermon were followed by a feast, or sometimes a series of feasts, and finally by visitations. During Christmastide, on their allotted days (the deacons on St. Stephen's, the priests on St. John the Evangelist's, the choristers on Holy Innocents, and the subdeacons on the Circumcision) members of the cathedral or parish would hold feasts and visitations, the most elaborate and sometimes controversial of which was the boy bishop, who visited community members with gifts and songs in the spirit of St. Nicholas.

The events of the *episcopus puerorum* demonstrate the varied and subtle ways that church festivals expanded into the outright theatrical world of plays and games. Variations on the festivities of Holy Innocents and its theatrical renditions abound. Boy performers were in costume, as numerous records detail the significant cost of elaborate vestments for the boy bishop as well as his extravagant feasts. There is also some evidence of the choristers performing plays during their festival—in one example wearing masks.[3] In another instance, a record in the late fifteenth century tells of the choristers at Winchester dressing as girls and dancing for nuns at St. Mary's convent, and across late medieval England the boy bishop festivities were multiple times censured for burlesque.[4]

Generally speaking, the boy bishop practices derived their intertheatrical energy from the Christmas season and its institutionalized revelry. This season of play included the Feast of Fools while it lasted, the especially raucous parties of the subdeacons, and the dances and entertainments that the appointed Lord of Misrule would facilitate at court, manor houses, and schools. The boys were viewed as performers, and some became famous. Francis Massingberd speculated in

1842 that Ben Jonson's verse commemorating a Queen's Chapel chorister named Salathiel Pavey refers not only to his playacting but also to his renown as a particularly talented boy bishop:

> He did act, what now we moan,
>   Old men so duly,
> That the three sisters thought him one,
>   He played so truly.[5]

"Old men," and Jonson among them, remember the performance roles that were "played" by choristers before they became famous for their masques.

The boy bishops' theatrical personas were aggregate forms of character composed of their own actions as well as those of clergy, household staff, play audiences, worshippers, and sermon writers. The performative facility of the boy bishop to represent his mimetic role and yet also to disclose his strategies for doing so—all in one action—is most apparent in his sermon, which was essentially a ventriloquized speech. And it is here that we get a clear sense of the performance event deploying its physical and illocutionary constraints to create an opportunity for the audience to respond to the performance's spiritual themes in the theatrical event itself.

The latest extant sermon was delivered by a chorister named John Stubs at Gloucester Cathedral in 1558. It exposits Jesus's command in the Gospel of Matthew, "Except yow will be convertyd and made lyke unto lytill children, you shall not entre in to the kyngdom of heaven."[6] Several times, the sermon's author, Richard Ramsey, refers to the boy's physical appearance and young voice as a way of simultaneously reinforcing his authority and exposing the homiletic and ceremonial artifice behind it, as when at the end of the sermon the boy bishop prays: "Consideryng my tendre age and infansy, I am constrayned to complayn with the wordes of the prophete Jeremy, . . . Lord God, behold I kan not speke, . . . because I am but a child."[7] The intertextuality and performativity of this scene (indeed, it is a scene) are impressive. The boy bishop addresses God in a prayer, citing his own youth while quoting a biblical prophet who only rhetorically calls himself a child, and in this procedure the boy purports to empty himself of any self-produced rhetorical ability or prophetic power. He then exploits and repurposes his ad hominem self-critique by drawing attention to this ceremonial—that is, theatrical—authority: "What then, good people? Because I kan not speake perfectly and eloquently shall I speake nothing at all? Why am I set up in this place? Why is this message committed unto me?"[8] In effect, the young homilist treats the theatrical scenario as a kind of icon, exposing and rhetorically rejecting the Christian festival's strategies of mediation and then offering his own preadolescent voice and bodily presence as a symbol for the audience to imitate in order to be "made lyke unto lytill children."

By drawing attention to his body, voice, and artificial ecclesial position, the boy bishop substitutes one form of mediation for another, ceremony for bodily immanence; but in the course of the scene, the two forms merge to performative effect, as they apply the power of the biblical prophecy to the very moment of the feast. We might extend the performative logic of this sermon—the festival's most direct self-description—to its other theatrical forms, including its liturgy, feast, visitations, dances, and even plays. Each, we can speculate, can be understood to compel audiences through the boy bishop's theatrical and self-effacing gesture. The message is clear: the festival transcends the moment through its symbolic presentation of time, liturgy, and prophecy, but it simultaneously appears in the form of a common chorister and contracts itself to the scope of the audience at hand.

What the *episcopus puerorum* represents (the biblical lesson) in this one event is duplicated in its theatrical medium (the festival) and reduplicated in the boy's performative gesture (his self-reference)—as well as potentially in the audience's reception (their imitation of childlike faith). This way of making meaning out of theatrical conditions is an example of the performative move that I examine in this book. These are echoes of meaning that rebound through the audience and event and are caught again by the performer in a move that may well remind us of modern performance art. It is a strategy that has its roots in medieval Christian practices and that persisted after the Reformation in evolving theatrical forms.

The Progress (and Regress) of Elizabeth I

Elizabeth I's 1559 coronation procession is another early modern performance that remained prominent in cultural memory through the lifetime of Shakespeare and elaborated a performance genre passed down from previous decades. The event has received scholarly attention as an inaugural statement of hoped-for political and religious stability and as an attempt to adjudicate the divergent ecclesial messages presented at the respective coronations of Edward VI and Mary I.[9] Many have noted the event's use of multimedia—speeches, pageants, texts, banners, coats of arms, fabrics, prayers, attendants, trumpets, and object symbols. While I do not presume to make any comprehensive statements about the procession's use of media here, I do want to briefly consider its inheritance from the same theatrical tradition that includes the boy bishop festival. At least as inflected by Richard Mulcaster, Elizabeth's progress demonstrates how such a political event shares in early modern performance culture's strategies, first, for creating the effect of a political and theological whole that is greater than its parts and, second, for theatrically dismantling this transcendent whole to make an opportunity for particular audience engagement. Like the boy bishop's performative stripping away of ceremony, the procession builds its copiousness of spectacle to the point where it becomes obstructive, and it is through its participants' navigation of the spectacle itself that queen and subject become present to one another in the mode of the theatrical—that is, within the holistic event's dispersal of meaning throughout its audience, role players, ornaments, scripts, and physical movements.

Like the boy bishop events, Elizabeth's procession took place in the greater Christmas festival season, on January 14, 1559. During the Christmas and Epiphany seasons leading up to the coronation, Elizabeth was in Whitehall, where the festival period was in full swing despite Mary's recent passing. Local maskers and choristers would have been in practice through the activities of the post-Christmas feast days (including Twelfth Night, which I discuss below), preparing for the spectacular scene of the progress. No doubt, the festival context was utilized thematically, as Elizabeth's royal office was "inextricably bound up with the Church's ritual calendar, and the king's [or queen's] ordinary household ceremonies [were] infused with liturgical symbolism to such an extent that reformed doctrine would find hard to touch."[10] Moreover, although a foremost aim of the progress was to reinforce England's return to Protestantism, it used theatrical devices from before and after the Reformation and even, I suggest, attempted to harness the productive tension perceived between Catholic and Protestant expressions.

For instance, the second device of the process at the Conduit in Cornhill included personified virtues and vices as in morality drama. This allegorical drama effectively integrated newer theatrical trends such as representing historical figures and having them and Elizabeth herself appear with older mimetic character types of morality virtues and vices. William Leahy reads the episode as "virtue being seen to reside in the Protestantism supplanting the Catholicism associated with Mary's reign."[11] Yet the persistent thread of old theatrical forms that ran through the performance—concluding with a mostly Catholic Mass at Westminster—suggests less a supplanting of one religious aesthetic by another than an integrated adoption of nostalgia and theatrical innovation, perhaps coloring the entire event as a "calculated exploitation of (Catholic) ceremonial theatrics in order to promote coherent Protestant policy and majesty."[12]

The procession included five pageants written by four prominent citizens and recorded by Mulcaster, among others. Its pageants lacked a single master author, and the event had the festival effect of interchanging performers and audiences. The event dispersed audience attention across time, spectacles, and sounds but also attempted to shape this attention into a vision of England's political and religious future, for ruler and subject alike. The performers included the queen, her attendants, members of the church, and "gentlemen, barons, and other [of] the nobility," as well as the thousands of spectators that lined the streets behind wooden barricades, manned pageant stages, and covered entire buildings with colorful fabric and tapestries.[13] We learn from the Corporation of London in 1558 that the city was to take on the costs of adorning Elizabeth and her company as well as the streets and stages themselves; the path from Whitehall to Westminster was to be "seemly trimmed and decked for the honor of the

City against the coming of our Sovereign Lady the Queen's majesty . . . with pageants, fine paintings, and rich cloths of arras, silver and gold" so as to surpass the coronation celebration for Mary I.[14] Understandably, scholars frequently compare such processions to the Corpus Christi Feast procession.[15]

The first pageant was a politically and religiously charged one: "The Uniting of the Two Houses of Lancaster and York," housing a triple-decked platform of three generations of monarchs, including Anne Boleyn. It was positioned near the Tower of London on Gracechurch Street, often the first stop on coronation entries. This is also where Queen Anne memorably paused during her own coronation process to see a Hans Holbein pageant of Mount Parnassus. In *The Queen's Majesty's Passage* Mulcaster describes a child at the "forepart" of "The Uniting" who was tasked with declaring "the whole meaning of the said pageant."[16] Mulcaster adds, "The two sides of the same were filled with loud noises of music. And all empty places thereof were furnished with sentences concerning unity. And the whole pageant garnished with red roses and white." The image is one of copious decoration—flowers, tapestries, fabrics, and *sententiae* filling every available space. The panorama of visual yet textual commentary especially in *sententiae* may aptly remind us of religious illustrations and title pages in the period, where engraved windowpanes and available spaces are filled with compendious scenes of preachers before congregations or sometimes raucous crowds destroying sacred images, appended with word scrolls protruding from figures' mouths. Perhaps not coincidentally, the "Uniting" scene particularly resembles the title pages of The Great Bible of 1539 and of the Geneva Bible first printed in 1560, densely decorated with word scrolls, banners, and scenes of prominent religious and political figures delivering the book to laypeople. And not insignificantly, one of these two books featured conspicuously in one of the pageant's curious and yet theatrically telling mix-ups.

In this instance, as Elizabeth approaches the next pageant featuring the figures of "Time" and his daughter "Truth," she is told that a copy of this vernacular Bible will be given to her, and, whether improvising or by plan, instructs a courtier named "Sir John Parrat . . . to go before and to receive the book."[17] Yet subsequently learning that the predetermined script is instead for the Bible to be lowered to her on a "silken lace," she calls Parrat back and moves her train forward to receive the book at the originally scheduled time. It is curious that Mulcaster, a commissioned writer, retains these details of progress and regress, but, in fact, the visible hiccup is rather characteristic of the pageant. One never knows where to decipher the line between the queen's improvisation and embarrassed backtracking. What is clear, though, is that in this all-important pageant dramatizing the return of Protestantism (or "Truth," the daughter of Time) Elizabeth is caught between the roles of performer and audience, or perhaps is asked to play both. The collective authorship and variously delegated performances of the procession's pageants make Elizabeth's own agency in the allegory of Truth and Time somewhat ambiguous: Does she take the book, or is it enforced upon her?

A similar and even more visible moment of loaded spontaneity occurs in "The Uniting of the Two Houses" just before the Truth and Time device. In this pageant as well, the interpretation of Elizabeth becomes conspicuously and ambivalently contingent on the theatrical apparatus itself. In a pivotal moment of illocution, the child at the front of "The Uniting" addresses the queen in the spirit of "trust":

> Therefore as civil war and shed of blood did cease
> When these two houses were united into one
> So now that jar shall stint, and quietness increase,
> We trust, O noble Queen, thou wilt be cause alone.[18]

The candor of the city's demands for Elizabeth to sustain peace is an expected feature of such pageants, though, of course, the monarchy wars of the fifteenth century were less relevant than the religious divisions enacted by Elizabeth's immediate predecessors. Notably, the demands to silence "jar" and create "quietness" could have struck the historical audience as even more ironic than they do us, given the noise and visual copiousness of the spectacle. In fact, Mulcaster notes that the "noise was [so] great by reason of the press of people" that Elizabeth could not hear the child speaker and had to move her litter so close that "she could not well view the personages" and asked to have them explained to her.[19] Afterward, she ordered "her chariot to be removed back and yet hardly could she see, because the children were set somewhat with the farthest in." This resulted in an anamorphic viewing experience for Elizabeth and also for the spectators, insofar as Elizabeth herself was performing for the crowds. Taking in the entire pageant required physical movement and improvisation on all sides. Mulcaster's apparent intention in retelling these interactions is to convey Elizabeth's adaptability and magnanimity, but his account also reveals the give-and-take of the performance and Elizabeth's approval of it. Mulcaster records the Latin sentences that littered the "void places" of the pageant, including many that issued warnings to the queen, such as "Those who inspire fear when united must fear when they are divided," and "Unity among the citizens will act as a firm defense of a kingdom."[20] The word scroll–like sentences represent the voice of the people in text—a synesthetic and perhaps more permanent textual visualization of the noise of the crowd.

The effect is that the performance appears bigger than both the audience and the queen. The queen is forced to acquiesce to the pageant's theatrical constraints, to surrender meaning to its extramimetic content. And through this manipulation, the performers compel her to strip away an aspect of her ceremonial poise, to become at visibly separate times an intimate listener to a chorister boy or a distanced admirer of copious decor. Thus the boy's statement of "trust" reveals itself to be conditional on the environment, as the injunction for "quietness [to] increase" provides the occasion to issue the indicative demand, "We trust, O noble Queen, thou wilt be cause alone." Such a performative statement is almost more effective in its mere sounding than in its language. Quietness here—meaning both "absence of noise or disturbance" and "freedom from legal restrictions"—apparently does not include silencing the crowd and its spectacle, which present themselves as contingencies of the queen's action.[21] Popular "trust" appears not simply as inherent to Elizabeth's title but also as dependent on the role she plays in the space created for her. Thus the performance defines authority and, indeed, creates trust by shifting the power of theatrical spectacle toward and then away from Elizabeth—in a kind of oscillation between divesture and regeneration, progress and regress—literally moving the queen and her attendants back and forth and drawing attention to the laden act of perceiving, where what appears "asserts more things than it grasps."²² Just as it does in its simultaneous exploitations of religious nostalgia and reform, the event makes performative use of its theatrical conditions simultaneously to celebrate and challenge the queen.

Twelfth Night

I have been arguing that these two performances—the boy bishop festivities and Elizabeth's coronation progress—expand their thematic and ritual reaches by breaking character, as it were, and by calling on audiences (including royal ones) to respond. This move is both characteristically medieval in its reliance on allegory and on the wholeness of the sacred occasion and also post-Reformational in its deployment of the rhetorical gesture of self-divesting for the sake of achieving a more direct and personally stripped-down appearance of bare, or plain, communication. A consistent element to this stripping-down gesture is the role of language, spoken or written. The boy bishop festivities, for example, owe their liturgical expression, their revelry, and their theatrics to an older Catholic tradition, but, at least in the post-Reformation text I examine, the chorister's sermon also shows signs of distinctly Protestant strategies, with its overt recognition of the distractions of rhetoric and theatrics and with its word-centered application of biblical prophecy to individual auditors. Elizabeth I's procession likewise centers on moments of verbal communication; or, more accurately, it unsettles the ceremonialism of the event in anamorphic scenes punctuated by concentrated moments centered on words—in the forms of the Bible and of the boy performer's speech. There is continuity as well as productive tension: the events *theatrically* demonstrate continuity with the medieval past, even while they *representationally* harness the dramatic potential found in religious reform.

Although Shakespeare's theater lacks the sacred setting of the first two examples, I want to call attention to a similar performative move in *Twelfth Night* and its own comedic occasion. Like many of Shakespeare's comedies, *Twelfth Night*'s generic spirit is festive, but, as in the previous two examples, it also takes advantage of its audience's immersion in this intertheatrical atmosphere to create the performative effect of character sincerity, which it accomplishes by both building and stripping its theatrical artifice.

Twelfth Night relates through Christian liturgical tradition to the boy bishop festival and Elizabeth's procession, as it too is a product of the long festival season. The title refers to the Twelfth Night of Christmastide, January 5, the Eve of the Feast of Epiphany—a reference that is frequently noted in introductions to the play but that has received relatively little critical attention, especially given that the title is not directly reinforced in the plot of the play itself. As is widely known, the Twelfth Night holiday involved a certain amount of license for social deviance, wassailing, costuming, masques, pranks, and expressions of social reversal. Epiphany is the Christian feast that celebrates the beginning of Christ's ministry and especially his visitation by the "wise men from the East," and the pagan legacy of the occasion seems to have inspired feasters to remember their own extra-ecclesiastical traditions.[23] The question of whether Shakespeare wrote the play specifically to debut on a Twelfth Night celebration—or even the unnamed play performed at court on January 6, 1601, by the Lord Chamberlain's Men—likely will never be answered, but the possibility that the play was written for a festival occasion persists in the form of John Manningham's well-known firsthand account of a performance on February 2, 1602.[24] This was Candlemas, the Feast of the Presentation and the final day of Epiphany and the greater Christmas season. The performance Manningham saw took place at Middle Temple, which, like many schools and houses in the period, would have been concluding its seasonal festivities. Like the boy bishop, both Twelfth Night and Candlemas traditionally employed a revel leader, known as the Lord of Misrule at schools, court, and larger houses. Two decades before the *Twelfth Night* performance, Middle Temple punished students for celebrating Candlemas—for "playing at dice or cards, outcries in the night, breaking open chambers, as by the Lord of Candlemas night," and for funding a "Lord of Misrule," a practice that had already been prohibited at the school.[25] These penalties occurred seemingly after the previous year's explicit "ordinance" and "admonition" against this sort of revelry: future transgressors were to be expelled. Regardless, the school's parliamentary minutes note similar events in future years, and we can assume that Shakespeare's play would have been received in the spirit of these earlier shenanigans.

Notably, Shakespeare's contemporary John Marston was a student with Manningham at Middle Temple during these years when he was beginning his career as a poet and playwright, and he is reputed to have had his own plays produced at Middle Temple Hall. Curiously, in 1601 Marston wrote a play that shares not only *Twelfth Night's* subtitle, "What You Will," but also many of its plot devices—mistaken identity to be recovered by the recognition of a birthmark, romantic love, disguise, and shipwreck. Its plot includes a group of boys, reminiscent of the milieu of young men at Middle Temple, who harass characters that are less inclined toward the comedic mood. Marston's play makes more of its own title than does Shakespeare's, especially in a two-character exchange before the "Prologus" and "*Before the Musicke sounds for the Acte.*" Here Doricus satirizes Marston himself and his newfound reputation for controversial writing that would eventually lead to imprisonment:[26] "Nay and your friend the Author, the composer: the *What you will*: seemes so faire in his owne glasse, so straight in his owne measure that he talkes once of squinting *Critickes*, drunken *Censure*, splay-footed *Opinion*, juicles huskes, I ha done with him, I ha done with him."[27] The two characters then retire "within the Curtaines" to heckle the rest of the play. It is possible, but by no means evident, that Marston's self-admitted reputation for attracting the attention of detractors had something to do with his temporary expulsion from Middle Temple. He was expelled "for non-payment of commons" and for suggestive and unspecified "other causes," and then was reinstated just in time for the 1601–2 Christmas season, including the performance of Shakespeare's play.[28] In Marston's play, the title "What You Will" represents the license afforded to its characters' revels as well as an invitation for the audience to inhabit the unique space of the comedic genre.[29] I suggest that Shakespeare's own *Or What You Will* similarly refers its audience to comedy's roots in Christian festival and in its borderless connections to performance culture, viewed comparatively.

In the occasion of *Twelfth Night*'s first recorded performance (regardless of whether it debuted then) we catch a glimpse of its intertheatricality with other plays and with the performance culture around the festival season and institutions like Middle Temple—the rule breaking by students who break into chambers or cry out in the night, and are censured or expelled, but also the plays and the cultivation of wit. The play theatrically reflects these old festival games and pastimes. Like the boy bishop festivities and to a lesser extent Elizabeth's progress, *Twelfth Night*'s principal character part was that of a boy actor, a role that evolved from that of the chorister and from children's parts in morality drama. All three performances involve vestments and/or costumes; and we might even compare the cross-dressing characters of *Twelfth Night* to the choristers who dressed as girls and danced for nuns at Winchester. The play's comic characters—Maria, Feste, Aguecheek, and Belch—are pranksters, just like the men at Middle Temple, who transgressively cry out and sing in the night. Shakespeare also includes a one-of-a-kind puritan character in Malvolio, who, interestingly enough, keeps the audience's thoughts in check, representing a pressure against histrionic play and affectation, though Malvolio ultimately relinquishes this attitude when he pursues Olivia. Moreover, this intertheatricality extends to the multimedia of the play itself, which is full of old ballads and ends with a clown song that relates to the tradition of the postplay jig. In fact, Feste's dual persona as the fool and as the company clown, probably Robert Armine, is yet another connection to medieval drama and its religious roots insofar as the clown derives from the Vice character in morality plays.[30] As clown, Feste prompts intermittent moments of metadramatic pause, when he faces the audience to sing or perform an acrobatic stunt as the recognizable clown player and to enlist the audience as "necessary helpers in the creation of theatre."[31] Though less politically charged than the boy speaker in "The Uniting of the Two Houses" discussed above, the clown is similar in his capacity for filling and extending the theatrical experience, forcing audiences to readjust their attention, and providing present-moment context for the fiction around him. He represents the festival of the playhouse itself.

Twelfth Night thus reaches the audience through the multiple and interrelated theatrical modes of fiction, festival, occasion, and clowning, among others. As C. L. Barber puts it, "So much of the action in this comedy is random when looked at as intrigue, so many of the persons are neutral when regarded as character, so much of the wit is inapplicable when assessed as satire" unless we attend to "how art develops underlying configurations in the social life of a culture."[32] Yet there's something more to *Twelfth Night*'s theatricality than its saturnalia. Shakespeare shares his wider performance culture's interest in the fluidity and immediate deliverances of theatricality itself, in the performative power at hand in making theatrical process the subject of drama. And in *Twelfth Night* Shakespeare sees one of many opportunities to create something out of the convergence of old and new theatrical devices. He utilizes the cultural attention paid to mediation that characterized the Reformation period, contextualized between revelries and schoolmaster prohibitions, continuities as well as breaks with the Catholic past.

In Viola's several disguised performances, for example, Shakespeare celebrates theatricality as a theme and guide for audience interpretation. In the fifth scene of act 1, Viola disguises herself as Cesario in an attempt to woo Olivia on behalf of Duke Orsino. What I want to highlight about this much-discussed scene is how Cesario's actions reflect the performative move of self-divestiture and audience engagement—where here the audience is on display in the form of Olivia. Cesario and Olivia's exchange begins before he enters the scene, when Olivia questions him through the medium of Malvolio—"What kind o' man is he?" "Kind" in this case invokes the period's primary term for literary and dramatic genre as well as the casting of character in which the world is a stage and everyone has a part (1.5.146).[33] Malvolio responds by detailing Cesario's appearance in its ambiguity and "erotic slippage":[34] "Not yet old enough for a man, nor young enough for a boy, as a squash is before 'tis a peascod, or a codling when 'tis almost an apple. 'Tis with him in standing water between boy and man" (151–54). William Slights notes this statement's precedents for sexual ambiguity in the popular myths of Narcissus, Actaeon, Venus and Adonis, and Salmacis and Hermaphroditus—with Actaeon, of course, making an appearance in Orsino's complaint in the play's first scene, associating Malvolio's description of Cesario's sexual qualities with Orsino's self-centered love musings in the first scene.[35] But Malvolio, in fact, is wrong. Cesario is not in "between" boy and man; he is *both* boy and man, and *also* woman. He is a boy playing the role of a woman impersonating a man. Cesario is thus introduced in an expression of the capaciousness of dramatic representation not only in the fiction but in the practicalities of play making. He enters the scene as a figure with a certain anamorphism, not unlike the boy bishop chorister or the boy speaker in Elizabeth's procession: the theatrical apparatus changes as the audience's perspective shifts.

Shakespeare dramatizes one of these shifts on stage. In addition to his eunuch disguise, Cesario pretends to have memorized a speech either composed or sanctioned by the Duke—"I can say little more than I have studied" (173). Olivia is at first irritated by this routine, complaining that the speech "is the more like to be feigned," but gradually this irritation turns into curiosity as she reads something hidden and perhaps unexpected within Cesario's performance (191). Eventually, of course, Cesario abandons his pretended "part" and delivers a speech eloquent enough to break Olivia's vow not to entertain suitors. Note that the authenticity that Olivia detects in Cesario is not actually a by-product of his poetry, his "loyal cantons of contemned love," but rather a performative phenomenon created by his construction of a conspicuously theatrical persona (262). In other words, Cesario's layers (or Viola's, or the boy player's—*whose layers are they?*) become conspicuous. He is something like a caricature of a character, drifting melodramatically into the presentational realm of the clown. Olivia even asks, "Are you a comedian?" (177). To truly strip away theatrical vesture in order to appear sincere, one would need to differentiate between the medium and the message, but this is not a distinction to which Shakespeare or his performance culture adhere.

In light of the play's intertheatrical connections, its multimedia, and the living cultural heritage it shares with other festival season performances, we can attend to how Viola's ploy puts theatricality itself on display. Shakespeare offers a step-by-step exposé of theatrical process, of moving from one form of mediation to the next, and the audience never doubts that the divested form of straight talk after Cesario abandons his memorized part is yet another form of theatricality, a new performance masquerading as character sincerity. And we might ask, is the audience less likely, as a result, to be convinced of Viola's sincerity than Olivia is? That is, to the extent that the audience witnesses Cesario/Viola performatively creating the trait of sincerity, does it also disbelieve this sincerity—as such is the quandary of performing a trait of honesty and authenticity?³⁶

Perhaps not, when we view the scene in its festival and intertheatrical contexts and when we consider the trans-Reformational history of Viola's performative strategy. Viola strips away one layer of her disguise, that of Cesario's overdone formality, and uses this maneuver not to foreswear theatricality altogether but to hone its audience's attention into the focal expression of lyric poetry, culminating in the willow cabin speech. Here we find a reiteration of the spectacle-word binary that characterizes many post-Reformational performances and particularly those that were overtly religious in nature, like the boy bishop festivities and Elizabeth's procession. Especially given the broader event of *Twelfth Night*'s production—including its clowning, ballads, festival namesake, and possible festival occasion—Viola's lyricism in the willow cabin speech may disown Cesario's false formality, but it retains the greater intertheatricality that surrounds it, including the ambiguity and social subversion of her boyishness and its connection to the season's saturnalia. And in fact, Cesario's "sincerity" continues to rely on the theatrical premise of his overdone "part," providing Cesario with a histrionic backstory that transforms into bare communication when it reaches Olivia, as she puts it, with "an invisible and subtle stealth / To creep in at mine eyes" (289–90). Viola's sincerity is itself intertheatrical in that it appears within the transition from one form of performance to another. Hence, Harold Jenkins says of the willow cabin speech's parodic nature that it "is of the kind that does not belittle but transfigures its original."³⁷ Viola's theatricality is transfigured, trans-vested, or at least transformed, into intrigue, beauty, and sincerity in the mind of her audience, Olivia.

Of course, most of *Twelfth Night*'s early seventeenth-century performances would have been, not within the confines of a school or house during festival season, but in the commercial playhouse. In these other stagings, Viola's theatricality is not shaded as much by the religious occasion immediately at hand, though the festival context persists in the play's title; and, in fact, that the title has nothing to do with the plot makes its role as an interpretive frame that Shakespeare intended to invoke all the more intriguing. Still, it is worth remembering that Viola's performative shedding of her theatrical routine works not against the liturgical occasion but with it. That is, as is evident in the first two performances I gloss, medieval and early modern Christian ceremony was the forebear of Viola's strategy, so even outside of Manningham's remarkable viewing opportunity Shakespeare trusts his audience's cultural knowledge. He constructs an especially personal and focalized character phenomenon of sincerity as an aggregate of intertheatrical associations to the festival season, to other performances of gender in the forms of boy actors, to games of misrule, and to an emerging Protestant investment in rhetorical divesture and bare speech.

BY LOOKING AT these three vignettes together, we see shared strategies for making performative phenomena—childlike faith, political and religious trust, and character sincerity, respectively. Each scenario offers a scene that looks out across itself to its larger event and then integrates its audience into this same perspective. Michael Fried terms this self-conscious dramatic moment a *coup de théâtre*, a movement of obvious theatricality where the characters and the audience behold the same spectacle at once. It involves the scene's own admission of theatrical strategy or stripping away of a layer of the performance so that the performer and the character inhabit a shared perspective. These three intertheatrical shows acknowledge the presence of the audience as constituting one of the event's defining conditions or interpretive barriers. They merge performer and character in what Erika Fischer-Lichte calls "multistability," where in modern performance art "aesthetic perception . . . takes the form of oscillation. It switches focus between the actor's phenomenal and semiotic body, thus transforming the perceiving subject into a state betwixt and between."[38] Yet unlike Fischer-Lichte's characterization of modern performance, the "perceiving subject" in these *early* modern vignettes is not so much "betwixt and between" the real and fictive worlds as dually present in both and grounded in the undivided fluidity of the larger event. Early modern performances characteristically make much of their occasional contexts, and these events create a continuum from fiction to theatrical participation, game, pastime, and play. The audience is affected by each characteristic of the performance event, and, as I argue in this book, each is never entirely separate from the others.

In the boy bishop festivities, Elizabeth I's coronation procession, and Shakespeare's *Twelfth Night*, this continuity is executed in part by the festival occasion, as performers and audiences find dramatic power by indulging the Protestant Reformation's renewed cultural sensitivity to mediation across theatrical genres and religious practices. But it is not just the Christmas festival season that animates the theatrical in these performances. Viewing performance genres comparatively, on a continuum, as I argue early moderns did, affects the way religion appears to interact with performance culture in the decades surrounding the Reformation. Religious nostalgia and reform exist on a continuum as well, sliding along the various courses of performance content, occasion, dramaturgy, character, ritual, and audience.

Early Modern Theatricality

Plays, cycle drama, royal entries, sermons, and ballads are all individual performance types, but their borders overlap and converge with one another and also with the borders of many other, less frequently recognized performance types, including Lord Mayor's shows, interludes, mummings, jigs, beggar songs, wait songs, minor liturgies, seasonal games and pageants, and the exercises of the London merchant soldiers in the Artillery Company. Scholars have become increasingly comfortable thinking of plays and related performances as events, and this "eventuality," as Michael Witmore calls it, reflects the multifarious motives that bring a performance into being—its economic, material, technical, conventional, religious, festival, and authorial causes.[39] We have much to gain by thinking of commercial plays, in particular, as intertheatrical events rather than merely as fictions or texts—in William West's words, "as made out of other performances.... [and] as belonging to a horizontally organized repertoire, never completed and slowly changing, of lines, gestures, characters, situations, genres, and other smaller elements that cumulatively allow for new performances and new concatenations of actions."[40] Plays are a central example of how performance events are "neither song nor dance nor drama, they are at once none of the above and yet all of the above," in that they can be seen as both whole and part—part of larger playhouse events that included music, jigs, and entertainment between the acts as well as in-action performances such as ballads, balls, prayers, orations, dumb shows, acrobatics, and games.[41]

Consider, for instance, the interpenetrating presence of music in a play event. Most obviously perhaps, music featured as part of the action of plays, as when a character sang, or as part of the setting, as in *Romeo and Juliet*'s ball. Yet this kind of represented music was relatively scant compared to what is sometimes called incidental music—music playing before and after a performance, during interludes in between acts, and at the end in a jig. Many plays utilized mum shows set to music before acts. Then, of course, there were numerous sennets, blasts, stately drums, and other symbolic sounds, as well as ambient music, such as that heard in *The Tempest*. And, not least, music surrounded the institution of the playhouse in the form of ballads—when characters sang ballads but also when hawkers standing outside the playhouse may have sung to audience members as they entered and left.[42] Ballads also infiltrated plays in their popular culture when their stories reappeared in broadside form and were re-embodied in spontaneous sung performances in alehouses, markets, homes, and workplaces.

Scholarly discussion of early modern theatricality has shifted over the last four decades from focusing primarily on plays and antitheatrical polemics to more recently expanding this evidence base to include dramaturgical and material aspects of performance—in short, from the textual to the social and phenomenological conditions of performance. In his influential *The Antitheatrical Prejudice*, Jonas Barish attempts to define some central essence to the theatrical world that puritans targeted in their tracts, and he omits aspects of playhouse culture that might be considered circumstantial. The result for Barish of focusing on plays and polemics—what David Postlewait says amounts to a collective "psychodrama" of "sacred and secular forces"—is a definition of the "equivocal nature of the theatrical," a version of theatricality defined as protean and progressive.[43] And while many continue to corroborate the protean capabilities of early modern plays, recent decades have seen a decisive push to include the so-called circumstantial factors of performance in characterizations of the theatrical, considering plays as "*embodiments* of theatricality as well as *vehicles* for representing the theatricality of fictional characters."[44]

Yet using a wider lens for identifying theatrical activity in the playhouse reveals that theatricality extends far beyond the play and its venue. For example, even though it was common for early modern writers to complain that the popularity of plays discouraged people from attending sermons, plays and sermons often fashioned themselves with descriptions taken from one another—as when Knapp argues that stage players came to constitute "a kind of ministry" comparable to church community and when John Donne the preacher acknowledges that auditors enter the venue of a sermon with habits of spectatorship "as ever they had been at the Stage."[45] And if Protestantism cultivated certain "attitudes toward the perceptual faculties, the structuring agents of human knowing," we should anticipate that performance types on both ends of the sacred-to-secular spectrum would share theatrical strategies.[46] Thus we can expand Barish's definition of the theatrical to encompass a network of practices that erases the distinction between the central and circumstantial elements of an event. As Henry Turner puts it, early modern theatricality is "an open set" of elements "that are shared across individual theatrical occasions."[47] The result is that there really is no strict difference between theatricality and what I have been calling the intertheatricality shared among performance types.

Such phenomenological approaches shift attention "from what beliefs 'mean' *intrinsically* to what they are *made* to mean, and what they accomplish for those who invoke and use them."[48] Early modern performances are invested in the situatedness of thought, with their accounts of the porous body, Aristotelian "common sense," psychophysiological passions, and largely antidualistic understanding of the human mind, among many other examples. The theatrical is dispersed through the sensible and spatial environment of an event, blurring the boundary, first, between representations and circumstances; second, between subject and object; third, between subject and subject as spectators embrace the social contingencies of drama; and fourth, between psychology and embodiment. In an essay on early modern notions of "performance," Mary Thomas Crane notes that "a preoccupation with the subversion/containment debate [in cultural materialist scholarship] conceals the constitutive binary that lies behind it and structures it, namely, the distinction between representation and experience, or discourse and embodiment, which might also be described as a distinction between semiotics and phenomenology."[49] To per-form meant to act or to do, and an overfocus on dramatic "representation" risks accounting for only one side of this. Emphasizing the embodiment of thought and the proactivity of early modern performance, phenomenological interpretations of drama by Julia Lupton, Kevin Curran, James Kearney, Michael Witmore, and Bruce Smith suggest some inherent parallels between the ways that early modern theater and modern phenomenology respectively approach consciousness.[50] These scholars aver a common hypothesis that early modern writings and especially performances demonstrate a marked acceptance of the social and physical structures of mutuality through which individuals understood and lived their own identities, even (or perhaps, especially) in the intimate areas of affect, sexual desire, and religion.

In what follows here and in the ensuing chapters I offer a historical phenomenology of "the theatrical" and show that early modern performances take pains to encourage their audiences to think about their perceptual practices and how such perceptual content might actively contribute to the material being represented in performance. For example, the Chester Whitsun cycle represents conflicts of perception, particularly in *The Fall of Lucifer*, where Lucifer erringly dissociates his perception of beauty (what it is) from his own creaturely response to beauty (how "what it is" implies a distinct relation to him). The play uses this suspense to prompt its audience to attend to the moral and spiritual stakes of the act of viewing the play. The cycle relies on this reflection and compels the audience to recognize that the pageant's sense of drama is grounded in reception—with the help of liturgy as a common intertheatrical experience. Across genres, audiences intend performances—perceive them as such and, therefore, constitute them—in multiple ways at once, as representation as well as social occasion, ceremonial function, and theatrical spectacle.

There is a manifest commensurability between early modern ways of thinking about embodiment, space, and knowledge and modern ways of describing phenomenological reflection. Moreover, on a general level, nonspecific to early modern drama, art can be understood as an instrument that aids the process of eidetic thought under the auspices, I propose, of what Edmund Husserl calls "imaginative variance." He suggests that fictional or literary works are useful to eidetic reduction because they oblige audiences to vary their psychological perspectives on a thing and to imagine the conditions of thought from multiple hypothetical angles: "In respect of the originality of the new formations, of the abundance of detailed features, and the systematic continuity of the motive forces involved, they greatly excel the performances of our own fancy, and moreover, given the understanding grasp, pass through the suggestive power of the media of artistic presentation with quite special ease into perfectly clear fancies."[51] For Husserl, forthrightly artful texts are helpful because they are explicit in their intention to describe something with creative license: they bracket their intentions. Fruitful reflection occurs in the recognition of this license by the audience, when viewers or readers embrace the transparently strategic nature of fictive and rhetorical speech acts and, in turn, become co-subjects, or intersubjects, with the performance around a particular theme.[52] Therefore, not only do the representational aspects of theater make it an insightful mode for describing phenomena, but also it is *in* the critical process of describing the conditions of a given representation that the observer learns about her own role in constituting the event. This is scholarship conceived as historical reflection on dramatic themes.

Where this reflexive practice appears most closely to characterize aspects of early modern drama is in the shared theatrical strategies of performance culture. Early modern performers and audiences seem to have been especially comfortable inhabiting a perceptual space within the overlap between what is understood to be performative and what is normal. Intertheatricality and social fluidity among early modern performance types contributed to a situation in which audiences understood individual characters, scenes, spectacles, and dialogues as modes of imaginative variation on the larger performance event. As with the gesture of Cesario divesting himself of theatricality, the audience may hold a dual intentionality toward the thing as represented and the thing as theatricalized, resulting in the creation of a phenomenon like character sincerity that is not so much *meta-* as *intra-* and *inter-*theatrical. Maurice Merleau-Ponty uses theatrical imagery to make the point: "In the action of the hand which is raised towards an object is contained a reference to the object, not as an object represented, but as that highly specific thing towards which we project ourselves, near which we are, in anticipation, and which we haunt."[53] Perception is like a dramatic gesture in that it "asserts more things than it grasps."[54]

In short, early modern performances do things, and audiences do things *with* them.[55] Through their intertheatrical relations and by enduing audience response with immediate meaning, they "accomplish precisely what they signify," constituting "a new, singular reality for the artist and the audience, that is to say, for all participants of the performance."[56] And through the materials and circumstances we might otherwise call incidental, early modern performances create something out of the excesses of representation, in particular when they repeat one another's theatrical strategies.[57] We have seen, for instance, how Cesario's presumption to speak plainly in his willow cabin speech relies not simply on the poetical language of the speech but even more so on the paradoxical surplus of character sincerity that results from the building and stripping of theatricality. The same gesture is performed in the anamorphism of Elizabeth's progress and in the blending of liturgy and theatricality in the boy bishop's sermon.

I am using *performative* here to denote the ability of a spectacle or theatrical utterance to create something, to blend with normal reality as known. This usage has its roots in J. L. Austin's well-known definition of the performative, but the performative speech act takes on layers of complexity when it occurs in a theatrical event. In a famous passage, Austin suggests that overtly theatrical representations cannot, in fact, be "performative": "A performative utterance will... be *in a particular way* hollow and void if said by an actor on the stage, or if introduced in a poem, or spoken in soliloquy.... Language in such circumstances is in special ways—intelligibly—used not seriously, but in many ways *parasitic* upon its normal use—ways which fall under the doctrine of the *etiolations* of language."[58] In other words, performatives can exist only "in ordinary circumstances." By the end of Austin's *How to Do Things with Words*, and as Derrida markedly observed, Austin himself questions this distinction between performative and constative acts, wondering if there really is a difference between the so-called ordinary and the theatrical. Hence, as Stanley Fish argues, any distinction regarding the performative that might include or exclude the theatrical should be made between a speech act's intended uses rather than between its genres: "By the same argument, the conventions (or rules) that define those acts cannot be said to be present in one kind of discourse and absent (or uninvoked) in another; for they are the procedures which make all discourse possible, and any distention one might want to draw must be drawn at a level of generality below that at which they operate."[59] Andrew Parker and Eve Sedgwick further elaborate the problems in Austin's exclusion of theatrical language from the performative by contending that the "relation between theatrical speakers and the words they speak" is not "fixed in advance, as definitionally consistent."[60] The implication is that theatricalized speech acts are "parasitic" only to the extent that "ordinary" speech acts are also parasitic—which, Parker and Sedgwick suggest, they always are.

Performativity is a term with different but overlapping meanings in the disciplines of cultural studies and performance studies, and as critics like Judith Butler have established, the performative is in no way restricted to spectacles that audiences would generally describe as artistic.[61] Parker and Sedgwick thread a string from Austin's performative speech act theory to more recent cultural performativity studies by putting pressure on his terming of the "etiolations" of theatrical speech acts, a word Austin uses to explain the "parasitic" quality of theatrical speech but whose biological history refers to plants that have been deprived of sunlight.[62] Gender studies, in particular, have used the notion of the performative to explain "the ways that identities are constructed iteratively through complex citational processes."[63] Cultural critique of performativity examines behaviors that perform and enact identities through repetition, and under that definition it is virtually impossible not to apply the same critique of iterative identity building to theatrical behaviors.

Theatrical exploits also do things performatively, especially within the bounds of their event, through the act of repetition. Whereas cultural performatives create perceptions by hiding their constitutive power behind the guise of the ordinary, overtly theatrical performatives create perceptions by reaching out into the world of the audience and suggesting the theatricality of what is otherwise understood to be normal behavior. Samuel Weber provides a useful way of differentiating between cultural performativity and performativity in theatrical settings: "Theater, in short, is that which challenges the 'self' of self-presence and self-identity by *reduplicating* it in a seductive movement that never seems to come full circle."[64] Even as we have seen in the three performance vignettes discussed above, the wholesale devotion to theatrical practice and occasion in these performances does not just blur the line between theatricality and reality but extends it out to an almost imperceptible horizon. Where, for example, does the theatrical behavior on display in Elizabeth's procession end? Which side is audience, and which is spectator? And what identity or event in the so-called ordinary world—imagined as truly divested of theatricality—is being represented in the event's network of pageants, speeches, texts, and movements, and its festival surroundings? Moreover, in the case of Manningham's viewing of *Twelfth Night*, we see the extension of the theatrical horizon through the play's repetition of elements of Manningham's and Marston's festival experience that may not be visible without the help of that intertheatrical frame. As Weber continues, a staged spectacle "involves a process of repetition that can never be entirely self-contained, insofar as its horizon is determined by an audience of spectators and not simply by the communication of a message."[65] It is the acknowledged presence of an audience—if not acknowledged in the represented content, then acknowledged at least in the theatrical frame and occasion—that makes the performative capabilities of the theatrical unique. The audience functions both to exclude and to extend the theatrical into the broader culture. Thus Austin's exclusion of theater from "ordinary" performative communication is actually, and ironically, what distinguishes the performative in theater, with the important qualification that at the same moment that the theatrical reduplicates the ordinary through the inherently repetitive practice of representation, it also referentially locates the ordinary within the confines of its event—in the audience, technologies, actors, and occasion. And the blatant conventionality implied by the ordinary in theater speaks back toward the theatricality of the ordinary in the lives of its audiences. In a word, the performativity of the theatrical event subsumes the real world of its audience, not revealing all to be *merely* theatrical but showing all to be *fully* real.

The audience's role as the immanent and circumstantial representative of the ordinary—the unfastened gateway that both closes and opens the *theatrum mundi*—helps to make visible the ways a performance can immediately shape a group of people, since the audience never fully inhabits a position inside or outside the fiction or illocution. One of the most important contentions of recent work on the materiality and historical phenomenology of drama is that early modern performances and their personnel often assume that the stage properties, spatial orientations, sensations, and emotions—together, the most immediate referents for the "ordinary" conditions of the performance—are just as manipulable, deployable, and, in short, performative as its represented content. The early modern period was a time when "the relationship between the performed and the real was much more complex and uncertain, with at least a possibility that the act of performing itself constituted an 'exercise' that effected material change in the world."[66] This is one of the distinguishing factors of early modern performance. Audiences seem to have been aware of their implication in the event and also of a given performance's involvement in a network of overlapping performances. In a sense, intertheatricality is a condition that executes the kind of repetition that constitutes performative behaviors.

Fried's well-known argument that the eighteenth century saw a shift in the visual arts toward audience absorption is a salient retrospective on how audiences in the early modern period were used to being positioned alongside the performance, looking out on the world of the ordinary without drawing any absolute lines between where they stood and where the spectacle appeared. He differentiates the emergence of dramatic "tableaux" from an early modern dramatic use of "coup de théâtre," a shift from acknowledgment to total "negation" of the beholder.[67] Fried frequently uses theatrical concepts to explain this shift in European visual art, and one of his central points is that earlier theatrical practice acknowledges the beholder by staging a sudden change "*within* the action," causing "dramatic illusion [to be] vitiated in the attempt to impress the beholder and solicit his applause." This is opposed to the tableau, which occurs "*outside* the action" and is designed to "neutralize" the "visuality" of the audience.[68] We should notice a trace of Austin's *etiolations* of language in the biological history underlying Fried's view that theater *vitiates* and *neutralizes* the audience. Regardless of whether the eighteenth-century audience's visuality is, in fact, neutralized, Fried rightly recognizes that theatricality appeared within the action of early modern performances and that this involved recognition of a theatrical effect he calls "visuality"—the performance's acknowledgment of the act and conditions of spectatorship. Visuality itself was on display through performative repetition, that is, because early modern performances were "co-extensive" in their staging of represented content and its eventuality, occasion, festivity, and genre.[69]

Thus a comparative approach to early modern performance culture approaches it at some point between cultural performative critique and a theory of audience reception. A performance could, at one time, have a representational or symbolic function and yet also a ritual function that was recognized by a given community to change things in the here and now, in Husserl's words, "by virtue of that bestowal of sense and of characteristics which is carried out intrinsically by the perceiving, the remembering, the phantasying, the pictorial representing, etc., itself."[70] It is not entirely rhetorical, for example, when *Henry V*'s Prologue demands that the audience's imagination "now must deck our kings."[71] Similarly, in sermon culture, the rhetoric of rightly receiving the word of God often demanded a certain immediate response from the audience—how they sat, where they looked, what they did and did not hear—conflating faith with the effort to listen well. It sounds all the more pertinent, then, when in a 1629 outdoor sermon Donne pronounced what we might call a perceptual imperative for the audience to engage the performance space: "They must *stay*, they must *stand*, they must *thrust*, . . . they must take pains to hear."[72]

Performative Religion

I've used the term *trans-Reformational* in describing how performance culture crossed with the theatricality of religious practice in an imbricate historical pattern. By this, I mean to invoke both the continuation of Catholic practices and habits of mind that has been elucidated by historians like John Bossy, Christopher Haigh, Alexandra Walsham, Eamon Duffy, and Michael Questier, and also how lived Christian practice builds connections to the theatrical world *across* the Reformation.[73] Just as I suggest that early modern audiences attended to a performance's fictional or representational content as well as to its theatrical scaffolding in overlapping and performatively productive ways, so too did many of these performances use theatrical strategies that were characteristic of both sides of the Reformation at once. This is not to say that the Reformation didn't inaugurate significant aesthetic shifts but that older aesthetic practices persisted in the performing arts after the Reformation, sometimes unqualified and sometimes sustained in tension (I argue, productive tension) with emerging practices.

We have seen, for example, performances of childlikeness and sincerity that exploit the dramatic power of the "Word" in dramatic scenes that paradoxically present a rhetoric of bare communication through elaborate theatrical scaffolding. Likewise, the record of Elizabeth's progress through London foregrounds the effort to engage the queen with the Bible and verbal descriptions of trust, to stretch her physically and theatrically into the aural space of a boy speaker. Yet while these aspects of performance reflect similar tendencies in emerging Protestant practices of confession and worship to favor word over image and personal expression over form, the same performances rely heavily on traditional, festival, and ceremonial behaviors characteristic of the old faith. Like a scene of *coup de théâtre* in which performer and audience share a perspective on the wholeness of the event and its horizon in greater liturgical life, this same performative of Protestant directness and reductionism is caught up in a larger dispersal of attention into images, acoustical spaces, ambience, and the seasonal labor of a performance event.

The very terms that scholars use to describe theatricality and audience reception—*presence, emotion, ambience, occasion, festivity, interiority, intention, (dis)enchantment*—reveal just how fundamentally tied performance culture was to trans-Reformational religion at the levels of perception and interpretation. It is no wonder that the notion of theatricality was in the foreground of the critical turn to religion in early modern drama studies spearheaded by scholars like Debora Shuger, Michael O'Connell, Stephen Greenblatt, Huston Diehl, Jeffrey Knapp, Paul Whitfield White, Ramie Targoff, John Cox, Beatrice Groves, and others. It is through increasingly detailed and comparative study of drama and religion that scholarship has moved beyond the binary terms introduced in Greenblatt's earlier statement that "performance kills belief."[74] Yet rarely in the past four decades have scholars doubted the multilateral and complex nature of the relation between theater and religion.[75] Put simplistically, early modern drama addresses religion not primarily institutionally, devotionally, or politically but theatrically. Many scholars have turned to a dialectical account of religion and drama, asserting that when the old ritualistic habits of mind dissolved, new ones emerged and manifested in theater, reinvented with a greater awareness of the processes of representation and subjective introspection.[76]

Further, responding in part to "latent religious content in critical thought and [phenomenological] discussions of alterity," scholars have increasingly explored a phenomenology of early modern drama as a way of describing the continuities—dialectical or otherwise—between theatrical and religious practice, suggesting that settings and objects constitute as well as mediate human relations in ways that are historically relevant to both drama and religion.[77] Critical attention has turned to how objects, bodies, spaces, and social customs appear in the perceptual conditions of performances of religious matter. Jennifer Waldron, for example, examines the body in post-Reformation theater by revealing the "somatic dimensions of Protestantism itself—

the many ways in which mainstream reformers such as Calvin and his followers in England tried to enlist the body and the bodily senses in the project of reform, both inside and outside the church."⁷⁸ Beckwith takes this a step further in arguing that the "enchantment" that scholars have often associated with the effects of religion (and religion in theater) is, in fact, antithetical to Protestant penitential values and thus also contrary to the theatrical practice of a playwright like Shakespeare. Enchantment, she argues, denotes the disconnection of people from one another—a kind of antisacrament—so she identifies drama's religious performative in its ability to reconnect people: "Only . . . without enforcement, without enchantment, can art yield its good works."⁷⁹

Styling post-Reformational theater and poetics as "sacramental," for some, is a way of filling a gap in sixteenth- and seventeenth-century devotional life left by the departure of transubstantiation and other mediatory forms of grace, such as auricular confession and penance. The representational facilities of drama, in this view, adopted a higher approach to "sign-making," one that "entails a radical understanding of signifying, one that points beyond the life and presence of the artist."⁸⁰ In such views, drama is incarnational insofar as it joins signs and things with greater assurance of metaphysical meaning and divine justice: "The plasticity of language and the mutability of experience are twin—or one—in their interinanimation."⁸¹ Yet any attempt to describe drama or poetry as filling a void left by the abandonment of Catholic sacramental theology is limited in treating a play audience as a microcosm of an entire society's felt lack of a metaphysical logic of salvation. Hence, recent interventions by Kastan and McCoy not only reject the usefulness of speculating about Shakespeare's religious confessions but argue that the broader search for ways that Shakespeare's plays may have contributed culturally to religious thought distracts us from the dramatic movements that primarily motivate his plays.⁸²

While Kastan and McCoy warn against approaches to drama and religion that threaten to benumb the effectuality of Shakespeare's art, it is equally worth considering the risk of oversimplifying theater's engagement of religion when comparing drama to ritual practices like celebrations of the Eucharist, confession, and baptism. I am suggesting that the comparison between theater and sacrament might, in fact, *over*-simplify how Christian poetics and cultural habits come together in the manifold perceptual world of a theatrical scene. Perhaps the theology of sacramentalism is not capacious enough!

Where the analogy of early modern theater as sacramental most closely approaches theatrical practice may instead be in the sacrament's own theatrical action—as opposed to its metaphysical claims. Specifically, I am referring to the sacrament as performative, that is, how the ritual of a sacramental utterance or act attributes mediatory potency to the senses and places enormous weight on a participant's intention.[83] As theatricalized speech acts, sacramental events in the decades after the Reformation in England involve activities of body, perception, and thought that in some ways exceed the metaphysical categories argued over in early modern treatises about sacramental theology. In this way, the notion of a "sacramental theatricality" participates in a broader intertheatrical category of what Groves terms an "incarnational aesthetic"—an integration of dramaturgical commitment to the image and spectacle with an increasing belief in the performative power of the word.[84] And even more broadly, such sacramental or incarnational traces in performance culture constitute part of what Helen Cooper means by the "total theatre" of the early English playhouse. Post-Reformation theatrical productions retained from medieval practice an iconic effect where "anything can be staged" and where visual elements of "plot structure," "visual iconography," and "stagecraft" not only represent but create connections between audience imagination and the "cosmic."[85] This phenomenality persists in England after the break with Rome in explicitly sacred forms such as the Eucharist and in baptism, but it can also be found in more person-bound utterances—such as marriage, confession and absolution, the contractual language of the Lord's Prayer, the Protestant notion of the divine "Word," and other theatrical representations of morality and faith. These speech acts were not new, but the commercial stage was new, as were the broadside ballad, the Protestant sermon, and new orders suppressing biblical cycle dramas and ceremonial liturgical practices; and with these changes came a nuanced sensitivity to the theatrical, especially as it informed and was itself informed by religion.

In sixteenth- and seventeenth-century England the barrier between the parallel trajectories of religious and theatrical practice was porous. One cultural discourse that markedly captures the interrelations of theater and religion is the ceremonialism controversy—the series of reforms, redactions, and polemics that debated the use of visual and physical media in worship, church practice, state spectacle, and popular festival. As I explore below in the context of Shakespeare's *Henry V*, differing views on the use of ceremonial images and objects in worship and even on the call to uniformity and adherence to the church calendar reflect competing understandings of how media relate to Christian devotion.[86] Significantly for a comparative study of performance culture, the line between the risks and promises of devotional media is often drawn along the question of perception—Exactly what sort of clarity of mind and perception is needed to access God's grace?

Consider, for example, how the puritan-minded sixteenth-century theologian William Perkins views religious rites as mediating but by the same token obfuscating faith. He devoted much of his writing to defining the role of the sacraments in this regard, arguing that the sacraments should be considered "voluntarie" instruments as opposed to "proper" instruments of grace, where a proper instrumental medium is one where the object or form that a person experiences can be said to objectively transfer grace.[87] Perkins offers the act of writing as a counterexample: "When the scrivener takes the pen into his hande and writes, the action of writing comes from the pen, moved by the hand of the writer." He disagrees with this properly instrumental formulation and contends that sacraments are voluntarily instrumental in that while they operate as "signes representing to the eyes that which the word doth to the eares," it can only be said that God himself transfers grace—the author, not the pen.[88] The distinction is subtle but prominent in the early modern theatrical imagination, for the implication of Perkins's Reformed distinction is that right sacramental worship depends heavily on the knowledge of the devotee—that is, on one's intention toward God as the sole cause of grace. Thus, in a treatise on how to discern whether someone is elect or reprobate—and, it might be added, in a formulation that curiously foreshadows Descartes's "clear and distinct" perception—Perkins describes the perception of grace as inherently unmixed with the perception of instrumental media: "The knowledge of the elect, is pure, certaine, sure, distinct, and particular: for it is joined with a feeling and inwarde experience of the thing knowne."[89]

Tellingly, Richard Hooker, a theologian who frequently wrote in support of tempering Protestant reforms and thus against Perkins's views, notably agrees that the root question that determines the problem of ceremonialism and devotional media is that of clarity of perception. Targeting the opinion espoused by Perkins, Hooker criticizes those people who "elevate too much the ordinary and immediate means of life, relying wholly upon the bare conceit of that eternal election, which notwithstanding includeth a subordination of means without which we are not actually brought to enjoy what God secretly did intend; and therefore to build upon God's election if we keep not ourselves to the ways which he hath appointed for men to walk in, is but a self-deceiving vanity."[90] Hooker grants that puritans recognize a certain necessity to the sacraments (in this case, baptism) but protests that they locate this necessity exclusively in God's "secret" intention. Those who hold this opinion are like "the old Valentian heretics" who ascribed salvation "unto *knowledge* only."[91] Salvation is mediated somehow, Hooker contends; and he asks, Which medium attributes more action to God, water or one's own knowledge? According to Hooker, although the sacraments "contain *in themselves* no vital force or energy," they are nonetheless "*moral instruments* of salvation," which Hooker compares to the notion of the human body as the form of the human soul: "Now even as the soul doth organize the body, and give unto every member thereof that substance, quantity, and shape, which nature seeth most expedient, so the inward grace of sacraments may teach what serveth best for their outward form."[92] In both camps, the sacraments are necessary intermediaries of salvation, but for Hooker the difference is in where one locates the efficacy of the sacramental sign, in God's secret intention or *also* in the material sign.

Hooker stresses that, in his opinion, the puritans advance only a partial truth. The efficacy of the sacraments and other devotional media indeed depends on a participant's knowledge, since knowledge is a component of faith, but because of the materiality of the human condition this knowledge is never disengaged from physical circumstances or purely inward. In a way—and especially given his project in *Of the Laws of Ecclesiastical Polity* of looking back before the Reformation and attempting to minimize unnecessary reform—Hooker's stance reflects the trans-Reformational tendency in performance culture of utilizing the performative power of Protestant rhetoric and antitheatricalism while still paradoxically foregrounding the theatrical scaffolding and occasion of the event to extend a performance's reach to the audience and beyond.

It is also notable that the question of God's ordinance regarding the institution of the sacraments is not really up for debate in the writings of theologians like Perkins and Hooker. The arguments center on human psychology and epistemology; they are about the relation between experience and knowledge, and about what kind of knowledge warrants action. We may well be reminded of Hamlet's musings to this effect. What, according to Hamlet, does he know about the Ghost, and what degree of certainty *should* be enough to motivate action? Recent scholarship on the soliloquy form and on Hamlet's in particular has challenged the view that soliloquy occasions a space of contemplative remove or skepticism, instead suggesting that Hamlet's soliloquies emphasize his theatrical entanglement, as moments of pronounced contact with the material world. Brian Cummings contends that "soliloquy is always *performative* rather than *cognitive*. Yet in the process he [Hamlet] becomes aggressively doctrinaire about his own distinctions, which are not perhaps as precise as he claims."[93] Similarly, David Schalkwyk suggests that such performances of inwardness on stage create "traces of exteriority that are borne in the very silent listening of the deepest inwardness."[94] Midway through the play, Hamlet confronts the reverse of himself in the player who delivers the emotional speech on Priam's death. Unlike Hamlet—self-characterized as "a dull and muddy-mettled rascal," "unpregnant of my cause"—the player has no real-life cause but "a mere fiction," and yet he can "force his soul so to his own conceit" (2.2.502–3, 487–88). Hamlet's self-diagnosed problem in this scene is that he is "unpregnant" with the Ghost's message, while he envies the player who impregnates his mind with the mere power of "his own conceit." Hamlet knows his cause for action, but he cannot seem to perceive it with the fixity and clarity of mind required to excite his emotions. He cannot render it "unmixed with baser matter" (1.5.104).

Shakespeare's depiction of uncertainty and inaction here reflects the greater performance culture's intersection with the religious controversy over ceremonial mediation. Hamlet's anagnorisis in act 5, where he turns to "indiscretion" and "rashness," leads him to a total submission to outward circumstance. Shakespeare "transforms theology into tragedy" as Hamlet embraces a new form of God—"a divinity that shapes our ends"—whose will requires none of the epistemological isolation that Hamlet associated with the spiritual reality of the Ghost. The answer, Hamlet decides, is not to "force his soul" to feel the conviction of knowledge but simply to act as if it did, not to fight for an unobstructed perception of reality but instead to treat the material accidents involved in the act of perceiving as pertinent intentional content in its own right—as instruments of grace. In short, Hamlet concedes the theatricality of knowledge and the materiality of belief. His future actions, he determines, will be "proper" instruments of God's intent—not *merely* instrumental but materially and objectively indispensable to God's plan. Hamlet abandons the attempt to realize the "inwarde experience of the thing knowne" and instead trusts whatever rash course of action "nature seeth most expedient."

Whether or not Shakespeare had theological debates over sacraments in mind when he wrote *Hamlet*, it is clear that the character of Hamlet is built around one of performance culture's predominant ideological pressures: the question of the purity versus the theatricality of thought.[95] Versions of Hamlet's alternations between theatricality and clarity, expansion and reduction, appear throughout performance culture in sermons, ceremonies, plays, songs, and street shows. Viewed across the Reformation period, the performances I investigate in this book explore the dramatic power found in the problem of theatricality and, by extension, in the paradoxes of mediating

God. As with Perkins, these performances include a gesture toward clearness and directness. And as with Hooker, they also affirm the usefulness and the inevitability of the theatrical. Further still, *as theatrical performances* they grasp the emotional and social power of the interplay between the two perspectives.

This is an artistically felicitous paradox that long predates the Reformation. Augustine, who influenced the development of medieval Christian aesthetics and whose arguments against aesthetically appealing spectacles in religious devotion reemerge in the writings of early modern antitheatricalists, uses this very problem of theatricality to frame his memoir of conversion. He opens his *Confessions* by drawing an analogy between the limitations of language and the impossibility of containing God: "We cannot think you are given coherence by vessels full of you, because even if they were to be broken, you would not be spilt."[96] Kristen Poole evocatively describes this as "a moment of spatial and spiritual vertigo," apt for how it links language and knowledge in the concept of capacity and material constraint.[97] Yet despite his felt ineptitude to describe God, Augustine, even in the ostensibly sincere and rhetorically divested mode of confessing, determines to try nevertheless: "What has anyone achieved in words when he speaks about you? Yet woe to those who are silent about you because, though loquacious with verbosity, they have nothing to say."[98] He applies the same principle to the topic of beauty in his well-known "Late have I loved you" prayer that appears later in the book. Regretting his misspent youth chasing sex and attending plays, Augustine simultaneously protests the aestheticizing of religion while also admitting that the human faculty of desire is in some sense divine: "The lovely things have kept me far from you, though if they did not have their existence in you, they had no existence at all."[99] Like Hamlet, Augustine comes to reject the notion that there exists a perspective on the divine that is free of the influence of desire, doubt, and theatricalization. In acknowledging the limitations and even aesthetic risks of his own writing and yet continuing to write with intended eloquence—"Woe to those who are silent"—Augustine performatively disavows and then reasserts the theatricality of the confessional speech act, foreshadowing the pattern of the examples I've discussed.

Early modern performance culture fosters the paradoxes of mediation that characterize devotional discourse across the Reformation. Yet can we really say that early modern performances like ballads and plays navigate these deep philosophical and religious questions or, even further, that they actively shape the religious ideas and activities of Christians at the time? The answer depends on what counts as evidence of religious engagement and practice—or better, what oppositions of belief and practice, institutional and popular, doctrine and devotion, are used to delineate the causes of religion. The discipline of literary studies has influenced early modern religious history especially by expanding what counts as religious life and by insisting on the ability of nontheologians and nonclerics to shape religious practice. In such spaces, to borrow from David Hall, "lay" performance-goers might be seen to enjoy "a certain measure of autonomy; here they become actors in their own right, fashioning (or refashioning) religious practices in accordance with local circumstances.... arising out of custom, improvisation, and resistance."[100] As it happens, "custom, improvisation, and resistance" are three terms that centrally characterize the critical focus of early modern drama studies as a whole over the last four decades.

As I represent it in this book, religion flexes in and out of performance culture at inter- and intratheatrically creative points. To view these theatrical expressions of religion requires lending performances a degree of autonomy, always qualified but never subsumed by historical narratives that locate the source of religion elsewhere. The history of early modern theatricality is *not* the history of post-Reformation Christianity in England, but the two are differentiated not as much by quality as by scope. And they intersect at more points than a mere survey of shared literary themes will produce. "The challenge," writes Robert Orsi, "is to study religion dialectically, on the levels both of the self and of culture, tracking back and forth between structure and agency, tradition and act, imagination and reality, and, in the process dissolving the solidity of such dichotomies."[101] In the playhouse, church, pageant carriage, and street, audiences both attend to and participate in activities that oscillate between "imagination and reality." Thus one of my central observations is that the contradictions that result from attempts to capture theological truths in "vessels" of human knowledge in specifically religious venues lead to the same maneuvers of rhetoric and contextualization—in short, the same theatrical strategies—in the world of early modern performance. And although the notion that religion and theater "share" characteristics misconstrues them as categorically separable in ways that I, for one, cannot justify, my language for their collaboration and compatibility necessarily depicts them as discernably separate, an ironic statement given that one quality that religious and performance culture can be said to share, I believe, is their acknowledgment of the ubiquity of the theatrical.

THE FOLLOWING CHAPTERS examine the intertheatrical connections and shared performative strategies of early modern performance culture. The contribution these studies make to the history of religion in England does not take the form of identifying specific denominational characteristics in given performances; nor do I argue that Christian practice deputized the stage or, conversely, that the stage secularized its religious content. Instead, these chapters grant a degree of autonomy to early modern performance culture as a network of sites and dramatic forms capable of receiving, reproducing, and advancing religious ideas and practices. In the course of identifying these ideas and practices—since they do not always fit a confessional agenda—I will turn to theological and popular devotional texts as the plays, sermons, ballads, pageants, ceremonies, jigs, and liturgies I discuss appeal to them. Still, the material I want most to offer in this book emerges within and between the performances themselves, in their attitudes toward the theatrical. In essence, this is necessarily also a statement about audience response, given my suggestion that one of the defining features of comparative early modern theatricality is its performative gesture toward the audience, as performances use the audience to expand their reach into spectators' bodies, into their visual and acoustic environments, into their spiritual sensibilities, and through their future actions.

Chapter Two

THE REAL PRESENCE/ABSENCE OF GOD IN THE CHESTER CYCLE PLAYS

Biblical cycle plays form one line of the dramatic ancestry of the theatrical in late medieval and early modern England. For certain parts of England, biblical dramas were perhaps the most elaborate form of popular theatrical performance. They were often huge productions that culled the resources of entire towns, enlisting guilds to produce and sometimes collaborate on individual plays performed on lavishly decked carriages. As narrative performances, aesthetic spectacles, technology exhibitions, and festival events, these pageant dramas and especially their longest generic form as biblical cycle plays encompass numerous interlinking performance types, including not only plays but music, dancing, games, Passion tableaux, vices, comedic dialogue, and cries—as when the crier would ceremonially announce the beginning of the play. And of course these intertheatrical connections increase when we account also for the contextual performances enacted by biblical drama's various liturgical occasions, such as Corpus Christi and Whitsuntide.

Religion centrally informs the theatricality of late medieval and early modern biblical play cycles, most obviously in their adaptations of biblical episodes; but identifying how Christian practice informs cycle drama's theatrical identity involves a deeper process of disambiguation, as these productions constantly blur the lines between author and performer, performer and character, and performer and audience. And just as biblical plays might be paired with ecclesiastical or civic events in different places and times, examining the devotion or religious celebration integrated into their theatricality requires locating religion not only in liturgical and ecclesiastical elements but also in their towns, craftspeople, local customs, competitions, commerce, and communities. In other words, while biblical cycles are full of spiritually iconic and sometimes didactic scenes that reenact and pay homage to traditional faith, they also engage faith in and of the present moment in acts of producing and witnessing the show, performatively creating scenes of faithful response designed to exist simultaneously in the sacred past and in the theatrical and urban present. In what follows, I turn to the Chester cycle plays as one example of this amorphous genre that initiates the performative gesture I outlined in chapter 1: an open acknowledgment of dramatic scaffolding and perceptual self-consciousness to the end of enacting thematic responses in its immediate audiences.

Biblical cycles' strategies for presenting religious material are to some extent inherited from their liturgical-theatrical predecessor in the medieval Feast of Corpus Christi—a festival celebrating the body of Christ sacramentally manifested in the Eucharist. Indeed, in the past some scholars have classified cycles like the Whitsun plays of Chester as "Corpus Christi" cycles because of their shared heritage in the feast, though the Corpus Christi "plays" found in the archives represent a wide variety of events that were produced during the feast, many of which have no apparently essential connection to Corpus Christi. Although there has been debate over the extent to which the cycles should be attributed to the liturgical festival, the festival occasion and the cycle dramas of Whitsuntide nonetheless intersect at many fascinating points, one of which is their shared futures of suppression in the decades following the beginning of the Reformation. All of the major English cycle plays were eventually suppressed for their connections to the old religion. Many of the conventional iconoclastic assaults were applied: biblical cycle plays were profane, vulgar, superstitious, and vainly ceremonious. Yet plays like the Chester cycle that survived at least into the 1570s should not be categorically lumped together with other forms of suppressed art.[1] Cycle plays existed among divergent opinions about their medium's suitability for representing sacred material, but scholars such as Kurt Schreyer, Beatrice Groves, and Lawrence Clopper have shown the complexity of their responses to criticisms.[2] Clopper has argued that vernacular drama emerged partly as a creative response to critical "attempts to suppress or rechannel lay festival behavior."[3] Such antitheatricalism unintentionally "opened a space" for more elaborate narrative forms of drama, carefully designed not to foreground overlaps with the "somergame" and clerical *ludi* and *miracula*. By focusing on the Chester cycle and its illuminating archive detailing its responses to post-Reformation critique, I want to advance a similar understanding of cycle drama as building into its text and dramaturgical strategies the very contextual tension between lay festival and ordered ritual from which it emerged and through which it continued to reform itself through the sixteenth century.

As represented in antitheatrical complaints against them, the plays indeed provide farcical opportunities for what some may have called idleness; but, as I will show, their festival contexts and subtle presentation of theatricality encourage spectators to imagine their management of the event's sensationalism as involving a moral strategy of its own. Hence, the Wycliffite author of the fifteenth-century "tretise of miraclis pleyinge" recognizes the force of the plays' attempts to mediate godly belief even as he condemns it, writing on the one hand that "miraclis pleyinge been verrey leesing as they ben signis withoute dede" but also that "they ben holden in mennus minde and oftere reherside by the pleyinge of hem than by the peintinge, for this is a deed bok, the tother a qu[i]ck."[4]

There is no critical consensus about how audiences received religion in the Chester plays, except perhaps that scholars often describe the plays as conveying or even embodying religion in forms that go somewhat beyond the mere representation of didactic and narrative content. As Theodore Lerud argues, cycle and miracle drama offers a "quick" (living) form of religious spectacle, bound up with powerful structures of religious mediation and in some supermimetic way seeking to manifest "Christ's living presence."[5] Focusing on the performers' perspective, Margaret Rogerson suggests that Chester's players may have experienced "affective piety" through the "imaginative meditation" involved in impersonating the deep emotions of biblical characters.⁶ Critics including Mervyn James, Victor Scherb, Gail Gibson, David Coleman, and Glynn Wickham tend to take a broader devotional or incarnational view of the plays, focusing on how they are infused with the divine from the top down and applying principles of devotional and sacramental aesthetics to the plays' symbolism and to the social bodies surrounding them.⁷ Beckwith's treatment of the York cycle takes these suggestions further by focusing on the plays' multivalent impersonations of the body of Christ and how these impersonations extend the drama of the Eucharist to the social body of the church and, indeed, of the plays themselves.⁸ Such ostensions, I would add, characterize the parading of the Eucharistic host in the reliquary that featured at the center of Corpus Christi processions. But it is a matter of theological and literary interpretation as to whether such forms as the Corpus Christi Feast, the procession, and even the liturgy and Eucharist should be viewed primarily as representing devotion to the exclusion of theatrical accouterments or as inspiring more overtly histrionic forms to celebrate biblical instruction and sacramentality.

I argue that the Chester cycle is one example of how biblical drama demonstrates the latter interpretation. The Chester cycle acknowledges conflicting attitudes of play-going yet also asserts its devotional power in a complex world of signification influenced in part by the habits of devotion represented in the Corpus Christi tradition. Further, I want to offer a qualification to the characterization of such drama as "sacramental theater": while the sacrament of Holy Communion is part of the cycle drama's theatrical history and is also dramatized in many dramatic episodes themselves, the Chester cycle does not seek simply to extend sacramental grace or symbolism: quite the opposite, it seeks to activate its audience's faith by calling attention to what I will describe as its disincarnate immanent spectacle. To explain this, I will examine several specific theatrical scenes in the cycle and the ways that they at once evoke and yet pointedly depart from their performative relatives in the liturgical tradition—relatives such as the Corpus Christi Mass itself. Hence, there is a sense in which the Chester cycle reverses the semiotic motto of its sacramental—and theatrical—ancestor. In describing the Eucharist in the liturgy for Corpus Christi, for example, the Sarum Missal instructs participants to understand that "signs, not things, are what we see," referring to the blood and body transubstantially present in the wine and bread and also to the imperative to believe in the miracle.[9] Yet consider also the broader theatrical atmosphere of the Chester plays, where local craftsmen don costumes to impersonate high-profile biblical characters, demarcated by recognizable spoken lines and conspicuous props. Imagine the ornate sets, large crowds, and surge of economic exchange during the festival—the cycle as a religious event as well as a regular enactment of regional identity, craft, and commerce. In the absence of an actual monstrance and altar, the cycle gives audiences *things, not signs*. That is, the theatrical effort of the plays viewed as an event is a constant reminder of the labor and property of the present, sensible scene.

The theatrical and the religious in the Chester plays, thus, can be said to cohere in the withdrawal rather than presence of miracle. Such divine invisibility directs attention to the condition of audience visuality as a perceptual limit that defines not only its aesthetics but also its presentation of the sacred—in effect, instigating a form of phenomenological reflection that dwells on the givenness of the spectacle. This is most evident in the disappearance of God in the first play, *The Fall of Lucifer* by the Tanners. In the play, God and his angels live in harmony until the audience experiences the stage directions: "*Then they sing and God shall withdraw.*"[10] God indefinitely vacates his throne and leaves the angels alone in heaven. At this point, things change: the teleological structure of God's creation is splintered by Lucifer's doubts and actions of self-exaltation; sin is born; and the cycle unfurls into play after play of confounded characters struggling to see God and reckoning with the sense-fallible condition of humanity. In a significant way, even the appearance of Jesus in *The Annunciation and the Nativity*, which begins with Gabriel's recital of the Ave Maria, finds its theatrical release in the rising action caused by the missteps of its preceding characters and typological foresights. As I will explore, the primordial event of God's disappearance changes the representation of religion in the play precisely because it dramatizes the obstruction of access to dogma and divine presence per se and shifts attention to the constraints of spectatorship and audience interpretation as sites of faith. In other words, the cycle in some ways defies notions of noncommitted mimetic representation and thus highlights its vernacularism and nonsacramentality. This observation might beg the question were it not for the plays' consistent gestures toward what they are not: they are not scripture, and they are not the transubstantiated host; and, according to their adaptations to Protestant doctrine after the Reformation, at least rhetorically, they are not Catholic.

Consider, for example, several convergences of drama and cultural censure in the year 1576. This was the year of the suppression of the Wakefield plays and the imposition of significant restrictions in York that prohibited the impersonation of God in plays. It was also the year of the opening of London's first commercial playhouse, the Theatre. Furthermore, 1576 was the year that a group of London actors visited York for a performance.[11] In a sense reflecting Chester's disappearance of God, the broader theatrical practice of impersonating the divine gave way to the birth of a commercial subculture where, as I will later demonstrate in plays like *Henry V* and *Doctor Faustus*, representations of the divine were frequently used not to refer the audience to institutional faith outside the playhouse but to extend the scope of theatrical media to include both sensational dramatic action and spiritual edification. Biblical cycle plays did this by emphasizing audience exposure to theatrical strategy and thus by revealing their representations of the sacred to be contingent on craftsmanship and on the audience's own perceptual activities. Thus the invisibility of God in the Chester cycle is not only a source of dramatic conflict within the plays but also a bearing point for exploring the relation between religion and theatricality in the transition to early modern drama. In this chapter, I look primarily at three plays in the Chester cycle — *The Last Supper*, *The Healing of the Blind Man*, and *The Fall of Lucifer* — and at the performative and religious consequences of the things and obstacles that limit sacred access. I attend in particular to the performative opportunities that obtain with the onset of Protestant restrictions on biblical plays, though in the end the play and its banns use these ecclesial pressures simply to enhance the play's strategy all along: to fortify a festive Christian society around divine disincarnation and the obfuscation of the sacred.

The Real Presence of Theatrical Gods

The plays of the Chester cycle include what a seventeenth-century playgoer in London might perceive to be overlapping purposes—religious instruction, civic celebration, liturgical event, commercial activity, and dramatic entertainment, among others—united in their shared festival occasion. Although caution is necessary when linking early English theater too closely with specific feasts, one way to examine the religious reception of the Chester cycle is by comparison to the Corpus Christi Feast and the theology that it propagated. Founded by a canoness known as Juliana of Liège, or Juliana of Mont Cornillon, the Corpus Christi Feast was added to the church calendar in 1261, roughly fifty years after the church officially approved the doctrine of transubstantiation. Much of the original liturgy for the feast's Mass has been attributed to Thomas Aquinas, which includes the sequence *Lauda, syon*, that I discuss below. The festival became a feast of Canterbury in 1317, and the thirteenth century saw the popularization of various forms of Corpus Christi processions to accompany the Mass, including in England. Eventually, performers found occasion in the feast to produce plays. Such plays were not so derivative from the feast as to constitute a specific "Corpus Christi play" genre, as Alexandra Johnston has discussed, but in certain regions the tradition of hosting a play during the festival eventuated in the late fourteenth century in the development of large-scale cycle drama, in Cheshire transferred to the Whitsun season.[12] Like other cycles, however, Chester's integration of religion at the levels of theater and occasion did not survive, historically speaking. Performances of the cycle were sparse during Elizabeth's reign; recorded performances occurred in 1561, 1567, 1568, 1572, and 1575.[13] In this section, I want to use the reasons for the cycle's suppression and also its relation to its Corpus Christi liturgical heritage as cultural contexts for suggesting some possibilities about its performativity as a religious production.

Sometime before 1540 the cycle's banns were rewritten in reaction to Protestant ideas about devotion and art. The banns are a prologue delivered before the plays that include an announcement of performance and a review of the individual guilds and their productions.

There are two extant versions of the banns, presumably from either side of the Reformation. The post-Reformation or "late" banns are almost entirely different from the pre-Reformation or "early" banns. The most obvious differences are the addition of a longer introductory announcement of the performance preceding the survey of individual guilds and the adoption of a second-person imperative voice from a third-person voice to announce the guilds. Thus, instead of "Semely Smythis also in Syght / a louely Caryage the will dyght," the late banns read, "You Smythes honest men yea and of honest arte / howe Christe amonge the doctors in the temple did dispute / to set out in playe comely yet shalbe your parte."[14] The tone of the revised second-person voice communicates a feeling of communal ownership over the plays in performance. There is also a self-critical tone to the late banns, as if making transparent their awareness of the fragility of certain forms of religious art in the post-Reformation landscape. Kurt Schreyer has studied the banns' sensitive balance between alienating and yet preserving the past. One remarkable artifact he examines is a manuscript copy of the pre-Reformation banns annotated by an antiquarian named Randle Holmes II in the mid-1600s. Holmes deliberately and meticulously crosses out verbiage associated with the old religion but then also draws attention to the survival of this deleted content in the manuscript by noting in the margin that such lines have been "erazed in the booke" — possibly referring to another copy of the banns or to another document.[15] Schreyer takes the deletions to have a "double effect" of "polychronicity": "They preserve the act of censorship but also cordon off and seemingly protect forbidden areas."[16]

Many of the more explicit remarks in the late banns that criticize the perceived Catholic content of the plays have a similar effect of drawing attention to the same theatrical material that is causing political conflict. Examples include the admission that apocryphal stories "intermingle there with onely to make sporte / some thinges not warranted by any writt" and also the request that audiences not "compare this matter or storie / with the age or tyme wherein we presentlye staye / but to the tyme of Ignorance wherein we did straye."[17] Notably, most of these acknowledgments of allegedly superstitious or outmoded religious material are mere apologies; the plays retain these "thinges not warranted by any writt" — with the conspicuous exception of the rhetorical "writt" of the late banns themselves. Schreyer's compelling account of the Chester cycle's banns depicts the city's guilds and performers as markedly independent and sophisticated in their understanding of the relation between theater and political-religious pressure. After the Reformation, Chester hosted extreme Protestant as well as traditionalist factions, and we should remember especially that Catholic resistance to reform lasted longer in Lancashire—just north of Cheshire, and sharing an archdeaconry in the Middle Ages—than almost anywhere else in England. Still, while from one perspective these trans-Reformational aspects to the Chester archive can be understood as part of a survival strategy for the plays and their tradition, it is also worth asking how this combining of past and present, visible and "erased," performance and "writt," is not only defensive but also creative and productive to the end of maintaining *and* adapting the plays' integrations of religion and theatricality in the festival drama.

In other words, the polemical arguments over iconoclasm and devotional media surrounding the cycle speak to its positive identity in addition to its pressures. Yet the antitheatrical controversy may not represent a coherent cultural conversation as much as several cross-cultural monologues. As Clopper reminds us, antitheatricalism did not operate according to consistently evolving rules through the medieval and Reformational periods: "Historians of the later Elizabethan stage have read Puritan attacks on the stage as the culmination of anticipatory antitheatricalism from earlier in the century. Such an argument confuses the Puritan attack on the stage with the antiludic medieval tradition."[18]

Substantial evidence of the controversy over the Chester plays in their august years can be found in the letter book of the extreme Protestant activist Christopher Goodman. Goodman returned to Chester in 1570 after a significant stay in Geneva, where he worked with the reformer John Knox. He appears to be especially concerned with the Whitsun plays, in one letter describing them as a popish plot to maintain Catholic practice, if only at a folk level.[19] Another letter from Goodman's book written by Archbishop Grindal condemns "the usuall plays of Chester" as containing "sundry absurd & gross errours & heresies joyned with profanation & great abuse of god's holy word."[20]

The argument here is often repeated in similar contexts: that the plays distract from and also misappropriate the scriptures by representing them visually in a popular performance. This criticism is distinct from more general iconophobic critiques and also, to a lesser extent, from earlier attempts to suppress seditious drama.

The same sort of accusation is leveled by the author of the fourteenth-century "A tretise of miraclis pleyinge," who complains that the emotion incited by such plays is false devotion because it "ben not principaly for theire oune sinnes ne of theire gode feith withinneforthe, but more of theire sight withouteforth."[21] That is, if one's spiritual zeal can be traced to outward sensory stimuli, then it does not constitute true repentance; and the plays, says this author, direct faith toward the visible rather than the invisible and thus create a distraction from true belief. This is more a denunciation of the representation of sacred persons and events than of the dramatic form as a whole.[22]

Another especially valuable source for the historical context of the Chester cycle is the *Breviary* of Robert Rogers and his son David. While Rogers's primary aim is to record the play as a civic custom, writing after the plays were suppressed, he does not shy away from casting judgment on the cycle as an "abomination of desolation with suche a clowde of ignorance to defile with so highe a hand the moste sacred scriptures of God."[23] Like the other criticisms, Rogers's identifies the misuse of scripture as the plays' chief crime, mentioning also the scale of the production, the crowds, and the elaborate spectacles as a misapplication of religious energy. What we see in the Rogers *Breviary* written in the years after the suppression of the cycle is a possible integration with more familiar Elizabethan antitheatricalism.

All of these censures of the Chester cycle and its miracle-play relatives express disturbance with the plays' mixture of the Bible (and the events it holds in sacred imagination) with vernacular performance. In particular, to various degrees over the decades of the cycle's performance, critiques seem to condemn the role of the human body in the dissemination and interpretation of Holy Writ, especially in the form of inappropriate sensory engagement in devotion—and in the sense of sight in particular. Attacks on religious drama do not seem to be so developed as to fit neatly into the later Protestant division of the Word of God as heard and read versus ascetic devotion as seen and touched. Rather, they voice alarm at the notion of the Bible being performed at the discretion of a town, out of control of the larger established church, and made into a popular spectacle. The logic of these attacks presupposes that authentic devotion should be differentiated from circumstance and environment, suggesting, with the author of the "tretise," that revealing the human strategy behind belief debilitates it. On the one hand, this logic pits theatricality against church-sanctioned representations of sacred material, as Waldron summarizes: "If common sense could be used to confirm the marks that God had inscribed in the world and in the sacraments, testing these divinely given images against dead idols of the human brain and hand, theatrical production confounded these distinctions, subjecting the senses to unnatural images masquerading as lively and natural ones."[24] Yet on the other hand, theatricality is not binary in this history, as the "tretise," the banns, and the *Breviary* do not target theatrical spectacle in general but only those spectacles that infringe on the more sacred iconographies and liturgical tableaux of the church—such as the impersonation of God.

One of the central observations of this chapter is that while the Chester plays do, in fact, infringe on such material they also use theatrical energy—technology, intertheatricality, dramatic suspense—to subtly elide some head-on collisions with alleged obscenity. The cycle's treatment of the body exemplifies this capability of the theatrical. The body is important, of course, not only for its part in the controversy over physically mediated devotion but also for the part it plays in the cycle's theological and festal indebtedness to the Corpus Christi tradition that celebrated the body of Christ as a devotional object. Mervyn James's article on the early English Corpus Christi festivities has shown how the ceremonial celebrations of the body of Christ played a significant unifying role for the social body, providing the city "with a mythology and ritual in terms of which the opposites of social wholeness and social integration could be both affirmed, and also brought into a creative tension, one with the other."[25] This social function is performative and, in a sense, worldly. The city guilds, in fact, contributed to the integration of the theatrical and the social in the Corpus Christi tradition even before the Whitsun plays began, by providing lights for the liturgical procession.[26] But the nature of such theatrical collaboration was as much controversial as unifying. Notably, Nicole Rice and Margaret Pappano have shown that competition among guilds for the most prestigious positions in the light-bearing religious procession, in fact, "cast Corpus Christi as a festival marred by dissent, mobilizing the drama to celebrate Whitsuntide as a new occasion for civic ceremonial" centered more on artisan drama and less on liturgical festival.[27] Such tensions may have created opportunity for reimagining some of the themes of Corpus Christi in a newly adapted, civically oriented collaborative cycle. David Mills thus has suggested that such social integration emerged even in the economic conditions of the plays' production, including companies sharing carriages and an awareness of mutual economic benefit.[28] While the correlation between festival drama and the ceremonialized body of Christ has long been noted, the new critical challenge is explaining how this thematic relation might take new forms given the complexity of cycles' economic and artisanal connections to the feast. Rice and Pappano suggest that "the York and Chester cycles not only represented but also performed artisan identity: the plays became major means for artisans to participate in civic polity, and the drama served as a vehicle through which local artisans made public claims to status."[29] I want to advance this transfer of attention from the Chester plays' representations to their performative functions, but I apply such evidence of performativity to the enactment of the continued religious role in its civic environment, where the body of Christ is theatricalized and represented wholly differently than it is in the Eucharist and in Corpus Christi ceremonies.[30]

One can look to ways that the cycle shared in the Corpus Christi tradition's interest in acts of perception as illustrations of its own devotionally inspired, though nonsacramental, treatment of the body. Especially in plays like *The Fall of Lucifer* and *The Last Supper* that dramatize episodes that inform theologies of the body, the cycle frequently addresses the body as a perceiving subject. William Newhall's "proclamacion"—the first document (from 1531–32) depicting the cycle as a civic scene of multiple plays—says that the plays have a threefold purpose, and these three aims are fairly consistent in the cycle's archives: "for the Augmentacion & incres . . . faith," "to exort the myndes of the common people . . . [in] doctryne," and "for the commenwelth & prosperitie of this Citie."³¹ Outside the role of the "Expositor" who provides commentary at the ends of episodes, the plays' dramatic conflicts turn upon moments of confusion, misinterpretation, and sometimes physical comedy. Likewise, their resolutions typically come by way of recognizable theatrical spectacles, *coups de théâtre*, and stage technology. In these cases, the emphasis is on the body's faculties of sensation and interpretation: the body as seeing, hearing, touching, ingesting, recognizing, anticipating, and sharing, with particular regard for the body's limitations—what it cannot see and cannot touch.

We can understand this aspect of the plays' theatricalizations of sacred material not primarily as representing theology or metaphysics but as dwelling on the phenomenon of sacred immanence. By *immanence*, I mean a principle of perception whereby any object of our attention is known wholly through the particularities of an encounter, where the limitations of access are endowed with just as much meaning as its disclosures. Or as Witmore has put it, it is the perspective that identifies things in actions and dramaturgical appearances rather than in "spatially discrete bodies or materially indifferent ideas."³² With its incorporation of theatrical circumstance and ambience into dramatic action, early English theater could be said to draw a continuous relation between its spectacle as it is perceived and as it is given to perception—between its theatrical and representational qualities, a self-disclosure of theatricality in the representation itself, not dissimilar to Fried's concept of the *coup de théâtre*.

I invoke a phenomenology of givenness in this characterization of the cycle's theatricality. In the Second Lecture of *The Idea of Phenomenology*, Husserl avers that any experience of a perceived thing, intellectual or physical, "can be made into an object of pure seeing and apprehension while it is occurring. And in this act of seeing, it is an absolute givenness."³³ For Husserl, scrupulously accounting for the particularities, limitations, and circumstances of a perceived thing— describing it in its "absolute givenness"—is not meant to detract from its ontological objectivity, just as the cycle's presentations of the sacred do not overtly oppose their metaphysically laden liturgical relatives. On the contrary, such attention to the perceiving act aims to approach objectivity more closely by gaining awareness of how our acts of seeing often unconsciously project so-called empirical data onto a thing. Bert States uses the term *frontality* to describe the givenness of theatrical phenomena.[34] The Chester cycle, like other forms of medieval religious theater, foregrounds its frontality and givenness, and I want to argue that this is its primary theatrical mode of engaging audience faith.

I do not mean to imply that this late medieval theatrical emphasis on immanence is a sign of secularization. A version of this secularization narrative might proceed as follows: as God became more transcendent and less perceivable in the order of the cosmos, people increasingly began to understand the meaning of the observable world in its bare observable facts. Yet while the Reformation marks a pivotal sea change in how Europeans thought of spiritual reality in relation to personal faith, theorists have recognized that the Reformation did not simply empty the world of transcendent meaning but narrowed certain physical channels of divine mediation "in order to make him [man] open to the intervention of God's sovereign grace, the only true miracle in the Protestant universe."[35] Secularization occurred, it is argued, through the dis-integration of God and creation that opened up space for a more direct access to God.[36] Thus there is a tendency to misunderstand how the secularizing of Europe around the time of the Reformation affected the ways people understood material phenomena. In general terms, Charles Taylor describes this gradual transition as moving "from a world in which the place of [human] fullness was understood as unproblematically outside of or 'beyond' human life, to a conflicted age in which this construal is challenged by others which place it (in a wide range of different ways) 'within' human life."[37] The framing of shifts toward immanence as "challenging" beliefs in transcendence would be a misconstrual of the Chester cycle's self-reflexive presentation of its beholder's perceptual acts. While the cycle indeed embraces its role as a Whitsun performance that does not—and cannot—purport to mediate divine presence as a sacrament could, it seeks to hone its audience's habits of engagement in ways that enlarge, rather than confine, the content of faith. In other words, its vantage on immanent phenomena is never merely explainable "systematically . . . on their own terms" but always in simultaneous reference to the audience's self-referential act of beholding, an encounter in which the sacred may at any point be both inherent and deferred.[38]

Far from inhibiting religious belief, the Chester cycle makes use of its civic, social, and technological scaffoldings to prompt its audiences to revisit the question of how one's disposition toward spiritual material promotes or inhibits faith. Thus the cycle's integration of theatricality with its promotion of faith takes the form of an aesthetic emphasis on the limitations of human perception and the corresponding apophatic and potentially transcendent realities of religious drama. This emphasis is closer to a shift than a departure from the theme of immanence in the larger Corpus Christi tradition. In the feast, for instance, the theme of immanence is manifest centrally in the Eucharistic body of Christ, both in Mass and in the procession where the host is carried in a monstrance. Yet importantly, in celebrating the Eucharist, the Feast of Corpus Christi commemorates, not primarily the sacrifice of Christ, but specifically the miracle of transubstantiation and its institution.[39] The focus of the feast is the Eucharist's ability to make Christ's body accessible and efficacious to those who behold it in the ceremonies, so its imagery stresses elements of biblical and liturgical scenes where—much as in theatrical scenes—participants attribute a spiritual whole to manifest parts. In other words, the feast celebrates the miraculous *sign* as such, not deferred or subsumed by the thing signified. We see the historical importance of this distinction in the fact that the late medieval reformer John Wycliff, along with the medieval realists and nominalists that influenced him, attacked Eucharistic theology for the same stress on nondeferred immanence that we find in the feast: that it brought together the particularities of human perception and supernatural grace in the collaborative acts of administration/elevation and reception/perception. Wycliff chose a different set of metaphysical laws to apply to sacramental dogma, such as the principle that "a quantity must be identical with the substance to which it is attributed."[40] Especially given Wycliff's influence on the Reformation, this comparison speaks to the nuance in the Chester cycle's coherence with the medieval Corpus Christi tradition, both before and after the Reformation.

Rancière's account of historical transitions in cultural aesthetics is helpful for theorizing how a performance event like the Chester cycle exercises a trans-Reformational form of theatricality, a form that persists through the Protestant Reformation's influences on thought about religious images and media. Rancière argues that new aesthetic regimes come about primarily as reorganizations of how sensibility is distributed; the delineation of the sensible defines the commonality of aesthetic practices, and it assigns who is included in this commonality.[41] Only in secondary ways does he consider shifts in aesthetic values, such as Protestant iconoclasm, to operate as direct rejections or subversions of previous values. Thus it is only in a secondary and problematic sense that the medieval Feast of Corpus Christi can be characterized as treating religious mediation as a bridge (as some conventional explanations would have it) and (proto-)Protestant reformers can be characterized as treating spectacle as a divide. To impose this bridge-divide binary would be a Protestant reading of the Middle Ages. The more radical and primary change with the Reformation comes from extreme Protestantism's reorganization of religious intelligibility—the establishment of a vocabulary and infrastructure that allowed for the creation of the binary of "bridge and divide" in the first place. As I discuss in chapter 1, one way to view the aesthetic binary that preceded the Protestant Reformation and from which Protestant aesthetics broke is as an opposition between human limitation and divine excess. As I've discussed, this opposition appears repeatedly in Augustine's *Confessions*: "We cannot think you are given coherence by vessels full of you, because even if they were to be broken, you would not be spilt."[42] Under this paradigm, the church encouraged visual and tangible devotional objects not because they bridged a divide torn by original sin but because human capacity for desiring God was limited and therefore should welcome all the sensory help it could get. Visual and performative events such as liturgies and icons were understood to exceed and spill over the composition of their parts. So when later reformers rejected this formulation, they did so not on its own terms but by introducing a doctrine of total depravity that canceled and rendered superfluous the sacred's aesthetic excess.

Thus, understood not in binary terms of access and obstruction but as a quality of perceptual surplus, the kind of theatricality available to the Chester cycle was not simply supplemental to its presentation of religion but an essential attribute of the devotion that it promoted. This distinction can be applied with particular salience to recent trends in describing the sacramental operations of morality drama and biblical cycles. Central to some scholars' readings of sacramental theater or poetics is the notion that the "real presence" of God in the sacrament so saturates incarnational devotion that it extends beyond the Eucharist even to theatrical performances. Sometimes this real presence is depicted as mystical, homologous, or more than metaphorical. Beckwith's work has been particularly influential in this respect, describing the impersonation of Christ's body in the York *Play of the Crucifixion* as "the sign that looks back, the real presence that exceeds the parameters of representational space and confronts the audience's detachment with the familiar, deeply reproachful spectacle of a suffering caused by that very detachment."[43] Christ's body is really present through its consolidations of audience affect. In this way, cycle drama is performatively sacramental, even as the actor playing Jesus in the Crucifixion scene is perceived to be at actual risk of physical harm, a kind of multistability that draws on beliefs in the multiple dimensions of theological signs. This way of using the term *real presence* purports to go beyond mere associations of emotion and to recognize that the social bonds created by Passion scenes are akin to the bonds created in Holy Communion. Given the reminder, via Rancière, that audiences of early English theater operated within an aesthetic binary of limitation and excess rather than of access and divide, this sort of hypermetaphorical invocation of real presence makes sense.

But how is such religious sensibility unique to the theatricality as opposed to the theology of cycle theater? The answer, I believe, can be found by examining the potential overlaps between theatrical performativity (accomplishing something in performance) and sacramental presence. The Chester cycle and other civic dramas seek not simply to absorb their audiences into the performance but to make them aware of the conditions whereby they might be absorbed into it, as well as the spiritual implications at stake. As I will demonstrate in more detail in the Chester plays, consider briefly the effects created when the vision of the Crucifixion in the aforementioned York play acknowledges the audience and its theatrical environment, the "waye or strete" of the city:

> Al men that walkis by waye or strete,
> Takes tente ye schalle no travayle tyne.
> Byholdes myn heede, myn handis, and my feete,
> And fully feele nowe, or ye fyne,
> Yf any mournyng may be meete
> Or myscheve mesured unto myne.[44]

A scene like this is more a *coup de théâtre* than a *tableau* in that it acknowledges itself as the spectacle that moves ("feele") its audience and characters at once. The command to "Byholdes" Christ's body also establishes a sensorium organized around the related imperatives in the words of Institution—"Take, eat" (15.90). The audience is forthrightly implicated in the theatrical event, and I want to suggest that any sense of sacramental presence must account for its self-reflexive theatricalization, or, insofar as it recalls the Eucharist, its retheatricalization.

Furthermore, such retheatricalization of the event constitutes a performative doubling where spiritual themes consummate in the audience's response. Broadly conceived, Christ exists in the Eucharist as a mystical presence that results from invocation and faith. In this way it is, more accurately, a coming-to-presence in the sense that it is always beheld in the ritual context of its transformation through prayer and belief, call and response. Yet the host does not simply appear; real presence is not purely God's presence as it was imagined to exist outside of the sacrament. It is contingent on the ritual as a limiting factor. It is performative as a ritual/speech act. Thus real presence is not the same as simple presence, if by the latter we mean the presence of Christ as it is understood to exist before and after the sacrament. Likewise, real presence is also not merely mimetic representation because real presence does not refer to the presence of something outside of the theatrical setting.[45]

The example of cycle drama suggests that real presence is a thing's presence specifically as transformed—as given—in the terms and setting of its absence, by way of the ritual. It is the performative creation of identity through the ritual and repetition of its performing. And this performativity is essentially worldly, since its intent to move audiences makes use of the transformative *yet not deferring* power of the theatrical, even though it draws an analogy to the sacrament. Speaking particularly of modern performance art—with which I believe trans-Reformational performing arts have a theatrical affinity—Fischer-Lichte suggests that a defining feature of performative acts is that they establish a limit to their representational functions: "Performative acts (as bodily acts) are 'non-referential' because they do not refer to pre-existing conditions, such as an inner essence, substance, or being supposedly expressed in these acts; no fixed, stable identity exists that they could express. Expressivity thus stands in an oppositional relation to performativity."[46] Theatrical performances like the Chester cycle exercise the ability to create a worldly real presence by acknowledging the viewer and the event—that is, by closing the gap between the represented and the theatrical.

And if Rancière is right that "artistic practices are 'ways of doing and making' that intervene in the general distribution of ways of doing and making as well as in the relationships they maintain to modes of being and forms of visibility," then it is the transformation, intervention, or theatricalization—the ritualization—of represented material that makes that material present in a new way.[47] The performative occurs as the audience's attention is directed toward a conspicuous absence and as the audience then witnesses drama in its becoming. The significance of the fact that it was the Painters in addition to the Pinners who produced the York *Crucifixion* is not that the spectacle might be more realistic than their two-dimensional functional paintings but rather that the spectacle is *living*, a *quick* picture, integrated into the real lives of city audiences in extrarepresentational ways.[48] The actors are neighbors, local painters and pinners; the success of the plays is the community's material prosperity; and the audience is acknowledged in performance.

Thus early English cycle drama is sacramental in the same sense that real presence emerges in the theatricality of the Eucharistic rite—

from how it repeats the sensory binary of human limitation versus divine excess. If we remove the Mass itself and its doctrine of God's direct intervention in that ritual, then what we are left with is a theatrical but *still efficacious* real presence, the sort we find in the Chester plays. As we will see, in *The Last Supper*, it takes the form of the objects that cross from everyday life into iconicity as well as the value of collective hospitality these objects inspire.

Making Sacred Bread in *The Last Supper*

The Chester cycle demonstrates a consistent awareness of the cultural tension between the extra- and intratheatrical presence of the spiritual—its divine presence and its real presence. Such awareness is recorded in the cycle's banns. The plays' scripted content increased through its performance life, and its most significant changes were made to its banns, where the Eucharist, in particular, is a point of controversy. David Mills has shown how the early and late banns differentiate between opposing Catholic and Protestant interpretations of the Eucharist. He notes that the post-Reformation banns provide a caveat to the Bakers' production of *The Last Supper*, instructing them to "see that with the same wordes you vtter / as Criste hym selfe spake them to be A memoriall / of that death and passion which in playe ensue after shall."[49] Mills observes that these lines seek to encourage a "memorial" interpretation of the Last Supper, but it should be added that the Bakers' play itself also contains potential for a dramatization that represents the sacrament in an older Catholic manner. To this end, *The Last Supper, and Betrayal of Christ* includes an elaboration on the biblical text in which the character of Jesus, seated at the table, addresses his disciples just before uttering the words of institution. We can imagine these lines heard by audiences in the 1520s and then again in the 1570s:

> For know ye now, the time is come
> that signs and shadows be all done.
> Therefore make haste, that we may soon
> all figures clean reject.

> For now a new Law I will begin
> to help Mankind out of his sin
> so that he may Heaven win,
> the which for sin he lost.
> And here, in presence of you all,
> another sacrifice begin I shall,
> to bring Mankind out of his thrall,
> for help him need I most.
>   (15.69–80)

Although the actual words of institution ten lines later generally follow the biblical rubric—"this is my body / that shall die for all Mankind / in remission of their sin"—they are prefaced by this provocative Johannine declaration that "signs and shadows be all done." In the context of the performance festival, these lines were spoken on Tuesday of Whitsun week, the second day of performances, so to most playgoers they could also be understood as one culmination of the foreshadowings of salvation from the previous days' plays. The rainbow of *Noah's Flood* and Melchysedeck's offering of bread and wine to Abraham are two examples of narrative moments that audiences could have identified as the "signs and shadows" to which Jesus refers—respectively, to the sacraments of baptism and the Eucharist. Still, given other thematic parallels to the Feast of Corpus Christi, and given also the proximity of these lines to the words of institution, Jesus's statement could also refer to the literal presence of his body in the historical Last Supper and its impersonation in the play.

So in the context of the two versions of the banns, this sacred event can be interpreted in at least two ways: either it is reformed through interpretation as a memorial and therefore as a reminder of the immanent spiritual access that Christians have to God directly through Christ, or it theatricalizes the miraculous immanence of Christ in the physical miracle of transubstantiation. Jesus's statements contain both expressions of immanence, as represented and as embodied in the present moment of Communion.

Yet perhaps the Protestant banns distract us from a common aspect in both interpretations, namely, the crucial fact of transformation—"here, in presence of you all." I am referring to the fact that the play impersonates a biblical event that is itself the basis of the preeminent Christian ritual of the Eucharist. Of course, there is no miracle in the play; there, the elements are transformed through artisanal craft and civic production as well as through a social faith in the performative process. Thus "Therefore make haste" also refers to the labor of the play: the immense amount of time taken for the performance, the organizational structure established over the years for producing the multistage progressive plays seamlessly, and the necessarily fragmented viewing experience of any given audience member. Julian Yates, in his book on the "object lessons" of early modern England, provides a useful illustration for thinking about the ways that aesthetic representations can make meaning out of their own reliance on the contingencies of interpretation and perception. His "object lessons" are technologies, moments, and things that turn perceptions into empirical lessons, the performative work that takes place when one's experience of an object becomes a lesson. With the phenomenological critique of empiricism and psychologism in mind, Yates looks for those literary moments of erring judgment that "[restore] the labor of the things or beings that perform the work of connection and are erased or forgotten in the process. These lessons restore another order of movement to the scene, a blurring of categories. Things speak, take on faces, appear to address us. And this movement permits us to understand the formal relations between things, to perceive the labor that conjunctions do in enabling scenes we tend to read as human drama."[50]

In other words, things happen in the moments that pass while an indiscernible shape or space resolves into a face or narrative scene. Compared especially to commercial theater, biblical cycle plays do not bother to erase the visibility of their labor but, instead, incorporate the "labor of things" into the performance event. This labor can be literal and technological, as when builders construct multitiered carriages and when people behind the scenes operate a theatrical device to lift Jesus into the clouds in *The Ascension*; or, as I will show, such labor can be semiotic, slowing, obscuring, and perhaps reversing the transition from thing to sign.

I want to demonstrate that the cycle's theatrical labor is also not just a way of making faith present; it is itself transformed into a kind of ritual real presence. Viewed as a religious performance, the cycle promotes faith as a way of seeing as well as a quality of action that induces this way of seeing. Jean-Luc Marion describes faith not as a confirmation or judgment on what is visible or invisible but as a constituting condition of visuality itself. "What we lack in order to believe is quite simply one with what we lack in order to see. Faith does not compensate, either here or anywhere else, for a defect of visibility: on the contrary, it allows reception of the intelligence of the phenomenon and the strength to bear the glare of its brilliance. Faith does not manage the deficit of evidence—it alone renders the gaze apt to see the excess of the pre-eminent saturated phenomenon, the Revelation."[51] Here, "Revelation" is not specified outside of the conditions of its own revealing. The Chester plays do not distinguish between theatrical and religious practice; both take form in a community of craftsmen performing the same expensive and largely unchanging play cycle, year after year, anticipating and recognizing the comic and godly characterizations of figures like Noah or Balaam, and performing—in the sense of accomplishing and enacting—the very devotion their narrative representations are intended to promote. This is in contrast to Erin Kelly's argument that through scenes of doubt that show contrived miracles, like those of the Antichrist, "the very form of religious drama [in the Chester cycle] could remind audiences that performance simulates outward signs and rituals of faith and thus generates doubt about religious truth."[52] Kelly suggests that such doubt was productive in "giving audience members the impetus to reinvigorate their faith by participating in church rituals or by reading scripture." This argument essentially adduces the cycle's secularity by dis-integrating theatricality and devotion in the period. On the contrary, the cycle treats Christian signs as more than mere simulations. Its biblical narratives, their symbols and icons, refer principally to the performance society itself "with, through, and against the religious idioms available" to it.[53]

We see this self-conscious performativity, for example, in how biblical plays like *The Last Supper* address audience members both as

The Real Presence/Absence of God in the Chester Cycle Plays 75

witnesses of a dramatic show and as part of the community that produces, represents, and reimagines it. Consider the play's supper table as an object, probably originally built by the Carpenters, themselves responsible for *The Annunciation and the Nativity*, and eventually coming into the hands of the Bakers.[54] In the beginning of the play, the stage directions describe Peter and John walking into the town to find a room to use for Passover supper: "*Then Peter and John shall go, and they shall speak to a man carrying a brick-coloured pitcher of water*" (15.36ff.). At this point, it is likely that the actors, already standing on the ground level, walk out into the audience in search of the man carrying a pitcher. There is something reminiscent of the Corpus Christi procession here or, for that matter, of the frequent instances when the Communion elements are paraded through a sacred space. The characters walk into the city—into the audience—and the "*brick-coloured pitcher*" transforms somebody into a character. Not only does the pitcher prefigure the chalice and water basin that appear later; it also becomes the frontal aspect through which that person's clothes transform into costume and through which his speech turn into a rehearsed part.

When the disciples find him, the three approach the carriage, which is likely curtained, and the audience experiences the first of several monumental reveals in this play. Each reveal shows a scene that calls attention to its own creation, thereby simultaneously building and shedding its theatrical persona in a performative application of the themes to the present performance situation. Here, the curtain or other barrier recedes for the Owner to offer the disciples the famous room of the Last Supper:

> Lo, here, a parlour all ready dight,
> with pav-ed floors and windows bright.
> Make all things ready as you think right,
> and this have you shall.
>
> (15.53–56)

The Owner's ekphrasis directs attention to details that audiences may not have automatically noticed in the Bakers' craftsmanship, since windows illuminate less when the room is outdoors and since many may not have been able to see the elevated floor of the carriage from the ground level. He presents the room as a blank canvas of sorts, where the largest unadorned space is the table itself. The second "reveal" occurs in the time that passes in the subsequent stage direction: "*Then they shall deck out the table and return*" (60f.). Altogether, the table of the Last Supper comes to presence through an engagement with the audience and a kind of dramaturgical exposé or divesting. The audience watches one of their own present the carriage, followed by Peter and John decking the table with its distinctive accouterments—wine, wine cups, and bread, of course, perhaps as well as the other dishes of the Passover dinner. The scene's use of audience interaction would have become particularly memorable over the years, especially because of the actors' custom of sharing the bread that the Bakers made with the audience. The late banns instruct the players to "caste god looves Abroad with A Cheerfull harte."[55]

It is significant that *The Last Supper* creates a scenario in which revelation depends on exchange—exchange between actor and audience, craftsman and scene, guild and city; such exchange creates the conditions for the sacramental moment being dramatized to be enacted in forms of hospitality at the performance event. One can trace a palpable narrative of this exchange in the bread itself. It begins with the Bakers, the most fitting company to produce a play about the breaking of bread (figure 2.1). An earlier charter from 1462 instructs them "to be redy to pay for the costs and expenses of the Play and light of Corpus Christi."[56] This charter refers to a play produced on the occasion of the feast as well as to the lights for the feast itself—separate events that, I argue, share theatrical as well as religious themes.

The most prominent of these "costs" goes toward the wheat, paying three pence for three "stryke of wyete."[57] In the surviving sixteenth-century manuscript of the Chester cycle, the bread—having been baked in preproduction—first appears in the hands of Peter and John, who use it to "deck out" the table, at which time the bread is transformed into a cue through which the audience anticipates the Last Supper—a sign of things to come. It is a prop, but like many edible props it is impermanent. It couldn't have been baked very long before

FIGURE 2.1. Guild of Bakers: Bakers at work. In *Ordinary of the Company of Bakers in the city of York*, ca. 1600, fol. 42b. Reproduced with the permission of the British Library, MS 34605.

the performance, which may convey, as Diane Purkess suggests, the distress and therefore prominence of the accidence of its presence—"a metonymic trope for all the effort that goes into bread."[58]

Predominately, this play begins as a scene of hospitality. The Owner opens the doors of his home in a spirit of welcoming, and two of the disciples work as intermediaries to make it specifically hospitable for others. Lupton describes the phenomenological dimension to hospitality as "a form of theater" that conditions relationships and, for this reason, is political. The "virtue of hospitality," she writes, "[requires] a certain virtuosity, an element of pure performance." It is "a labor of display, not only the laying of foods on trenchers of wood, plate or sugar, but also the display of self and household for the assembled company."[59] What Lupton calls the "pure performance" of a scene of hospitality I would call also a scene of pure theatricality. It is a setting of the scene, and it represents something—such as the historical room of Maundy Thursday or the wedding feast of the lamb—only in a way that is secondary to its immediate use. This moment is a fitting example of the political or social performative of such biblical theater, in that there is really no gap between its representation of Communion and its instrumentalization of community mediated by props and spaces. Hospitality returns *in extremis* at the end of the play when Jesus dons a servant's towel and washes the disciples' feet.

The Last Supper uses its bread to incite audiences to attend dually to the sacred of the past as represented and also to the familiar theatrical setting as enacted in the present. The analogy of divine and earthly food has a long history and makes its way even into the Corpus Christi Mass, and specifically in the Gradual—the liturgical song based on the Psalms that is sung after the reading of the Epistle. The preceding Epistle reads, "For I have received... the Lord's body," and the first two of the Gradual verses follow: "The eyes of all wait upon thee, O Lord: and thou givest them their meat in due season," and "Thou openest thine hand: and fillest all things living with plenteousness" (figure 2.2).[60] Here, the Mass frames the celebration of the Eucharist in a voice of general thanksgiving and sustenance.

The Chester play communicates a similar analogy in its professed aim of contributing to the prosperity of the city. Of course, the scene in *The Last Supper* will be viewed in some reference to playgoers' oc-

The Real Presence/Absence of God in the Chester Cycle Plays   79

FIGURE 2.2. *Cena Domini* and *Manna Datur Filiis Israel*. In *Speculum Humanae Salvationis*, 1375–1400, fol. 037v. Reproduced with the permission of the Morgan Library, MS M.766.

casional appearances at Communion itself, but possibly the more prevalent reference is to the variety of theatrical events derived from the original Corpus Christi Feast. Besides the Whitsun plays, these include the Corpus Christi liturgy, its procession, the various Corpus Christi plays, and perhaps the Midsummer festival and play. Like other theatrical and liturgical forms, these events intertheatrically link the sacrament to a theme of general provision.

Insofar as the play depicts apostles preparing a table, moreover, it mirrors the moment in the liturgy during which the Eucharistic elements are offered by the celebrant to God to be remade as body and blood: "We . . . entreat thee to accept and bless these gi+fts, these pre+sents, these ho+ly unspotted sacrifices, which we offer to thee."[61] The fruits and grain of agricultural labor are offered in the spirit of Abel as the first yield. Yet, once again, the differences between the church and play contexts are more instructive about the scene's religious performativity than are the similarities. The entire production—story, props, actors, table—is offered as familiar objects of community practice and transformed into those same practices of social production and hospitality. To quote again from Weber, a theatrical scene such as this one "involves a process of repetition that can never be entirely self-contained, insofar as its horizon is determined by an audience of spectators and not simply by the communication of a message."[62] The play thus performs a scenario of building, cooking, table setting, serving, and acting, but these activities stream, almost without resistance, into the town, its people, and their day-to-day work—which, we should remember, includes the upkeep of materials and resources for its several festivals.

The audience's role in completing and extending this performative circle is especially visible when Jesus and the disciples are seated at the table where they at last assume the iconic pose—"*Then Jesus shall recline, and John shall sleep in his bosom.*" Here the audience witnesses the play's most climactic reveal—"*Then Jesus shall take bread, break it, and give it to his disciples*" (80f., 88ff.). In this process, the audience flashes between symbolic and immanent ways of seeing. In the hands of Peter and John, entering the carriage with the pitcher-carrying man from the crowd, the bread is familiar, while at the theatrical moment when Jesus breaks the bread it becomes referential and symbolic, representationally transformed into the body of Christ at the scene's center, reminiscent of the reliquary that held it in the Corpus Christi procession. The play's dialogue temporarily gives way to Christ's voice, an intertextual echo of the priest in the consecration liturgy:

> This bread I give here my blessing.
> Take, eat, brethren, at my bidding,
> for, lieve you well, without leasing,
> this is my body
> that shall die for all Mankind
> in remission of their sin.
>   (89–94)

In contrast to most of the cycle's homages to liturgical language, this instance uses English for the words of institution, and since Latin would have been understood as an obvious reenactment of a holy moment in the Mass, we can interpret this decision to use the vernacular as pulling back slightly from their iconicity—and it may have even been the case that repeating *Hoc est corpus meum* would have too flagrantly crossed the line. This is one of the scenes most prominently cited in the post-Reformation banns when they highlight the cycle's use of the vernacular: "These storyes of the Testamente at this tyme you knowe / in A common Englishe tongue neuer read nor harde / yet therof in these pagentes to make open shewe."[63] Before the Reformation and even up to the Act of Uniformity in 1559 the English-language Sarum rite was in use in churches and at Chester's Abbey of St. Werburgh, which was dissolved in 1540 and then resurrected the subsequent year as the Protestant cathedral. The consecration liturgy and words of institution in the 1559 Prayer Book were entirely in English, but the Sarum rite was still in Latin.

In particular, an emblematic passage like this of the words of institution puts more pressure on how its context is perceived, how its sacredness, ingratiation, even profaneness is determined largely by the performative intent that the audience locates in the performers' demeanor, the scene's aesthetics, the audience's collective behaviors, and knowledge of the play's tradition. *The Last Supper* is an "event object."[64] We might identify a given scene or object in the play, and yet this object comprises a "constellation of appearances" that, in Martin Seel's words, transition into "the state of an occurrence *on* the object." That is to say, objects like the Bakers' bread appear in a process that includes ordinary, aesthetic, ritual, and utilitarian perceptions of it: "A processuality becomes apparent in them, and through this processuality they acquire the status of aesthetic object," or, as I've described it, the status of ritual-theatrical presence. Insofar as the play differentiates itself from the Communion liturgy, it does so by shifting focus to the subjective and collective experience of the audience. Likewise, audiences come to intuitively identify the bread as part of a process itself, the process of the play, in which objects like the bread come into the service of a drama that has its own ends. Yet rather than imagining that the bread loses its former identities—while it is baked and stored, in the process of being laid on the table in the play, and before it is taken by Jesus—we can think of its role in the theatrical scene as an assembly of its identities throughout the process. In a way, such processual and cumulative identity echoes the thematic focus of the Corpus Christi Feast on the miracle of Christ's transubstantial real presence rather than on his mere divine presence. The bread and its related objects provide unique lenses of imaginative variance, to use Husserlian language. The characters, the town, and the audience assemble these objects (*assimulare*, to collect but also to seem together, to imitate), and the exposé of this process of assembly takes on a ritual function performatively akin to the consecration liturgy.

Audiences may have been less cognizant of these objects than they were of the events themselves of the liturgical elevation and words of institution, but even here the play prompts the audience to perceive the scene dually in its symbolism and in the present enactment of Christian community it symbolizes. We see these perceptual intentions blend especially as we imagine the audience's sensory memory of church contexts—what Walter Ong calls the audience's "sensorium," the embodied perspective and sensory habits of a viewer at Mass.[65] The play is reminiscent not only of the language and spectacle of the liturgy but also of its subjective feelings and of the ways it directs audience attention. The upheld bread in the play is an object of visual belief, a sign presented to the physical senses intended in lieu of understanding the Mass's language. Yet in *The Last Supper*, audiences uniquely experience a confluence of sight and vernacular understanding. Whether the audience adopted a bodily disposition of reverence toward the scene through sensory memory of the Mass is an open question. Does the fact of the bread's greater accessibility here contribute to its symbolic weight or detract from it? Even physical proximity to such prop-bread may have heightened theatrical self-awareness. In pre-Reformation performances, this sense of accessibility was heightened by contrast to the visual inaccessibility of the sacrament at church, where rood screens conditioned viewers' engagement of the Mass by actually obstructing their vision of liturgical action and sometimes by influencing it through what were often elaborate designs and ornamentation. By the 1570s, rood screens existed primarily as an artifact torn down or placed aside, but for the majority of the cycle's late medieval and early modern performances the scene's lack of a screen is noteworthy as a visible example of how the play combines iconic symbolism with sensory immanence. The use of vernacular and the visual immediacy of the scene project a nuanced kinesthetic and gustatory identity onto the sacred symbol of the bread and combine it with the attitudes of perception that the audiences carried over from their liturgical lives in Cheshire's churches. Paradoxically, the absence of such barriers of visibility, language, proximity, and even ecclesiastical-legal obligation for attendees at the play reinforces the fact of the performance's effort to convey the theatricality as opposed to the ontology of Christ's real presence.

The bread's penultimate stop on its journey through the play is in the hands of Judas. Dramatically, it would make sense for there to be a pause in dialogue after Jesus says,

> For more together drink not we
> in Heaven-bliss till that we be
> to taste that ghostly food.
> (15.102–4)

After the audience allows the transformation from real to "ghostly" food to sink in, the stage directions instruct: "*Then he shall eat and drink with the disciples, and Judas Iscariot shall have his hand in the dish*" (104ff.). Judas holds the bread in his hand for longer than we might expect, as it is not until fifteen lines later that "*Judas shall reach into the dish*" (120f.). The theological pose of the elevation moment has passed, and, suddenly and perversely, the play leaves the liturgy behind as Judas now grips the same bread in his own kind of elevation.

One might consider this moment in the context of reformers' theological objections to transubstantiation that often parodically invoked the medieval question of an animal that consumes fallen crumbs of the Eucharistic host, still relevant for seventeenth-century reformers like John Milton: "Even the most wicked of the communicants, not to mention the mice and worms which often eat the eucharist, would attain eternal life by virtue of that heavenly bread."[66] Christ's body, mystically contained in the bread, has been clutched and eaten by Jesus's betrayer, and when Judas leaves the room, the mystical bread is replaced by ordinary food, as Jesus exclaims in his own stage direction, "Brethren, take up this meat anon!" (15.137). What, in fact, is the audience eating, Jesus's body or the mouse's crumbs? Thus the bread's journey from the familiar, to the sacred, and finally to the profane leaves the loaves in a kind of limbo between symbol and food, and between holy relic and defilement, until they finally reach the hands of audience members. The Bakers "caste god looves Abroad" to the audience, who restore the bread to its original status as regular sustenance and who continue to enjoy the performers' hospitality.

The bread is visible throughout play, but its journey is slow—slowed by the movements between theatricality and representation, by the transparent display of the Bakers' hard work and by the play's interaction with the audience. It starts and falters in a sort of theatrical counter-rhythm to Jesus's command to "make haste." Furthermore, much of the theatrical labor of *The Last Supper* is focused on what differentiates it from the sacrament through both comparison to and digression from the Corpus Christi tradition. What returns from the theatrical ritual, therefore, is a kind of religious elevation of the process of *becoming sacred* through the work of cooking, building, decking, hosting, speaking, holding, dipping, tossing, sharing, and ingesting.

The Supper Table—Then, There, and Here

Objects like the Chester play's bread can shift theatrical identities in an instant, and they also can assemble multiple identities at once. Jonathan Gil Harris adopts Michel Serres's perspective on the "polychronic" and "multitemporal" qualities of objects in early modern drama. Far from remaining static or merely representative, objects "collate diverse moments in time" and materialize "diverse relations among past, present, and future."[67] As Schreyer has shown, Shakespeare's appropriations of theatrical props from late medieval theater were likewise multidimensional in how they prompted audiences to interpret them. He offers the extended example of the ass's head in *A Midsummer Night's Dream*, suggesting that Shakespeare intended audiences to import the sensationalism and antipapal imagery traditionally associated with the ass's head but to do so with self-awareness of their interpretive strategy—in a sense, treating the object as a lens of early modern historiography.[68] Most relevant for my purposes is the argument that Shakespeare was not necessarily novel in his willingness to use props with manifold interpretive potentials. Such interpretations include a prop's economic practicality (when the company already owned it), its conventional symbolic associations, and also the interpretive playfulness that results from an object that is transparently referential, even self-referential to the community at hand. In a similar fashion, I have highlighted the process and multistability of the bread in *The Last Supper*, its ability not only to be identified in multiple historical moments at once but to assemble (or "seem as") multiple things at once—where identifying a *thing* results from the combined effort of the context of its presentation and the perceptual limitations of the beholder. Not only do objects sustain multiple temporal contexts simultaneously; they also can give real form to what they signify. In other words, these props are parts, but, in the same moment they are parts of different yet simultaneous wholes brought into collaboration—sacred and profane, church and city, referential and immediate. We imagine this multidimensional viewing experience cultivating an audience that was attuned to dramatic and liturgical memory on the one hand and to their own embodiment of religious community and theatrical participation on the other.

The theatrical furniture of the supper table in *The Last Supper* is like the bread in its convergence of the symbolic and immanent but with heightened interaction with the community as a mediating body and performative limit. In the context of the religious cycle play, the table is more than just a bridge between people; it is a mirror that reflects and a platform that supports the excess of divine grace. Whereas this specific symbolic table is normally visible only when ceremonialized in the singular event of the Eucharist, in the play its work as a symbolic *and* transformational medium helps the audience to straddle several interpretive contexts at once. Should we view the table as representative of an altar, with all the perceptual attitudes of sacramental access that come with it, or should we view it as a stage prop that either sat in a storage house or served normal, nontheatrical purposes throughout the rest of the year? Or alternatively, with J. L. Austin, do these questions risk bifurcating the theatrical and nontheatrical and thus misunderstanding the extensiveness of theatrical acts and their relations to cultural performativity?[69]

Hannah Arendt notes the paradox of mediation performed by tables as both ceremonial and practical objects in an anecdote: "The weirdness of this situation resembles a spiritualistic séance where a number of people gathered around a table might suddenly, through some magic trick, see the table vanish from their midst, so that two persons sitting opposite each other were no longer separated but also would be entirely unrelated to each other by anything tangible."[70] Commenting on this passage, Lupton adds, "The table, unlike the couch, distributes distance while also creating the possibility of the face-to-face; it is quite literally the support not only of plates, notebooks and Sabbath candles, but also of the very spacing that sustains human relationship."[71] The very experience of intimacy in dining or dialoging is achieved through an object that is both screen and window, limiter and distributor of space. In this way the table is a metonym for the phenomenology of religion as it appears in Chester's theatrical scene. In the liturgical setting, where the altar table sat adjacent to a wall—the celebrant and congregation facing the table in the same direction—the table mediates not a physical but a spiritual and imaginative intimacy between participants. I want to imagine this "communion of the saints" to be the performative effect of the altar table: through ritual, an object of hospitality transforms people into a spiritual community across time. Whereas the altar table in liturgy is understood to be supernaturally performative through the metaphysical doctrine of the sacrament, the Chester play's table joins two scenes of mediation: narratively among the disciples and Jesus, and theatrically among the Chester audience and the performers.

We have no way of imagining the particularities of this table today, of course, but the Chester play's text emphasizes its personnel, its mediatory function, and notably its setting, the stage and room. Among the many famous images of the Last Supper from medieval and Renaissance Europe, Leonardo da Vinci's is in the small minority that positions its occupants on only one side of the table in a pose overtly, or theatrically, oriented toward the viewer/artist. Another common arrangement is circular, with some occupants' backs facing the viewer, often with their heads turned sideways to show profiles. A still less common rendition looks down on the disciples from above, often depicting the table as a circle. Albrecht Dürer, for instance, experimented with woodcuts of the first two positionings. An important difference between the two arrangements in visual art is the question of to whom the supper table is oriented: Does it mediate the disciples and Christ with each other, or does it present (deck, elevate, theatricalize) the entire group to the viewer? Mark Morton observes that "the three-sided positioning . . . tends to impose an emotional distance between the viewer and the subject matter," and I would say the same of the bird's-eye view.[72] While this may be true for visual art—and particularly for the absorption that Fried describes in later paintings—it is certainly not the case in premodern plays like *The Last Supper*, where the scene's interactive acknowledgment of the audience identifies them as festival members, co-laborers, and even enactments of the performance's religious material. As I have argued, early English theater drew on a religious aesthetics grounded in doctrines of divine excess and perceptual limitation rather than the later Reformational binary of bridge and divide. In the performance culture of sixteenth-century Chester, theatricality created dramatic suspense and emotional intimacy at once.

Even in missal and Mass book illustrations, there is hardly any consistency to the disciples' arrangement around the table. It is probable, however, that Chester's *The Last Supper* positioned its actors around no more than half of the table so that Jesus would be visible at a wider angle. One illustration of the Last Supper—reprinted in other texts—that shares some remarkable features with the Chester play comes from a sixteenth-century Sarum Missal printed in Paris by William Merlin in 1555 (figure 2.3). As the red-letter print beneath it reveals, this image illustrates the narrative origin of the Feast of Corpus Christi, making it especially relevant as a cultural companion to the Whitsun *Last Supper*. The most apparent difference between this image and the scene in the cycle is the circular arrangement, but we can nevertheless observe some dramatic parallels that are representative of the Corpus Christi tradition. For one, here the figures are in action. Christ is central and still, but the rest of the disciples are speaking, gesturing, and embracing. While in the Communion liturgy the scene would have been configured according to set, nonmimetic movements, its accompanying image in the missal shows the moment of institution as a narrative snapshot, as is frequently the case in liturgical illustrations of the Last Supper. In this way, the illustration invokes a historical process — a day, an event, a dinner — as illustrative of the iconic moment.

Moreover, like the play, the illustration couples the symbolic with the quotidian. Two of these details are especially reflective of the Chester play's description: the owner's portrayal to Peter and John that the house has "pav-ed floors and windows bright."[73] Along with the figure of Christ, the scene centers on the cooked paschal lamb in a dish, prominently set to play up the hospitality and ritual specificity of the occasion. Further, Judas is distinguished, as he often is, both by his lack of a halo and by the bag of money in his hand, contrasting his motion of clutching to Christ's elevation of the bread that occurs just moments later. Like the Sarum Missal's woodcut, *The Last Supper*'s fusion of such details as both signs and things collapses the emotional distance between the audience and the body of Christ. It presents the body of Christ as a dinner host and a guest, occupying a room that has particular details and belongs to an inhabitant of the city.

The play makes a point to show the audience the table at three perceptually different moments: before it is prepared, while it is in use at the words of institution, and after it has been defiled by Judas. Although there is a brief centering on Jesus's elevation and prayer, as is the case in the bread's parallel journey, the main distinction from the Mass and Corpus Christi liturgy is that audiences of the play are privileged witnesses of the domestic and dramaturgical labor of cycle theater. *The Last Supper* shows more than just the Last Supper, a narrative hinted at in the missal's image; it also distributes the space and time required for the moment depicted in the illustration to come to pass. As a result, audiences are allowed to live with the sacred event in a familiar element. This may indeed contribute to the meaning of Jesus's words when he refers to the "presence" of the occasion — "in presence of you all, / another sacrifice begin I shall."

In contrast to Mills's argument that there is no "present" in the drama of the Chester cycle, the present time, in fact, is enacted by multidimensional objects such as the bread and table.[74] The present in the play subsists performatively in these objects as fulfillments of the "signs," "shadows," and "figures" that Jesus tells his disciples to

FIGURE 2.3. *On the Feast of Corpus Christi.* Illustration in *Missale ad vsum insignis ecclesie Sarisburiensis*, Paris: Guillelmum Merlin, 1555, fol. P1r. Reproduced with the permission of the Huntington Library, Bridgewater 62286.

"reject"; they are fulfilled in the narrative, in the Mass, and also in the play itself. The Passover was *then*; the biblical history was *then*; the Mass is *there* in the representation and behind the festival; and the play is *here* in front of the carriage and within the festival. Although the play's dialogue does differentiate between signs and mere things, its emphasis is on the ways that signs and things mutually empower one another, a formulation also found in the Corpus Christi Mass.

A pointed demonstration of this is found in the Sequence of the Feast of Corpus Christi. The Sequence is a song in the communion liturgy that precedes the reading of the Gospel, in this case, from the Gospel of John where Jesus says, "My flesh is meat, and my blood is drink indeed."[75] The Corpus Christi Sequence by Thomas Aquinas speaks to the miracle of the Eucharist, but rather than simply telling the story of the Last Supper, it offers a semiotics of the scene that evokes several temporal relations at once. Its description begins by setting the "table," as it were, and by reminding auditors of the benefits of the sacrament: the altar table "to-day before us laid / the living and life-giving bread."[76] Gradually, the song makes the table, bread, and wine feel like familiar accouterments, musically invoking the historical setting that we see visually in the missal's illustration of the traditional Passover meal and dramatically in the Chester play. The table on the carriage becomes "the same which at the sacred board / was by our incarnate Lord / given to his apostles round."[77] The liturgy depicts the scene dramatically, with characters surrounding the "board" (*mensa*) that held the original Last Supper, as if to say that what was palpably familiar to Christ has been elevated to the status of liturgical furniture but is now lowered, once again, to the parish or cathedral altar table.

Thus the first of the Sequence's lessons on the semiotics of Corpus Christi is that the old symbolic and typological system (*phase*, Passover) is over and that a new form of access to "reality" (*veritas*) has taken its place.

> On this table of the king,
> our new Paschal offering
> brings to end the olden rite.
> Here for empty shadows fled
> is reality instead;
> here, instead of darkness, light.[78]

Without announcement, the historical dining table is transformed poetically into the sacramental altar table. The passage's diachrony connects the "empty shadows" *then* to the immanent communion *now*. Notably, the Sequence makes a point to emphasize a hard transition, as the first three lines of the stanza contain three adjectives for "new": *novi regis, novum Pascha, novae legis*. Definitively, the new "thing" has to replace the old "shadow." We see this same transition in the Chester plays, during Jesus's first statements after being seated at the table: "The time is come / that signs and shadows be all done / . . . / all figures clean reject" (15.69–72). The Sequence encourages auditors to approach communion with a renewed feeling of wonder as well as with recognition of its transformative power.

Two stanzas later, however, the Sequence shifts focus from the sacrament's accessibility to its inaccessibility and its invisibility to faculties of human sense.

> Hear what holy church maintaineth
> that the bread its substance changeth
> into flesh, the wine to blood;
> *Doth it pass thy comprehending?*
> *faith, the law of sight transcending,*
> leaps to things not understood.
>
> Here beneath these signs are hidden
> priceless things, *to sense forbidden;*
> *signs, not things, are what we see;*
> Flesh from bread, and blood from wine,
> yet is Christ in either sign
> all entire confessed to be.[79]

The song reinstates the sacrament's status as a sign by carefully differentiating between a shadow and a sign. Where a shadow is a typological figure that anticipates the coming truth, a sign is the appearance of a "thing." The shadow is the Hebrew ritual, and the thing itself is the sacrament. Yet in another way, the shadow-sign analogy could be applied to the sacrament and its own multidimensionality. Once transformed, the elements and their visual appearance are no longer mere shadows but signs of the presence of Christ into which they have transformed. Indeed, this is the sort of cognitive confidence in perception that the Corpus Christi liturgy consistently encourages. What differentiates the signs here from the shadows that have passed away earlier in the Sequence is the sign's appearance (*speciebus*). This rhetoric of appearing and visuality is carried through from "the law of sight" a few lines earlier, literally suggesting that "what you do not grasp and do not see [*Quod non capis, quod non vides*] noble faith holds firm beyond the order of things [*rerum*]." The rhetorical play of the vocabulary for thing (*res*) and sign (*signum*) is essential to the song's doctrinal precision, as the Sequence creates a continuum with shadows on one end, sacred things on the other, and signs in the middle. Encountering signs *feels like* encountering things, but they *are* ontologically the things themselves.

This relation between the thing and its appearance is highly nuanced, and the song's repeated yet varied forms of these terms attempt to reflect the fullness of its vision of truth (*Christus totus*) despite humans' limited capability to see it. Thus, despite being historically and contextually removed from the Whitsun plays, the Corpus Christi Mass exercises a similar performative gesture of prompting its participants to practice a certain "way of seeing" in the present. The Sequence includes the more familiar transition from the historical "shadows" of the Passover meal to the biblical "signs" of Maundy Thursday in a heuristic for perceiving the relation between "signs" and "things." Once again, we see the influence of this strategy on the performative pattern of the Chester play: the dramatic emphasis of *The Last Supper* is on its setting and quotidian objects, empowering those things and the dramatic conflict with which they are entangled to prompt acts of faith in a histrionic theatrical procedure that helps to perceptually train audiences to experience a sacramental theatrical procedure *in absentia*.

It has been noted by one nineteenth-century translator that the Sarum Missal's Sequences display "an abrupt and fanciful wildness... which may not unfitly be likened to the style of choral odes in Greek plays." He continues, "Their meaning is often very obscure, and the symbolic allusions are exaggerated, and difficult to discern."[80] I would add that the Sequence is like a dramatic ode also in its act of calling auditors, like the ode's tragic characters, to step back for a moment and consider the pattern of action. Just as the Corpus Christi Sequence discourages overthinking the semiotic nuances of the Eucharist and prompts auditors to think circumspectly, the Chester play seeks to embed its audience in the drama and its *in situ* perceptual details. It looks to its immediate surroundings for evidence of the transformative power of its Last Supper theme.

Clearly, the play is not purporting to reenact the Mass, and neither is it exactly replaying the historical narrative of the Last Supper. Instead, it is attempting to establish a pattern of repetition extended into a specific community. The late banns thus instruct the Bakers:

> see that with the same wordes you utter
> as Christ hym selfe spake them to be A memoriall
> of that death and passion which in playe after ensue shall
> the worste of these stories doe not fall to your parte
> therefore cast god looves Abroade with A Cheerfull harte.[81]

The banns treat "The Last Supper" as a memorial of the event and also as a preparation for the Passion narrative, so the guild is tasked with promoting "A Cheerfull harte" through the familiar as well as symbolic activity of sharing bread around a table. As an event and a production, the play consists of things that are also signs. It encourages audiences to see both at once and to adopt an attitude of imitation, recognizing that the mimetic or representational nature of the play blends with the actual performance of mutual charity and hospitality.

Despite its lack of a proper sacrament, in this respect it follows the Corpus Christi theme as established in the Sequence, encouraging its audience to practice faith by engaging confidently in the objects that they can understand—their community, their cheerfulness. Likewise, in the second episode in the play, the foot washing, Jesus reiterates that his actions are intended to establish a pattern of behavior: "Sith I have washen your feet here— / Lord and Master—in meek manner, / do eachone so to other in fere / as I have done before" (15.165–68). And after the disciples wash one another's feet, he charges them to "love together in all thing / as I before, without fletching, / have loved you truly ay" (174–76). Dramatic representation (shadows) and actual imitation (shadows) converge. *The Last Supper* thus is certainly not sacramental in offering any Eucharistic form of real presence beyond a string of representative associations. Yet its stagings of objects and iconic moments in positions of multistability celebrate the performative capabilities of the body of Christ—historically, religiously, popularly, and profanely—especially as summoned and shaped by the drama and festival.

Ah Lord! Disincarnating Faith

My argument has been that the Chester cycle's theatricality maintains the co-presence of signs and things that is also prominent in the Corpus Christi tradition, but the cycle shifts emphasis onto things, the "real" presence of the event, its audience, and its community. Essentially, I am suggesting that the Chester plays operate primarily as enactments rather than reenactments. They present people, props, spaces, and dialogue in their roles as narrative signs, rather than the other way around, where signs masquerade as things. This is a subtle but specific distinction in critical thinking about the incarnational capabilities of medieval drama. Glynne Wickham has offered an influential critique of the view that biblical plays attempt to "reenact" mimetically sacred history on the basis that it is simply impossible to reenact a miracle. Instead, he argues, the purpose of such plays "is to nourish and sustain faith . . . to supply in three-dimensional, realistic, visual images an outward, theatrical figuration of an abstract concept."[82]

Scholars have developed a broad-ranging critical vocabulary for cycle drama's aim to render abstract devotional content "three-dimensional" and "theatrical," variously understanding the plays to memorialize, symbolize, represent, sacramentalize, or reform their biblical content and the liturgical heritage of the Corpus Christi Feast. In recent years, scholars have turned especially to the theological rhetoric of sacramentalism to provide alternative accounts of theater's mediation of spiritual meaning. David Coleman proposes what he calls the "sacramental sociology" of religious art and argues that early English drama reflects controversies and anxieties over the sacraments, implying, furthermore, that the church was losing its ability to connect with devotees through the sacraments as traditionally administered.[83] In a sense, this is an essentially secular use of the term *sacramental*: the church, for various reasons, is unable to offer an embodied and accessible form of sacred encounter, so such encounters transfer to a less ecclesiastical context, in this case, cycle theater. Such a view adduces the religious capabilities of drama, but it does so only by implying that the church was devotionally deficient, an ancillary suggestion that is more difficult to substantiate.

Another prominent view is that medieval drama influenced religious life as a tool for memorizing sacred material. Lerud and Scherb see such plays as theatrical counterparts to devotional images and so stress the memorializing nature of their performances.[84] This does not imply that drama performed a surrogate function for the church, but it does depict the religious purposes of theater as in service to a form of devotional life that was fully centered in and defined by the church—in other words, reproduced in the plays. Other approaches, alternatively, have advocated for the ways that cycle drama constitutes the divine incarnation itself in the form of community. Beckwith defends the capacity of cycle theater "to cause what it signifies, to perform a bond of love in the community of the faithful."[85] Gail McMurray Gibson's description of an "incarnational aesthetic" understands these plays to mediate the divine but with the reminder that the Incarnation was a cultural concept that reached beyond church contexts, even enduing "crudely popular" forms with the "deliberate and conscious effort to objectify the spiritual even as the Incarnation itself had given spirit a concrete form."[86] And Beatrice Groves locates this "incarnational aesthetic" in drama's legacies of "ritualistic display and meta-theatricality," in fact, "for the whole emphasis on the visual and concrete in late medieval devotion."[87]

I would emphasize that, at least as is demonstrated in the Chester cycle, biblical drama generated a positive religious identity in its theatrical mode, and not primarily as a surrogate or supplement for the church and its devotional practices. The Corpus Christi liturgical tradition bears testimony to the theatricality of its own events, so cycle theater did not attempt to give new form to otherwise abstract devotion but rather gave new embodiment to a religious tradition that was already material and social itself. To be clear, the connection I'm drawing between the Corpus Christi liturgical tradition and the Chester cycle is not in the development of genre but in shared strategies for theatricalizing religious themes. The cycle used manifest, theatrical religious practices and semiotics as models for dispersing religious practice into the drama of theatrical appearing. The objects in *The Last Supper* provide an example of the cycle's commitment to a semiotic arrangement where sacred excess interacts with the limitations of human perception.

I want to look now at the other side of this semiotic excess, at the meaning that the cycle creates out of the limitations of perception, the fact of being "to sense forbidden," as the Corpus Christi Sequence says. The Chester cycle adopts artificiality as a theatrical as well as thematic premise. It foregrounds an immediate experience of the mundane, the temporal, and even the doubtful as it asks audiences to see something that is forthrightly *made* and yet to have faith in its power not only to bring prosperity but to transform a community in faith and practice.

From a broad perspective, one way that the Chester plays create a purposely obscured engagement with the sacred is through widespread use of literary typology and prophecy.[88] There is a centripetal structure to the cycle, with Christ's passion, death, and resurrection in the center, preceded by stories of faith and salvation that foreshadow Christ, and followed by plays like *The Harrowing of Hell*, *The Resurrection*, and *Emmaus* that dramatize characters' recognitions of Jesus after the Resurrection and so look backwards toward the Passion events. Generally, plays overlap and interact with one another, as we see in the episode of the foot washing's prescription of imitation and also in *The Last Supper*'s dual function of fulfilling shadows and foreshadowing Christ's death yet to be performed. Viewed as a whole, the cycle presents Christ to the audience in his mediated presence through prophecies, types, and moments of anticipation and recognition—the habitat of theatricality. That is, the narrative structure of the Chester cycle flows toward Christ, but it does not culminate in a revelation of Christ himself. It lingers purposely in a state of *towardness*, looking forward and looking backward toward where Christ should be, where faith and theater perceive his outline.

And the attitudes of interpretation prompted by this towardness—among others, anticipation, dramatic irony, doubt, recognition, and laughter—are both the means and the performative effects of the cycle. To a large extent, this feature of cycle drama differentiates it from liturgy by further emphasizing the horizontal over the vertical and by further exploiting obfuscation as a constituent part of religious experience and dramatic festival. This is not to say that the plays encourage disbelief; just the opposite, the post-Reformation banns make it clear that the cycle's aim is to promote belief: "thereof in these pagentes to make open shewe / . . . . / to sett out that all maye disserne and see / and parte good be lefte beleeve you mee."[89] One might imagine the towardness of the Chester cycle as an extension of the worldly and immanent media that promote active encounters with sacred representations by obscuring them. We might find religious-theatrical parallels in churches that shrouded the crucifix during Lent and in commercial theater, for example, when Shakespeare's Paulina draws back the curtain on Hermione. At times, the cycle seems to evoke the sacred only to hide it behind a proverbial roodscreen of dramatic conflict or anticipation.

We see this strategy at play in the cycle's rendition of *The Healing of the Blind Man*. The play begins with the episode of the healing and then moves to Jesus's visit to Mary and Martha and the resurrection of Lazarus. Among other distinctions, the more domestic and intimate scene with Mary and Martha is separated from the healing episode by the latter's public setting, full of accusations and arguments. These differences are appropriate given that the healing of the blind man on the Sabbath dramatizes Jesus's controversial defiance of Jewish law, while the raising of Lazarus has the tone of a personal conversation among friends. The Glovers assume the formidable task of bringing cohesiveness to these different scenes, and they do so by highlighting the related themes of visuality and belief, the same issues that are prominent in the stories' source, the Gospel of John. In Chester's *The Healing of the Blind Man*, the Pharisees' unwillingness to "hear" the account of the miracle and to "believe . . . as you see" contrasts with the Blind Man's readiness to accept Jesus's revelation—"Thou hast him seen with thine ee" (13.203, 245, 232). The stage directions at the end of this episode take spectacular liberties with the biblical source, reading: "*Then they shall gather stones, and Jesus shall suddenly vanish*" (289ff.). This was one of the cycle's many stage tricks and crowd pleasers. Jesus symbolically embodies the Pharisees' spiritual blindness by becoming physically invisible.

Several lines later, after the Pharisees leave the stage in frustration and perhaps after the carriage's curtain closes and reopens, Mary Magdalene appears and complains of the absence of Jesus during her brother's death—"Ah, Lord Jesu" (306). I want to attend to this particular exclamation—"Ah"—and its importance in this play as an expression of the theatricalized divide between the immanent and the transcendent, communicating Mary's inability to reconcile her belief with what she sees or, in this case, does not see. It is this "Ah" and its exclamation of immanent shock that introduces suspense and conflict into the episode. For this reason, we hear Martha echo the same versatile sound to express recognition rather than blindness when Jesus finally reappears—"*Then Jesus shall come*"—saying, "Ah, my Lord, sweet Jesus!" (313f.–314).

Mary and Martha transpose the spectacular effect of Jesus's sudden disappearance onto his long and torturous absence during Lazarus's sickness. Interscenically, this adds force to Mary's complaint that "in feeble time Christ yode me fro" (Christ went from me) because, according to the preceding episode, Jesus can appear and disappear whenever he pleases (309). Yet the characters' doubt also prompts the question of whether Mary and Martha share the Pharisees' blindness, especially since Jesus's disappearance in the preceding episode creates two opposing effects at once—as a show of Jesus's power but also as a reminder that this is entertainment and that narrative events like Jesus's absence obviously serve the theatrical purpose of giving occasion to stage a sensational resurrection. Why did Jesus choose not to come to Lazarus's aid earlier? The play has a threefold answer. Narratively, his delay reveals Mary's and Martha's lack of belief. Both thematically and theatrically, it also provides occasion for Jesus to differentiate between the conditions of faith and the "open shewe" of his power, theatricalized by an exciting stage technology. And performatively, Jesus's delay allows the play's theatrical strategy to inform and even shape the interpretation of the miracle that it represents.

As in many of the cycle's plays, Jesus's followers vacillate between belief and doubt. In a fashion consistent with the cycle's superimposition of later Christian revelation onto earlier biblical characters, Martha understands that Lazarus "shall rise the last day," but she does not believe in the full extent of Jesus's power now (387). This *now*, the present moment of immediate encounter, is contained in her "Ah"—an utterance that directs attention to the theatrical conditions of visibility and obfuscation. Unlike the common dramatic expression "O," which acoustically beckons sensory attention toward the speaker, in the Chester cycle "Ah" projects attention outward.[90] It aligns the audience's perspective with that of the speaker and directs its attention toward a common spectacle. Just so, Martha uses the same utterance in a momentary lapse of belief when Jesus orders the tomb to be opened, exclaiming, "Ah, Lord, four days be agone / sith he was buried, blood and bone. / He stinks, Lord, in good fay" (440–42). Jesus's emphatic reply commands attention, not only because he stands in a dramatic pose *"turning his back and with hands upstretched"* but also because, for once in the play, Jesus is claiming to speak "openly" (446ff.):

> Father of Heaven, I thank it thee,
> that so soon has heard me.
> Well I wist, and soothly see,
> thou hearest mine intent.
> But for this people that stand hereby
> *speak I the more openly,*
> that they may lieve steadfastly
> from thee that I was sent.
>   (3.447–54; my italics)

In one way, to speak "the more openly" means to pray loudly enough for his companions to hear him in the hopes that they will follow his example of faith. It also refers to Jesus's frequent caveats in the Gospel of John that his teachings are intentionally obscure until a certain point when he will speak more "plainly" to his followers, as was emphasized in *The Last Supper*.[91]

There is thus a Johannine emphasis on suspended revelation and a corresponding test of faith in the activities of interpreting and anticipating dramatic signs. Yet when one considers the play's preoccupation with witnessing and believing what is witnessed, Jesus's "open" speech can also be understood to refer to the visual spectacle of Lazarus's resurrection and the moment when the sacred comes out from behind obscurity. He speaks "openly" at the inauguration of revelation. However, once Jesus has performed the miracle and Lazarus has appeared, the opportunity for faith has passed, as has the momentum of dramatic action. Open show and open speech thus appraise faith but do not occasion it.

Mary Magdalene appears repeatedly in the gospels of Matthew and John, perhaps most prominently in her visit to Jesus's tomb, where as she turns from the tomb to look for Jesus in the city, the Geneva version reads: "Behold, Jesus also met them, saying, God save you." This echoes the earlier phrasing through which the empty stone is removed to reveal the empty tomb—"And behold, there was a great earthquake."[92] As in the biblical account, the Chester play *The Resurrection* grounds its drama, and therefore its power to promote belief, in the obfuscation of Jesus and the delaying of sacred revelation. "Behold," "Ah," see an empty tomb but understand by faith the imperceptible miracle that has taken place: "Ah, hie we fast for anything / and tell Peter this tiding" (18.362–63). Then just a few lines later, Mary relays this news to Peter and John, saying, "Ah, Peter and John, alas, alas! / There is befallen a wondrous case. / Some man my Lord stolen has / and put him I wot not where" (370–73). It is not unimportant that Mary misunderstands the angel's message and, as in the biblical account, acts upon faith while it is yet unconfirmed by Jesus himself. Especially in episodes like these Resurrection scenes that include noticeable visual spectacle, the outward projection of both doubt and wonder encapsulated by exclamations like "Ah" promotes audience faith by creating a "pure performance"—framing the scene as both a symbolic spectacle and an embodiment.[93]

Mary's and Martha's "Ah" is used in perceptions of Christ's absence or obfuscation as well as in announcements of his appearing; and in this way it communicates the perceiver's confrontation with the sensory binary of human limitation and divine excess. In other words, the expression conveys visuality and biblical revelation as given. The play uses the same utterance for the human reactions to both hiddenness and revelation and thus reflects the cycle's greater emphasis on the "disincarnation" of God. I take this term from Emmanuel Levinas's essay *Totalité et infini*, where he describes the capacity of the face of the "other" for offering knowledge of God. Yet, Levinas insists, "The Other is *not* the incarnation of God, but precisely by his face, in which he is *disincarnate*, is the manifestation of the height in which God is revealed."[94] For Levinas, it is not that the human face is mystically present, as in a sacrament, but simply that the kind of ethical confrontation enacted by the face hones one's focus into the "irreducible structure upon which all other structures rest," including structures "which seem to put us primordially in contact with an impersonal sublimity." Thus the notion of the sacred *désincarné* reflects the performative process whereby a theatricalization of a biblical moment like the Lazarus episode can create the conditions for faith by positioning its audience toward a God who isn't currently there—demonstrating a posture of towardness.[95] I have elsewhere contrasted this "ritual poetics from "incarnational" poetics by the former's emphasis on the absence of transcendence and by the opaqueness of human appearing.[96] *Ah!* speaks to the potential for faith that preceded it, a potential predicated on the withholding of revelation. Thus, like the supper table, Mary and Martha serve as spectacle as well as mediation, both liturgical furniture and prop. They represent the audience and character at once. It is characteristic of early English theatricality to stage a critical spectacle within the action, so allowing the spectacle to be seen by both the audience and the characters, and it makes this experience self-reflexive as audience members witness the characters' responses while they manage their own.

This performative effect is not only metatheatrical. The Chester cycle is like an empty monstrance of sorts, historically adjacent to the Corpus Christi tradition but also conspicuously missing its sacramental status performed by the elevation of a priest. *The Healing of the Blind Man* and *The Last Supper* seek to promote belief by foregrounding their emptiness and their practical familiarity, illustrated by the moment when Mary Magdalene turns from the tomb to behold Jesus standing behind her. Yet the plays' strategic displays of theatricality are more than reflective and more (or perhaps less) than meta-, since the play conjoins dramatic action with the conditions of its production and also with the audience's activities of spectatorship.

It should be no surprise, therefore, that Lazarus's response to his own resurrection—after the miracle—takes a different form. It expresses wonder but not theatrical faith. Among twelve "Ah's" in the second half of the play alone—more than any other play—Lazarus's "Ah" expresses the same activity of perception and nonperception that it does for Mary and Martha; but where the women fail to believe, Lazarus's "Ah" reflects a kind of deductive reasoning and thus circumvents an experience of the disincarnate: "Ah, Lord! Blessed most thou be, / which from death to life hast raised me / through thy mickle might" (456–58). Jesus "most" (must) be "Blessed" because his power is "mickle" (abundant); his power is evidence, incarnate. Lazarus too has faith, but it is not the same sort of unmediated faith that the audience is invited to experience alongside Mary and Martha.

The Healing of the Blind Man presents the invisible as an object of faith. The play creates tension between revelation and obfuscation, but it reveals this tension to be dramatic and temporary. Its episodes show some of the more extraordinary miracles that Christ performs in the cycle, but the challenge presented to the audience is that of having faith without the need for an "open shewe" of divine power. By showing the audience the spectacle and the activity of beholding, the play exposes the strategy behind theatrical appearing. It treats faith and theatergoing as contingent on the same conditions of hesitation, inscrutability, and doubt.

Believing in the Invisible in *The Fall of Lucifer*

Obscuring the sacred and creating dramatic conflict are part of the same theatrical process. Both require certain amounts of wonder and self-doubt, affirming T. G. Bishop's statement that "perception is liable at any moment to become the theatre's subject, so that theatre is always about to suggest a theory of itself."[97] In this respect, the first play of the Chester cycle, *The Fall of Lucifer*, is the most important in establishing a constructive attitude of perception. It tells the story of Lucifer's ascension to God's throne and consequent damnation. It grounds the cycle in an initial conflict based in an obscured vision of God. Sin enters in the form of Lucifer's faulty interpretation of divine withdrawal. From a theological perspective, *The Fall of Lucifer* is particularly noteworthy because it takes on the task of explaining the provenance of sin within a perfect universe, and while it does not go as far as to answer the accusation that Daniel Defoe would later level against *Paradise Lost*—that it does not address the "main problem" of how "the spotless seraphic nature could receive infection"—it might well remind us of the Miltonic tradition in its humanizing of Lucifer in that the play's interest in the origin of evil is a worldly reflection on visuality and beauty.[98] It refers directly to the conditions of sight in the spectacle of theater, treating Lucifer as a kind of theatergoer himself. *The Fall of Lucifer* dramatically asserts two conditions: first, that the obscurity of God is a fundamental component of Christian faith, and, second, that this obscurity creates the conditions of dramatic conflict. The cycle's first play thus offers itself and its instigation of dramatic conflict as a kind of training in popular, festive devotion.

Consider, for instance, the first four-line stanza of the play. This opening contains perhaps the most brazen and potentially controversial combination of divine imagery and theatricality in the entire cycle.

> GOD   Ego sum alpha et oo,
>   primus et novissimus.
>   It is my will it should be so;
>   it is, it was, it shall be thus.
>   (1.1–4)

These first two lines also open plays 2 and 24, the latter being the final play of the cycle, *The Last Judgment*. They use a somewhat phonic version of commonplace Latin, the language of the Eucharist and of the Bible, and subject it to the craftsmanship of human authorship, acting, and the festival atmosphere. On paper, these lines convey the perfection, timelessness, and omnipotence of God, and these aspects of his character are buttressed by a series of theological Latin commonplaces in the ensuing lines:

> The whole food of parents is set
> in mea essentia.
> . . . . . .
> Peerless patron imperial
> and Patris sapientia.
> . . . . . .
> All mirth lieth in mansuetude
> cum Dei potentia.
>   (1.7–8, 11–12, 15–16)

Three liturgical songs sung by the angels, two of which are entitled "Dignus Dei" and "Gloria tibi Trinitas," reinforce this trait of God's totality or absoluteness (96f., 136f., 224f.). As the play progresses, God's lines increasingly stand out as shorter, sometimes rhyming, and often songlike. The sonic effect is to associate God with the sounds of liturgy and with symbolism of transcendence.

However, if we imagine these first lines in their historical performance, we might imagine a carriage that the pre-Reformation banns describe as "the heuenly mancion," outfitted with a heavenly scene above and a hell-dungeon below where the fallen angels later appear. We see a man in a god costume with a gold-painted face delivering the plays' first fifty-two lines, replete with Latin and Trinitarian theology, most of which is intended to sound over the top to average Cestrians.[99] In this light, we might speculate that the dominant impression of God's declaration "It is my will it should be so" is of the cycle's grandeur and ambition. That he is depicted with conspicuous anthropomorphism is apparent, but the character's artificiality underscores the fact that the absolute "will" of the "alpha et oo" is being imagined from the perspective of human will, crafted for theatrical opulence, and impersonated by an actor with a gilded face from the Tanners.

In addition to a costumed and gilded actor playing God—a practice that would play a significant part in the cycle's suppression—the play integrates the limitations of human perception into its depiction of divine will. There is a sense in which the Creation itself is treated as theater. It is something that must be interpreted, whose beauty can be misleading when taken out of context, and whose right context is the festival community. In his initial speech, God claims a logical necessity between his absolute will (as in line 3, "It is my will it should be so") and his creative will—the license that he exercises in creation, including poetic creation. He elaborates:

> Both visible and invisible,
> all lies in my wielding.
> As God greatest and glorious,
> all is in mea licentia.
> (1.17–20)

In the form of "licentia," God restates his claim to comprehensive control over the universe, but here he adds that the things of his "wielding" comprise two categories of perception: the "visible" and the "invisible." This is the first hint of dramatic conflict in the cycle, as God alludes to an invisible will that is unknowable to creatures, and it is the lack of knowledge that leads to error.

The term *licentia* may well have accumulated meaning over the cycle's long performance history, especially in Reformation England, where it also meant licentiousness or dangerous speech. This context is confirmed in the post-Reformation banns, where the audience is told that the author "was nothinge A freayde" to cite biblical texts in the vernacular "with fear of hanginge breninge or Cuttinge off heade / to sett out that all maye disserne and see."[100] In both late medieval and early modern productions of the play these lines self-allude to the process of mimetic creation and to the poetic freedom that allows the visible to stand in for the invisible. We see this meaning reinforced in the lines that follow, dropping heavily with a feeling of empowered poetic freedom:

> Prince, principal, proved
> in my perpetual providence,
> I was never but one
> and ever one in three,
> set in substantial soothness

> within celestial sapience.
> The three trials in a throne
> and true Trinity
> be grounded in my godhead,
> exalted by my excellency.
> (1.23–32)

The alliteration in these lines is excessive to the point of being provocative; their explicit craftedness may even suggest *licentia* in the form of boldness of speech. They constitute a challenge, in a sense, to anyone who wonders whether the cycle will really exercise its theatrical license over its sensitive theological content. And with such license, God establishes a precedent that characters will varyingly accept and reject. He creates a performative narthex through which audiences enter a play grounded in the paradox between God's absolute will and the blatantly crafted and rhetorical creation that is the play itself.

Opening the three-day festival, this speech introduces the problem that leads to the foundational conflict of the play, Lucifer's rebellion, framing it as a failure to recognize the marks of divine creation in the immanent pieces and vacancies of experience. In his opening monologue, God presents himself both as a being that asserts total will and also as a sign, or possibly as a potentiality that contains signs:

> The might of my making
> is marked in me,
> dissolved under a diadem
> by my divine experience.
> (1.33–36)

At one and the same moment, God declares that his creation is evidence of his absolute will but also that this teleology is unknowable, "dissolved under" the idea of his very existence. He echoes the words of the Corpus Christi Sarum Mass, where the true sacred object is hidden beneath the sign and is accessible only in its manifest appearing. This is the problem that sets the drama of the cycle in motion: the choice that creatures have to interpret bodies and objects either as signs of God's will or as mere things. There is a perceptual gap between God's absolute perfection and his imperfect creation, so true belief is a matter of making the right interpretative decisions. Those who find faith will not do so by seeing God but by trudging through the obscurities of typology, prophecy, and theatrical craft and seeing them as extensions of the divine creative will.

For this reason, the dialogue of *The Fall of Lucifer* continually returns to language about the creating and forming of things. Early on, God predicts Lucifer's apparent unsettledness in the face of the unknowable, so he warns of the dangers of overaspiring to comprehend creation, once again echoing the Corpus Christi liturgy's exhortation not to overquery the nature of the Eucharist: "For craft nor for cunning, / cast never comprehension" (1.73–74). By contrast, God constantly asserts his own right to possess the knowledge of creation, claiming that the subjective act of perceiving and the objective ontological reality that is being perceived converge in him:

> The world, that is both void and vain,
> I form in the formation,
> with a dungeon of darkness,
> which never shall have ending.
> This work is now well wrought
> by my divine formation.
> (1.79–84)

The play introduces dramatic conflict by making belief contingent on Lucifer's ability to accept the invisible absolute in the visible phenomena of creation. Ironically for latter performances that withstood pressure from London, Lucifer impersonates God by attempting to fuse the perceptual and the ontological, literally taking God's place. Moreover, dramatic conflict is introduced into the play-scape through this allusion to the "dungeon of darkness," probably a cavity that the Tanners constructed beneath the carriage's main stage where the devils will later be imprisoned. The significance that God attributes to the cosmic creation—"angels nine orders of great beauty"—also metatheatrically applies to the dramaturgical creation of the festival performance. The dramatic action that unfolds does not propagate dogma about God but instead compels audiences to recognize the faith-inducing and faith-compelling capabilities of human artifice, just as Lucifer is charged to accept how the cosmic artifice illustrates the divine attributes stated in the play's opening—God's omnipotence, comprehensiveness, and absolute will.

It is with narrative satisfaction, then, that Lucifer's original sin is instigated by the disappearance of God, as I noted in the opening to this chapter. Before God vacates his throne, he warns Lucifer that his beauty should not tempt him into pride, cautioning that before long he will become "revisible" (135). Then the stage directions read, "*They sing and God shall withdraw*," and immediately Lucifer issues his rebellion (136f.):

> Aha! That I am wondrous bright
> amongst you all shining is full clear!
> Of all Heaven I bear the light
> though God himself and he were here.
> All in this throne if that I were,
> then should I be as wise as he.
>
> What say ye, angels all than been here?
> Some comfort soon now let me see.
> (137–44)

Consistent with the play's central conflict of visibility and invisibility, Lucifer marvels at his own physical brightness and insinuates that his luminescent body positioned on God's throne deserves to possess divine authority. Rice and Pappano conjecture that Lucifer's claim as a light-bearer in the first pageant refers to earlier disputes that led to the Chester mayor assigning the disgruntled Tanners Guild's position in the torch-bearing Corpus Christi procession. Just as such competition over brightness leads to the angels' fall, so "the pageant text suggests that the privilege of light-bearing coexists uneasily with the maintenance of a stable hierarchy."[101]

This history of brightness and preference speaks also to the pageants' thematic focus on vision and sacramental obscurity. Lucifer's lines introduce a voice that is more personal and subjective than anything the play has yet offered. They also suggest a strong interpretation by the audience in acknowledging the difference between Lucifer's claim that he shines the brightest "Though God himself and he were here" and the sight of God actually being there. Error has already made its way into rhetoric. Thus Lucifer's character is decidedly perspectival, and this individuality shows the more brightly when juxtaposed with the angels' song, as music is often a mark of liturgy and conventional religious symbolism in the plays.[102] The play presents the original angelic fall as a response to the limitations involved in being a creature with subjective vision. Sin results not from making but from idolizing, not from partitioning God but from Lucifer's unwillingness to operate as usual within the perceptual conditions of doubt and divine obscurity.

As a cohesive narrative involving devices of anticipation, conflict, and resolution, the Chester cycle takes on the perspective of Lucifer to popularize biblical material, especially insofar as his perspective draws attention to what is visible and immanently knowable. The episode continues by staging arguments between Lucifer, his sidekick Light Borne, and several orders of angels—Virtues, Cherubim, Dominations, Principalities, Seraphim, and Thrones. Eventually God returns to the stage, rebukes Lucifer, and banishes him to the dungeon of hell situated beneath the carriage, where the fallen demons regret their pride. Still, it is not until God disappears and Lucifer rebels that the play assumes the theatrical character that the cycle carries through *The Last Judgment*: characters reveal unique personalities, dialogue becomes more conversational, and the audience's perspective is subject to dangerous bias at any given moment. In an unexpected way, Lucifer's perspective acts like the dinner table of *The Last Supper*. God disappears, and consequently the play becomes more familiar. *The Fall of Lucifer* clearly condemns Lucifer's sinfulness, but the theatrical setting explicates this lesson by providing opportunities for audiences to relate materially and spiritually to the blindness and perspectival vulnerability that constantly lead characters astray. The fact that God's authority is partitioned and no longer patently visible in his anthropomorphizing actor adds a layer of verisimilitude and turns perception itself into a bearing point for dramatic action. For the audience, sin is not the presence of doubt; it is the inability to accommodate self-doubt.

It is also worth noting that Lucifer's expressly limited perspective in this play is marked by a series of exclamations, drawing a parallel between God's disappearance here and Jesus's disappearance in *The Healing of the Blind Man*. Yet here the order of revelation and misinterpretation is reversed, with God's presence and verbal explanation preceding Lucifer's rebellion. Lucifer's first statement of revolt begins with an "Aha," and his subsequent interjections begin with other utterances of surprise:

> Distress? I command you for to cease
> and see the beauty that I bear.
> (1.153–54)

> Go hence? Behold, seigneurs on every side,
> and unto me you cast your een.
> (1.189–90)

Notice that each expression, beginning with the original "Aha," is followed by a statement that points to something immanently visible—"see the beauty," "Behold, seigneurs," "cast your een." Lucifer's argument thus questions how the angels can be expected to remain loyal to a disincarnate authority when his own beautiful body is manifest right in front of them.

These expressions culminate in Lucifer's reversal of the theme of created immanence that was introduced in God's opening monologue. Lucifer takes God's throne and commands his onlookers, "Behold my body, hands and head— / the might of God is marked in me" (199–200). The command "Behold" insinuates a completely different understanding of belief and visuality than it does for the character of God and in the biblical account in Matthew discussed earlier. Lucifer's mistake is not his attention to beauty; rather, he sins by terminating the meaning of beauty in the sensory object that is perceptually given—that is, not grasping it in its givenness at all. He falls because he does not see the divine will in his own luminescent body.

The Fall of Lucifer creates an ongoing relationship between aesthetics and morality, and theatricality bridges this relationship as both a form of creating and a mode of spectatorship. Lucifer, as we have seen, misinterprets the immanent beauty of his own body when God's bodily presence is obscured. On the other hand, God's warnings to Lucifer consistently emphasize his role as the creator and Lucifer's status as a creature. I would contend that there is something more sophisticated being dramatized here than a mere caveat about the dangers of rebellion against one's maker. The Chester author(s) constantly returns to language of visibility and invisibility as well as to sign-object terminology, such as God's "The might of my making / is marked in me" and Lucifer's parallel "The might of God is marked in me" (1.33–34, 20). This blunt language that links making and marking, or signifying, is common enough to the biblical cycle tradition to appear also in the York play *The Fall of the Angels*, where Lucifer proclaims that "all the myrth that es made es markide in me."[103] In the same play, upon discovering Lucifer's revolt, Deus retorts, "Those foles for thaire fayrehede in fantasyes fell / And hade mayne of mi mighte that marked tham and made tham."[104] The potential to create, the act of creating, and the act of signifying come together in these plays' renditions of the first sin—might, making, and marked. These plays suggest that the key to having faith is not to separate any one alliterative term from the other two. Yet where the Chester and York plays are perhaps especially sympathetic to Lucifer is in their broader treatment of "marking." No character argues against the fact that Lucifer is luminescent and beautiful. The point is that perception occurs in a context, and Lucifer's context is within the defined roles of the hierarchy of angels. Whereas Lucifer's arguments always refer to what is visible, God's arguments emphasize the ontological ramifications of perception.

Furthermore, God does not apologize for the potential obscurity of his divine appearance in creation, even in his own absence. Instead, he expects the angels to understand that objects are signs and that an experience of beauty refers to more than is perceptually given. Lucifer himself realizes this error immediately after his "fall"—"*Now Lucifer and Light Borne fall*," once again beginning with an expression of immanent observation: "Alas!" (240f.).

> Alas! that ever we were wrought,
> that we should come into this place!
> We were in joy; now we be nought.
> Alas! We have forfeited our grace!
> (1.241–44)

The manuscripts of the play reveal an important textual transition here. The first fallen angel to speak, whom we presume to be Lucifer, is no longer identified by name. Beginning with these lines, Lucifer and Light Borne are named generically as "Primus Demon" and "Secundus Demon."[105] Perhaps the fallen angels were also visually represented by generic-looking demon costumes, denuded of their previous splendor. Whereas before they were "in joy," now they are simply "nought," reflecting an Augustinian conception of the contingency of existence on goodness. This transition describes the angels' change in nature and dramatizes the theological *and* theatrical convergence of immanence and ontology. Lucifer is now identified merely as the First Demon.

The play ends with God creating the first day, and this serves as a kind of benediction that unites perception and ontology, experience and transcendence:

> As I have made you all of nought
> at mine own wishing,
> my first day here have I wrought.
> I give it here my blessing.
> (1.309–12)

The creation of the first day begins with "Lightness and darkness," the very conditions of visibility and invisibility that have made it possible for Lucifer to rebel (303). Yet in addition to announcing their reunion, God reminds the audience that any perceived divide between aesthetics and morality—we might transpose *representation* and *theatricality*—is unoriginal. Somewhat audaciously, then, God closes the play in a manner that in one way reinforces the preeminence of his absolute will but in another subtly highlights the ambiguities of interpreting his will even when it is *désincarné*—"at mine own wishing."

THE CLOSING BENEDICTION to *The Fall of Lucifer* also serves as the prologue to the rest of the cycle, the "first day" of many more to come, each full of error and doubt. It provides the first palpable link to the real world, in which unfold twenty-three additional plays, and as such, it carries the perceptual conditions of original sin into the rest of the cycle. The plays' many moments of typology and prophecy, as well as of humor and doubt, trace their dramatic ancestry to the first disappearance of God.

And these heightened scenes of towardness center not only on characters and their decisions but on objects. Objects retain their roles as assemblies of the theatrical process. The table and bread in *The Last Supper*, for instance, present the cycle as a spectacle to behold as well as a compilation of objects to physically hold. One might contend that these overlaps in representation are simply due to the fact that such early drama is not yet stabilized by playhouses and commercial companies, but the plays' language itself suggests that there is something thematically purposeful about their overt theatricality. By fully embracing their craft and artificiality as religious artistic media, the Chester Whitsun plays are able to facilitate simultaneously dramatic and religious practices from the also simultaneous activities of creating and beholding—producing them and watching them. Unlike its sacramental counterparts, the cycle gives itself to the audience primarily as a compilation of fundamental elements—time, place, objects, hospitality, and bodies—and it stays there, never asserting its theological claims or ontological status except through conflicts born from potential errors of perception. Viewed as drama, these theatrical conditions can be understood to intentionally obscure anything that might be seen as an "open shewe" of divine presence.

Chapter Three

HENRY V AND THE CEREMONIES OF THEATER

> O pardon, since a crooked figure may
> Attest in little place a million,
> And let us, ciphers to this great account,
> On your imaginary forces work.
> —Prologue, *Henry V*

In the Prologue of *The Life of King Henry the Fifth*, the Chorus's "crooked" O shape before "pardon" and also in the play's first line is a paradoxical symbol of emptiness and wealth. As an utterance, it "seeks a listener," sounding out the acoustical promise of a listening space, a kind of vocal sennet for the words that follow.[1] Yet despite its reputation as a distinct aural sound, Shakespeare's Prologue wants his audience to visualize O as a shape, as if it were read in the form of "ciphers" on a page that either represent nothing or add value to the numbers they follow. As owner of 12.5 percent of the Globe, Shakespeare could be imagining the ciphers in records of stage expenses, as Philip Henslowe repeatedly and painstakingly details in his diary: for example, "Lent unto the company the 5 of maye 1602 to geve unto antony monday & thomas deckers. . . . Layd owt for the companye the 16 of maye 1602 for to bye a dublett," and so on, to the sum of "22^{li} – 07^s – 00^d."[2] Shakespeare's metaphor, thus, joins the utterly logistical with the theatrically embodied. In early modern England, a cipher was a conspicuous trope for visual nothingness. Figurative uses often adopted derogatory meanings. Sometimes ciphers are flatterers who, though "nothing of themselues," yet "puffe men vp" like added zeros, or, as in one Protestant sermon, ciphers are those who "take a roume" in the church pew but "signifie nothing" because they "hatest to be reformed."[3] Antitheatricalists often applied the cipher trope to players, as when William Prynne depicts playacting as the "true etimologie" of a hypocrite: one who "acts anothers part."[4] As I discuss in chapter 1, Hamlet wrestles with this paradox when he compares his own inaction to the player who can manipulate his face, body, and voice—"his whole function"—for the part he plays, for the "nothing" of Hecuba.[5] *Henry V*'s Prologue curiously invokes this antitheatrical context when, in a move of disillusionment, he refers to "us"—the players currently performing on the platform.

The context of potential hypocrisy and antitheatricalism that the Prologue introduces haunts the remainder of the play in the form of *cipher*'s political counterpart, the king's *ceremony*. In subtle yet important ways, Shakespeare relies on ceremony in *Henry V* as an intertheatrical trope with overlapping problems in political symbolism, Christian devotion, religious festival, and the playhouse scene. Like the cipher, in some contexts ceremony shares an early modern polemical vocabulary with hypocrisy, especially in religious controversy. I am referring specifically to the ceremonialism controversy, where writers argued over the dangers and merits of the physical and liturgical mediation of devotion that defined the Reformation period's developments in church practice.[6] The Prologue admits that drama is not real life but only a cipher, and this remains as the metatheatrical echo of King Henry's continuous struggle with the alleged emptiness of monarchy's "idol ceremony" (4.1.237). Perhaps Henry's ceremonial authority, he reasons, is just a cipher and, therefore, the virtue of his symbolic apparatus merely utilitarian. As the antitheatricalist believes the playhouse to do, the king uses rhetoric and pageantry to manipulate his subjects. According to one conventional reading of the play, Henry ultimately takes a stance against his own ceremony, forswearing the theatricality exercised by his forbearers and, in the St. Crispin's speech, motivating his overwhelmingly outnumbered army bravely into battle with the French. According to this explanation of Henry's motivations, ceremony's theatrical nature lacks real substance; it is the instrument of Machiavels and hypocrites.

However, in *Henry V*, Shakespeare creates a scenario where theatricality and politico-religious ceremony share each other's fates, so the apparent problem that has always plagued the interpretation of Henry as an iconoclast of ceremonial authority is its nearness to interpreting him also as an iconoclast of theatrical ceremony, as condemning all of the physical and ideal materials from which we get *Henry V*. The Prologue's rhetoric fits unnervingly well into Stephen Gosson's puritanical charge never to forget that a player is really a false "cypher": "If anye Player belie me in your hearing vpon the stage, you would rather consider of the person than of the speach, for a Player is like to a Marchants finger, that standes sometime for a thousande, sometime for a cypher, and a Player must stand as his parte fals, sometime for a Prince sometime for a peasant."[7] For Gosson and Prynne—and problematically for Shakespeare—the Chorus's identification of "us" as ciphers demands recourse. By invoking overlapping early modern controversies surrounding theatricality and ceremony and by positioning these questions at the center of the play's celebrated historical character, Shakespeare might be seen to set up a divide between the content of political power and its theatrical appearance, a divide that might imply duplicity and emptiness—even if such theatricality is victoriously torn down by the triumphant Henry.

Given this problem, we would do well to include *cipher*'s other noteworthy meaning. Besides being a zero, an encryption, and a hypocrite, a cipher is an exposition. Especially in its use as a verb—"To cipher what is writ in learned books"—a cipher can be the act of decoding or even the key itself; it supplies meaning where meaning is hidden.[8] This latter meaning is notably positive rather than derogatory. In fact, ciphering a thing is often the opposite activity to iconoclasm. With this meaning in mind, it is no surprise that much of Henry's own description of ceremonial authority comes through the dense Christian symbolism of his long soliloquy in act 4 and in the prayer that follows it—a scene thick with inter- and metatheatrical visitings. Religion and specifically the context of the religious ceremonialism controversy allow Shakespeare to summon and then bridge a binary between the king's authority as symbolized and as it really exists legally, between the theatricality of "the sword, the mace, and the crown imperial" and the anointed person it represents (4.1.258). This is, at the same time, a trans-Reformational bridging of the medieval period of Shakespeare's source and its reflection of the contemporary political scene.

As I will argue, in *Henry V* Shakespeare explores the performative capabilities of theater. He draws audience attention both to the artifice of theater and to the potential hypocrisy of that artificiality, and he uses religion as a psychological and intersubjective vehicle for creating audience appreciation for the theatrical connections among Christian ritual, political ceremony, and the process of theatrical appearing—how each depends on the audience's complicity as a performative limit. In this manner, the Prologue points to theatricality itself as the cipher or key for decoding the apparent emptiness of the play—the "wooden O" itself that creates a "swelling scene" within "the girdle of these walls" (Prologue 13, 4, 19). We can reimagine the "crooked figure," therefore, as the Prologue player himself, his bending body and curved mouth enunciating O's, and his reliance on the audience's belief in the play—what Bruce Smith calls a "semantic emptiness . . . [that] stands as testimony to . . . embodied fullness."[9]

Further, in taking seriously Shakespeare's exposé of theatricality in this play, this chapter disputes one popular understanding of Henry as "a pattern of Protestant monarchy" who strips the altar of his kingly ceremony in order to inspire his troops to victory over the French.[10] Such interpretations hinge on discovering either a major transformation in Harry's character, with its climax in the soliloquy of act 4, or a pragmatic Machiavellian duplicity.[11] By contrast, I argue that in so transparently putting the audience's "imaginary forces [to] work" in collaboration with theatrical ceremony and its correlative "idol ceremony," the play resists the didactic monument that Henry's conversion could potentially become (4.1.237). In the end, the play's most climactic moments—Henry's soliloquy and the St. Crispin's speech—do not mark points of character transformation for Henry but instead assert the dependence of both monarchy and theater on the performative capabilities of ceremony and its paradoxes.

With reference to the broader performance culture, *Henry V* addresses a concern relevant to all of Shakespeare's plays, namely, the moral question of theatricality, and it magnifies this question by placing it in the context of political power. Yet rather than taking a side on the moral question in the terms provided by the antitheatrical polemicism, I argue that Shakespeare opts for the vocabulary and theatrical concepts of religion to reinforce the importance of perception, theatrical environment, and audience engagement as critical aspects of the play-going experience. Thus Shakespeare draws a parallel between the *covertly* coercive ceremonies of political power and the *patently* coercive ceremonies of the playhouse, and he encourages productive slippage between them. Shakespeare takes advantage of Protestant energies of iconoclasm and reform by harnessing their capacity to create depth of character, but he also reconciles this energy with nostalgia for traditional religious symbolism. The effect is that the play not only creates awareness of the conditions of political symbolism but also invites the audience to view all ideological symbols anamorphically, in the court and cathedral as well as in the playhouse—using religious models of ceremony to expose and empower the process of theater across genres.

Pardoning the Play

In the mode often used by early modern dramatic prologues, *Henry V*'s opening speaker begins by rhetorically demystifying the stage and calling on his auditors to help populate it with their imaginations. The Prologue—"a priestly officiant celebrating the stage events"—stands both with and apart from the audience, as together they consider the nature of theatrical spectacle.[12] The Prologue's ambivalent attitude toward theatrical artifice—always self-conscious but often assertive—parallels Henry's own journey through both doubting and experimenting with the artificial fronts of his own symbolic power. And so the Prologue affords a unique opportunity to think about how the play establishes a working understanding of theatrical ceremony as the subject as well as the medium of Henry's struggles. As I hope to show, the play's Prologue and Choruses convey the ritual aspects of theatricality as it is represented in speech and as it is actualized by the audience's response.

With its address to the audience's "imaginary forces," the Prologue foregrounds the material conditions of theater in 1599, when the play was first performed at the Curtain or perhaps at the new Globe. He metatheatrically calls attention to the "stage," "this unworthy scaffold," "this wooden O," and "these walls" (Prologue 3, 10, 13, 19).[13] The player acknowledges, in other words, that he is standing on wooden floorboards that creak in tune with the audience's wooden benches and stools. Visually, if the theater is open-roofed, the audience sees the "brightest heaven" above them as well as the partial roof that is painted like the "heavens," reminding them that they paid admission to enter a physical wooden enclosure that is otherwise a wholly familiar environment but for its "invention" (2). Moreover, the Chorus alludes to the playhouse's architectural resemblance of a "cockpit" and by extension to the nearby bear-baiting theater, an association that brazenly solicits Stephen Gosson's accusation that Elizabethan theaters "turne reasonable Creatures into brute Beastes" (11).[14] And "when we talk of horses," the audience's imagination is assisted by the ubiquitous noise of animals "printing their proud hoofs i'th' receiving earth" just outside (26, 27). In fact, the ambient effect of the Chorus is notably different from that of dramatic rapture that the player invites. In making it difficult for the audience to forget that there is an outside to this inside "O," the Prologue reveals the human strategy to his and all plays.

In addition to explicitly referring to the theatrical atmosphere, the Prologue positions the audience in an attitude of active response particularly through its use of imperative verbs—*pardon, suppose, piece out, make, think, carry, admit* (8 and 15, 19, 23, 25, 26, 29, 32). These imperatives can be considered "categorical intentions" in that they imply unsaid yet operative judgments about the objects they intend—in this instance, the visible anatomy of the theater—and in that they reflect the distinction between theatrical meaning as represented and theatrical meaning as present and collaborative.[15] We might view the Prologue's strategy alongside Merleau-Ponty's statement that the act of perception "asserts more things than it grasps."[16] In an absorptive sense, the audience responds with focus to the Prologue's and the Chorus's requests to imagine the scene unfolding, but in a more foundational sense, these imperatives compel the audience to change their intuitive disposition, to understand the play as a certain kind of spectacle—a *coup de théâtre* that conscripts the audience in the creation of wonder. For instance, to "piece out," the audience first must first intend the play as a potential whole, while to "make," one first must implicitly recognize the play as unmade. Even more, to "think," one must in some fashion acknowledge that the play is theoretically not-yet-thought and could possibly not be intended categorically as a play. I use *intend* here to express the basic perceptual relation between a mind and an object of its attention. The Prologue's commands to think about the play imply modes of intention that precede fully articulated thought. Before the audience begins piecing, making, and thinking, the play is a contiguous collection of wood, sky, noise, circularity, outside, and inside, and the Prologue and Chorus draw affective awareness to the audience's implication in the creation of spectacle.

The most frequent and performative of the Prologue's imperatives is the request that the audience "pardon" the play's material limitations. Responding to the Chorus's "O Pardon," the audience takes up the grammatical role of a present participle in *pardoning* those violations of reality that are necessary for theater. The effect is an explicitly cipher-like manifestation of theater, incorporating the term's several meanings as a nothing and a fullness, both obscuring and explicating meanings. Samuel Weber notes that performance texts acquire the qualities of the present participle in their dual function of both presenting and re-presenting material at once: "A text that does not merely 'reproduce' and yet also does not simply 'create' or 'produce.' Its object is situated in an unusual and complicated relationship to its 'pretext.' It is involved in an operation that, like the 'hymen,' expose the interval 'between' texts and in so doing allows something else to 'enter' the stage or scene: a certain theatricality, which has as its grammatical earmark the present participle."[17] The pretext—the matter from which the performance comes—in this case is performance culture, suggested by the Prologue's many references to the building structure, its environmental features, and the audience's acquired habits of spectatorship.

In *Henry V* Shakespeare highlights this transition from general theatricality to a specific stage representation. The character of Henry himself is the most advanced articulation of theatrical becoming, but, as we will see, his character too intersperses among the symbolic and theatrical sensorium around him. This process begins with the Prologue and its resistance to audience absorption. The Prologue unravels theater's material and intentional conditions in a way that resists disappearing into the sublimity of the history of England's king. It is notable, moreover, that the Prologue's part was not included in the Quarto. The earliest performances of the play may not have included the opening Prologue. Playgoers who saw both versions of the performance may have received the Prologue simply as a trendy addition; or, we can imagine, perhaps they saw its variant status as yet another mutable condition of theater that needed to be pardoned.[18] The Prologue's textual and theatrical history is a reminder, in a sense, of the very ephemerality of which he and later Choruses warn. And like textual critics, I would suggest that its variant status adds to the play's continual foregrounding of its ceremonial process and its evolution through various forms.[19]

Taking the Prologue at its word, to some extent, suggests that, more than simply representing an illusion of history, the play grounds its impression of wholeness in the parts and properties of theater. One such property is the cloak that Henry borrows from Erpingham for disguise. It is the pretense—and pretext—upon which is built the phenomenon of honesty as a character trait. The cloak (a textual variant, like the Prologue) is one important example of a scenic object or medium that draws on specific audience perceptual acts in ways that ultimately contribute to a belief in character interiority.[20] Interestingly, this impression of Henry's sincerity, like Viola's in *Twelfth Night*, occurs through a conspicuous process of theatrical dressing up and then divestiture, here focalized in a literal vestment. Bert States comments on the nuanced identity confusion of stage props like Erpingham's cloak, suggesting that a cloak is not actually a cloak insofar as it is used and intended as a prop.[21] Like the Prologue's imperatives, the clothing object operates beyond its representational uses. In covering and obscuring, it alleges that there is something to be revealed, and, as in the disappearance of the Chester Cycle's God, it is through dramatic obfuscation that audiences engage in dramatic belief.

Henry, in his role as a character, treats the costume as a fictional prop, disguising himself as one of Erpingham's captains in a military class somewhere between his character's supreme social position and that of his common interlocutors, Bates and Williams. As an article of clothing, the cloak has a simple function, but as a prop—or, a double prop, both to Henry and to the player—it is the nucleus of a broader perceptual vicinity of disguise, embodying and distributing the Prologue's statement: "Your thoughts that now must deck our kings" (Prologue 28). For instance, aurally, do the tone and pitch of the player's voice change in this scene? Does the noise of the audience—floorboards adjusting, people chatting, shuffling, responding—grow quieter when they realize that somebody on stage is representing himself to his fellow characters deceptively? Visually, does the cloak shadow the king's eyes and hide the gaze that the audience had previously associated with authority? Physically, does the cloak fasten at the neck? Or perhaps the actor playing Henry holds the collar together with his hand, leaving a closed fist positioned over his chest, conveying insecurity and perhaps sincerity. Does the player crouch or turn his body deliberately in order to avoid being too directly spied? Might the audience wonder if Williams will catch a glimpse of royal vesture between folds or perhaps recognize a slip in Henry's presumably altered voice? While all these details are speculative, of course, we can recognize the give-and-take between the audience and the decisions of stagecraft that contribute to a sense of Henry's whole character. What I want to call attention to is how the introduction of the cloak and its acts of hiding Henry cast the scene within an appearance-reality duality separated by an interpretive distance that may project in various ways a sense of character interiority.

The audience's participation in ciphering (i.e., deciphering) the scene through its imperatives and props affects how we can interpret this scene's dialogue. In the beginning of act 4, the three "soldiers" discuss whether the king's ceremony is simply a strategy for hiding incompetence and neglect, and much of the argument is over vocabulary. Is there an opposition between the king's outward show and inner motivation, or, as Henry ultimately contends, is this a false dichotomy? This scene's treatment of ceremony overlaps with those of the Prologue's and Chorus's in that it is concerned with self-representation and role playing. Bates, for one, holds that whatever the king "may show" outwardly is at odds with his inward "wish," but the discussion fails to resolve this important question (4.1.113–14). The only point on which the characters seem to agree is an acknowledgment of ceremony's inscrutability, that the king's reliance on such symbols as title and pomp paradoxically distance the very subjects that they purport to inspire. In this view, ceremony cannot provide assurance of whether the king's "cause" is "just and his quarrel honourable" (127–28). Bates argues that the justness of the king's cause is irrelevant, since a soldier is morally exempt through obedience to the king, while Henry retorts that individuals are responsible for their own spiritual standing, despite their cause of death (127–33). Bates and Williams are willing to concede that the king has responsibilities to his subjects, but they are not willing to grant the reciprocal responsibility of subjects to submit to the king's ceremony as if it carried the whole weight of his authority. Ceremony, for them, has purpose but no substance—no real presence—and, therefore, should be stripped when its cause is questionable.

The disguised Henry's conversation with Bates and Williams dramatizes the critical questions of whether ceremony contains any real substance, whether there is anything to decipher at all, and whether discussing the justification for ceremony makes it any more palatable. We might remember, however, that the very discussion itself is mediated by the cipher of disguise. The cloak expands Henry's character phenomenon by both obfuscating and disclosing him. We see Henry in it and behind it, as the audience intuits an implied secret performance behind the player's main performance of Henry. The imagined "real"—that is, undisguised—space of the play is made fully visible only in the brief moment of Erpingham's interruption to Henry's soliloquy, the sole moment when Henry simply responds without disguise or effusive self-reflection (4.1.282).

Yet the play's insistence on Henry's appearing in spectacle, rhetoric, disguise, or overt theatrical forms like soliloquy has the effect of foregrounding the burdens as well as the constitutive influence of theatrical strategy on the formation of character. An example of this paradox is the theatrical phenomenon of touch enhanced by Erpingham's cloak. How might the garment itself evoke affective responses to the sense of touch and the prop's unfamiliar weight? Does the wrapped-up king perhaps attune the audience to the chill of the night? I would suggest that the sense of touch accentuated by this prop crosses affectively with the audience, by way of something like what Sedgwick has called "touching feeling," a form of "intimacy" that "subsist[s] between textures and emotions."[22]

Affect is a useful way to describe the speculative and ephemeral but nonetheless real phenomenon of character intimacy generated by specific theatrical elements, and especially how these elements—like Chester's bread and table—traverse the divide between symbol and object. "Affect arises . . . in the capacity to be acted upon," such as the capacity to feel conjured by Erpingham's cloak. It "is found in those intensities that pass body to body . . . , in those resonances that circulate about, between, and sometimes stick to bodies and words."[23] In a sense, this scene releases the audience from any constraints they might experience in identifying Henry merely imaginatively, in turn grounding his character interiority in a greater sensorium of touch and, more specifically, in the subjective interactions between touching and feeling that we experience ourselves. The audience vicariously experiences "the pleasure of tangibility and the objects' appeal to the sense of touch beyond any purely visual and imagistic import," and this heightened sense of touch "calls the object home to its 'proper' place of self-identity."[24] In this case, because the cloak's true owner (Erpingham) inhabits a space offstage, the sensory appeal of Henry's cloak and our awareness that the player is touching it locates the "proper" home of the cloak, and thus the home of the Prologue's world, within the physical ambience of the theater—the objects, people, props, and perceptual structure of the playhouse. Repeating the performative move introduced in chapter 1, the prop contributes to the "real" Henry not by stripping all theatricality and clothing but by locating character within a progressive series of stagings and costuming, robing and disrobing. Materially, we are given only a player in two sets of clothes, and yet we are theatrically conditioned to "pardon" and "piece out" an unseen but whole character beneath the clothes.

Fischer-Lichte's notion of performative "multistability" describes how in performance art the audience's attention tends to shift between the different persons being theatricalized. This aspect of modern performance art is also in effect in early modern scenes like this one, heightened in the post-Reformational context by a renewed sensitivity to sensory mediation, especially in ceremonial contexts. The audience oscillates "focus between the actor's specific corporeality and the character portrayed."[25] In Henry, there are three persons and multiple angles between which to oscillate. The first pair is that of the player and the character of Henry, and the second is the character of Henry and the part he is playing for his interlocutors—the performance within the performance. Among all three persons, the body remains the same. It is performative in creating something that exists uniquely because of the moment of its performance. When spectators witness the scene, they also shape it into a unity that bridges the immediate and imaginary worlds. Such unity is the effect of devices like Erpingham's cloak, which adds meaning to Henry's attempt to demystify and personalize the struggles of a monarch: "His ceremonies laid by, in his nakedness he appears but a man" (4.1.105–6). Ironically, Henry only "appears but a man" because he put on, rather than "laid by," a costume. This is the productive paradox of ceremony: Henry's inner character is a function of the very theatrical accouterments that fitfully plague him.

Wiggling Henry: The Character Phenomenon

Scholars have often taken a theological approach to explaining ceremony in *Henry V*, since the play is full of language derived from the Protestant ceremonialist controversy. One common conclusion views the play as a conversion narrative in which Henry discovers a kind of proto-Protestant understanding of authority that disavows the superstitious trappings of ceremony. Yet these readings of the play have difficulty accounting for the seeming contradictions in Henry's treatment of ceremony, at times appearing to throw off "the sword, the mace, and the crown imperial" and at others ritually memorializing his bloody scars incurred in battle (4.1.258). Maurice Hunt and Jeffrey Knapp have offered more moderate interpretations, with Hunt arguing that Henry is a champion of religious tolerance and Knapp finding in Henry an antimaterialist version of sacramentalism.[26] The persistent difficulty, however, is the challenge of reconciling the extremes of Henry's contradicting words and actions as well as locating his ceremonial or anticeremonial conversion within Shakespeare's larger commentary on theatricality itself. To this end, I build on Hunt's and Knapp's readings and suggest that religion provides much more than a topical context for Henry's struggle with ceremony. By consistently framing Henry's exercise of power within theological vocabulary and contexts—even from the first scene with Ely and Canterbury—Shakespeare introduces an enriched framework for Henry's struggle with political symbolism and ceremony by troubling the distinction between mediation and presence.

As we have seen in chapter 2 with regard to the "real presence" of biblical cycle theater, religious contexts often serve as prompts to ask how the theatrical becomes the performative, how something is created or accomplished within the performance event beyond the constraints of the perceived divide between theatricality and representation, and how the material is transformed in the immediate moment via theatrical or ritual processes. I have discussed how character undergoes a transformation through its multistability and through the play's slippages between audience absorption and disillusion. Indeed, character is a performative effect—and affect—of the theatrical environment and its objects, and in *Henry V* character serves to explicate the paradox of ceremony. By *character*, I mean something like what Bert States terms the "character phenomenon": "As we say, character 'develops.' So what is it in the character phenomenon which persists? If character changes with every scene, or within single scenes, or even constantly, where do the eye and ear get the notion that something called character is iterating itself, always being itself, in this chaos of different and differing phenomena in the stage world?"[27] In other words, what are the theatrical devices that remain out of focus yet serve to create a singular impression of character? I turn now to the scenes that are typically understood to dramatize Henry's conversion—his turn to egalitarianism or to pragmatism, depending on how one interprets it—observing several ways that Henry uses the framework of trans-Reformational ceremonial devotion to exteriorize his inner struggle by distributing it into the processes of theater. The trans-Reformational context of ceremony accommodates symbolic as well as immanent representational models, and my argument is that this combination of symbolism and immanence, or representation and performative, maps onto Henry's own character development.

Many of the often-polarized responses to Henry's character over the years can be attributed, in the first place, to the play's style. It is written with the stylistic awareness that viewing a history play about Henry V might feel like the experience of viewing a monument. By *monument*, I refer to a memorialized object that its audience immediately recognizes as designed to represent something in the past—with emphasis on the recognition of an original design or intention. I specifically want to invoke the didactic ways that people tend to know monuments and how we classify the kind of knowledge that comes from institutionalized symbols. Spectators characteristically position themselves before a monument as visitors observing a work of art whose historical content or referent is imagined to have compelled the artist to cast it in a certain way—or in performance terms, a work whose representational qualities are imagined to predetermine its theatrical appearing. The presumed strength and stability of the original thing represented are assumed to delimit the contours of the monument's design. It should be "respectful," we might say. The sense of the monument alleges that *beholders* change while *the event* stays the same. It harkens to a time past, or at least to an interpretation of a time past. Foucault's metaphor of criticism as archaeology underscores this modern tendency to see monuments as self-descriptive: "There was a time when archaeology, as a discipline devoted to silent monuments, inert traces, objects without context, and things left by the past, aspired to the condition of history, and attained meaning only through the restitution of a historical discourse; it might be said, to play on words a little, that in our time history aspires to the condition of archaeology, to the intrinsic description of the monument."[28] *Henry V* strategically gives the superficial stylistic impression that there is a simple subject-object relation between the audience and the play, as if it speaks for itself and as if its knowledge is inherent. And this false impression is reinforced by the extended soliloquy Henry gives in act 4 and specifically by its soliloquy form. He bares his soul, makes transparent his self-doubts, and then delivers a confident, rousing speech bolstered by the theatrical phenomenon of sincerity. Any ambiguity, the monument insists, must have been resolved; the inner Henry has been revealed.

And yet, nothing could be further from the truth of Henry's theatrical identity. As Henry dwells on the complexities of political ceremony, he becomes entangled in the logic and baggage of religious ceremony, with its language of idol, sacrament, and inner versus outer substance. In act 4, the spiritual psychology of religion initially enters Henry's imagination in the conversation he has with Bates and Williams over the souls of soldiers killed in battle. Williams introduces the question: "Now, if these men do not die well, it will be a black matter for the king that led them to it" (4.1.143–45). The disguised Henry responds that "every subject's duty is the king's, but every subject's soul is his own," and he imagines the dying soldier as "every sick man in his bed" who is culpable for his own conscience—a reference that with a heavy hand remembers Falstaff in his deathbed earlier in the play, described by his friends either as tormented in conscience because of Henry's betrayal of him or as too delirious to make a valid spiritual statement (175–79). From this point in act 4, Henry continues to use religion as the conceptual context for wrestling with ceremony.

The Chorus's repeated exposé of theatrical artifice as well as Henry's own self-revelation of political strategy constantly hammers upon and unsettles the foundation of the play's styling as a kind of performance monument. The effect is a reinforcing of the play as an evolving event and of character as a process. Viewed from the phenomenal complexities of ceremony that the play evokes, *Henry V* presents itself as something that is molded and felt by the audience and its characters, subject to the worldly methods of human perception and the externalization of thought. We have already seen the physical side of Henry's character phenomenon in his cloak and the audience's identification with the "real" Henry's sense of touch. Theater delivers a sensory and emotional impression before it is digested into rational thought, and, significantly, it is the primacy of *feeling* over remembered thought that consumes Henry's struggle with ceremony.

For instance, when Bates remarks that he would rather the king "were here alone, so should he be sure to be ransomed," Henry's unsympathetic response writes it off as a rhetorical tactic: "howsoever you speak this to feel other men's minds" (4.1.121–22, 125–26). *Feeling* is a concept that can refer to a subject's activity of feeling an object (she feels it), an object's own subjective perception of that feeling (it feels her touch), or, abstractly, the general sensory or emotional faculties possessed by the perceiver (she has feelings). In early modern medical thought, emotional and physical types of feeling were interrelated with the intellect, such that feeling is a kind of early modern analogue for phenomenological intersubjectivity. Viewed discursively, Henry's statement intends to suggest that Bates must be trying to discover his opinions, to feel them out. This is a meaning similar to that used by Edmund in *King Lear*: "He hath writ this to *feel* my affection to your honour."[29] Viewed intersubjectively, however, Henry also understands Bates to be trying to rouse his emotions, and in this way, to feel other men's minds is also to incite feeling in other men's minds, acknowledging that interrogation and performance are not one-way activities. Thus Bates's feeling of his interlocutors' minds is a gesture that momentarily circumvents rational dialogue; it is a feeling-out of his companions to see if they share a mutual understanding about the king.

There is an intersubjectivity at play here among characters' perspectives and positions. The king is the topic of conversation, yet the king and his "cause" for war are never directly identified by the characters. The audience senses this conspicuous absence in the form of dramatic irony enacted by the physical yet hidden presence of the king himself. The characters strike up a spontaneous conversation and express different perspectives on the idea of the king—his vulnerability, responsibilities, and culpabilities—and because the conversation is fabricated by Henry's disguise, it is dramatically hypothetical. And it is also full of hypothetical thoughts: "So would I he were here, and I by him," "But if the cause be not good," "Now if these men do not die well," "But when our throats are cut" (115–16, 134, 143–44,

191–92). Henry's longest statement in this discussion is an extended hypothetical that compares the deaths of an imaginary "son that is by his father sent about merchandise" and "a servant" who is robbed and killed to the soldiers who die under the king's orders (147–84). Who is responsible for their souls? Even Henry attempts to feel the minds of his subjects, as they try to imagine the perspectives of one another toward the king and as Henry offers his soldiers the perspectives of a father and a master. Moreover, the overarching hypothetical silhouette of the scene is a steady reminder of the fact that Henry is still playing the part of a soldier—a dramaturgical *what if* in the flesh.

Ceremony is often associated with such affective dimensions to feeling in early modern drama. For instance, *Julius Caesar*, probably written very closely after *Henry V*, is particularly concerned with the sometimes untrustworthy political sway of ceremony, as illustrated in Flavius's iconoclastic command to "disrobe the images, / If you do find them decked with ceremonies," as well as in Caesar's reputed superstition "of fantasy, of dreams and ceremonies" (1.1.65–66, 2.1.196). Yet *Julius Caesar*'s most sophisticated discussion of ceremony appears in the first scene where the tribune Murellus accuses the Romans who celebrate Caesar's triumphal entry of being "worse than senseless things" (36):

> And when you saw his chariot but appear,
> Have you not made an universal shout,
> That Tiber trembled underneath her banks
> To hear the replication of your sounds
> Made in her concave shores?
> (1.1.44–48)

Murellus depicts this ceremonial celebration as an echo, relaying both the frivolity of the event and its lack of substance. The "replication" of its "sounds" echo back to its spectators and consume their senses with the surface of the event rather than its cause—in this case, the defeat of Pompey. For Murellus, spectators who get wrapped up in ceremony are "senseless": they lack feeling. Likewise, in *Summer's Last Will and Testament*, Nashe observes that when people encounter ceremony or theater, they come face to face, in a sense, with themselves, with the limits of their own encounter. Consider the court fool. Autumn describes ceremony's superficiality as indicative of court fools who do not think beyond the limits of their felt impressions: "A foole conceits no further than he sees; / He hath no scence of ought, but what he feeles."[30] As fools are the actors of the court, their morality—their "ought"—is constituted by feeling.

Henry's soliloquy complicates matters even further by considering these very affects of ceremony while deploying the especially theatrical, and thus self-presentational, medium of soliloquy. Referring to the ceremonial symbols of his kingship, which he bemoans as his "hard condition," Henry describes ceremony as a "great greatness," a phrase that is unable to point to an authority beyond its own expression (4.1.248). The king's authority, he says, is "twin-born with greatness, subject to the breath / Of every fool whose *sense* can no more *feel* / But his own *wringing*" (231–33, my italics). Henry says that to be stuck in ceremonial existence, in constant performance, is to think no further than one can feel, perhaps at the expense of considering the justness of the king's true cause for invading France.[31]

Hence, *feeling* in *Henry V* is in an important way counterpoised to the substance or content that is imagined to be behind ceremony, motivating and empowering it. In other words, Henry doubts the validity of political representation because of its theatricality. He opens act 4 by encouraging his captains to remember that despite the ominous outlook of battle, "There is some soul of goodness in things evil, / Would men observingly distil it out" (4.1.4–5). This metaphor compares the promise of ill-omened battle to distillation, probably referring to distilling plants or liquids for perfume and medicine. To distil an unfelt rationale of goodness out from the felt experience of fear is, as Shakespeare expresses it elsewhere, to retreat to "reason," to use "the fineness of their souls" rather than the soul's embodied feeling.[32] Yet, while in the beginning of act 4 Henry imagines authority and inspiration to be rarified and soul-like, his soliloquy tells a different story, admitting that his own fineness of mind is jealous of his subject's "gross brain" (4.1.279).

From one perspective, there might seem to be disparity between the dramatic form of soliloquy and the speaker's desire for the grossness and physicality of thought. It may seem more natural for the speaker of a soliloquy to champion "fineness" of rarified thought since that is the ostensible reason for a character removing himself from everyone else, attempting to avoid encounters of intersubjectivity. Yet recent discussions of dramatic soliloquy suggest just the opposite. Scholars have shown that soliloquy especially in Shakespeare's plays is in no simple way an expression of interiority or individualism but is, in Cummings's words, "the *locus classicus* of the problem of self."[33] Soliloquy is an act of self-reflexive doubt. By virtue of its inward gaze and self-address, more often than not, it renders the self visible in ways that betray the very soul-searching motive for which the character soliloquizes. De Grazia observes the obvious but often ignored fact that soliloquy also increases the visibility of the audience and its implication in the scene. In soliloquy, "The exiting of the other characters clears a space not for pure solipsistic thought but for direct contact with the audience."[34] The audience of *Henry V* is positioned to both constitute and unravel the illusion of the play, but through both activities the audience also extends Henry's struggle with ceremony into the performative reaches of spectatorship more broadly, into performance culture and its applications in religion and politics. Richard Preiss suggests that the attempt to discover a pure "interiority," as the audience might be inclined to do in act 4, results from searching too much outside the playhouse for secular historical signs of modern individualism. "When we consider the world *inside* it, fittingly, rather than the world around it, we can better understand interiority as a site-specific technology, a practical invention."[35]

What we have in Henry's soliloquy is a conspicuous use of the theatrical-ceremonial technology of soliloquy in an examination of the question of ceremony's own reliability for mediating the truth. Further, Henry's turn to prayer at the end of the soliloquy brings this question to a head. If we were to understand the play to dramatize a conversion of character, we would treat this part of the soliloquy as the climactic moment of transformation when Henry turns his attention away from the superstitions of ceremony and directly toward God, free from the distractions of the idols of pomp and symbolism, and no longer hiding behind disguise. But this is not, in fact, what happens. To the contrary, the prayer amounts to a dizzying mixture of theological angles, as it theatrically searches for a suitable "form of prayer," to quote Claudius in *Hamlet*, to free him from the trappings of self-representation. And as with Claudius, Henry's prayer to the "God of battles" constitutes a last, futile attempt to free himself from ceremony—and the play's final rhetorical nod toward monumentalism.

The central paradox in the prayer joins a Catholic model of ceremonial devotion to a Protestant model of iconoclasm. In response to his inherited sin—"the fault / My father made in compassing the crown"—Henry asks God to recognize the "chantries" that he built "where the sad and solemn priests / Sing still for Richard's soul" (4.1.289–90, 298–99). Such a request would be out of the question to any anticeremonialist and to most English Protestants because of its explicit appeal to Catholic practices of repose prayers and works-based soteriology. However, in a complete reversal of theological affiliation, Henry ends his prayer with recognizable Protestant *sola fide* soteriology:

> More will I do,
> Though all that I can do is nothing worth,
> Since that my penitence comes after all,
> Imploring pardon.
>   (299–302)

Henry reverses his position, claiming that any acts of penitence that he conducts or commissions are "nothing worth," and that the preeminence of sin ("all") causes him ultimately to rely on "pardon" alone.[36] Henry's prayer is more exploratory and processual than it is conclusive.

The structure of this prayer takes us on a theological historical journey. It progresses from Mosaic intercession, to a statement of the restitution and penance he has performed, and finally to reductionist Protestant reliance on faith. Yet, interestingly, even this final cry for unmediated mercy is voiced on behalf of his subjects. This is both an exercise and a failure of Henry's priestly function.[37] It is priestly insofar as it is intercessory, but it fails, in a sense, because he performs this prayer in private; that is, there is no symbolic representation of Christ—or the political equivalent—if there is no one watching. The reentrance of Erpingham immediately before the prayer reminds us that, as far as stage directions are concerned, Henry is still wearing the cloak, which now sits as a kind of humble cope or chasuble and contrasts markedly with the "interissued robe of gold and pearl" that Henry has bemoaned just moments before (259). We might think of the many medieval illustrations of vested celebrants kneeling and gazing up at the altar during Mass, or we might even remember the many miracle and biblical drama performances that drew on the imagery and staging of Eucharistic celebration, as in the Croxton *Play of the Sacrament* and in Chester's *The Last Supper*. The only audience for Henry's prayer, however, is the playhouse audience, who, all things considered, views the prayer not as a liturgical mediation but as Henry taking another stab at figuring out his ceremonial identity, feeling around for a theological foothold rather than experiencing a deliberate conversion from ceremonialism to rarified thought.

Note also that the prayer ends by "imploring pardon," using a term that has a significant theological history and also echoing the Prologue's request for pardon and so invoking the attitude of response and recognition that it earlier induced in the audience. Imploring "pardon," in this play, is associated with artificiality and a reliance on the processes of theater. Recall, for instance, Henry's earlier complaint about "every fool whose sense can no more feel / But his own wringing" (4.1.232–33). In the prayer, Henry implicates himself as one of these fools and proffers the underlying activity of "wringing" as universal to anyone subject to ceremony, including the ceremony of the stage. His prayer is a kind of wringing-out of ceremony for forgiveness, a spongy pressing of his own "gross brain" for something persuasive, and a prayerful gripping of his hands in a gesture of desperation. Henry's character does not undergo a linear transformation from the materiality of superstitious ceremony to the fineness of soul-like anticeremonialism—or from Catholic to Protestant.

An additional question that Henry's soliloquy raises is whether he has the ability in the first place to embrace or, alternatively, throw off ceremony—or, to state it in terms of theatricality, whether ceremony is such a thing that can be thrown off. Is there any way to get beyond a sense of one's own wringing? And what kind of character change should we expect from a play purposed, in part, on exposing the entanglements of theatrical appearing? Clearly, one of the performative effects of Henry's soliloquy and prayer is the implication that there is an inner agency driving his frustrations, that there is a person *represented by* the ceremony that he cannot shed. Shakespeare cauterizes this "hard condition" by continually situating Henry in narrative situations where he is forced to add to his theatrical persona and perform before others. I am thinking of his disguised conversation with Bates and Williams and of the St. Crispin's Day speech, but also of the barely masked semblance of a council in the first scene with the clergy, Henry's theatrical exposure of the English traitors in Southampton, and even his courting of Katherine—"It is as easy for me, Kate, to conquer the kingdom as to speak so much more French" (5.2.185–86). Although the soliloquy of act 4 presents Henry in isolation and presumably in a state of honesty, the play's preoccupation with constant performing, with the activities of the audience, and with the transparent scaffolding of the theatrical environment forms a texture that asserts itself upon any moment—like Henry's prayer—that might appear at first to reveal something beyond the theatrical.

One way to understand the performativity of Henry's struggle is as the object of the audience's dual intentions toward his representation of inner self, on the one hand, and his overt theatrical strategies and performances, on the other. On this point, we might consider the Merleau-Pontian notion that perception emerges "in the crossing of the body and the world."[38] All physical perceptions are dual perceptions, occurring simultaneously, of the perceptual object as well as of the body that is performing the act of perceiving. Thus, when Henry perceives the symbolic yet real objects of his ceremonial authority— "the balm, the scepter and the ball"—he also remembers the feeling of them, discovered from the alternative perspective of Henry's disguise (4.1.257). The younger King Henry expresses the novelty of this phenomenon in *Henry IV, Part 2* to the Lord Chief Justice when he first encounters the royal garments, saying, "This new and gorgeous garment, majesty, / Sits not so easy on me as you think."[39] In the scope of the Henriad, the metaphorical meaning of these lines gives way somewhat to the literal fact of feelingness. Traces of Henry's envy for someone else's body, for a body whose touch is not always mediated by ceremony, can be seen in his envy for the peace of mind that even the supplicant beggar enjoys: "Canst thou, [idol ceremony] when thou command'st the beggar's knee, / Command the health of it? No, thou proud dream / That play'st so subtly with a king's repose" (253–55). His memory records the crossing of his sensing body and the objects that adorn it. At the same time, the audience becomes accustomed to seeing Henry in modes of performance and acquires a sensitivity to the strategies he uses toward others.

A phenomenology of theater recognizes that dramatic content is a product of dramaturgical and scenographic variations on a theme—such as the theme of character, or authority, or religion—and *Henry V* insists on making these variations transparent to audiences historically caught between arguments of iconophobia and ceremonialism.[40] David Morris offers a tangible experiment that speaks to the composite and anamorphic creation of scene and character that this play is intent on exposing, and to how the changes in perspective particularly between soliloquy, monologue, dialogue, and spectacle contribute to and thus unify theatrical phenomena. Imagine character to be like a cork:

> Obtain a wine cork. Lay the cork on a table so that it can roll on its long axis across the table. Rest your hand beside the cork so that your finger and thumb drape down, just grazing its circular ends. Close your eyes and relax, bracketing any assumptions or claims about the cork and what it should feel like. Hold your hand very still for a minute or two, exerting as little pressure as possible on the cork, yet touching it. Then lift your hand off the table, keeping your wrist and hand relaxed so that the cork just hangs between your fingers. Now wiggle the cork.[41]

The experiment is meant to disrupt one's habits of perception and attribution of ontology, to slow down the tendency to move beyond the theatrical. When one holds the object with relaxed fingers and, as much as possible, when one brackets assumptions about what the object between one's fingers is, one's physical sensations of the cork's ends feel independent of each other, and the feeling of the object is lost in the feeling of the act, which becomes a property of the feeler (she has feelings). Yet as soon as one squeezes and wiggles the cork, the feeling returns as the property of the object (it feels like a cork). The habit of perceiving a singular object of perception—the cork—is unavoidable, as ultimately the experiment shows the object to appear in the crossing of one's fingers and the world: "The unity is in the wiggle." In some sense, too, the unity of Henry's character, his authenticity and the common humanity that may exist beneath its ceremonial guise, obtains in the wiggle. Such unity is only ever manifest in the movements and contacts between the perceiving and perceived bodies of the theater in the mode of the present participle (she is feeling the cork). The play's larger unity also emerges through this anamorphosis and intersubjectivity, in the imaginative variants that it offers us, and—as early modern audiences would have experienced it—through its many problematic intertheatrical connections to ceremony.

Anticipating *Henry V*'s most powerful moment of soliloquy, the Chorus that precedes act 4 encourages this kind of felt connection between audience and character. The Chorus verbally depicts Henry "walking from watch to watch, from tent to tent," addressing his subjects as "brothers, friends and countrymen" (4.0.30–34). Henry's strolling the ranks can hardly be shown on the stage, but the audience's imagination preempts his confrontations with Pistol, Gower, Fluellen, Bates, and Williams in the following scene and creates an impression of Henry in solitude and thought, visible in the dark night only to those close enough to be in conversation. The Chorus emphasizes the audience's intimate perception and even invasion of this privacy and solitude, noting the details of Henry's face: "Upon his royal face there is no note / How dread an army hath enrounded him" (35–36). And so whatever host of people has "enrounded" Henry in the camp, the audience is positioned within this circle. This phenomenon of theatrical intimacy and authenticity arises in the crossing of the actor's body with the audience member's, manifested in Henry's look:

> His liberal eye doth give to every one,
> Thawing cold fear, that mean and gentle all
> Behold, as may unworthiness define,
> *A little touch* of Harry in the night.
>   (44–47, italics added)

This emphasis on Henry's gaze frames the audience's "sense of depth and space" within the confines of the theater and in relation to him. The theatrical feeling of intimacy, further, helps to establish the roles of the theater—player, character, and audience. Relations between bodies, such as Henry's ceremonial body and the supposed real bodies of his subjects, are "not simply rooted in the crossing of one's body and the world, but in the crossing of one's existence and an other's existence."[42] Synesthetically, we are told to visually "behold" Henry's own act of seeing and then to feel its "touch." We are instructed to attend to Henry's eye and activity of looking, provoking "a warping of our own space" and, by consequence, an impression of another out from the visual condition of the playhouse.[43] This moment of *coup de théâtre* exposes the visuality of the scene—that is, the presence of the audience perceiving. It builds on the Chorus's rhetorical call for audience interaction, and it enacts this interaction through the theatrical strategies of disguise, intimacy, and space. Thus "a little touch of Harry in the night" not only personalizes Henry's character by referring to him as the more casual "Harry" but also uses the sensory atmosphere of intimacy and soliloquy to suggest a heightened sense of character.

Henry's soliloquies in act 4 demonstrate that his character is constituted by felt experiences that unfurl before the audience who inhabit the same sensory and perceptual space. And yet, despite these attempts to create a feeling of selfhood, at the end of the prayer to the God of Battles there is still no resolution to the problem of ceremony.

"All Things Are Ready, If Our Minds Be So": A Performative Occasion

What might be made, then, of the surprisingly decisive resolve of the St. Crispin's Day speech?[44] The speech has been called "the climax of the king-and-commoner dialectic of the Henriad" and even "the thematic climax of the entire Henriad."[45] I don't challenge the thematic significance of the speech, but I would question the notion that it culminates with Henry stripping his ceremonial authority, "liberating himself and his society from bondage to idol (therefore idle) ceremony," as Richard Hardin describes it.⁴⁶ Up to this point Henry has not garnered momentum towards an expected anticeremonial conversion, especially given his lack of clarity in the preceding soliloquy. At the same time, in the tone of the Prologue and Chorus, the play's persistence in revealing its own theatricality reinforces the role of the ceremonial and theatrical as important aspects of character and human relation.

A more consistent reading of the St. Crispin's speech, I suggest, focuses on the performative work it does through ceremony, and from this perspective it proves to be more like a conditioning of the mind toward its social and physical surroundings than a rhetorical defense of the king's cause. Just before the French attack the English on the morning of the Battle of Agincourt, Henry offers a noteworthy description of the rhetorical intent of his recent speech, saying, "All things are ready, if our minds be so" (4.3.72). Given the contortion on display in his soliloquy, this statement might make us wonder how and when Henry himself went from "imploring pardon" to being "ready." Some might suspect that Henry's readiness is pragmatic and designed to excite the same feeling in his subjects, but this interpretation assumes that Henry has left his soliloquized doubts behind and has become comfortable with a utilitarian approach; and even this demands that Henry reach an ideological position in between scenes. As in the prayer to the God of Battles, the St. Crispin's speech presents contradictory views of ceremony, stripping as well as reinforcing it. Yet there is a third option between anticeremonialism and pragmatism that may explain Henry's motivation in this speech. The readiness that Henry exhibits is a belief in the performative potential of ceremonial power—not as an allegedly empty rhetorical instrument but as a theatrical act that both *represents* and *does* things. And it is to religious ceremony, invoked in the form of nostalgia for the old religion, that Henry turns for a performative model and medium.

This speech is frequently understood as an activity of iconoclasm and social leveling, but this explains only one aspect of the speech act. From one angle, the speech is inundated with ceremonialist and sacramental imagery. Hunt provides a summary of this imagery, which includes, among others, references to the relics of his soldiers' scars, the Eucharistic notes in the "host" of soldiers being "familiar in his mouth," the "flowing cups" that are "freshly remembered," and, of course, the brotherhood of martyrdom that Henry extends to "he today that sheds his blood with me."[47] Additionally, Henry's language of disrobing to express his pure and naked motivation—exclaiming that "It earns me not if men my garments wear" because "Such outward things dwell not in my desires"—is undermined by the earlier paradox of putting on garments in order for his "ceremonies" to appear "laid by" (4.3.26–27). Even Henry's pretended disrobing has a prop-like quality, what Rayner imagines to inhabit an "in-between space" that "breaks down the dualism between world and stage in what might be called an aspect of *'readiness.'*"[48]

Notably, though, the speech also engages in repurposing anti-ceremonialist rhetoric. Henry readies his troops by addressing his representative soldier as "he that shall see this day." To put it in religious terms, such language superficially strips—disrobes—ceremony's power of mediation between the devotee and the sacred object (4.3.44). With the disposition of a present participle, the audience is witnessing the memorialized event as it is being memorialized. Henry's apparent rhetorical strategy is to position his military audience as a direct witness of the event and thus to marginalize their awareness of being mediated by ceremony. However, the play has heretofore made the play audience self-aware of its constitutive activity of pardoning theater's artificiality and has also conditioned the audience to recognize the felt experiences and theatrical contingencies of Henry's rhetoric. So while we might imagine the audience of soldiers to be absorbed in the spectacle, the playhouse audience is particularly attuned to strategies of mediation. In his continuation of Marlowe's *Hero and Leander*, George Chapman personifies the goddess "Ceremonie" in a similar fashion, forwarding her nature as the mere face of devotion but, in so doing, also asserting the necessity of ceremony all the more. Leading religion "in a chain," Ceremony appears to Leander and commands him to observe proper "nuptial rites":

> all her bodie was
> Cleere and transparent as the purest glasse:
> For she was all presented to the sence;
> Devotion, Order, State, and Reverence,

Her shadowes were; Societie, Memorie;
All which her sight made live, her absence die.⁴⁹

Like Henry's emphasis on memorializing the battle—the impending victory that "shall be remembered"—the goddess Ceremony takes the form of shadowy "Memory." She makes memory ready to act for the good of "Devotion, Order, State, and Reverence," goods that were frequently associated with ceremony. Yet she also nods to the primacy of "substance" and so is, in the same moment, wholly sensory and wholly transparent. Like Shakespeare's, Marlowe's treatment of Ceremony suggests no contradiction between simultaneously grounding meaning in the immanent spectacle and deferring meaning to the substance behind it.

As I have been arguing, this is a characteristic of early modern performance culture in general. While certain performances, including *Henry V*, might introduce and use the imagined binary between representation and theatricality as a device for creating dramatic action, they are no less confident in the transformative power of the theatrical for doing so. Just so, Henry's speech adopts this purposeful binary of mediation and real presence, but it does so with confidence in the performative power of theatrical becoming.

Perhaps one reason why Shakespeare amplifies Henry's rhetorical use of the St. Crispin's feast is that England's holidays and civic festivals were the most wide-ranging examples of this ambivalent yet confident expression of ceremonialism. Throughout the latter sixteenth century, higher-profile festivals inherited from the medieval and early Reformational periods instigated a flurry of polemicism over their morality and usefulness. Given Henry's concern with his inherited authority, the well-known history of the Wars of the Roses, and the contentious status of Queen Elizabeth's own idiosyncratic uses of religious ceremony, two political and religious festivals that Elizabethan audiences might have associated with Henry's speech—besides St. Crispin's—are Elizabeth's coronation procession and the commemorative annual Accession Day festival. The latter occurred on November 17 of each year, the anniversary of Elizabeth's succession.⁵⁰ For the Accession festivities, the court hosted a ceremonial tournament, and the public celebrated by ringing bells, lighting bonfires, and attending sermons written for the occasion. Still, the event was highly contentious, surrounded by the typical arguments of ceremonialism and anticeremonialism, such as the pragmatic power of memorialization and, contrariwise, the distraction and idolatry of ceremonial mediation.[51]

Notably, though, support and dissidence for the celebrations did not always follow a Catholic-Protestant divide. For example, whereas the puritan Robert Wright argues that the Accession Day festivities treat Elizabeth as if she were a god, we also read the Catholic William Rainolds accusing the nation of pagan idolatry in celebrating the event.[52] Idolatry is a flexible accusatory label. Nevertheless, English Protestants predominantly valued Accession Day as a kind of ceremonial counterceremony, as it were, to the abuses of Rome—polemical in its position but pragmatic and even nostalgic in its tactics. Roy Strong cites a manuscript of another speech written for the occasion that views the festival as a commemoration of the queen's mediatory presence as monarch. It states that through Elizabeth, much as through a ceremony, "we enjoy withall . . . the gospel preached amongst vs, the peace of conscience, the reconciliation betwene god and our soules."[53] Others likewise admiringly compared Elizabeth on Accession Day to Solomon, Josiah, and the Queen of Sheba.[54]

Proponents were not limited, however, to defending ceremony by extolling the value of the thing being ceremonialized—the queen, in the case of Accession Day. Sometimes, writers ignored the message and focused on the medium, commending the experience of ceremony itself as an activity. In essence, these statements defend the performativity of ceremony for its effects on the attitudes and social habits of participants. For example, decades before Elizabeth's succession, Sir Thomas More describes a secular use of ceremony in *Utopia*. The Utopians' religious practices embrace typical devices of ceremonialism—"They burn incense, scatter perfumes and display a great number of candles"—but are quick to clarify that such rituals have an experiential rather than instrumental benefit: "not that they think these practices profit the divine nature in any way. . . . They feel that sweet smells, lights and other such rituals somehow elevate the human mind."[55] The "nature" of the divine object of worship, More says, can be neither more nor less perfectly represented; it can only be more or less profitably ceremonialized—that is, more beneficially performed.

It was common for writers to engage the questions of ceremony and mediated devotion with specific regard for what we might call their ceremony's affective and performative value. Addressing the many reformers who specifically rejected the sensory experience of such religious ceremony, the ceremonialist theologian Richard Hooker notes the inconsistent treatment of ceremony's basic mediatory qualities: "To solemn actions of royalty and justice, their suitable ornaments are a beauty. Are they only in religion a stain?"[56] Of course, and as I have discussed, some reformers also targeted the alleged abuses of political ceremonial practice, but what is most salient to my discussion about these divergent and sometimes inconsistent opinions is their habit of marginalizing consideration of the thing ceremonialized in favor of quibbling over the activity and affect of ceremonial mediation itself.

We see this focus on the theatrical environment of ceremony in accounts of Elizabeth's coronation procession that I highlighted in chapter 1. On January 14, 1559, Elizabeth was carried on a golden litter through the streets of London, stopping to receive gifts, hear speeches, and watch pageants. The queen's coronation procession is relevant to *Henry V*'s treatment of ceremony for at least two significant reasons, despite occurring several decades before the play's first performance. The first is that the procession's first pageant, of five, was a symbolic pyramid dramatizing "the uniting of the two houses of Lancaster and York," the historical setting of most of Shakespeare's history plays, including *Henry V*. The second point of relevance is that *The Uniting of the Two Houses* was performed on Gracechurch Street, the very street where Queen Anne Boleyn, Elizabeth's mother, enjoyed a coronation pageant in her own honor.[57] As for Shakespeare's Henry, the ceremonialism of Elizabeth's reign was interpreted through concerns about legitimacy and inheritance. Still, Malcolm Smuts reminds us that the details of the pageants' scripted speeches and specific symbols "often bear little relationship to what most spectators actually saw." Yet Smuts's comment is more applicable to the speeches than the spectacle, since the copious ambient environment would have proved easier to see than the speeches were to hear.[58]

Above I've discussed Richard Mulcaster's observations about the anamorphic aspects of the pageants as well as their congested visual ornamentation. The pageants' pictorialized allegories appear crowded with figures, multiple stages, and symbolic relations between characters, and Mulcaster notes that while each stage was full of people, decorations, banners, and trim, even the gaps between ornaments on the stages' physical structures were filled in with *sententiae* expressing the pageants' themes. The dominant impressions of the ceremony were of its exuberance and noise, how its dense sensory atmosphere echoed, like Caesar's triumph in *Julius Caesar*, off its many surfaces.

One nuanced response regarding the merits of these sorts of ceremonial festivities comes in a letter from William Cavendish, the Earl of Newcastle, to Prince Charles. Cavendish affirms the opportunity provided by royal ceremonies like the coronation and Accession Day festivals by observing a certain spatial and phenomenological "distance" that is created between kings and their subjects through ceremony: "What preserves you Kings more than ceremony[?] The cloth of estates, *the distance people are with you*, great officers, heralds, drums, trumpeters, rich coaches, rich furniture for horses, guards, marshal's men making room, disorders to be laboured by their staff of office, and cry 'now the King comes'; . . . aye, even the wisest though he knew it and not accostumed to it, shall shake off his wisdom and shake for fear of it, *for this is the mist is cast before us*, and masters the Commonwealth."[59] Beyond the impressiveness of the spectacle, which is intended to represent kingly pomp, Cavendish also encourages Charles to embrace moments of distance building. *Distance*, here, draws on several early modern meanings. One is the distance between military ranks, as is seen in the ceremonial entourage.[60] Yet another more ambient meaning is the distance between the monarch and his audience cast by the ceremonial environment, an interpretive distance composed of the figurative "mist" of horns, colors, voices, and drums. This distance paradoxically connotes both close proximity and expanse. It is like the Prologue's cipher in its ability to expand a figure into a "million" and then to collapse it into "nothing." It can bring kings and subjects together but then use that same relation of proximity to create a divide. Ceremonial distance is the active ingredient in creating the character phenomenon. Cavendish thinks of ceremony as we might imagine the cork; it causes its beholders to feel the thing represented and then, alternatingly, to feel their own engagement, flashing back and forth and discovering a unity of the thing itself through this anamorphic activity. In the play, Henry articulates both sides of ceremonial distance, at one point bemoaning its self-isolating qualities and at another declaring that "this day shall gentle" the "condition" of any man who fights alongside him (4.3.63).

Henry's use of the feast day, in particular, as a vehicle and conceptual model of religious ceremony is a careful maneuver of manipulating the phenomenal "distance" of the event. The St. Crispin's feast day serves to make "ready" his troops in a way that joins the representation of authority with the transparent theatricality that Henry no longer wants to hide. He achieves this by remaking the ceremony *for* and *before* his immediate audience, infusing the ceremonial feast day with new meaning.

> This day is called the feast of Crispian.
> He that outlives this day and comes safe home
> Will stand a-tiptoe when this day is named
> And rouse him at the name of Crispian.
> He that shall see this day and live old age
> Will yearly on the vigil feast his neighbours,
> And say, "Tomorrow is Saint Crispian."
> . . . .
> This story shall the good man teach his son,
> And Crispin Crispian shall ne'er go by
> From this day to the ending of the world
> But we in it shall be remembered.
> (4.3.40–46, 56–59)

This is a remarkable instance of ceremony making, of filling the cipher of ceremony with the experience of its audience. Henry reestablishes the ceremony by making the traditional shoemaker's feast day germane to the battle at hand.[61] By adding a new memorialized event to St. Crispin's Day, and by playing up this expanded meaning, Henry elevates the immediacy of his soldiers' ceremonial experience, treating their immanent presence as a self-referential icon. He continues this strategy of superficially rejecting ceremonial pomp while asserting the purported accessibility of the intimate and the personal later in the play when he refuses to display his battered armor in his triumphant procession after the battle, with the Chorus explaining:

> he forbids it,
> Being free from vainness and self-glorious pride;
> Giving full trophy, signal and ostent
> Quite from himself to God.
>
> (5.0.19–22)

His insistence on a quiet return reinforces the importance of the actual moment of ceremony making over the deferred remembrance of it.

The play imposes no contradiction between Henry's use of ceremonial affect and his iconoclastic rhetoric. Compare, for instance, the speech as recorded in Shakespeare's source, Holinshed's *Chronicles*, which reads: "If they would but remember the just cause for which they fought, and whome they should incounter, such faint-harted people as their ancestors had so often overcome. To conclude, manie words of courage he uttered, to stirre them to doo manfullie, assuring them that England should never be charged with his ransome, nor anie Frenchmen triumph over him as a captive; for either by famous death or glorious victorie would he (by Gods grace) win honour and fame."[62] Especially noteworthy among Shakespeare's several elaborations on this historical account is that Henry directly mentions his "cause" for war. Not only does he declare it to be "just," but he makes the power of memory—his strongest rhetorical tool—contingent on his soldiers' comprehending and agreeing with this cause: "Remember the just cause for which they fought." In *Henry V*, Shakespeare omits this reference to the cause from the speech and relocates it to Henry's earlier discussion with Bates and Williams. I would suggest that the reason for Shakespeare's omission of the king's cause for war from the Crispin's speech is his decision to emphasize the performative action of the speech that occurs between Henry and his soldiers. The inspiration is neither the king's motive alone—his cause and responsibility—nor that of the soldiers. It comes to being, rather, as a relation between the past that Henry invokes and the present that he enacts. Henry refuses to limit the meaning—or "rouse"—of his speech to "something that is either completely outside of the world or completely encapsulated within some point of it"—neither totally represented nor totally theatrical.[63] He gives form to the speech—that is, he per-forms it—with an awareness of its power as a speech act that mediates the remembered event and its theatrical reiteration in the feast day. As in Chester's *The Last Supper*, where Jesus infuses a potentially memorialist interpretation of the Eucharist with the fact of his own unmediated presence, Henry duplicates a ceremony "here, in presence of you all."[64]

The feast is further infused with meaning by the contrast between the readiness of Henry's soldiers and the idleness often associated with festivals back at home. Reformation England underwent a series of reforms to the church calendar in the mid-sixteenth century. The first major reduction of observed festivals was ordered by Henry VIII in 1536, followed by significant revisions from Edward VI.[65] While the reductions fit generally into the Reformational paradigm of minimizing distractions from spiritual devotion, the monarchs' express rationale was headlined by their complaint that celebrating too many festivals meant that there were too many days when people abstained from working, a policy that draws on the conventional Protestant condemnation of idleness—adding an auditory pun to the soliloquy's "*idol* ceremony." Shakespeare shows his awareness of the historical revisions to the liturgical calendar in Henry's first soliloquy in *1 Henry IV*.[66] Here, Hal overtly links "idleness" to the celebration of "playing holidays."[67] This anticeremonialist connection returns through a remark made by Westmorland in *Henry V*, the comment that instigates the St. Crispin's speech. Westmorland says, "O that we now had here / But one ten thousand of those men in England / That do no work today!" (4.3.16–18). Presumably, these idle Englishmen are those who refrain from work for the holiday. Had they not celebrated the feast day, or had the calendar already been reformed, perhaps England's odds would be less dismal. The detail of Westmorland's complaint is a notable addition to Holinshed, where Henry merely hears someone say, "I would to God there were with vs now so manie good soldiers as are at this hour within England," with no mention of those "that do no work today."[68] With this in mind, there arises an alternative interpretation of Westmorland's newfound readiness to fight where he says, "Perish the man whose mind is backward now" (72). There is no reason to think that the pessimistic Westmorland suddenly believes that the justness of the king's cause will mystically fight in their favor. Rather, the readiness of Westmorland's mind occurs through Henry's recreation of the saint's day, from something memorialized to something memorializing in the immediate work of the speech.

It is unlikely that most of Shakespeare's playhouse audiences would have been especially devoted to one side of the religious ceremonialism controversy. Henry's rhetorical and theatrical uses of ceremony are more significant, instead, for how they heighten awareness of mediation in theater and in politics. The notion that ceremony creates a form of "distance" that can be controlled and even rhetorically collapsed, as Henry demonstrates, acknowledges the importance of the body and its surroundings in a political or ritual event, and this same preoccupation with the physical conditions of spectacle is found in early modern antitheatrical writings. Many early modern tracts about theater evaluate its moral status not only by appraising its represented content but also by attending to the question of affect. Stephen Gosson, for example, criticizes the ambience of theater as "noysome too the body" and not just to the soul, emphasizing the bodily confusion caused by what Henry calls the "rouse" of ceremony.[69] Gosson complains that theaters emit "straunge consortes of melody, to tickle the eare; costly apparel, to flatter the sight; effeminate gesture, to rauish the sence; and wanton speache, to whet desire too inordinate lust."[70] This phenomenology of theater targets the physiological infiltration of inordinately strange and pleasing sensation, fearing that it might "slip downe into the hart, & with gunshotte of affection gaule the minde, where reason and vertue should rule the roste."[71]

Notably, these effects are precisely what More and Cavendish find potentially *profitable* about ceremony. Likewise, against accusations that the adornment and visual sensuousness of theater turn it into an idol, Thomas Heywood's *An Apology for Actors* avers that, from its provenance, theater utilizes ambience—costumes, sets, colors—as visual media for identifying character types and especially character morality.[72] This view of theater corresponds to traditionalist religious positions, such as that of the Catholic bishop Stephen Gardiner, who describes religious ceremonies as "gates to our sences."[73] Heywood embraces the phenomenology that Gosson condemns by preferring to think of theatrical ceremonialism as ciphering its content rather than distorting it.

Heywood suggests that it is not always disorderly to elevate physical and perceptual stimulation above intellectual comprehension, and that the theatrical utility of ceremony can sometimes take moral precedence over its representational functions. With this in mind, he writes, "I hope there is no man of so unsensible a spirit, that can inveigh against the true and direct use of this quality," speaking specifically of the ways that color can be used to decipher the moral lessons of theater, those that Gosson judges to "flatter the sight."[74] His use of *unsensible* engages in a melee for the term among ceremonialist polemics of the period. The vocabulary of sensibility covers a range of meanings, including the subjective ability to physically sense something, an object's capacity for being sensed by a person, and general intellectual sensibility, such as was frequently said to differentiate humans from animals. We can compare it to the multivalence of Henry's allegation that Bates is merely trying to "feel other men's minds"—to induce, detect, or manipulate feeling. In polemical writings, and especially in religious polemic on ceremony, the physical and intellectual meanings of the sensible and the unsensible were often intentionally conflated, so that an unsensible person, according to a protheatricalist, would take issue with the sensory effects of plays and songs precisely because he refused to consider how feeling something in the body could be useful for teaching the mind. For instance, in a song praising John Case's then recently printed treatise called *The Praise of Musicke*, William Byrd attests that Case "soundly blames the senceless foole, & Barbarous Scithyan, of our dayes."[75] Like Heywood, Byrd implies that the sensible person is the one who brings physical perception and intellectual understanding into harmony.

Moreover, by calling antitheatrical polemicists "vnsensible," Heywood implicates the audience and its understanding of the relation between sensation and reason. Consequently, writers like Heywood and Byrd echo the 1549 prayer book injunction "Of Ceremonies," which recommends religious ceremonies that "stir up the dull mind of man to the remembrance of his duty to God."[76] When a mind is dull—or when one's "sense can no more feel / But his own wringing"—it is warranted to combat feeling with feeling, for the sake of being ready to receive moral instruction through aesthetic spectacle (4.1.232–33).

In the Crispin's speech, Henry repeatedly highlights the process of translating the physical into the intelligible, often couching sensibility in the language of measuring expense. Weighing costs, in a sense, is like participating in religious ceremony or viewing a play in the action of crediting the physical with worth exceeding its bare material presence. Henry declares that he is "not covetous for gold" or the "cost" of war but would rather "covet honour"; and he accuses the idle men who do not fight of "thinking themselves accursed" and of holding "their manhoods cheap" (24–28, 65–66). He imbues the physical cost of battle with meaning that can be realized by his subjects only if they fight *and* are willing to think beyond their own feeling, if they have a sensible "spirit," as Heywood calls it, that approaches feelings intersubjectively, aware of the ways that a spectator participates in the creation of a monument.

In addition to physical sensation, sensibility, for Henry, involves an interpretation of time and, in particular, a religious ceremonial understanding of time—in the sense of vertical time as opposed to linear time, "prefiguring and unfolding all which happened once-upon-a-time."[77] This intertemporality repeats the basic gesture of the "shadows," "signs," and "things" of Chester's *The Last Supper*. There are at least four moments of "time" aggregated into the Crispin's speech. There is the original event celebrated by the festival, the Feast of Saints Crispin and Crispinian, who were martyred under Diocletian. Commemorating this event, there is also the accumulated time of tradition, centuries of Europeans celebrating the feast in what became known as a holiday for shoemakers.[78] Then there is the specific historical celebration of this feast occasioned by Henry's speech as described in Holinshed. And, of course, there is the immediate moment of the early modern play performance. Each moment has its own history, but Shakespeare harnesses them all through the occasionality of the playhouse and the persistent explication of ceremonial becoming throughout the play.

Scott Trudell has elaborated on what he calls the "media dispersal" into the music, space, technology, and crowd of early modern occasional entertainments, such as those I examined around the Chester cycle.[79] "Immanently distributed through their environment, entertainments manifest the labour involved in *carving theatricality out of occasion*."[80] Time itself becomes sensible, in a sense, through the occasion of the performance. It is a moment set apart for reflection on what it means to bring the past into present form and also what it means for a form to embody a time past. Shakespeare invokes the interpretive attitude of a festival occasion in the Crispin's speech, where the theatrical apparatus of the feast day envelops the speech itself, and the two combine as the larger scope of time manifests in the immediate moment.

The playhouse takes on the face of an occasion both fictively and theatrically through the ways that Henry's rhetoric appears to the audience. After all, his speech follows a scene of disguise and performance, and another in which he vulnerably decries ceremony itself. The audience is attuned to the inevitability of the performative both for the imagined historical figure of Henry and especially in the playhouse, so the artfulness of Henry's language appears as part of a process of artifice and strategy. His character is dispersed into the occasion of its performing, into its atmosphere and into the audience's intentionality, creating in the referential festival occasion itself "an excess of the theatrical form."[81] What may have appeared to some polemicists to be a disagreement over whether ceremony divides spectators from the object of ceremonial representation or bridges them to it subtly becomes the older theological binary of human limitation and divine excess. Henry intervenes not in the controversy itself but in "modes of being and forms of visibility" through which themes like courage, power, and character sincerity are made intelligible to characters and audiences.[82] This redistribution of sensibility in theater is laid bare in the manner expressed by Merleau-Ponty when he writes that language "is never the mere clothing of a thought which otherwise possesses itself in full clarity"; it is, rather, a simultaneous appearing in thought and performance.[83] The "accent" of artful language, Merleau-Ponty continues, "is assimilated little by little by the reader, and it gives him access to a thought to which he was until then *indifferent* or even *opposed*."[84] Shakespeare's play does not strive to communicate content with which the mind is already familiar and accustomed. Instead, the play manifests its content simultaneously with the manifestation of its phenomenal conditions to create performative effects of scene, character, and the inspirational spirit of the Crispin's speech.

Although the sixteenth-century revisions to the festival calendar, like the sacramental imagery of the St. Crispin's speech, may have brought some uniquely Protestant reforms to the minds of audience members, Shakespeare's theatrical strategy of presenting images simultaneously as signs and things is trans-Reformational. Shakespeare's use of the festival occasion shows both sides of the ceremonialism controversy to be reliant on forms of theatricality.

In my reading, Shakespeare invokes the opposing logics that view the sacramental medium as voluntary or as instrumental, and he mixes them together in an exposition of the performative power of theater. With this view of theater, Shakespeare has an ally in the world of theology of ecclesiastical reform. Just as Richard Hooker views sacramental elements as instruments of soul formation—"So the inward grace of sacraments may teach what serveth best for their outward form"[85]—so does he blur the line between ceremony and substance in his discussion of the question of the inherent holiness of certain times and places: "No doubt as God's extraordinary presence hath hallowed and sanctified certain places, so they are his extraordinary works that have truly and worthily advanced certain times, for which cause they ought to be with all men that honour God more holy than other days."[86] Hooker writes as part of a milieu that seeks to reconsider the pace and aim of religious reform in England, and he generally argues that many of the objects and structures of the old religion retain value as physical media and should be appropriated into the new religion without fear of their past uses. He locates feast days in both the past and the present, and grounds them in the immediate moment of the sensible: "The days which are chosen out to serve as public memorials of such his mercies ought to be clothed with those outward robes of holiness whereby *their difference* from other days may be made *sensible*."[87] This might be described as a typological or even sacramental theory of ceremony, but, more accurately, Hooker's description is ritualistic and performative in the sense that it is at once transparent about its artificiality and insistent on its ability to transform itself and its participants through use.

That Henry submits his speech and feast day to the transformative power of use is evinced in his frequent references to the moment at hand and in the indicative move it creates. "*This* day," Henry declares, "is called the Feast of Crispian," and "He that outlives *this* day / Will stand a-tiptoe when *this* day is named." He who fights with him will never forget "*this* day to the ending of the world," and "*this* day shall gentle his condition." Henry turns the present moment into an occasion. Its power lies in its hypothetical future remembrances. "He that shall live *this* day" will "remember / What feats he did *that* day." *This* day, of course, has become compound. It is the moment of the ceremonial and the performative, remembered and memorialized. Shakespeare's audience is brought processively through the unresolved journey of Henry's struggle with ceremony. Shakespeare's king, then, is like the iconoclast who, in destroying sacred objects, incidentally—or occasionally—acknowledges their spiritual power.[88] By showing the place of the future scars to be inflicted on his arm, Henry makes transparent the felt conditions through which the mind is made ready, and, like a disguise, even Henry's acts of iconoclasm dress the altar of ceremony and power before it can be torn down.

IN THE END, Henry's use of ceremony to ready his troops for battle evades the important questions we initially expect it to answer: the questions raised by Bates and Williams about who is responsible for the souls of fallen soldiers. He never explains his justification for war—what the play refers to as the king's "cause." It is noteworthy that these lingering concerns constitute the would-be substance behind the political and theological ceremonies that Henry uses; they are the imaginary meaning behind the sign. To many Elizabethan Protestants, it is ultimately the integrity behind ceremonial actions that justifies them. A ceremony's affective or performative power is justified only insofar as the devotion it incites is theologically sound. So despite the play's dramatization of the famous English victory there remains a dark note, reminding audiences of the dangers of theatrical cipher and, therefore, also of the political cipher.

In this light, my interpretation of Henry's inconsistency, lack of resolution, and embrace of ceremony intends, not to prove that the play is ceremonialist through and through, but rather to show that its theatricality and intertheatricality make most sense viewed trans-Reformationally, as building the scene out of the performative capabilities of theatrical and ceremonial mediation that exist in a post-Reformational moment of change and nostalgia alike. However, in demonstrating that it at least is not iconoclastic, we are faced with the question: What is Henry's character if he is not a ceremony-stripping champion of Protestantism? There are, of course, many answers to this question, but there is one I want to highlight. Henry is a character who experiences genuine intellectual and moral conflict, and this conflict manifests in explicit allusion and phenomenal likeness to the religious and theatrical ceremonialist controversies of post-Reformation England. Thus, somewhere between the Chorus and the historical figure, Henry is a bearing point for the audience's physical, emotional, and ethical experiences of theater, however paradoxical they are. Beginning with the Prologue and stretching through to the St. Crispin's speech, in *Henry V* Shakespeare incorporates state and religious ceremony into the performance culture that facilitates the crossing of the body and the world. He exposes the shared theatrical strategy behind dramatic, religious, and political action, and he then sanctions this strategy, sets it apart, gives it occasion, and demonstrates its performative effect.

Chapter Four

GOD'S IDIOMS

Sermon Belief in Donne's London

God's idioms are the topic of a sermon "Preached at St. Paul's, Upon Christmas Day, 1628" on the theme, "Lord, who hath beleeved our report?"[1] The biblical theme presents the voice of a divine messenger—a prophet, a letter writer, or Jesus—who returns disappointed that his people failed to listen to God's Word. The sermon exhorts auditors to acknowledge God's interventions in personal and national affairs, and it offers instruction on how to hone one's sensitivity to divine action. The 1640 folio edition relays what immediately would have struck Donne's audience as out of the ordinary at the sermon's outset: the omission of a citation for the verse. Donne addresses this in the first sentence: "I have named to you no booke, no chapter, no verse, where these words are written: But I forbore not out of forgetfulnesse, nor out of singularity, but out of perplexity rather." His perplexity stems from the fact that versions of this sentence—"Lord, who hath beleeved our report?"—appear so frequently in the Bible that the question acquires special status. It becomes, in Donne's words, an "idiom": "I am sure you have all observed, that many men have certaine formes of speech, certaine interjections, certaine suppletory phrases, which fall often upon their tongue, and which they repeat almost in every sentence; and, for the most part, impertinently; and then, when that phrase conduces nothing to that which they would say, but rather disorders and discomposes the sentence, and confounds, or troubles the hearer" (8:292–93). Idiomatic phrases render communication "not the better beleeved, but the worse understood," but as Donne contends, they are not entirely without use, as spiritual comprehension entails much more than mere cognitive understanding.

Donne invites his auditors to ask why the scriptures include such idioms at all if their effect is to inhibit understanding. According to Donne, scriptural idioms are God's attempts to condescend to ordinary communication, to soften biblical lessons with verbal cushions that delay and echo the argument in order to assist human understanding at a subdidactic level. The specific rhetorical device in this case is *epiplexis*, but Donne probably also has in mind the general training in rhetorical copiousness and ornamentation provided in schools. In a practice slightly different from the modern use, Donne uses *idiom* in reference to its contribution to pathos. He explains that "out of an accommodation and communicablenesse of himselfe to man" God sometimes deploys "certaine idioms, certaine formes of speech, certaine propositions, which the holy Ghost repeats several times, upon severall occasions in the Scriptures" (8:292–93). The *OED* defines this usage of *idiom* as a "form of expression, grammatical construction, phrase, etc., used in a distinctive way in a particular language, dialect, or language variety; spec. a group of words established by usage as having a meaning not deducible from the meanings of the individual words."[2] Yet beyond its semantic meanings, Donne also utilizes the situational, spoken, kinetic, and phenomenological dimension of idiomatic speech acts to change the way that his audience understands belief—specifically, belief in sermons. An "idiom," in Renaissance terms, has a meaning that is "not deducible" from the individual words of the phrase itself but is created by repetition in culture and is established in the context and reception of the speech act of the immediate occasion. Idioms grant privileged status to the "suppletory" (marginal, peripheral) aspects of communication. "Lord, who hath beleeved our report," then, communicates something more than just a complaint about the disbelief of God's people; its meaning is "established by usage" and by the *in situ* experience of its auditors. In essence, it is performative and phatic, applying the meaning created by patterns of use and by the cultural repetition of a certain rhetorical tone and form to the situation of the auditors at hand.

In fact, Donne, along with other preachers and early modern writers on sermon-going, consistently foregrounds the "usage" of his sermons and in so doing acknowledges a performative dimension to how sermons communicate information and to how they promote belief—a dimension that is particular to the early modern performing arts and that contributes to the permeation of the culturally imagined divine Word in post-Reformation England. And such an understanding of the way that sermons interact with auditors on experiential levels extends from the example of the idiom to the theatrical dimension of the greater sermon event. The theatrical aspects of sermons were distributed through the spaces that they filled, the perceptual situation of the audience, the social occasion of the event, and the habits of interpretation by which they were received. Contemporary writings show that seventeenth-century sermons in London were distinctly invested in the environmental, social, and physical conditions of their delivery, even as the same writings often complained about these conditions. There is a kind of internal tension between the theatricality of sermon events and the sacred Word so imagined, but, similar to the superficial tension between ceremony and character in *Henry V*, this tension serves also to legitimate sermon theatricality as essential to religious edification. Preachers and writers on sermon-going harness this invoked tension to incite an attitude of self-reflection and interactivity in audiences. Audiences thus hear their own audition in the sermon; they conceive of the event as what we might call a dynamic *coup de théâtre* and an exercise in audition. In this way, as sermons incorporate their environments and their auditors' situatedness into their rhetorical representation, they echo the performativity of the broader performance culture. This self-consciousness about the theatricality of sermon-going, what I am calling the idiomatic quality of sermon events, affords an opportunity to consider the interplay between the theologically informed rhetorical practices of early modern sermons and their embattled social and physical spaces.

Using Donne's high-profile preaching venue at St. Paul's Cathedral as an illustration, the first sections of this chapter will explore how the archive of the sensory environments surrounding early modern London sermons emphasizes their theatrical and environmental qualities. From a rhetorical perspective, the sacred Word in these settings is the imagined object of belief, but from a performative perspective the manifestation of the Word is also the situational product of the activity of sermon-going itself, accumulated across sermon culture. The latter sections of this chapter address how we describe the relation between Protestant religion and performances of the sacred. The sensory, diffuse, and idiomatic character of sermons functions not only to distract auditors' attention but to provide an opportunity for the kind of embattled concentration that constituted belief in a sermon setting. Early modern urban sermons shaped experiences of belief in such a way that their didactic contents were continuous with their phenomenal contexts, including their spectacles, acoustics, distractions, mnemonic practices, and other so-conceived inessentials. Finally, I will discuss how this refusal to differentiate between a sermon's accidents and substance created a kind of real presence to sermons: not metaphysically but phenomenally as an imperative for auditors to pursue and search the perceptually dense sermon for its efficacious core and therefore to adopt an attitude of engagement and perceptual discernment that presents itself as what I call "sermon belief." What Donne will extol as the "Word preached" thus imagines the salvific efficacy of sermon-going as subject to an activity of sensory and perceptual warfare that not only accesses the divine Word but transforms it into something that both resists and relies on embattled attention.

The Voice of St. Paul's

What Donne describes as idiomatic in scripture takes the form of theatricality in early seventeenth-century sermons. Michael O'Connell remarks that "the sermon can be understood perhaps as the quintessential form of Protestant drama, one in which a solitary figure assumes the role of conveying and interpreting God's word."[3] The patent theatricality of early modern sermons also appeared in much less centralized ways; it spilled out into the aisles and pews, into the crowds and market stalls in the back of the nave, and into the robust attempts of auditors to grasp the Word of God with their bodies and minds. That is to say, sermon culture can be documented by far more than printed editions and the choreography and rhetoric of preachers. As part of godly performance culture, sermons were multifarious perceptual events that echoed the diffusion of the playhouse in subtle yet resonant ways.

Consider, for instance, the occasion and venue for the aforementioned sermon in 1628: Christmas services at St. Paul's Cathedral. The sermon would have been delivered as part of the evening prayer office, and the congregation would have notably included London's aldermen and mayor. At sermon time, the city leaders ceremoniously put on their cloaks, walked up to the quire where the pulpit stood, and sat to hear the sermon. Likely counterbalancing this ceremony, however, was the noise of visitors and children playing, as evidence suggests that on major festivals like Christmas children were allowed to play in the cathedral in the evening, "whence comes that inordinate noise which many times suffers not the preacher to be heard."[4] Such confrontations between ceremony and perceived disorder consistently follow St. Paul's through the period. Even visually, as the tallest structure in London, until at least 1561 when its towering spire was destroyed by a fire, it stood as a symbol of magnificence as well as change. The conspicuously missing spire combined with the cathedral's physical marks of religious reform—its lack of ornament, decaying roof, and reputed dereliction in ringing its bells. The cathedral's physical decay may have also reflected its increase in secular uses, including the leasing of space to tradesmen and the book trade outside the nave.[5]

At the same time, from an anticeremonialist perspective, like other major churches, St. Paul's was known, often discontentedly, for its extravagant music, its use of surplices, its kneeling rails and practices of genuflecting, and other high-profile inheritances of the old religion.[6] An author by the pseudonym of Philonax Lonekin, in his 1661 tragedy *Andronicus*, dramatizes divergent views on the devotional effects of huge church spaces like St. Paul's in a short exchange of differing opinions:

> *Cleobulus.* I love no such triumphant Churches —
> They scatter my devotion; whilst my sight
> Is courted to observe their sumptuous cost,
> I find my heart lost in my eyes;
> Whilst that a holy horror seems to dwell
> Within a dark obscure and humble cell.
> *Crato.* But I love Churches, mount up to the skies,
> For my devotion rises with their roof:
> Therein my soul doth heav'n anticipate.[7]

The speakers describe the effects of cathedral-like structures by the ways that "triumphant" spaces either fill their senses or, inversely, are filled by their senses, either scattering devotion through the inflammation of sensory experience or elevating devotion by pulling the "soul" up to "heav'n" through the senses. Cleobulus and Crato represent the ambiguity of *feeling* that accompanies many theatrical responses to religious ceremony: whether a felt experience informs the perceiver about the object (how it feels) or about himself (his feelings) often determines his opinion on ceremony. Cleobulus, for instance, comments that the church's opulence pulls his devotion away from him, whereas it has the reverse effect in Crato, taking root in his "soul" and transforming his senses. In St. Paul's, a congregation's devotion could not sensorily fill the building without encountering reform and decay along the way — symbols of this now old debate. One gets the sense that the cathedral was just so large and had undergone so much disrepair that anyone — conservative or reform-minded — could find some reason to complain, and still, as we will see, such complaints serve as the backdrop of a performative theology of sermon-going.

One common complaint was about the building's nave, called Paul's Walk. To see Paul's Walk was to see a marketplace in the back of a giant church, a venue crowded with people, stalls, and posted notices, what Bruce Smith calls a "heterogeneous throng."[8] And to hear Paul's Walk was to hear distinctive merchants' calls, the whispers of city gossip, and even the lectures of clergy for hire offering a sample of their product. In his 1629 *Micro-cosmographie*, Bishop John Earle depicts the Walk as "a heap of stones and men, with a vast confusion of languages.... The noise in it is like that of bees, a strange humming or buzzing, mixed of walking, tongues, and feet.... It is the synod of all parts politic,... the market of young lecturers,... [and] the general mint of all famous lies."[9] Of course, church authorities attempted to curtail civic commotion in the church, as is indicated by John Chamberlain's observation that St. Paul's had established a "new devised order to shut the upper doores in Powles in service time, whereby the old entercourse is cleane changed, and the trafficke of newes much decayed."[10] Yet despite such attempts, it maintained a reputation for not only accommodating but even inviting the commotion of society and spectacle.

I would suggest that a holistic understanding of St. Paul's Cathedral as London's center for preaching—with the city's most popular sermon venue, Paul's Cross, just outside in its churchyard—should include this extraliturgical atmosphere. The tunneling quire and the nave with its steep lancet arches and countless pillars provided a singular acoustic identifiable as the sound of St. Paul's (figure 4.1). Together with Paul's Cross, the cathedral served simultaneously as a barometer for developments in reform, a social hub, and a theater for the voice of the English preacher.

As the grand model for London's sermon culture, the cathedral's aural eminence, its voice, as it were, surfaces even in specifically visual media. One such instance is the cathedral's roof as represented in a 1559 copperplate map depicting St. Paul's in relation to other important city structures, including Christ Church and Newgate Market (figure 4.2). In comparison to the roofs surrounding the cathedral, which are shaded on one side to show angularity and elevation, for St. Paul's the engraver chose to abandon this regularity and instead to portray its distinctive wooden roof, multiple times repaired, here detailed by parallel lines rather than shading. This characteristic is often repeated in other sixteenth- and seventeenth-century map depictions of St. Paul's. The lines of the roof over the nave and quire curiously angle in and up toward the steeple. The immediate effect implies that the cathedral's steeple is the perspectival center of the map, which it is not. Perhaps it is simply large enough for the topographer to provide stylized shading, as if it were so enormous that any structures

FIGURE 4.1. Wenceslaus Hollar, *Interior of Old St. Pauls*, 1656. Reproduced with the permission of the Yale Center for British Art, Paul Mellon Collection, 32914–B1977.14.16214.

within its eyeshot would be in perspectival reference to it. In addition, the upward and inward angled roof conveys the curvature of the vaults that it covers and provides an awareness of the building's acoustic interior, a first-person perspective of looking down the deep nave and even hearing the echoes of crowd and preacher that mirror the repetitious curves of its vaults and arches.

FIGURE 4.2. *St. Paul's Cathedral Precinct.* Copperplate map of London, 1559. Reproduced with the permission of the Museum of London, image no. 006081.

The angled roof also draws attention to the building's steeple, here elongated to the extent that the church is taller than it is wide and reflecting the visual and aural prominence of its bell tower and bells. An antagonistic view toward the bell tower and its steeple's grandeur might interpret this imbalance in light of early modern literature's many comparisons of religious structures such as St. Paul's to the arrogance associated with the Tower of Babel. Thomas Dekker's is perhaps the most famous of these associations. In *The Dead Tearme*

(1608), Dekker personifies the steeple itself in "Paules steeples complaint," where the steeple looks down at the "shuffling," "halking," and "humming" of Paul's Walk and laments: "I verily beleeue that I am the Tower of *Babell* newly to be builded vp, but presently despaire of euer beeing finished, because there is in me such a confusion of languages."[11] St. Paul's spire was a symbol of incessant noise, as it is for Dekker's steeple, and yet also a singular mark of the focalized sound of the preacher. Moreover, in the copperplate map, just to the right of the spire is Paul's Cross. The pulpit itself is portrayed in an excessively large and empty churchyard, relative to the greater area of the map and to the space just below the cathedral. The topographer's emphasis on emptiness and spaciousness conveys the acoustic and social capacity of the cathedral precinct. Thus the asymmetry between these two elements of the map—the elongated spire and the spatially enlarged outdoor preaching area—shows how a maker of visual media relates to them as an auditor who alternately hears its steeple from a distance and also hears its human sounds from within earshot of the preacher.

The recently published *Virtual Paul's Cross Project* demonstrates that the noise and acoustics of a space like the cathedral's outdoor pulpit dramatically affected how auditors heard a sermon and even *what* they heard (figure 4.3). For instance, when the churchyard was filled to the brim with upwards of six thousand people, a common auditor standing over 150 feet away from the pulpit lost certain pitches and resonances of the preacher's voice. From across the churchyard, birds, horses, and bells might indeed be louder than the preacher's voice and competing for the same acoustic space. By contrast, a privileged listener, such as an alderman, might sit near the pulpit in the sermon house, where the preacher's elocution resonated and echoed with a musical quality, integrating with more continuity into the psalm singing and call-and-response liturgy that accompanied the sermon.[12] In this way, socioeconomic status affected more than just a listener's apprehension of the preacher's words.

The voices of the cathedral's interior and outdoor spaces—their preachers, crowds, echoes, and ambience—affect both their historical and current depictions, demonstrating the aural pervasiveness of London's preeminent sermon venue, perhaps the noisiest of them

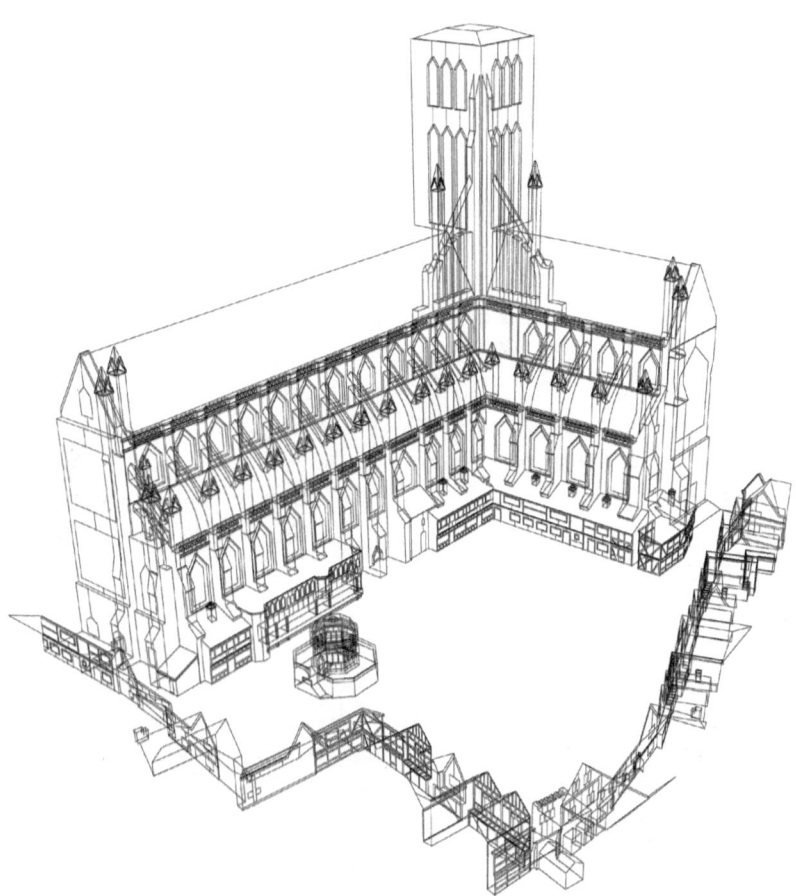

FIGURE 4.3. Wire frame image of the acoustic model, Paul's Churchyard, the Cross Yard, constructed by Joshua Stephens and reproduced with the permission of the Virtual Paul's Cross Project.

all. Donne's own preaching voice, then, although preeminent, is not alone. It is in competition with other sights and sounds, but it also draws its voice from the cathedral's distinct atmosphere. Donne crafts his sermons for the space with awareness of how it shapes sound and in anticipation of competition with distracting noises—jostling the mapmaker's sense of proportion. Donne's voice in this Christmas sermon, self-reflexively idiomatic as it is, looks and sounds like its environment, and it prompts the question of how homiletic reflections on the sermon-going experience, like Donne's, attest to the influence of sermon theatricality on sermon belief.

The Idiomatic Things of God: Sermon Literacy

Donne channels the conflict between the sermon and its environment in the Christmas sermon of 1628. This sermon is an extended consideration of unbelief and specifically of not heeding the messages of God's prophets. Donne finds the statement "Lord, who hath believed our report" repeated by three biblical authors—Isaiah, John, and Paul—and the sermon methodically addresses each instance in turn. They constitute a genealogy of unbelief that ends with his own auditors, who, he says, are most to blame because they have received the fullest revelation.

My interest in this sermon as an example, among others, of "sermon belief" is its depiction of belief as a somatic and social response not just to God's message but to its accidents and environment. Thus Donne turns the idiom "Lord, who hath believed our report" into an imperative for belief. The environment itself becomes a contingency of faith insofar as faith arises in a sermon event. Although it "conduces nothing to that which is said" and is outside of the content of the sermon, the biblical theme takes on a new voice as the noisy, peripheral environment that separates those who lack belief from those who are "sensible" to the unexpected reaches of God's Word (296).

So it is that Donne directs this rhetorical question at the church itself. "The act," Donne says, "is to beleeve," and "The Object, the next, the nearest Object of this Belief, is made the Church; that is, to beleeve that God hath established means for the application of Christs death, to all, in all Christian congregations" (309–10). Donne refers to not only belief in Christ as the "means" to salvation but belief in the church as the "means" to Christ. So while *church* here primarily indicates the Christian body interspersed in individual congregations, it also refers to the precinct that environs this specific speech act—the place of hearing. Keeping in mind that this sermon was delivered on Christmas evening, and that most in attendance would have received

Communion at the cathedral or at another parish earlier that morning, it is with some irony that in the same breath Donne accuses his auditors of lacking belief and also draws attention to the means of salvation, most immediately embodied in the congregation's physical presence at the sermon, sitting in the quire, standing next to pillars, gathered around the pulpit, or hearing the preacher's resounding voice as they paused outside at the nave doors.

Donne calls the church both an "Object of this Belief" and the "established means for the application of Christs death." That is, sermons are objects and media, and this multistability is informed by the event of sermon-going as a battle for attention. Illustrations of sermons such as John Gipkyn's diptych painting of Paul's Cross (figure 4.4) often show a crowd gathered around the pulpit, concentrating on the sermon in the front and showing signs of distraction farther away, talking with each other, playing with dogs, sleeping, or just passing by. While the Christmas sermon was delivered indoors, the atmospheric elements remain the same—the sexton whipping the dog, the noise of horses, and the presence of people passing by and talking in the periphery. Moreover, these different circumstances reflect the variety of motivations for attending sermons. A sermon could be a dutiful habit of devotion, a social opportunity, a business transaction, a civil ceremony, a spontaneous pop-in, a rhetorical display, or a law school class assignment. Still, while one might expect Donne simply to extol the biblical theme as the only worthy didactic focus of attention, he does not. He says that the conditions of audition, like idioms, are the Holy Ghost's tools for order, form, and accommodation to human experience.

Whereas theologically Donne identifies the belief content of the church narrowly as the Word and sacraments that it protects and administers, his discussion of believing in the church implicates these essentials in the inessential conditions of their appearance. The "Word," he says, does not consist of all of the individual words that might be taught in the church but only those that are "inspired by the holy Ghost." The Word of God, in this sense, is "not Apocryphall, not Decretall, not Traditionall, not Additionall supplements" (8:309–10). We remember that the "suppletory" things of God's Word serve the purpose of condescending to the conditions of human understanding,

FIGURE 4.4. John Gipkyn, *Old St Paul's (sermon at St Paul's Cross)*, 1616. Reproduced by kind permission of the Society of Antiquaries of London.

but Donne's point here is to further define the "Act" of profitably attending a sermon as the discretion exercised when isolating "the true Church" from among its supplements and then identifying "what the true Church proposes to us"—with emphasis on the activity of isolating. To illustrate this, Donne takes a common sermon topic, the question of what early moderns termed ceremonial *things indifferent*, and applies it to belief and sermon-going. He mentions "problematical points" that people debate, the mistake of focusing on inessential aspects the Bible, and an individual believer's idiosyncratic preferences and biases as examples of potential distractions from the central content of a sermon, and he imagines all of these as if they were book marginalia. He compares the peripheral beliefs of *things indifferent* to "those marginal and interlineary notes, that are not of the body of the text." For literate auditors, a textual example is at hand in the prayer book and Geneva Bible, as well as in practical religious handbooks, and in many of the godly broadside ballads printed from the 1620s through the 1640s, where margins are filled with scriptural citations and explanatory notes. Additionally, an aural element of a sermon's marginalia includes "those often periodicall murmurings, and noises" made by auditors in response to the sermon—sounds of agreement, understanding, or dissent—frequent enough to cause Donne to complain that even people out of earshot of the sermon itself "will give a censure upon it, according to the frequencie, or paucity of these acclamations" (10:133–34). Such statements reveal that while Donne is conclusive about what is truly essential to the church's salvific function—the Word and the sacraments—he nevertheless continually insists that sermons are full of marginal objects of perception that must be brought to auditors' attention in order to be marginalized, that is, to be perceived as "marginalia."

The reason for Donne's positive insistence on auditors dismissing peripheral noise and spectacle is his understanding of hearing as phenomenally prior to believing—or at least, his suggestion that this is a beneficial perspective to adopt. To this point, Donne relays a scriptural motif that served as a commonplace defense of preaching in the seventeenth century: "Men cannot be saved without calling upon God; nor call upon him acceptably without Faith; nor beleeve truly without Hearing; nor heare profitably without Preaching" (8:308). At the heart of this statement is a rhetorical concatenation of hearing. Donne's auditors are to hear the sermon with an aim toward believing. Audition is the medium as well as the most immediate object of sermon belief, and in this dual capacity *hearing* takes on the multistable identity of a medium that points to itself. Donne's language is full of rhetorical ambiguity that results from his understanding of sermon-going as both an object and a medium of belief—a voluntary and instrumental medium, to use the terms of Perkins and Hooker. He charges the hearer to interpret the "body of the text" apart from its context, but with full awareness that the body of the sermon is also found in his congregation's immediate embodiment of it.

The same ambiguity is discernable in his command to focus selectively on ideas that are instructive, essential, and unbiased in the sermon. This approach draws on the Protestant parlance of describing the Word of God as "plain," as in Perkins's statement that "it is a very by-word among us: *It was a very plaine sermon. And I say againe, the plainer, the better.*"[13] Richard Younge in 1657 goes further and conveys plain hearing as a kind of interpretive method. Hearing the plain Word of God is a form of practical devotion. It is performative in the sense that to speak plainly combines "saying" and "doing" God's ordinances. There is no room for duplicity or idleness in plain hearing:

> Pastors are the glasse, the school, the book,
> Where peoples eyes do learn, do read, do look.
> The learned Pastours words, though plain;
> To plain men truth may preach:
> But Pastours pious practice doth,
> A holy life them teach.[14]

Younge's point is to challenge the autonomous virtue of plain preaching, particularly when the preacher himself is not a virtuous person. He argues that plain teaching should be received by plain hearing and offers the final caveat that even when executed this way, instruction is ineffective without the example of a holy life, that is, the behavior exhibited by a congregational body. The vocabularies of plain hearing and preaching demonstrate the extent to which such moral imperatives were grounded in the occasion of their pronouncement.

In the 1629 Christmas sermon, which shows particular interest in sermon-going, Donne consolidates his several statements on the multimodal and dynamic activity of hearing a sermon into a kind of church literacy. Church literacy is an aptitude for interpreting a sermon's message in light of its immanent context and an exhortation to recognize God's direct interventions into major events in England's history. The key to reversing the complaint "Lord, who hath beleeved our report" is to acknowledge that major historical events are "of the right hand of God"; they result from God's providential "judgement" and are not mere "accidents" (8:305). Donne cites the storm that destroyed the Spanish navy, the discovery of a letter that unraveled the Gunpowder Plot, and the unseasonably cold weather to which England attributed the alleviation of plague as examples of society misunderstanding God's judgments to be merely accidents of human experience. Yet as a way of contextualizing this literacy within the church itself and in his sermon-goers' bodily presence at St. Paul's, Donne applies the concepts of "accident" and "judgment" to his auditors' personal experiences of life and faith: "But then, in every such letter, in every judgement, God writes to me too; and that letter I will open, and read that letter; I will take knowledge that it is Gods hand to me, and I will study the will of God to me in that letter" (8:306). Those who neglect to actively engage history on the individual level where God's judgments are manifested in seemingly mundane accidents have "fallen lower then [sic] under the Prophets increpation, *non credidi.*" Such people are unable to answer the prophet's complaint—"Lord, who hath believed our report?"—and are guilty of disbelief because they have removed God from the idiomatic conditions of faith. Donne again uses a term that is popular also in realms of religious ceremonial writings and theatrical polemics: such people demonstrate "*insensibleness* to future calamities" (8:300, my italics). That is, their perceptual senses are out of coordination with their interpretive senses; they mistakenly ignore certain feelings as irrelevant.

The language that Donne uses to express the ambiguity and also the fullness of perception suggests that he insists on considering belief within the firsthand and perspectival activities of believing. Because the accidents of God's judgment are necessary aspects of the interpretive process, Donne uses the extended metaphor of God's handwriting to draw attention to the cognitive and kinesthetic activities of a congregation that usually go unnoticed. "All comes from Gods hand," Donne says, "by way of hand-writing, by way of letter," but at the same time, "to acknowledge it to be Gods hand, and not to read it" is "a slighting of God" (8:305). Truly believing God's report means reading his writing on the deteriorated walls of St. Paul's and recognizing it as the hand of God. Thus profitable sermon-going means reading

God in the dispersed interior architecture of its nave, in the current events that may have occasioned the sermon, and even in one's onsetting drowsiness at the forty-fifth minute of its delivery. These things may be particularities of embodied circumstances, repetitions that, in Donne's words, "discompose the sentence" of God's writing, but Donne affirms their centrality in the act of believing.

The Art of Hearing and Not Hearing, Seeing and Not Seeing

The Christmas sermon of 1628 is among several of Donne's that address the topic of how to hear sermons well, how to "heare profitably."[15] The art of hearing sermons constitutes its own printed literary genre in the seventeenth century. Such books have titles like *The Day of Hearing, Hearing and Doing, The Boring of the Ear, The Difference of Hearers,* and *The Poor Man's Help . . . Hearing of the Word Preached*.[16] They often serve as companions to books on how to compose and deliver sermons well. In addition, books on the sensory faculties sometimes include exhortations on how to hear God's Word preached beneficially. Wilhelm Zepper's *The Art or Skil Well or Fruitfullie to Heare the Holy Sermons of the Church* (1599) reminds readers that "to make Sermons, and to heare them, are (as we say in schooles) relatives."[17] Thus, in addition to making good sermons, "we must know, that it is a point of no meane or common skill and paine also, to heare holy Sermons well." In a sermon at the noisy outdoor venue of Paul's Cross in 1629, Donne similarly expresses the strain required in the act of listening to a sermon as a feeling of pain. Particularly in the case of the poor, who hear fewer sermons because they cannot afford to hire chaplains to preach to their family, cannot leave their work for public sermons, or possibly cannot afford seats, beneficial hearing is painful: "They must *stay*, they must *stand*, they must *thrust*, . . . they must take pains to hear" (9:123).

Painfully hearing a sermon, according to many authors, can be achieved through a threefold approach. A sermon by Gryffith Williams aptly titled *The Fruitfull Knocking*, printed as a folio in 1636, provides a representative example of this prescription:

1. Preparation, before we come to the Church.
2. Attention, while we heare the Word.
3. Meditation, after we have heard the same.[18]

This process is patterned on the traditional exhortations to prepare, attend, and reflect on receiving Holy Communion. The Elizabethan Prayer Book instantiates it in the two prayers that bookend the administration of Communion—each respectively beginning, "We do not presume to come this thy Table" and "Almighty and Everlasting God, we moste hartely thanke thee."[19] The intended effect of preparing, attending, and meditating, Williams says, is that "in hearing them [sermons], you heare, not onely them, but you heare the *voice* of Christ through them." Art-of-hearing treatises describe in great detail practices of "meditation," and one frequently endorsed practice for hearing Christ's voice in a sermon is repetition—literally, repeating the sermon and its main points afterward, often over a meal with family and servants who were unable to attend.[20] In Donne's words, this allows a "good hearer" to be not only a "Doctor to him that sits by him" in church but also "in his repetition, when he comes home" (4:118).

Practices of preparing for, attending to, and meditating on a sermon can be understood as concentrating—compacting and isolating—the general perceptual and psychological activities involved in attending a sermon, especially at a venue like St. Paul's. Implied in these hearing treatises and in Donne's discussions of good listening are exhortations to convert the overall sermon experience into an essential "Word." But as I have been arguing, there remains a significant emphasis on the Word as perceived by bodies in a space and in weekly or even daily sermon-going routines. The legacy of printed sermons can give the false impression that there were strict beginnings and ends to sermons when in fact the event was more processual. Auditors encountered prayers, scripture readings, and benedictions, and they participated in social mingling, call-and-response liturgy, and sometimes psalm singing. These interactive elements distribute the meaning—the Word—into the contingencies of the event and space, and thus they reflect the broader performance culture of London. In another sermon, although he clarifies that he prefers the behavior of his own time to that of the early church, Donne makes this comparison of the sermon event to theater explicit:

> When we consider the manner of hearing Sermons, in the Primitive Church, . . . it testified to a vehement devotion, and a sense of that that was said, by the preacher, in the hearer; for, all that had been formerly used in Theaters, *Acclamations* and *Plaudites*, was brought into the *Church*, and not onely the vulgar people, but the learned hearers were as loud, and as profuse in those declarations, those vocall acclamations, and those plaudites in the passages, and transitions, in Sermons, as ever they had been at the Stage, or other recitations *of their Poets, or Orators*. (10:132)

The scene he depicts is striking in its description of audience response, especially during "transitions," like interludes, as well as the specification of an audience composed of different social groups that include the "vulgar" and the "learned." While Donne does not condone a raucous atmosphere, he endorses the example of "vehement devotion" manifest in the responsiveness of the auditors. It seems reasonable to him that auditors would grasp the "sense" of a sermon in the same ways that they do a play—in the theatrical idioms of the time.

Much like the atmosphere of music and entertainment that surrounded play performances, the atmosphere of sermons may have proven to be more perceptually dominant than we expect, as is suggested by preachers' preoccupation with exhorting their congregations to employ all of their sensory and emotional faculties in activities of intent listening. In a Whitsunday sermon, Donne suggests that it is partly within the process and activity of psychologically rendering the sermon into an object of attention that edification arises: "Our errand . . . is to heare, and to heare all the words of the Preacher, but, to heare in those words, the Word, the Word which is the soule of all that is said, and is the true Physick of all their soules that heare" (5:56). Donne's comments move from the general sensory experience of ambient sounds, tiredness, and distracting spectacle to the words of the preacher, and finally to the auditors' role in deciphering within those words "the soule of all that is said." There is an expansive view of the sermon implicit in the command to render the sermon-going experience into its essence. We can compare this perspective to that of Shakespeare in his presentation of theatricality in *Henry V*. In purporting character interiority, Henry conspicuously relies on costumes and acting; and to give the impression of anticeremonial egalitarianism in the St. Crispin's speech he must utilize the ceremonialism of the feast day and the occasionality that extends even into the play event. Likewise, to empower the central Word of God in a sermon, Donne must utilize and acknowledge the mediatory power of the event itself, its distribution into space, rhetoric, society, and the bodies of his auditors. Thus, Donne says, "The Word of God is made a Sermon, that is, a Text is dilated, diffused into a Sermon; but that whole Sermon is not the word of God. But yet all the Sermon is the Ordinance of God" (5:56). For Donne, distilling the "whole" sermon into just the "Ordinance of God" involves a systematic engagement and categorization of the various aspects of the sermon-going experience.

Donne discloses, in Derrida's words, the process of re-marking—the "basic gesture" of ambience whereby some perceptions are marked as "significant." Timothy Morton describes the re-mark as "a kind of echo" because attributing significance—the marking of foreground over background and voice over noise—always manifests as a repetition of perceptions, both sensory and intellectual.[21] In one way, when a sermon-goer repeats the sermon in a new environment, he reamplifies the echo of the preacher's voice, but, for Donne it is also important that the original physical sermon environment joins in this activity of reiteration as it repeats the sermon in the form of acoustical echoes: "The Church is his [God's] Eccho; a redoubling, a repeating of some particular syllables, and accents of the same voice" (6:223). Early modern sermon-goers in particular responded to the imagery and phenomenality of the acoustical echo at sermons. One seventeenth-century traveler observes that English cathedrals during sermon time can be "so lofty that the Ecco drowns the intelligableness of the voice."[22] However, as in the "pain" and "thrust" of hearing, sermon-goers should not passively hear the echo as if it were just any re-mark of voice over noise but should actively "apply themselves to the Eccho of his Church, when perchance otherwise, they would lesse understand the voice of God, in his Scriptures" (6:223).

Donne's description of the sermon echo is performative. As the sermon is repeated—acoustically, socially, to one's household, or privately written in one's note tablet—it is reiterated, not only retold but also reheard. What auditors repeat in note tablets or at home to their households is a rendition of the event, formed from their physical effort and psychological negotiations. The sermon is stretched into a pattern of hearing and, therefore, of straining, paining, rendering, and re-marking; and this pattern of behavior enacts sermon literacy and faith in the present practice of religion and in performance culture broadly.

Donne conflates the echo of the church interior with the echo of the preacher's voice as it is concentrated and retransmitted by active listening and repetition. He uses the echo trope to insist on the relentless impact of one's auditory environment on the profitability of hearing in a sermon delivered to a royal audience at Whitehall in 1627. The sermon is on the apt biblical theme "Take heed what you hear," and it lays bare the process of heeding as a series of echoes that are produced ambiguously by the aural environment and constituted by the hearer's attentive faculties. Donne describes the ear as an organ for "acquiring knowledge" of all kinds, wanted and unwanted (7:408). That the sermon had a royal audience may explain Donne's choice of examples for describing the ear's vulnerability. Rhetorically addressing those who keep dangerous company with blasphemers and political dissenters, he warns that people who stand in "an ill ayre" of dangerous voices may themselves be diffused into their company's "cloud" of blasphemy. He compares the ear to "the clift in the wall, that receives the voice" of a speaker, while "the Echo is below, in the heart." The echo exists both outside the preacher in the soundscape and within the auditor, "in the heart," while the Word itself is imagined to manifest somewhere in between. Blending the architectural and the metaphysical, Donne suggests that the echo helps auditors absorb what is most profitable in the holistic sermon experience. "The Echo returnes the last syllables; the heart concludes with his conclusions, whom we have been willing to hearken unto." An echo represents the inevitable affects of soundscapes on hearers. This suggests that Donne's theme, "Take heed what you heare," is not as simple as it may at first sound. For heeding what you hear often depends on heeding *where* you hear.

In addition to directing auditors toward profitable listening, art-of-hearing literature addresses how *not* to use the other four senses. The way that Donne frames the art of hearing, through the concept of reading God's judgments in the accidents of human experience, synthesizes one of the more popular themes of hearing treatises: the notion that the profitable hearing of God's Word depends on successfully navigating through sensory distractions and on prioritizing hearing over the distractions of sight. John Brathwaite's *Essay Upon the Five Sences* summarizes post-Reformation England's celebration of hearing above the other senses: "Hearing is the organ of understanding, by it we conceive, by the memory we conserve, and by our judgment we resolve: as many rivers have their confluence by small streams, so knowledge her essence by the accent of the *Ear*. As our *ear* can best judge of sounds, so hath it a distinct power to sound into the centre of the heart."[23] Besides offering a psychological account of the ear's supremacy, Brathwaite notes the ear's competence in engaging an entire soundscape and distilling it into what is worthy of being resolved and believed. He suggests that the ear is better suited than the other sense organs to focalize the marginalia of auditory knowledge, organizing the "small streams" and indistinct "sounds" of its environment around other more significant sounds that constitute the soul of the sermon. It is well known, of course, that many English puritans distrusted theater for its incitement of idolatry yet endorsed sermon attendance, but we can think of this differentiation of theater and sermons also in psychosomatic terms, a kind of cleansing of the senses as conduits for belief.[24] Authors of the treatises understand sermons as opportunities to begin with a theatrical sensory experience and then to discipline one's senses and intellect so as to hear only the Word of God. Essentially, auditors are instructed to reform their spiritual environment, to inhabit it with acts of profitable hearing; or, as Donne puts it in his description of sermon literacy, "I will . . . give him my reformation for his information" (8:314).

An important component of the phenomenology of sermon-going is the notion that, unlike plays and despite their diffuse atmospheres, sermons were imagined to have identifiable centers. One reason for this is that sermons had single authors, single speakers, a central theme, and usually a single source (the Bible), whereas plays were often anonymously authored, had many speakers—requiring entire troupes to be realized—and typically had several sources with which they took considerable liberties. In contrast to plays, the imagined center of sermons drew on the vocabulary of the singular "Word" of God and so adopted its authority (or Authority). The ability to find the theoretical center and to hear it beneficially, however, was itself an activity of faith. In practice, the center of the sermon was a psychological focus for managing the holistic sermon-going experience. Thus the act of perceiving was psychologically and environmentally continuous with the object being perceived. On this point, Jean-Luc Marion describes preaching as a mode of revelation that always refers back to itself. This is because the first-person experience of a sermon auditor "cannot reach Jesus historically as its intentional object because the received lived experience (preaching), as a screen, returns the spirit of the *I* to itself in a repeated lived experience (faith)."[25] Because preaching is a further revelation of an imagined original revelation—the gospel as history—the most immediate object being revealed to the auditor is the fact of revelation itself. And the content of this fact of revelation is what Marion calls the *I*: the "lived experience" of the sermon and its "real immanence in consciousness."

Early modern sermons induce this same dual intentionality toward the event and the sacred Word, as they blend theology with the particulars and inessentials of the first-person experience of the event. Robert Orsi comments that the idiomatic aspects of a religious practice are not merely situational "windows onto wider social or cultural realities"—as if, for instance, sermon belief were defined merely by theology—but are central to religion insofar as religious speech and action occur in forms of practice.[26] So if it is true that revelation is the heart of early modern sermons, then the salvific core of a sermon has the power to save exactly inasmuch as it is revealed. Consider again Donne's description in 1628 of the literacy of divine writing: "God writes to me too; and that letter I will open, and read that letter; I will take knowledge that it is Gods hand to me, and I will study the will of God to me in that letter" (306). Particularly in the context of the church—which, according to Donne, is the first object of belief for the sermon-goer—opening, reading, identifying, and studying make up a specific perceptual disposition, an attitude toward sermons that concentrates them into conduits of belief, even if at face value they are anything but centered on theological instruction.

In short, replacing the eyes, the ear becomes the organ of church literacy that reads God's univocal judgments through the dissonance and dispersal of sensory environments. At work in the process of hearing a sermon is a kind of synesthesia where not only is the congregation charged to privilege the ears over the eyes, but true belief occurs in the transformation from viewing to listening as one's primary form of engagement. This reveals something vital about early modern theatricality: when a performance is aware of its own theatrical conditions and even incorporates them into its represented content, the perceived social or spiritual benefit of the performance—edification in sermons or instruction and example in drama—emerges in the interaction between the theatrical and the represented, or, specific to sermons, between their environments and their messages. Sermon-going, like play-going, is anamorphic. The "unity is in the wiggle," at the "crossing of the body and the world," as I have described it.[27] Writers often emphasize the necessity of moving from merely hearing the Word to actually doing it, but the activity of belief happens in the overlap, where the acts of selectively perceiving and bracketing the object of perception cross. In other words, the direct application of sermon-going is in the activity of sermon-going itself—in managing one's senses and thoughts, in acknowledging the social body at hand as the body of Christ, in rendering the event into a sacred core, and sometimes in repeating the sermon afterward.

Hence, perhaps the most frequently addressed topic of sermon-going in art-of-hearing treatises is actually the practice of ignoring things. Early modern sermons and hearing treatises warn auditors of common distractions and, in so doing, create a third category of sensory experience: in addition to the sermon and its insignificant environment, there are significant distractions. Writers draw attention to certain ambient sensations much as Donne assigns significance to scriptural idioms. Common distractions of noises and sights include acoustics, the sounds of hard materials, animals, and human commotion. The extreme boisterousness of St. Paul's Walk was unlike other churches, but writers still note the shuffling of human bodies during sermons elsewhere, such as the prebendary John Lee's complaint that men, and especially young men, walk into churches during service time just to have a look around without being respectful of the sacred space: "I have seen them from my seat (and not seldom) so walking or standing."[28] Although preachers often recommend that auditors stand during the sermon if they feel too tired to concentrate, movement and chatter appears to have been a common problem. One sermon-goer, also targeting younger attendees, conjectures that many treat the church as a gathering for eligible singles and so create a distraction: "When a man comes to hear a Sermon, there is a Sermon and the Market, there is a Sermon and a friend to speak withal; and so many young people will go abroad to hear Sermons; What is the end of it? It is, that you may get wives and husbands many of you."[29] Another sermon-goer complains of the opposite occurrence of people taking too little interest in the sermon and leaving at disrupting moments: "as I have seene divers begin to hem, and to hum, and to hang downe the head, to yawne, raspe, and stretch (as being weary with long sitting) saying that they have businesse, and therefore must away."[30] Furthermore, a recent essay by John Craig demonstrates that three of the more prominent noises making up the soundscape of parish churches were parishioners' groans in response to the sermon, barking dogs, and the crack of dogwhipper's whip.[31] These sounds, like many others, were both allowed and disallowed. For instance, some dogs were strays and others were pets; some audible audience remarks affirmed the sermon while others distracted from it. The relative disturbance of certain noises would vary depending on individual parishes and parishioners. More reform-minded puritans, for example, might take issue with psalm singing and bells, while traditionalist auditors might not.

Allowing for disagreement on what counts as a distraction, perhaps the most exhaustive list of the cacophony of disturbances during sermon time is found in Henry Mason's 1635 *Rules of Right Hearing God's Word*. Mason's long-winded complaint mentions "men and women . . . clapping their pew doors, and . . . redoubling the knock," people disturbing the service by entering late, children crying and the spectacle of "the Nurse [who] carieth him out of doores," dogs barking and the sexton's whip, insinuations of people flirting, and even the potential distraction of a preacher who is too "furious in his actions," "fluent in his words," and "vehement in his exclamations."[32] Whereas other sounds such as the flipping of book pages or horses walking outside are rarely noted, writers observe the distractions listed by Mason more frequently and thus attribute significance to them insofar as they are things that should be ignored. Their presence as distractions represents the *profitable hearing* space that such distractions vacate when auditors ignore them. Believing in the sermon means also that parishioners know what perceptual ambience is flagged as especially distracting and actively shun it.

Sermons and art-of-hearing treatises also address the practical problem of where to look while one listens. The idea is that disciplining one's eyes affects profitable hearing. A common strategy is to look straight at the preacher, even at his eyes, "lest gazing on other things, your eyes withdraw your minde from the doctrine deliuered."[33] Some writers, however, take the opposite approach and recommend intentionally looking away from the preacher, with one writer even instructing auditors to look at nonstimulating objects, so as to hear the preacher's words without seeing his animated facial gestures.[34] Another suggests looking down or covering one's eyes in an attempt to nullify visual distraction altogether.[35] These recommendations treat vision as a tool for controlling the attention of the ears in addition to the eyes. According to Walter Ong, such synesthetic combination of sense activities results from the different ways that sense organs locate subjects in relation to their objects. He writes: "Sound situates man in the middle of actuality and in simultaneity, whereas vision situates man in front of things and in sequentiality."[36] Sermon-going, as early modern writers imagine it, is a kind of tug-of-war between the spatial and directional perceptions enacted respectively by sound and sight and manifesting in a continuous relation to auditors' thoughts about such embattled attention. More specifically, the aim for many hearing-treatise authors is to execute hearing as if it were seeing, attempting to locate a sight-like perceptual line through the nonlinearity of the church soundscape. Such mixing of directionality and space sheds new light on Stephen Egerton's comment in 1623 that truly isolating and obtaining the message of a sermon is like finding one's way through a maze or navigating the ocean by the stars.[37]

We can ask, therefore, with an understanding of the sermon sensorium and its psychology: What does this synesthetic directional hearing *look* like? Writers imagine the directing of sermon-goers' auditory attention as an effect of their visual focus or lack thereof. Sight perceives objects in directional reference to the seeing subject, whereas in "profitable hearing" sermon-goers strain (or thrust, or "take pains") to see only the preacher and his eyes. Moreover, through *visual* strain they hope to *hear* only his voice. Auditors close their eyelids or stare at objects such as rafters, arches, or the floor—things they imagine to exert little visual stimulation. They are instructed to look at objects they believe do not pollute sound with sight. Such objects imaginatively function as exclusively auditory media, space through which only sound travels without the distractions of other sensations, but we can also think of these objects as occupying intentionally irrelevant space—space that is outside of the perceptual *line* of hearing that is created by the straining of the eyes. The church ceiling, the floor, and the darkness of closed eyelids do not place the perceiver "in front of" any significant visual object of sight but instead are thought to orient the hearer in front of the sound of the preacher's voice exclusively. This confirms Steven Connor's observation that "there can only really be a... *point of audition*" in terms of a "somewhat strained and optimistic analogy" to a *point of view*.[38] The church environment, with its distractions and marginalia, becomes significant for sermon belief through auditors' imagined remodeling of their point of view into a point of audition, overlaying lines of nonsight onto spheres of hearing, sanctifying some spaces, things, senses, and body parts as homiletically profitable and others as impairing.

Hearkening Is the Hearing of the Soul

What I have been calling "sermon belief" has at least three distinct kinds of objects toward which auditors orient themselves, and each is a part of the sermon as a holistic occasion for belief. First, believing in a sermon means believing in the ideas expressed in its words, what is typically called its content as imagined from a didactic or representational perspective, but I want to describe believing as a perceptual and social activity that extends beyond intellectual assent. Thus a second part of sermon belief is the sermon's context, including its distractions, ambience, and theatricality. These are critical components of belief insofar as auditors attribute significance to them as oppositional to profitable hearing and insofar as the activity of bracketing sensory marginalia itself contributes to belief. A third part of sermon belief is the very activity of attending to a sermon, including intellectual concentration, sensory control, preparation, repetition, and spiritual digestion. This last kind of sermon belief is a performative disposition toward the sermon that reflects Protestant beliefs about the saving properties of the spoken word. That is, sermon-going activities are sermon-like in that they seek to assign salvific properties to the sermon as an interactive event that requires rigorous attention, and the performative effect is the reciprocal real presence of God's Word and the potential salvation that occurs through the "vehement devotion" of sermon-going.

Sermon belief is the focus of Donne's Christmas sermon of 1628, where he defines efficacious belief as acknowledgment of divine intentions in their manifest accidents. In fact, the Christmas sermon, in particular, plays up the "manifest" quality of faith in one's activities and objects of attention. The word *manifest* and its derivatives occur eight times in the sermon, always referring to the historical contexts of the biblical idiom "Lord, who hath beleeved our report?" Donne explicates three specific biblical instances of this question, and each instance represents a further manifestation of the means for salvation. The last of these means is the church itself, which Donne metaphorically depicts as a tree that is planted publicly "here in his terrestriall paradise, and not in heaven; in the manifest ministery of the Gospell, and not in a secret and unrevealed purpose, (for, faith comes by hearing, and hearing by preaching, which are things executed and transacted here in the church)" (8:310). Donne's repetition of the Protestant maxim that "faith comes by hearing" signals the kind of manifestation that he has in mind: the "ministery" of sermons. But as we have seen, this language of the "root" and transaction of faith could easily mislead one to assume a too-simplistic hearer-object relation to sermon belief.

On the contrary, Donne and his contemporaries often describe hearing as composed of much more than audition. Early modern preachers and authors of sermon handbooks use *hearing* metonymically to represent a soulful activity. In a sermon in 1624, while discussing how to avoid hypocrisy in sermon-going, Donne states that attentive bodily awareness and physical "religious posture" are necessary for the soul to have a true religious experience, although the body cannot truly hear unless the soul is also listening (6:101). This soulful listening is what Donne calls "hearkning," which is "the hearing of the soul." Donne elaborates on this complex relation between hearing and believing: "As the soul is infused by God, but diffused over the whole body, and so there is a *Man*, so *Faith* is infused from God, but diffused into our *works*, and so there is a Saint" (6:100). We can interpret "hearkning" to express the interdependence between the idioms of sermon experience and its sacred center. There is an element of hearkening that occurs in the body. Paradoxically, one achieves the hearing of the soul not by abstractly attending to things of the soul but by honing the manifest bodily nature of sermon belief. For "Practise," or efficacious belief, "is the *Incarnation of Faith*" and not the extraction of faith from its physical incarnations: "Faith is incorporated and manifested in a body, by works; and the way to both, is that *Hearing*" (6:100). Ultimately, hearing that bears fruit in true faith "amounts to this *Hearkning*, in which, one essentiall circumstance is, that we . . . apply our selves to the *Ordinance, Come,* and *hearken* unto *me*." Hearkening is the "hearing of the soul" as it manifests in body and space.

Insofar as profitable hearing results from both engaging and dismembering a sermon's environment, we can describe the sermon's soul as phenomenally composed of its body. In the sermon culture of the early seventeenth century, sermons are depicted as having an inner substance, a singular object of auditors' deepest attention. Recent discussion about sacramental drama provides a theological framework for the difference between a religious performance's outer and inner qualities.[39] Scholars argue that after the break from Catholicism, early modern England became exposed to certain gaps in aesthetics, devotional practice, and social ceremony created by the Reformation's rejection of Thomistic sacramentalism. Without the pervasive sacramentality of Catholic theology and ceremony, the question becomes: How does Protestant belief turn into efficacious saving faith? Or, what is the objective sign for saving faith? We can find indications of these questions in the puritan's wrestling with salvation anxiety, or in what has become known as "staging faith" in Renaissance theater, and perhaps even in what Stephen Greenblatt has called the "regenerative" activities of iconoclasm.[40] These are examples of ways that early moderns arguably attributed sacred meaning to activities that were not otherwise. According to Regina Schwartz, in post-Reformation England, high-profile Catholic doctrines, like transubstantiation, "displace their [material] longing for that sacred world onto other cultural forms," such as the emerging mechanistic philosophy, Shakespearean tragedy, erotic mysticism, monism, and poetics.[41]

We should remember, of course, that any discussion of early modern England's latent need for lost sacramental meaning is speculative, and also that Protestant English theology was technically still sacramental or at least continually fraught with questions about what degree of sacramentality was Protestant/orthodox/biblical.[42] Moreover, I want to stress that these various "regenerative" forms of worship are often less novel than we sometimes suggest.[43] For instance, the performative move of Donne's sermons is essentially the same gesture made by the boy bishop sermon that I discussed at the outset of this book—an open acknowledgment of the theatricality of belief in an effort to cast the sermon-going act itself as an act of faith. In fact, this is the same maneuver that Henry executes in the St. Crispin's speech discussed in the previous chapter. All three examples presume the pre-Reformational origins of their integration of theatricality and religion. Here, I am averring that something like a sacramental logic remained in the church as well as in the larger theatrical patterns of performance culture, and that "sermon belief" in Donne's London is particularly illustrative of its the real presence—which is to say, its performativity.

Put simply, sermon belief involves a logic of inner and outer or, in Scholastic terms, of substance and accidents. And while sermons do not claim to provide access to salvation via divine miracle as in sacramental theology, there is congruence between the apprehension of sacramental real presence and the process of a sermon-goer transforming a sermon event into the divine Word. Moreover, this transformation and the many descriptions of it we find in sermons and art-of-hearing treatises are motivated by a desire for a form of inward grace manifest in the accidents of outward conditions, often articulated in metaphysical terms. Of course, this is a desire that also motivated the continued celebration of the Eucharist, but because Communion was administered so infrequently and because many early moderns regularly attended sermons weekly or oftener, sermon-going took on a substance-accident duality, loosely speaking, that in many ways mirrored the logic of sacramentalism found in old practices and doctrines. In fact, it may be the case that the growth of sermon culture away from celebrations of the Eucharist had a greater effect on the development of a sacramental logic to sermon culture than did the loss of Catholic sacramental theology, since sermons came to replace not only Thomistic sacramentalism but, to an extent, also Protestant sacramentalism. As I have argued, attending to the performativity of sermons means considering the theatrical excesses and purported transcendence that comes to presence through the performance itself, not as a transcendent intervention or miracle, but as the product of theater as ritual. Thus whatever sacramental presence can be identified in sermons is found in the encounter of their environments and in ways that audiences find a disincarnate event and attempt to transform it through faith and aggressive attention—in short, it is found in sermon theatricality.

According to sermons, art-of-hearing treatises, and the archive describing sermon events and their atmospheres, the activity of hearing sermons transforms a text or theme into an almost personified entity or *logos*, to which auditors ascribe a body and a soul. The sermon's body is its diffuse environment, and in a sense it is conflated with the body of the sermon-goer. The transformation of the sermon text into a bodily presence is evident in the ways that the vocabulary of the divine "Word" developed within the culture of early modern sermon-going. In sermons and hearing treatises, two common renditions of

God's Word are the "word as heard" and the "word preached." For instance, in 1616 Thomas Granger explains that he prefers a "verbatim" translation of a Pauline clause about hearing the Word, *"when yee receiued of us the word of the preaching of God."*[44] Granger favors an alternative translation because Paul "speaketh here especially of their act of beleeuing, the first degree whereof is hearing." Verbatim, he renders it: *"because receiuing the word of hearing from us of God."* The latter focuses on how the Word is applied to auditors and also conveys the Word as a compound with its sensory reception. The object of belief in this case is not the Word that they heard but the phenomenologically bracketed Word-of-hearing that was spoken to them "of God." A similar conflation of the activity of the sacred Word and its appearance occurs in usages of the "word preached." An anonymous large poster entitled *Some plain Directions for the More Profitable Hearing of the Word Preached* (1650), designed to be posted in public places for sermon-goers to read, discusses the importance of attending sermons habitually: "Long absence from the *word preached*; the sound of it being long from the ear, a Christian is too apt to forget what should be the behaviour of his soul in hearing" (my italics). Like Donne's "hearkning," the profit of the soul depends on the disposition of the body; in this case, it depends on the "ear" being in habitual familiarity with the specific act of hearing a sermon—shutting out distractions in order to uncover the sermon's substance. Attending to the posture of the ear implies that there is an inner hearing manifest in, and attainable through, outer hearing. Both the "word of hearing" and the "word preached" combine the theatrical and embodied activity of hearing with the representational content of what is heard. The effect is to syntactically present sermon-going as accidental to the substance of the sermon yet inseparable from it and thus to reinforce the notion that sermons have souls within their bodies.

Donne's own uses of the "word preached" directly refer to the sacraments, in one sermon calling the Word preached the "Sacrament of faith" and in another comparing its saving power to the "Sacraments administred in the Church" (5:262; 3:302).[45] Sermons are like sacraments, he suggests, insofar as the implication of accident and substance—body and soul, periphery and center—operates according to the sacramental understanding that any performance of the sacred alleges to give form to a sacred substance that precedes the performance. Thus, in another usage of the "word preached," Donne describes the physically perceived sermon as a kind of adhesive for the soul: "God made us with his word, and with our words we make God so farre, as that we make up the mysticall body of Christ Jesus with our prayers, with our whole liturgie, and we make the naturall body of Christ Jesus applicable to our soules, by the words of Consecration in the Sacrament, and our soules apprehensive, and capable of that body, by the word Preached" (3:259–60). Donne again portrays the audible sermon and its environment as God's handwriting that requires a unique literacy to apprehend.

His comparison of the "word preached" to the Eucharistic consecration liturgy is especially noteworthy because of the careful yet ambiguous way that English theologians handled Eucharistic theology. With the suppression of the elevation of the host and of the accompanying sacring bell, the consecration prayers in the 1559 order for Communion came to rely more heavily on the spoken language itself, and especially on the words of institution for indicating sacramental presence. In fact, one sees in the consecration prayer a building up of supplications, preparations, and narratives that suggest themselves as a kind of prayerful outer casing for the inner transformative power at the center of it all, not unlike the marginalia and theatricality of sermon-going. I've elsewhere referred to this ritual step as the greater activities of "Oblation," where the focus is momentarily on the bare, disincarnated elements of language and labor.[46] Even the words of institution—"Take, eat, this is my body"—appear marginalized in the syntax of the prayer as part of a subordinate clause that begins, "who in the same nyght that he was betraied, toke bread."[47] The priest then repeats the words of institution during the actual administration of the sacrament, after the elements are formally consecrated, perhaps as a kind of echo.

As a result, the language representing the most transcendently performative speech act of the liturgy appears in a slightly marginal grammatical position and, by consequence, bears witness to the performative power of the periphery of liturgy.[48] This same logic is at play in the "word preached." Donne suggests that sermons are like consecrations: they connote what is preparatory, audible, and environmental to salvation.

A final and especially pointed illustration of this sermon-shaped space is Donne's instruction on the appropriate posture of "comming" to a sermon. According to a sermon preached at St. Paul's exactly two years prior to the Christmas sermon of 1628, how one attends a sermon is analogous to how one prepares to receive the sacrament, echoing the language of the Communion liturgy. Donne states that "there are many commings to Church, commings for company, for observation, for musique." In typical religious practice, such as prayer, these ulterior motives are "unwholesome," but in the context of the Eucharist they are "deadly." If an auditor succumbs to distraction at a sermon, he simply neglects to hear "the Sermon of the Sermon," whereas bringing ulterior motives to the sacrament "ends not in the losse of a benefit" but "procures . . . damnation" (7:293). What Donne means by the "blessings of Gods ordinance in that Sermon" is ambiguous, but at the very least we can understand him to mean that a sermon's inner power is not its logic, rhetoric, ethic, or poetry. Rather, it is the "Sermon of the Sermon."

In this passage, "Comming" is a synonym for hearkening and perceiving the Word-as heard. Like hearkening, "comming" involves a host of rigorous activities, such as navigating through multiple sense stimuli, keeping the right motivation in mind, and, most importantly, ignoring the rhetorical flourishes of the preacher's words. Donne's condemnation of "collaterall" coming is one that he repeats elsewhere: "When thou comest to meet him [Christ] in the Congregation, come not occasionally, come not casually, not indifferently, not collaterally; come not as to an entertainment, a show, a spectacle, or company" (6:100). Collateral sermon-going primarily means having the wrong motivations, but it also means assuming a disposition that rejects the emotional and physical sensations one would experience in an entertainment, spectacle, or show. Even though Donne exhorts auditors to marginalize psychologically the theatrical aspects of sermon-going, these same aspects remain in many ways essential to the performative transformation of the "word preached" and profitable "comming." Donne's caution against collateral coming implies that sermons are constructed in such a way that demands the imposition of *uni*-lateral attention from their audiences. Such unilateral attention and the phenomenon of a singular object of attention, indeed, are created by Donne's rhetoric of the collateral and how it interacts with the sermon environment. "Comming" thus illustrates the inevitably idiomatic way that Donne and his contemporaries think about sermons, but it also indicates the role that idiomatic or collateral experiences can play in directing sermon-goers to perceive more deeply and to collectively construct the soul of the sermon. In fact, it is precisely because of sermons' perceived relation to more overtly theatrical performance genres that devout "comming" is able to distinguish itself and to induce an activity of faith.

WHEN AUDITORS HEAR through the idiomatic aspects of a sermon into its soul, they are transformed from accidental hearers into intentional hearers; they learn to read God's handwriting in the church; they convert the venue's soundscape into the "word preached"; and they consolidate a decidedly "collaterall" dispersal of attention into a singular object with the aim of attaining its salvific properties. It is clear, however, that the theory of sermon belief expressed by Donne and like-minded contemporaries is not an exact science. Diffuse sermon conditions persist despite admonitions to dismiss them, so theatricality coexists with theological instruction despite their contradiction in the minds of many early modern writers.

Auditors are instructed to hear sermons selectively but also to engage with their environments. They are told to hear profitably by selective looking or, alternatively, by selective not-looking, as the significance of a sermon's content operates by attributing significance to its context. As a result of these instructions, sermons are like sacraments in their performative logic though not in their theology. In all, portrayals of a congregation's relation to a sermon take on various metaphorical faces, including topographical illustration, marginalia, literacy, echo, body and soul, coming, and even sacrament. These models are neither opposed to one another nor entirely coherent. Rather, Donne and his contemporaries seem to embrace this variety as part of the multifarious experience that early modern sermons constituted for sermon-goers.

Although Donne has served to provide the primary examples for my analysis of early modern sermon belief, it is worth briefly acknowledging that the significance Donne attributes to the environment and conditions of sermons reflects his attitude towards the physical world in general, especially his treatment of the human body. In his *Devotions*, Donne claims that he can read his soul in his body, as if it were a physical effigy of his spiritual self—that "thou dost effigiate my soul to me" in "the state of my body"—an ability much like what I have called church literacy.[49] Although the state of his body involves aspects of complexity and decay that do not directly represent the state of the soul, still the corruption of the human body reflects the general depravity of the soul and, indeed, creates the intellectual occasion for conceiving it. The correspondence between the sign and the thing is, according to Donne, decidedly accurate, if nonetheless wholly nonempirical and caught up in the details of the body's accidents. In a similar way, Donne's biblical idiom—"Lord, who hath beleeved our report?"—can be read as a commentary on the idiomatic character—or body—of belief in early modern sermon-going. Truly efficacious belief technically may be reducible to faith in Christ, but believing is a largely extratheological activity environed by society and sensations. The sermon, understood by Donne and his contemporaries as a phenomenon of firsthand experience, is a kind of effigy of the activity of faith.

Sermon belief, then, exists in an auditor's ability to transition from the eye to the ear and to identify a sacred substance in the accidents of a sermon and its environment. In a post-Reformation culture that is often described as word-centric, Donne's Christmas sermon provides an alternative model to metaphysics for understanding the attainment of saving belief. Instead of witnessing with faith the elevation of the transubstantiated host, where the substance of God is dogmatically manifest in physical accidents, Donne's auditors witness the acoustical and familiar voice of the preacher and discern the saving Word manifest in its people, spaces, noises, and idioms.

Chapter Five

PERFORMING RELIGION IN EARLY MODERN BALLADS

I turn now to a network of performance events that may in some ways seem worlds apart from that of the early modern sermon, and yet it is a milieu whose theatrical strategies are surprisingly similar to those found in one of Donne's perceptually diffuse sermons. Even though religion and morality were not the most popular ballad themes in early modern England, measuring by the mere scope of broadside ballad print and circulation, it is possible that "godly" ballads—as scholars have come to call them—constituted the most frequent religious performances of the period. And as we have seen in the contexts of play events, ballads intertheatrically overlapped with virtually every other mainstream performance type. At the same time, if we judge by the perceived distance between the popular conditions of ballad production and the institutional settings usually associated with established religion, the godly ballad might also be the most so-called secular form of religiously themed performance in early modern England—if by *secular* we mean to convey a "conception of literature as the product of a purely human activity of poiesis."[1] The financial motives of ballad producers and sellers were explicit; many of the most popular ballads were owned in a registered ballad stock. Professional ballad singers and hawkers were often criticized for their vagrancy. And once a broadside was purchased, the future of its performance was subject entirely to the lifestyle and travels of its owner.

It is no surprise, then, that the topic of religion in English printed ballads has a tenuous critical history. Ballad scholars tend to assume that these material factors shifted hearers' agency away from engagement with devotional culture, rather than assuming that ballads could be themselves a form of devotional culture with other forms of material and religious culture, so historians often depict ballad religion as superficial, existing under the auspice of some other primary cultural factor—propaganda, polemic, sensationalism, commerce, or mere entertainment. A common assumption is that the popular contexts in which ballads were performed edged out the potentially authentic religious intentions of balladeers and audiences, resulting in an excessively conventional genre where religious expression was rarely original.

Some early moderns, in fact, held a similar opinion about the potential for ballads to carry religious themes. Henry Chettle criticizes various social vices in his pamphlet *Kind-hart's Dreame*, including that of balladeering in the city, condemnable especially for its consequence of "with-drawing people from Christian exercises, especially at faires, markets and such publike meetings."[2] Like early modern invectives against play-going, the complaint that ballads distracted people from godly activities was common. As they did with commercial theater, antitheatrical writers frequently pitted balladry against the more desirable activities of churchgoing, quietness, and hard work. "Alderman Pennington, with some hundreds following him," presented a list of complaints in the Root and Branch petition at the beginning of the Long Parliament in which ballads are likewise accused of "withdrawing of people from reading, studying, and hearing the Word of God."[3] The petition in general seeks to strip ecclesiastical authorities of excessive power and carries an anticeremonialist tone. It is interesting that something about the idolatry and alleged corruption of ceremonial authority related, in the petitioners' minds, to the idleness of popular balladry: both religious ceremony and ballads withdraw people from sermons, and both are also mediated by theatrical conditions. We might imagine this argument occurring in Shakespeare's *Henry V* with its play on idle/idol ceremony. Hence, although ceremonialism and balladry were on opposite sides of the spectrum of cultural performance, to some they shared the characteristic of being "subject to the breath / Of every fool, whose sense no more can feel / But his own wringing!"

Yet despite these criticisms, we must attend to the fact that there were still hundreds of godly ballads circulating in early modern London. According to Stationers' Registers, more than one-third of the ballads registered during the majority of the Elizabethan period were religiously themed, and Samuel Pepys in the following century categorized 110 of his ballads under "Devotion and Morality." Moreover, many writers seem to have differentiated explicitly between godly ballads and bawdy ones. As early as 1549, for instance, William Baldwin expresses his wish that godly songs "myght once driue out of office the baudy balades of lecherous loue that commonly are indited and song [sung] of idle coutyers."[4] Baldwin's sentiment reflects those of numerous writers and publishers of godly songs in the mid-sixteenth century, including those of *A Compendious Book of Godly and Spiritual Songs*, published in 1567, as well as Sternhold's and Hopkins's 1562 *The Whole Booke of Psalmes*, which sets the psalms to ballad stanza and simple tunes in an effort to reroute popular music from the profane to the biblical.[5] And as with plays, it was not the generic features of ballads that opponents attacked—stanzaic verse, tune, and a central narrative situation—but rather the conditions of their production and performance. Ballad singers were often disparaged as drunks and vagrants, and their voices were criticized as jarring. Others complained that the broadside sheets themselves littered the city, overflowing every market stall and pasted "on euery post."[6]

As we have seen in biblical drama, boy bishop festivities, commercial plays, political processions, ceremonies, and sermons, the theatricality of early modern performance culture was much broader and holistic than what Barish describes as the protean nature of plays and their representation of content. Rather, theatricality consisted of an overlapping spread of conditions that included the occasional, environmental, circumstantial, technological, social, and religious—many of which themselves derived or evolved from medieval practices. Moreover, in performance events that engaged religious themes, religion was often used as a primary model or vehicle for incorporating the specific and sometimes idiosyncratic conditions of performance and audience experience into the overall thematic meanings.

Studying performance culture comparatively demonstrates that early modern theatricality interacts in productive ways with religious habits of practice and thought. In terms of the transparency of human strategy, the performative use of theatrical environments, and the perceptual habits of audiences, it is virtually impossible to differentiate strictly between the theatricality of events like sermons and ceremonies and that of so-called secular productions like commercial plays and ballads.

I am suggesting that we should not measure the religious salience of a performance type merely by the extent to which it falls within boundaries of religious practice as delineated exclusively by nontheatrical forms. As this chapter in particular demonstrates, we can also accredit performance events with the power to shape and define a historical vantage on religion, and, thus proceeding, we can better recognize the overlaps between theatrical and religious practices. For religious practice within as well as outside of performance is an often improvisational activity that combines multiple human motives, strategies, and receptions. Moreover, our decisions about the motives, strategies, and receptions that are dominant influence whether certain aspects of other cultural forms count as legitimate expressions of religious devotion and instruction. More than an assent to a creed or obligatory attendance at church, religion in early modern performance culture can be described, in Orsi's words, as a theatrical form of "religious practice and imagination in ongoing, dynamic relation with the realities and structures of everyday life."[7]

The aim of this chapter is to espouse the sophisticated interplay between theatricality and Christian practice in early modern ballad performances and to describe how ballads tie their religious identity to the manifestation of the song in space, music, print convention, and audience community. In large part, locating religion in ballad performance is a matter of looking for belief in the bustling and diffuse world of street performance, in many ways like that of the outdoor sermons at Paul's Cross. My treatment of Christian practice in performance culture in this book has emphasized its trans-Reformational flexibility. Early modern performances—inside and outside of overtly religious occasions—exist on a spectrum of shared theatrical strategies, environments, histories, and audiences, and this spectrum is characterized in part by its creative and performative interest in theatricality itself, as a network of intertheatrical forms of presentation and audience reception that drew on the Reformation's contentious attitudes toward aesthetic media—reform as well as continuity. Thus we can look to the theatricality of godly ballads in order to uncover some overlooked avenues for Christian edification, devotion, and faith. As scholars such as Ian Green and Natascha Würzbach have shown, ballad religion is dispersed into many different perceptual pieces and motivations, and sometimes these pieces appear primarily under ulterior purposes—for example, as the balladeer's market cry or as a series of repeated ballad commonplaces. Those things that scholars have sometimes considered inessential to the ballad tradition—to some extent, including performance itself—are actually definitive of ballad theatricality and therefore definitive also of the godliness of godly ballads. That is to say, the perceptual conditions of a ballad performance are just as relevant to the appearance of belief in godly ballads as are theological and moral instruction. What godly ballads represent in their narratives and characters converges, in many cases, with the situation of performance at hand. Like other performance types, they expose the labor and process of their coming-to-be, and they use their audiences' sensitivity to mediation and theatrical strategy as a way of encouraging response to their moral imperatives and thus substantiating the integrity of the godly ballad in the performance event itself.

Defining the Godliness of Godly Ballads

From the early twentieth century, discussions of early modern ballads have shown a degree of discomfort with treating the godly ballad as a religious genre. Part of the trouble is defining the "ballad" in the first place. Scholars have struggled to determine the degree to which religion—understood in these discussions as a body of practices authorized by theology and institutional precedent—is commensurate with the broader genre. Conversely, definitions of the ballad often preclude the vocabulary commensurate with some understandings of religious practice. For instance, one would be right in assuming that the average passerby who caught a few verses of a godly ballad being performed by a monger outside, say, the Globe Theatre in Southwark would probably not have had an experience of personal devotion akin to private prayer, but few have considered the possibility of a tone and attitude of religious practice that might be specifically formed by the culture of balladry. Examining, as I have done, the diffuse and theatrical nature of big sermons as well as the nuanced religious contortions of theatrical ceremony invites comparative investigation of the intersections between ballads and Christian practice at the levels of dramaturgy, audience reception, and environment. Ballads come to be through authorial, economic, material, theatrical, and cultural processes, each of which has the capacity of furthering a ballad's theme and each of which intersects with religious practice at different points. Thus I search for religion in the lifestyle of ballad singers and in their interactions with audiences in performance. I query as well the flexible border between print and song, unlatching preconceptions about what normative religion might be in a ballad performance and beginning instead with the ways that ballads reflect "people's perceptions, values, needs, and history."[8]

In 1932 Gordon Hall Gerould proffered a definition of the "Ballad of Tradition" as "a folk-song that tells a story with stress on the crucial situation, tells it by letting the action unfold itself in event and speech, and tells it objectively with little comment or intrusion of personal bias."[9] Especially noteworthy is Gerould's stress on the "objective" quality of ballads — "the idea of the ballad as a 'pure,' 'traditional' oral form that is expressive of a communal 'folk,' and that, most importantly, is uncontaminated by print."[10] According to this definition, a balladeer's first allegiance in singing a song is to the story itself as it is known in ballad lore and as it is told in ballad idiom. Gerould's definition is intended to cover ballads authored and performed from the early modern period through more recent decades, so, like Barish's treatment of theatricality, it expectedly distances ballads both from their conditions of production and from the first-person experience of their performances in an effort to capture an essence over time. More recently, David Atkinson renewed this notion of objectivity through a reception theory that stresses the generic conventionality of ballads. He calls this conventionality the genre's "horizon of expectations." Defining the ballad requires understanding its "interpretive context": "a kind of reception that is bounded in terms of its parameters or horizon of expectations; it imposes a 'reading imperative', the requirement that the text be interpreted in accordance with the nature and assumptions of its idiom."[11]

It is interesting how anthropological approaches often cite the orality of ballads as reason essentially to exclude the aural conditions of performance from their definitions of the ballad genre. They focus, instead, on ballads' imitative and conventional characteristics. They reflect an understanding of a certain oral folk song form that we refer to as the "ballad," even across continents and centuries, and that has always been written and sung in the awareness of its own tradition. In a certain way, this aspect of balladry seems consistent in the early modern period; even at the level of print and distribution, ballad authors and producers prioritized continuity of conventions, design, and musicality. Yet scholarship specifically on the early modern ballad has tended also to emphasize the material and cultural factors of ballad production, seeking to subject the anthropological definition to the scrutiny of print history, object studies, social networks, and what Fumerton has called "ballad publics."[12] The early modern English ballad industry involved numerous personnel, including ballad authors, printers, sellers, hawkers, buyers, spontaneous singers, and even owners, as when a group would purchase a specific ballad stock. Once a ballad was written, it would be taken to one of several specifically sanctioned printers—often identified on the broadsheet—and then later sold either by a bookseller or by the iconic ballad hawkers who purchased ballads at wholesale cost. "What has plagued and delayed the emergence of scholarship of the broadside ballad in its full multi-dimensional 'thingness,'" argues Fumerton, "is that the word 'ballad' has traditionally prompted, and continues to prompt for the general public, thoughts not of a thing but of a non-objectifiable aural song, specifically a narrative 'folk' song."[13] And the critical preoccupation with the folklore of ballads has been to the neglect of their theatricality in performance.

Despite the popularity of godly ballads in the sixteenth and seventeenth centuries, defining ballad religion as a material as well as theatrical phenomenon must first account for the poignant decline in godly ballad printing in the seventeenth century. According to Tessa Watt's calculations, the circulation of religious ballads seems to have dropped from 35 percent of all ballads registered from 1560 to 1588 to 9 percent from 1625 to 1640.[14] These numbers do not account for unregistered ballads, which outnumber ballads in the Registry when based on the surviving body of extant ballads. Still, measuring the popular reception of godly ballads, however one might define the "popular," is more complex than looking merely at registration percentages. Reception involves the political and religious conditions of a specific decade or even year that may have influenced ballad authorship, print, registration, and circulation. Registry numbers are also altered by the increase in popularity of news ballads in the seventeenth century, where the rise of one ballad subgenre may overshadow the continued popularity of another without necessarily suggesting decline of interest in the older type. Third, we should account for the ballad stock of 1624–25, where a group took ownership of a large body of ballads predominately from the Elizabethan period, registered with the Stationers' Company. As Watt observes, the ballad stock purchase shows a higher percentage of godly ballads (30 percent) relative to the production of new nonstock ballads in adjacent decades, indicating that these religious and moral ballads enjoyed an especially lasting popularity among audiences.

What these production factors reveal is that godly ballads remained popular commercial products well into the seventeenth century and perhaps beyond despite diminishing numbers. Godly ballads had a unique identity among ballads of other themes. Watt suggests that this identity is mosaic-like, retaining some aspects of older devotional practices but also embracing Protestant ideas about salvation. If godly ballads did appeal to traditional religious tastes, could this mixture of the old and new be intentional? Might we describe them, as Schreyer does of medieval drama, as engaging in a practice of "synchronic diachrony," where their cultural survival is due in part to their continuity with a past that is represented in a nonthreatening way? One significant point of continuity with the past is godly ballads' dramatic employment of music as a vehicle for issuing moral exhortation, not unlike the music we find in liturgy and biblical drama. As we have seen in Chester's *The Fall of Lucifer,* such theater music often takes the form of liturgical song, simultaneously connecting the cycle drama to and differentiating it from the liturgical performances of Corpus Christi and Pentecost.

A distinctive feature of the godly ballad's use of music is the way it connects to a narrative past and prompts a general attitude of reflection—alternatively harkening to or criticizing former times. A large portion of religiously themed ballads adopt a speaker voice that recollects past times of waste or vice and then uses these to call for moral reform or to demonstrate reform in the speaker's character. For instance, deathbed ballads posthumously use the speaker's life to encourage auditors to redeem the time. Similarly, prophecy ballads recall recent events through which they interpret God's judgments. And, of course, biblical ballads reproduce a familiar story and present it as a moral lesson, as when, at the end of "The Story of David and Berseba," the speaker reflects:

> The scourge of sinne thus you may see,
>   for murther and adultery.
> Lord grant that we may warned be,
>   such crying sinnes to shun and flie.[15]

Such ballads' tunes theatrically signal to audiences that the past is being narratively remade as a fable for moral instruction. Ballad music resonates with music across performance culture in creating a sense of vertical time. I'm suggesting that ballads harness the performative potential to invoke time past in the present and that this strategy connects intertheatrically to a similar phenomenon in each event that I've discussed in this book: the festive contexts of the boy bishop events, Elizabeth's coronation pageant, and *Twelfth Night*; the multitemporality of the "signs" and "things" in the Chester Whitsun plays; the connection that Shakespeare draws between ceremonialism and theatricality in *Henry V*; and the many ways that the activities of early modern sermon-going carried through attitudes and sacramental logics that also characterize liturgies before and in the early years of the Reformation. Likewise, godly ballads contextualize the present moment within the sacred tradition of the past, and they also orient the present occasion as an antitype of the eschatological future. Music in godly ballads is far from liturgical, but like many customs it embodies a popular response to a tradition of festival established in the Christian calendar.

In particular, a ballad's music anticipates the song's moralistic end. This is apparent in the seventeenth century's most popular godly and moral ballad tune, "Fortune my Foe," a tune whose title invokes the theme of human preparation for change in fortune over time, projecting the past into a rule for future moral action. Thus music in moral ballads also points to the more immediate past of the ballad tradition and ballad production, through processes of recycling and renaming ballad tunes. In this way, anthropological definitions of the ballad are accurate to the early modern broadside in that the ballad tradition itself—and its music in particular—becomes a performative reference for converting stories of the past into moral imperatives in the present. Even the tune imprint on "The Story of David and Berseba," which simply reads, "To a pleasant new tune," invokes the ballad past and the balladic convention of representing the past through the same theatrical device it uses to announce its novelty.

Music is a component of balladry that also helps facilitate the convergence of the theatrical and the practical, as ballads integrate recognizable music into the culture of cheap print. Yet it is at intersections such as this one—where an aspect of familiar moral theatricality meets cheap print and commercial transaction—that scholarly opinion diverges. For many, theatricality implies motives of entertainment and sometimes the unrestrained use of the sensational. Contained within such understandings of the theatrical are assumptions about the authenticity often associated with religious practice and, opposed to it, the forthright disclosure of creative and commercial strategy in performance genres like balladry. For instance, Watt acknowledges the thematic representation of religion in deathbed ballads but insinuates that their sensationalism may have overridden their religious reception. Likewise, she suggests that while Protestant martyr ballads survived their audiences' lack of religious enthusiasm, they did so merely as "cardboard cut-outs" of the "emotional religious core" of the martyrdom narrative.[16]

Some appraisals of ballad religion have viewed performance merely as an extension of ballad production, print, and dissemination.

As a result, scholars have identified a certain derivativeness not only in ballad patterns print and lyric but also in ballad performance and, in turn, have interpreted religious ballads as outliers, of sorts, in the ballad tradition. Ian Green contrasts the numerous godly ballads of the sixteenth century that typically include an authorial attribution with the later seventeenth-century broadsides that were anonymous and often stock, and he suggests that the "picture that emerges gives much greater weight to the role of the publisher" in the production of godly ballads.[17] Moreover, he states that the decreasing presence of an authorial attribution renders religion especially routine and unintentional as a ballad theme: "The great majority of the cheap works which sold best were neither the product of 'godly' authors' pens nor would have been acceptable to them." Green points to early modern ballads' reliance on print conventions, cliché, and lyrical commonplaces as evidence of their unserious treatment of religion, writing that "one is forcibly struck by . . . the incompleteness of the teaching and the repetitiveness of the language and ideas" contained in godly ballads.[18] He continues:

> The elements of Protestantism in these ballads, such as a focus on the teaching of the Bible, salvation through faith, or the example set by Protestant martyrs, were so small that what one is looking at here is something much more akin to a secular ballad—on seduction, drunkenness, war, or "strange news" from Germany or Lincolnshire—with a change of focus and a few, safe, undemanding clichés that even sincere supporters of "prayer-book religion" (whose standards are generally assumed to have been much lower than those of the "godly") would have found inadequate.[19]

One significant presupposition here is that the secular in cheap print is rooted in ballad style; thus the fact that godly ballads do not present religion in a style more familiar to "prayer-book religion" means that their allegedly insubstantial religious content is overwritten by their worldly conventions.

Natascha Würzbach makes a similar argument about what she views as the worldliness of godly ballad performance conditions. Würzbach attributes the decline in godly ballad print between 1550 and 1650 to a correspondence between emerging secularism and a public demand for less routine and more personalized textual voices. "The reasons for this, from the point of view of textual intent, is to be found not only in the unsuitability of presenter communication practices of religious and theological moral themes, but more in the principal function of a speaker who assumes sole responsibility for conveying the subject of communication. Where this subject of communication is part of an unquestioned, fixed world view orientated towards salvation and redemption there is no necessity for a personalized statement."[20] Such opinions about the unsuitability of ballad print and performance for facilitating religious practice overlook how the routine form and conventionality of ballads might create the conditions for the kind of performative creativity and improvisation that characterizes certain patterns of religious practice at the time.[21]

At stake in these arguments is an evaluation of the authenticity of religion in godly ballads: How can a ballad really express or incite belief if it is so excessively conventional and cliché-driven or if it is unoriginal? And how can a genre so tied to self-imitation and cheap print purport to convey serious religious instruction from a "fixed world view"? As I have discussed in previous chapters, religious themes in drama before and after the Reformation have consistently made use of the constraints and conventions of their genres and industries. Theatrical events relied on theater's dramaturgical conventions, technology, property, personnel, and audience habits at hand to extend their religious themes.[22] Balladry was no different. To this point, Louise Pound in 1920 encouraged scholars to first consider ballads' stylistic and theatrical constraints before making conclusions about which themes were suitable for the genre. She wrote, "Ballad creation has for its motivating impulse the circumstance that characters and their story are to be brought before hearers, not in a narrative to be read, but briefly and memorably and dramatically in a recitational or song way. Only stories which lend themselves well to such handling are eligible material."[23]

A greater focus on ballads in performance foregrounds their stylistic, conventional, and theatrical characteristics, and it creates room for exploring how ballads may have contributed to different cultural discourses, not least of which is religion. Advancing this focus on ballads in performance, Bruce Smith and Christopher Marsh have approached early modern balladry as a specifically musical medium that promotes what Smith has described as a "kinetic" form of knowing its content.[24] Smith suggests that we look to how ballads "interact in highly volatile ways with the physical body, with soundscapes, with speech communities, with political authority, with the singer's sense of self," treating the body as the "common denominator" among the various parties involved in a ballad performance, from balladeer, to audience, to scholar.[25] Marsh similarly describes the performance and reception aspects of balladry as epistemologically and physically continuous phenomena, with music serving as a kind of common denominator similar to Smith's description of the body.[26]

Exploring how different performance types support varying ways of knowing things in collaboration with performance environment, sensation, perception, and psychology also encourages alternative ways of theorizing religion in performance culture. Godly ballads exist in cheap print culture, but they also exist in a performance culture that, as we have seen, exploits the constraints of performance situations for creating unique opportunities for theatrical and religious engagement. For instance, we can compare the martyr ballad tradition, as an example of a popular religious performance, with Foxe's *Actes and Monuments of these Latter and Perillous Days*, a book that is firmly cemented in Protestantism's literary heritage and that appears in churches and other formally orthodox contexts. Placing "A Ballad of Anne Askew" next to the *Actes and Monuments* reveals how the theatricality of the ballad form may have created the conditions for a religious practice that both imitates and differs from that of Foxe's more institutionally established book. If we were looking for the kind of devotion promoted by readings of the *Actes and Monuments* in ballads, then we might conclude that religion is unseriously executed in them. Yet it is important to remember that even sermons and other performed religious texts were theatrical and drew on the idiomatic conventions of their delivery. In 1570 a copy of the second edition of Foxe's *Actes and Monuments* was ordered to be placed in every collegiate church in England, just like the Bible, and both books were read privately and also aloud—and, hence, performed.

Performing Religion in Early Modern Ballads 205

Thus even the story of Ann Askew reached auditors through the drama and ambience of a sermon or prayer office. Through Foxe, auditors heard the Askew story in a performer-audience scenario, possibly amid environmental distractions; they may have taken notes or employed other strategies for profitably receiving instruction in church; and, as happened with sermons, they may have even repeated the story back at home, redistributing the performance afterward.

Still, one of the aspects that audiences of "A Ballad of Anne Askew" would have found distinct from the Foxe rendition was the lyrical ballad idiom, designed both for a certain tune and for the ability and practices of ballad singers—a body of performers who acquired a kind of collective reputation by the late seventeenth century.

> For such sinners as the Scripture saith,
>   that will gladly repent and follow thy word:
> Which I will not deny whilst I have breath,
>   for prison, fire, faggot, nor fierce sword.[27]

There are no comparisons between the style of the Askew ballad and Foxe's account, the former a short moral song and the latter an elaborate annotated record of events. The Askew ballad does not try to emulate Foxe. Instead, it converts the Askew story into the tradition of martyr ballads. This distinct theatrical form of the martyrdom theme is further suggested by the fact that, in several extant examples, the Askew ballad is printed on the same page as another female martyr ballad called "A Rare Example of a Vertuous Maid in Paris"—a song that ends with similar emotional fervor:[28]

> When all these words were ended,
>   then came the man of Death,
> Who kindled soon a fire,
>   which stopt this Virgins breath

Such ballads are printed, decorated with woodcuts, set to tunes, and sung by hawkers and ballad owners in an array of different settings. The musicality of the event has the performative effect of charging the singer's position and voice with the authority of the godly ballad tradition and also of converting the story into an occasion for remembrance. That is, the ballad event itself, as Pound suggests, takes a famous martyr legend and translates it into the social idiom of ballad singing—a memorable tune, an attractive broadside, and an opportunity for audiences to participate in the redistribution and continual performance of an endeared religious story.

Just as occurs with comedy and bawdiness in ballads, religious themes take root in the circumstances of ballad appearance. They borrow from and imitate aspects of other performance types and ballad themes, and these imitations acquire new meanings. Martyr ballads, we might say, adduce the balladic nuance of martyr stories and their popular religious import. Generally, the notion of "popular" religion tends to be interpreted as "the space that emerged between official or learned Christianity and profane (or 'pagan') culture," but as, Orsi suggests, we can expand what counts as a "theologizing" practice to include "the improvisational power of theology as a component of lived experience."[29] The singular, personal voice of the ballad speaker and singer—often conflated—indeed implies a perceived effect of authenticity, as if the account of the song is an individual expression. But what is in fact "authentic" about the song, what is true to itself, is its participation in collective ballad culture. In performances of "Anne Askew," audiences participated not in religious practice abstractly but in religious *ballad* practice, when they were moved by the narrative and in the phenomenal act of attending to the experience as a coherent performance of godliness, compiling it from among its ulterior conditions—its balladeer's musicality, its costumers' exchanges of currency, its audience members' physical proximity to each other, and its recognition of ballad commonplaces.

PARTICIPATION, IN A broad sense, is a defining aspect of ballad performance culture and informs an understanding of the theatricality of godly ballads. A particularly practical form of this occurs when audience members browsed broadsides while songs were being performed. *Bartholomew Fair*'s Cokes "*Runs to the ballad-man*," exclaiming, "Ballads! hark, hark! pray thee, fellow, stay a little. . . . What ballads hast thou? let me see, let me see myself."[30] We imagine him rummaging through the hawker's basket. Cokes then demonstrates another common form of audience participation by singing the burden (or refrain) at the end of each verse with the balladeer. These occurrences—in addition to dancing, purchasing broadsides, applause, and other reactions—are obvious forms of participation, but I want to suggest that audiences participated on more basic perceptual and intellectual levels through the activity of recognition and the social attitude of familiarity.

As simplistic as it may sound, audiences part-icipated in (from *pars* and *capere*, "to take part in")—and thereby assembled—godly ballads by recognizing the theatrical constraint that religion is dispersed into different perceptual objects and intentions in the multimedia performance event and by holding these parts together through their presence as audience. By *parts*, I mean the perceptual pieces of the ballad object, its verses, design, and ornament; but I also refer to the parts of a whole performance event—its environment, audience, props, and perceived motives—that, as *Henry V*'s Prologue suggests, audiences "piece" together through their attention. As I will discuss, ballad performances position audiences in attitudes of response and ideological conference, so the presence and self-consciousness of a ballad audience are a performative function of the conditions of ballad performance. Godly ballad theatricality relates to ballad lyrics as a set of constraints that invite audiences into a musical and often public form of religious interaction. The theme, its lyrical attributes, the environment, and the singer become aspects or fronts of a whole, and when the ballad is decidedly religious, as with the Askew ballad, there arises the potential for the audience to experience the ballad's sensible parts through the organizing lens of religion, and especially religion as found in performance culture. "We take the object *as* whole, and the part *as* part, and we intend the part *as* a part of the whole, and articulate it in a judgment": *the ballad is godly*.[31] Godly ballads enact a unique distribution of the sensibility of religion that, in practice, highlights opportunities for godly action that are perhaps most accessible to the ballad form.

I suggest that we can examine the parts of ballads in print and especially in performance and treat them as points of audience access to the ballad theme, or, if you will, variations on the ballad theme. Ballad performances make no attempt to hide the process of their event—the labor of their production, their imitation of other ballads, their reliance on the audience, and their economic motives. Likewise, ballad religion consists of performative behaviors by the singer and audience that propose to treat any given step in this process as religious, and specifically as contributive to a theatrical tradition and local community of religious exchange. Ballads do more than just to show the visuality of the audience; they implicate the visuality of the audience in an intimate performance situation.

I turn now to two different aspects of the *whole* of Christian practice in balladry and its corresponding forms of participation: (a) ballad imitation and conventionality and (b) the audience's physical actions that piece together the ballad as an embodied experience of communal religion. It should be noted that I am covering many decades of ballad making and performance, but this is often a necessary challenge when one is describing early modern ballad themes and subgenres. When possible, I speculate about a ballad's production in relation to its historical moment, and I also attend to trends of broadside design and topical allusion. Still, such historicization has its limitations, especially since ballad performances extend far beyond the moments of their original authorship. They were printed several times, sometimes changing ownership, and participated in a kind of aggregate culture of street and private performance habits—all variables that point to the importance of situational audience response in a way that is commensurate with the shared theatricality of performance culture.

THE CONVENTIONALITY OF BALLAD RELIGION

Early modern ballads thrive on imitation. They imitate their own genre's conventions as well as the conventions of other religious texts and performances. In fact, their habits of extensive imitation, allusion, and recycling probably contributed to their popularity and survival. Readers and audiences of ballads wanted to read and hear what they expected to read and hear. Atkinson provides a useful list of some of these expected formal characteristics: "Repetitive textual, metrical, and melodic structures; patterned arrangements of narrative and conceptual components, or parallelism in phrase and idea, including so-called incremental repetition; conventional vocabulary and epithets; recurrent, formulaic phrases, lines, and stanzas; formalized refrains . . . a recurrent vocabulary of melodic, rhythmic, and dynamic techniques, as well as ornamentation, designed to meet the emotional and metrical demands of the song texts."[32] I would add to this list recurrent themes and habits of standard allusion to stories and phrases that popular society would readily recognize, such as allusions to the Bible, traditional English lore, current events, and the political establishment.

When I refer to ballad conventionality, I mean the general ballad conventions of verse form and refrain, such as the common opening call to hearers; the even more general employment of commonplaces and godly sayings found in ballads and other forms of religious cheap print; the use, reference, repurposing, and grouping of ballad tunes and woodcuts; broadside design patterns, including layout, ornament, marginalia, and illustration; and narrative and voicing conventions, such as a closing didactic moralism and first-person speaker retrospection. Describing these aspects of ballad style as imitative reflects the fast rise of the ballad form, including its engagement of virtually every aspect of public interest. Imitation also reflects the trendiness of these conventions insofar as variations on ballad themes can be traced in ballad production from decade to decade. As moral songs, ballads emphasized the same social challenges targeted by antitheatricalists and anticeremonialists—indictments of idleness, raucousness, wastefulness, and indecency; and so, just as in theatrical and ceremonial discourses, vehement reaction against the legitimacy of godly ballads also implies an unstated recognition of their influence and cultural power.

In an early modern spiritual climate characterized by liturgy, radical ecclesiastical change, high illiteracy rates, the growth of the public sermon, and a dynamic performance culture, the conventionality and overt theatricality of godly ballads should be understood to heighten their emotional intensity and their ability to incite audience response. Take for example a godly ballad from the 1624 stock, "A most Excellent Ballad of Ioseph the Carpenter," reprinted later in the seventeenth century. To summarize that this ballad is simply about the annunciation and birth of Christ from the perspective of Joseph misses how significantly the ballad's imitativeness shapes its meanings. The verses are not separated into spaced stanzas but are differentiable by the rhyme scheme of *aaab, cccb, dddb*. The first eight lines read:

> *Joseph* an aged man truly,
>   Did marry a Virgin fair and free,
> A purer Virgin did no man see,
>   Then [*sic*] he chose for his dear his dear.
> This Virgin was pure, there was no nay,
> The Angel *Gabriel* to her did say.
> Thou shalt conceive a boy this day,
>   The which shall be our dear our dear.[33]

This ballad was popular in the seventeenth century, and it is representative in its black-letter physical layout: a title, woodcuts (in this case, two), the song, and a printer's advertisement at the bottom. If we focus on the presentation of this well-known story and how Joseph's perspective comes to presence in the ballad's conventions, perhaps the most immediately striking observation is how much the religious content is shaped by the ballad's auditory characteristics. We might even say that the story of Joseph and the Virgin is co-opted by its theatrical appeal in performance. Not only does it have a regular and simple rhyme, but it is filled with interior rhyme and consonance. The soft "g" (or, for the listener, the phoneme /j/) of the first line's "aged" reappears in the second line's "Virgin" at about the same point in rhythm. Furthermore, lines 5 and 6 share a subtle internal rhyme in "there" and "her," while lines 7 and 8 internally rhyme "conceive" and "be." The overall rhyme structure centers on the repetition of "dear," used in different grammatical positions, in the first person and then the third person. Although this ballad does not indicate a specific tune, it is possible that the refrain-like "dears" were sung with emotional intensity and were the most recognizable aspect of the ballad in performance.

To an extent, these aural aspects perceptually antecede the biblical content in the four lines devoted to confirming that the virgin was "pure." The ballad's theatrical sounds assert themselves before the thematic lyrics do. Perhaps one motive for the author including this effusion on Mary's purity, especially compared to the scant space afforded to describing Christ's actual birth, is its position in the burden, given the fact that burdens are repetitive and lend themselves to sing-alongs. Yet the pervasive conventionality of the purity theme also helps to establish the ballad among other godly performances and to create space to introduce some godly moral themes that are applicable even in the immanent occasion of the ballad performance. The repeated "dears" serve to emphasize and celebrate the important detail of Mary's purity—a detail that also enjoys prolonged expression in other early seventeenth-century broadsides, such as "The Angel Gabriel, his Salutation to the Virgin Mary," which devotes virtually the entire song to communicating Mary as "Virgin," "never toucht," "pure in thought and deed," "a spotless Maid," and so on.[34] Mary's repetitive purity in "A most Excellent Ballad of Ioseph the Carpenter" disclaims originality and conspicuously refers to other religious expressions in nativity ballads and cheap print.

Biblical details such as Mary's purity function as a kind of citation or allusion not because they directly reference a dogmatic text but because they nod to the importance of patently recognizable theological detail. The details themselves are less important than their inclusion as *standard* details. In other words, they present a safe theological commonplace, but they also speak to the religious importance of the activity of recognizing it and of the process of making a convention recognizable.

The ballad's reliance on convention and familiar citation suggests that the balladeer is advertising the fact that, as presented to auditors and customers, his ballad is historically and theologically accurate, that if you purchase this broadside then you will have brought an object of entertainment as well as godly instruction into your home for a penny or half-penny. In a sense, ballad subgenre conventions like these promote the reliability of a brand. We see this near the end of the ballad, when the Holy Family searches for a place for Mary to give birth. The direct effect of the stanza is to impart the familiarity of the details it mentions and their theatricalization in song.

> But when to *Bethelem* they were come,
> The Inns were filled all and some,
> When *Joseph* intreating every groom,
>   Could get no bed for his dear his dear
> Then was he constrained presently,
> Within the Stable all night to lye,
> Wherein they did Oxen and Asses tye,
>   With his true love and Lady dear.

The stanza emphasizes the most familiar aspects of the narrative, that the inns were full and that the stable housed animals. The almost cameo appearance of the "Oxen and Asses" is another allusion or imitation of sorts, if only in reference to these two animals' ubiquity in other verse and graphic renditions. As nonspecific as this allusion may seem, it is a good example of the kind of widespread cultural imitation for which ballads aim.

Yet it is this kind of automatic appropriating of biblical detail that leads Green to assume that ballads like this one must not be "the work of a 'godly' author" since they hold "the *verba ipsissima* of the Bible in low regard."[35] This critique echoes the complaints expressed by early modern writers who doubted ballads' ability to instruct or profit hearers. In 1582 Richard Stanyhurst complains that ballad authors and balladeers are "a frye of such *wooden rythmours*" who suffer from never learning Greek and Latin in school, and William Webbe in 1586 describes the sound of performances as "the vncountable rabble of Ryming ballet makers."[36] Besides registering cultural opinions, complaints like these also help to identify the aspects of ballads that society recognized as distinct of the genre. As is also true of sermon culture's art-of-hearing treatises, the very aspects of the genre that opponents target may also be the most operative in theatrically shaping the themes that ballads engage, including religion. In the case of Stanyhurst and Webbe, then, we might consider how the apparently unlearned and allegedly over-rhymed elements of godly ballads can be understood as particularly central to ballad godliness.

This is precisely the case in "A most Excellent Ballad of Ioseph the Carpenter":

> The Virgin fair thought it no scorn,
> To lye in such a place forlorn,
> Which night she had a young-Son born,
>   Even Jesus Christ our dear our dear

These lines contain the actual moment of the Nativity. Jesus appears, however, in a subordinate clause about the Holy Family's acceptance of their animal-infested housing. The relation between theatricality and religion in this ballad follows the same pattern found in Chester's *The Last Supper*, in Donne's sermons, and in the Prayer Book's consecration prayer: the representation of the sacred itself is decentered in the performance. Or more accurately—like cycle drama, sermons, and liturgy—ballads foreground the towardness of the theatrical act and thus suggest the performative potential for devotion of their immanent environments. The emotional and perceptual focus is on the phenomenality of the song, on the aspects of the scene that are most characteristic of the form and that are most in touch with the specific performance situation, just as is the case in other performance types. In this case, that "Jesus Christ" immediately precedes the ballad's refrain—"our dear our dear"—has a performative function. Stanyhurst and Webbe might well argue that it marginalizes the moment of Incarnation by positioning the name of Christ—the first time it appears in the ballad—alongside a representative example of allegedly superfluous and repetitive rhyme. Yet we should also notice that situating the moment of Incarnation next to "our dear our dear" is to position Christ adjacent to the telltale musical convention of the ballad. The moment of the Nativity is memorialized—even mnemonically—through the ballad's most recognizable musical motif.

This Nativity ballad's participation in ballad convention, in fact, grounds the religious participation of the audience in its theatricality. Jesus may seem decentered, but like King Henry he appears in the "wiggle." Like many godly ballads from the sixteenth and seventeenth centuries, "A most Excellent Ballad" adopts a perspective of human society and labor as opposed to a theological or hermeneutic one. This is demonstrated especially through its use of dialogue as opposed to declamation. Dialogue, especially between men and women, is a common feature of ballads of all types. It is also noteworthy that an uncommonly large proportion of the ballads that are titled as "Jigs"—any number of which may have been employed as the jigs performed at the end of commercial plays in the period—are also dialogue ballads, suggesting an affinity between ballads and a number of intertheatrical genres, including plays.[37] As a dialogue ballad, "A most Excellent Ballad of Ioseph the Carpenter" intertheatrically submits its religious content to the practices of the broader performing arts. Joseph's and Mary's expressed doubts are primarily directed toward one another, questioning not whether the miracle is true per se but, rather, whether the other will believe the miracle. The ballad confirms Mary's constancy and faithfulness ("By God alone, and I undefil'd," "true and faithful," "true and constant"), but it undergoes the kind of spousal (or prespousal, in this case) interrogation that ballad audiences heard in comic and bawdy dialogue songs, many of which conclude without the characters reconciling.

Criticisms like those of Stanyhurst and Webbe, that ballad authors are unequipped for effectively communicating moral instruction because they are unschooled in Greek and Latin, help us to understand where godly ballads locate their power to edify. Most ballad authors do not have the educations of theological divines, but they do have access to a cheap print medium and theatrical form that encourages them to imitate and borrow their religious material from other texts and performances and thus to invest in the emotional immediacy of their content in performance.

A 1593 ballad entitled "The Heartie Confession of a Christian" demonstrates how imitation and citation can serve to foreground the event of godly reception. Here we can detect traces of the performance conditions and their interaction with the religious content of the ballad in the design of the broadside itself (figure 5.1). Although this broadside consists of much more than stanzaic verses, the lyrical song is a confession of sin and an example of the process of prayerful repentance. The speaker begins by admitting that he is "drowned" in "*sin originall*." He asks for forgiveness of his "violence and treacherie" and then confirms the renewal of his "state in heaven."[38] The stanzas are spattered with biblical allusions, including the comparison of Christ to Moses's *"brazen snake"* and the tripartite title of Christ as "Prophet, Priest, and King." The fourth stanza illustrates the extensive use of general allusion and imitative language:

> 3. *Where I ungodly am, and superstitious,
> Unreverent, profane, and irreligious,
> Leading my life after a worldly fashion
> Against the rule of my heavenly vocation,
> And thus am set in an *ilfavor'd case*;
> Christ is my *perfect holiness, and grace:
> Him, as that *holy of holies*, if I frequent,
> My blottes, and blemishes shall soone be spent.

In a moment of narrative destitution in "an *ilfavor'd case*," where a sermon or prayer might typically seek to convey the individuality of a confessional speech act, the ballad speaker uses stock phrases of popular theology that actually depersonalize the confession. References to *"perfect holiness"* and the temple *"holy of holies"* as well as the euphemistic alliterative pairing of "blottes, and blemishes" are apt for the ballad's theme, but this same effect of aptness seems to drive its choice of imagery and citation rather than any authorial identity or thematic nuance.

Similarly, the speaker's self-description does not so much convey a sense of original confession as offer a patently imitational example of contrition—a confession that can be interpreted only in the manner of an *exemplum*. It is still emotionally driven and potentially sincere—to whatever extent we can measure a quality like sincerity—but what I want to observe is that, as a confession, it is remarkably undramatic, that is, nonsuspenseful and even recitational. The list of "ungodly" attributes—"superstitious, / Unreverent, profane, and irreligious," and so on—serves simply to show that the ballad is somewhat theologically relevant, as it is able to depict sin in at least seven different guises. Whereas "A most Excellent Ballad of Ioseph the Carpenter" conventionalizes and memorializes biblical details primarily through rhyme structure and musicality, "The Heartie Confession of a Christian" conventionalizes biblical details through allusion and popular idiom.

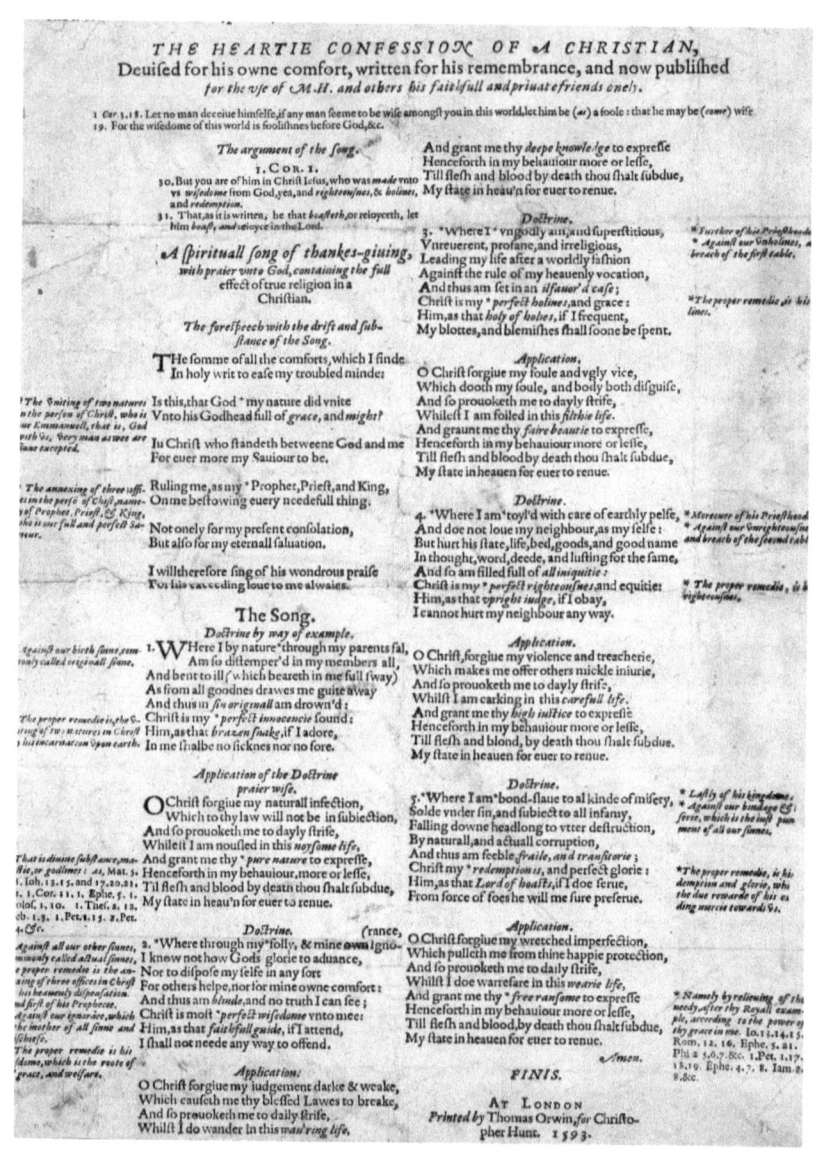

FIGURE 5.1. Ballad, "The Heartie Confession of a Christian," 1593. Reproduced with the permission of the Huntington Library, Britwell 18278.

Musicality is less prominent in the broadside of "The Heartie Confession" than style; and in performance, where music is perceptually prior to the lyrics, the balladeer would endeavor to capture this feeling of conventionality and theological appropriateness—vocally reproducing, as it were, the tone of ballad performance and broadside culture. Although the Duchess of Newcastle's opinions about ballads may have been somewhat idiosyncratic, her description of ballad "Tone" in a 1664 letter provides a commentary for understanding this ballad's imitative style in performance. She writes: "Neither should Old Ballads be sung so much in a Tune as in a Tone, which Tone is betwixt Speaking and Singing, for the Sound is more than Plain Speaking, and less than Clear Singing."[39] What seems to be culturally consistent about Cavendish's statement, written decades after "The Heartie Confession" was authored, is not that balladeers always lacked skilled voices but that ballad performances had a "Tone" consisting of much more than their well-circulated melodies. She describes this tone as circumstantial, organically arising from common labor, in this case comparable to the sounds of "good housewives" spinning thread and to "the noise the wheel makes in the turning round." Her attention to the popular circularity and perhaps circulation of ballad tone, as opposed to the grander circular "Musick of the Spheres," emphasizes its imitational qualities. Ballads—and godly ballads in particular—circle each other as they also circulate the theological and moral knowledge of popular culture through imitating and alluding to it.[40] And, like Cavendish, many found such circularity endearing.

Audience participation in godly ballad performance is also reflected in their physical appearances. The form of black-letter broadsides became more or less regularized by the end of the seventeenth century, but earlier ballad authors and printers often experimented with different ways of framing them. Broadside design went through trends. The particular design of "The Heartie Confession"—its use of multiple types, heavy marginalia, no woodcut, and sometimes graphic ornamentation—was especially popular among similar epitaph-themed ballads in the 1560s and 1570s. So by the 1590s this layout would have been recognizable for certain patterns of ballad voice, including confession and remembrance. This layout and its uses of imitation and citation remained popular into the 1620s–1640s, another period with a relatively high density of godly ballads, given the stock of the 1620s. These later decades might even be described as experiencing a nostalgic resurgence for the old religious broadsides (not all of them ballads) printed a half century earlier.

Especially notable in "The Heartie Confession" and in ballads of this type are the printed marginalia. They are composed of short theological explanations and citations. Where a ballad verse says, "Where I by nature* through my parents fal," a corresponding asterisk appears in the margin with the doctrinal explanation: "*Against our birth sinne, commonly called originall sinne._" Or, where the ballad refers to "Christ my *redemption," the margin explains: "*The proper remedie, is hi[s] [re]demption and glorie, w[ith] the due reward of his ex[cee]ding mercie towards us._" The margins also contain abbreviated biblical citations, as in "That is divine substance, majestie, or godlines: as, Mat. 5.48. Joh. 13.15. and 17.20.21.22," and so on. These bits of doctrinal exposition and biblical citation suggest a great deal about how authors conceived of the religious facility of the ballad form. They tell us that ballad makers were aware of their referentiality, that ballads were conceived as a genre not primarily designed for issuing doctrine but for repeating it, and that such repetition or reduplication comes to performative effect in moments of reading and performance.

In the late sixteenth and early seventeenth centuries, godly ballads practice repetition through effusive annotation. Their doctrinal annotations and citations serve as a frame for their verses. They function as categorical intentions of ballad songs, framing them as the kinds of performances that require doctrinal encasing. Like "A most Excellent Ballad of Ioseph the Carpenter," "The Heartie Confession" is an expression of remembrance, summary, confession, and example. Each is an imitative quality, and each affects aspects of the broadside design. Stacked above the ballad are a didactic epigraph, a title, Bible verses, and the "*forespeech._" Below are the printer's advertisement and the date, and in the margins lie doctrinal glosses and biblical references. A statement printed above the title announces the ballad's role as a repeater and summarizer of religious instruction: "There bee many that speake much of Jesus Christ, and beare a faire shew of his holines and vertue: but none are able to conceive (much lesse to declare) the sweete comforts of his heavenly grace, saving such as hold faith in a good conscience, without hypocrisie, pride, and covetousnes, and be reformed in their lives with charitie, peace, and unitie." The statement differentiates between hypocrites who "speake much of Jesus Christ" and those rare few who "are able to conceive . . . his heavenly grace." True *conception* leads to true *repentance*. Moreover, the ballad grounds this conception in "charitie, peace, and unitie," three Christian attributes that are especially social and, as I will argue, even native to godly ballad religion in performance. This deeper conceiving, he continues in the "*forespeech*" that precedes the first stanza, is given not by doctrine alone but by a "somme" (sum) of it, "to ease my troubled minde."

In some ways, godly ballads are composite and intertheatrical imitations of other religious forms. They often piece together different kinds of speech—instruction, preface, citation, title, note, illustration—and they also imitate the forms of other prominent religious literature and performance. Most noticeably, "The Heartie Confession of a Christian," with its crowded margins, typographical variety, italics, prefaces, and stanza titles, resembles the print layouts that were popular in devotional and theological books at the time, many of which would not be classified as particularly "cheap" print. The most highly visible of these might be the sixteenth-century Book of Common Prayer and the Geneva Bible in England (figures 5.2 and 5.3).

Both books were frequently read aloud in post-Reformation England, not least in churches. This excerpt from the burial liturgy is representative of how the Prayer Book served as a kind of performance text, with indented white-letter liturgical directions for movement—for example, "Then shalbe sayde or song"—interspersed among black-letter decorative text to be read aloud and marginal citations to be noted silently.[41] "The Heartie Confession of a Christian" likewise presents a scriptural reading and sung response, not only alluding to such books of institutional church practice but also alluding to their theatrical uses.

Consider, for example, that corporate confession was a central component of many of the Prayer Book's liturgies, including the morning and evening prayer offices, Holy Communion, and baptism.

The order for the buryal
of the dead.

The priest meeting the corpes at the church stile, shal say, or els the priestes and clarkes shal syng, and so goe eyther vnto the church, or towards the graue.

Iohn.xj.

I am the resurrection & the lyfe (sayth the Lord.) He that beleeueth in me, yea though he were dead, yet shall he lyue. And who so euer lyueth and beleeueth in me, shal not dye for euer.

Iob.xix.

I know that my redeemer liueth, and that I shal ryse out of the earth in the laste day, and shalbe couered agayne with my skinne, & shal see God in my flesh, yea, and I mee selfe shal behold him, not with other, but with these same eyes.

i.Tim.vi.

Iob.j.

We broght nothyng into this worlde, neyther may we cary any thyng out of this worlde. The Lord geueth, and the Lord taketh away. Euen as it pleaseth the Lorde, so commeth thynges to passe: Blessed be the name of the Lorde.

When they come at the graue, whiles the corpes is made redy to be layde in the earth, the Priest shal say, or the Prieste and Clarkes shal syng.

Iob.xix.

Man that is borne of a woman hath but a short tyme to lyue, and is ful of myserie, he commeth vp, and is cut downe like a floure. He fleeth as it were a shadowe, and neuer continueth in one stay. In the myddest of life we be in death. Of whom may we seeke for succour but of thee, O Lorde, whiche for our sinnes iustly art displeased: Yet O Lord God most holy, O Lorde most mightie, O holy and moste mercyful sauiour, deliuer vs not into the bitter paynes of eternal death. Thou knowest Lorde the secretes of our hartes, shutte not vp thy mercyfull eyes to our prayers: But spare vs Lorde moste holy,

FIGURE 5.2. "The order for the buryal *of the dead.*" In *The boke of common praier, and administration of the sacramentes,* 1573, sig. P7v–P8r. Reproduced with the permission of the British Library, C.25.m.4.(1–2).

At the buryal of the dead.

holy, O God moste mightie, O holy and mercyfull sauiour, thou moste woorthie iudge eternall, suffer vs not at our laste houre for any paynes of death to fall from thee.

Then whyle the earth shalbe cast vpon the body by some standing by, the Priest shal say.

FOR as muche as it hath pleased almightie God of his great mercie, to take vnto hym selfe the soule of our deare brother here departed: We therfore commit his body to the grounde, earth to earth, asshes to asshes, dust to dust, in sure and certayne hope of resurrection to eternal lyfe, through our Lord Jesus Christe, who shal chaunge our vile body, that it may be lyke to his glorious body, according to the mightie woorkyng, whereby he is able to subdue al thynges to hym selfe.

Then shalbe sayde, or song.

I heard a voyce from heauen, saying vnto me, Wryte from hencefoorth, Blessed are the dead whiche dye in the Lord: Euen so sayth the spirite, that they rest from theyr labours.

Then shal folowe this Lesson, taken out of the. xv. Chapter to the Corinthians, the first Epistle.

CHriste is rysen from the dead, and become the first fruites of them that slept. For by a man came death, and by a man came the resurrection of the dead. For as by Adam all dye : Euen so by Christ shal al be made alyue, but euery man in his owne order. The fyrste is Christe, then they that are Christes at his commyng. Then cometh the ende, when he hath deliuered vp the kyngdome to God the father, when he hath put downe all rule, and all aucthoritie, and power: For he must raigne till he haue put all his enimies vnder his feete. The laste enimie that shalbe destroyed, is death. For he hath put all thynges vnder his feete. But when he sayth, all thynges all put vnder hym : it is manifest that he is excepted,

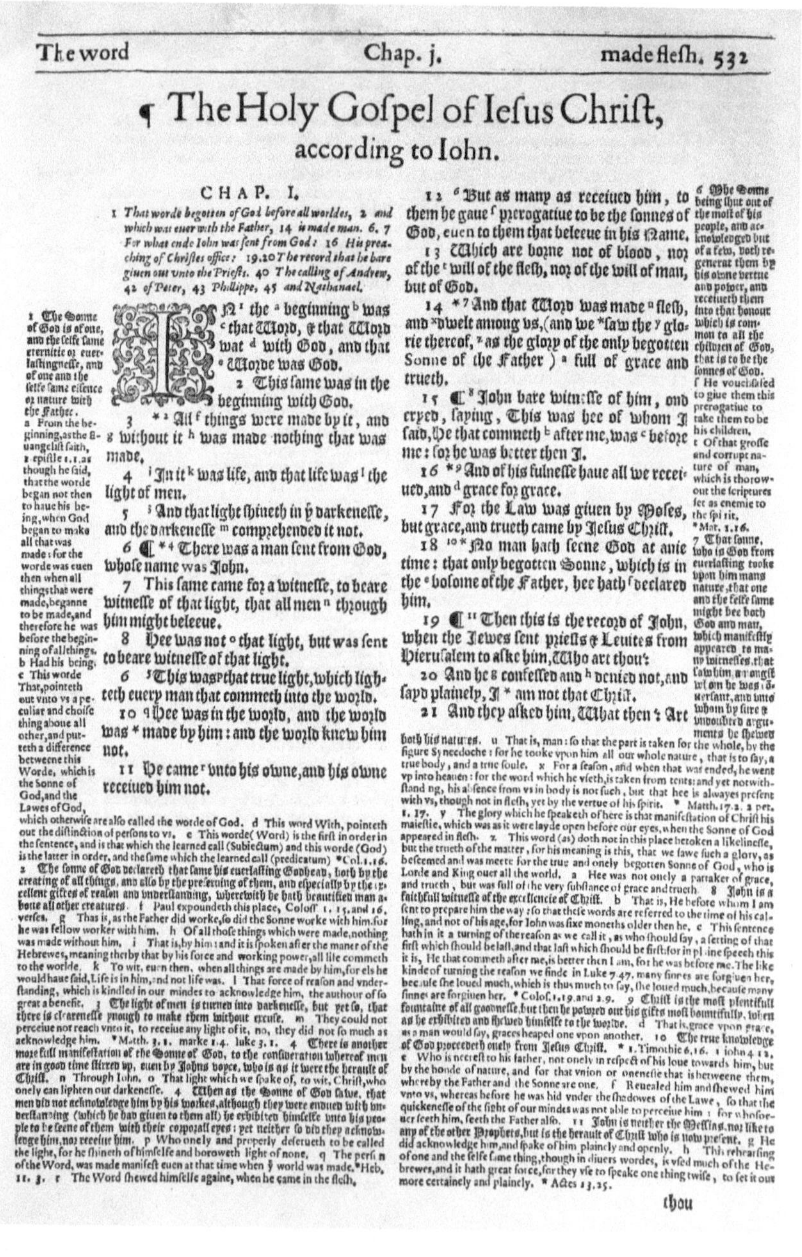

The word Chap. j. made fleſh. 532

¶ The Holy Goſpel of Ieſus Chriſt, according to Iohn.

CHAP. I.

1 That worde begotten of God before all worldes, 2 and which was euer with the Father, 14 is made man. 6. 7 For what ende Iohn was ſent from God: 16 His preaching of Chriſtes office: 19. 20 The record that he bare giuen out vnto the Prieſts. 40 The calling of Andrew, 42 of Peter, 43 Phillippe, 45 and Nathanael.

1 The Sonne of God is of one, and the ſelfe ſame eternitie or euerlaſtingneſſe, and of one and the ſelfe ſame eſſence or nature with the Father. a From the beginning, as the Euangeliſt ſaith, 1 epiſtle 1. 1. as though he ſaid, that the worde began not then to haue his being, when God began to make all that was made: for the worde was euen then when all things that were made, beganne to be made, and therefore he was before the beginning of all things. b Had his being. c This worde That, pointeth out vnto vs a peculiar and choiſe thing aboue all other, and putteth a difference betweene this Worde, which is the Sonne of God, and the Lawes of God,

IN[1] the [a] beginning [b] was
[c] that Word, & that Word
was [d] with God, and that
[e] Worde was God.
2 This ſame was in the
beginning with God.
3 *[2] All [f] things were made by it, and
[g] without it [h] was made nothing that was
made.
4 [i] In it [k] was life, and that life was [l] the
light of men.
5 [3] And that light ſhineth in ẏ darkeneſſe,
and the darkeneſſe [m] comprehended it not.
6 ¶ *[4] There was a man ſent from God,
whoſe name was John.
7 This ſame came for a witneſſe, to beare
witneſſe of that light, that all men [n] through
him might beleeue.
8 Hee was not [o] that light, but was ſent
to beare witneſſe of that light.
9 [5] This was [p] that true light, which lighteth
euery man that commeth into the world.
10 [q] Hee was in the world, and the world
was * made by him: and the world knew him
not.
11 He came [r] vnto his owne, and his owne
receiued him not.
12 [6] But as many as receiued him, to
them he gaue [ſ] prerogatiue to be the ſonnes of
God, euen to them that beleeue in his Name.
13 Which are borne not of blood, nor
of the [t] will of the fleſh, nor of the will of man,
but of God.
14 *[7] And that Word was made [u] fleſh,
and [x] dwelt among vs, (and we *ſaw the [y] glorie
thereof, [z] as the glory of the only begotten
Sonne of the Father) [a] full of grace and
trueth.
15 ¶ [8] John bare witneſſe of him, and
cryed, ſaying, This was hee of whom I
ſaid, He that commeth [b] after me, was [c] before
me: for he was better then I.
16 *[9] And of his fulneſſe haue all we receiued,
and [d] grace for grace.
17 For the Law was giuen by Moſes,
but grace, and trueth came by Jeſus Chriſt.
18 [10] * No man hath ſeene God at anie
time: that only begotten Sonne, which is in
the [e] boſome of the Father, hee hath [f] declared
him.
19 ¶ [11] Then this is the record of John,
when the Iewes ſent prieſts & Leuites from
Hieruſalem to aſke him, Who art thou?
20 And he [g] confeſſed and [h] denied not, and
ſayd plainely, I * am not that Chriſt.
21 And they aſked him, What then? Art

6 The Sonne being ſhut out of the moſt of his people, and acknowledged but of a few, doth regenerat them by his owne vertue and power, and receiueth them into that honour which is common to all the children of God, that is to be the ſonnes of God. ſ He vouchſafed to giue them this prerogatiue to take them to be his children. t Of that groſſe and corrupt nature of man, which is thorowout the ſcriptures ſet as enemie to the ſpirit. *Mat. 1. 16. 7 That ſonne, who is God from euerlaſting tooke vpon him mans nature, that one and the ſelfe ſame might bee both God and man, which manifeſtly appeared to many witneſſes, that ſaw him, amongſt whom he was conuerſant, and vnto whom by ſure & vndoubted arguments he ſhewed

which otherwiſe are alſo called the worde of God. d This word With, pointeth out the diſtinction of perſons to vs. e This worde (Word) is the firſt in order in the ſentence, and is that which the learned call (Subiectum) and this worde (God) is the latter in order, and the ſame which the learned call (predicatum) *Col. 1. 16. 2 The ſonne of God declareth that ſame his euerlaſting Godhead, both by the creating of all things, and alſo by the preſeruing of them, and eſpecially by the excellent giftes of reaſon and vnderſtanding, wherewith he hath beautified man aboue all other creatures. f Paul expoundeth this place, Coloſſ. 1. 15. and 16. verſes. g That is, as the Father did worke, ſo did the Sonne worke with him, for he was fellow worker with him. h Of all thoſe things which were made, nothing was made without him. i That is, by him: and it is ſpoken after the maner of the Hebrewes, meaning therby that by his force and working power, all life commeth to the worlde. k To wit, euen then, when all things are made by him, for els he would haue ſaid, Life is in him, and not life was. l That force of reaſon and vnderſtanding, which is kindled in our mindes to acknowledge him, the authour of ſo great a benefit. 3 The light of men is turned into darkeneſſe, but yet ſo, that there is cleareneſſe ynough to make them without excuſe. m They could not perceiue nor reach vnto it, to receiue any light of it, no, they did not ſo much as acknowledge him. *Matth. 3. 1. marke 1. 4. luke 3. 1. 4 There is another more full manifeſtation of the Sonne of God, to the conſideration whereof men are in good time ſtirred vp, euen by Johns voyce, who is as it were the herault of Chriſt. n Through Iohn. o That light which we ſpake of, to wit, Chriſt, who onely can lighten our darkeneſſe. 4 When as the Sonne of God ſawe, that men did not acknowledge him by his workes, although they were endued with vnderſtanding (which he had giuen to them all) he exhibited himſelfe vnto his people to be ſeene of them with their corporall eyes: yet neither ſo did they acknowledge him, nor receiue him. p Who onely and properly deſerueth to be called the light, for he ſhineth of himſelfe and boroweth light of none. q The perſon of the Word, was made manifeſt euen at that time when ẏ world was made. *Heb. 11. 3. r The Word ſhewed himſelfe againe, when he came in the fleſh.

both his natures. u That is, man: ſo that the part is taken for the whole, by the figure Synecdoche: for he tooke vpon him all our whole nature, that is to ſay, a true body, and a true ſoule. x For a ſeaſon, and when that was ended, he went vp into heauen: for the word which he vſeth, is taken from tents: and yet notwithſtanding, his abſence from vs in body is not ſuch, but that hee is alwayes preſent with vs, though not in fleſh, yet by the vertue of his ſpirit. *Matth. 17. 2. 2 pet. 1. 17. y The glory which he ſpeaketh of here is that manifeſtation of Chriſt his maieſtie, which was as it were layde open before our eyes, when the Sonne of God appeared in fleſh. z This word (as) doth not in this place betoken a likelineſſe, but the trueth of the matter, for his meaning is this, that we ſawe ſuch a glory, as beſeemed and was meete for the true and onely begotten Sonne of God, who is Lorde and King ouer all the world. a Hee was not onely a partaker of grace, and trueth, but was full of the very ſubſtance of grace and trueth. 8 John is a faithfull witneſſe of the excellencie of Chriſt. b That is, He before whom I am ſent to prepare him the way: ſo that theſe words are referred to the time of his calling, and not of his age, for Iohn was ſixe moneths older then he. c This ſentence hath in it a turning of the reaſon as we call it, as who ſhould ſay, a ſetting of that firſt which ſhould be laſt, and that laſt which ſhould be firſt: for in plaine ſpeech this it is, He that commeth after me, is better then I am, for he was before me. The like kinde of turning the reaſon we finde in Luke 7. 47. many ſinnes are forgiuen her, becauſe ſhe loued much, which is thus much to ſay, ſhe loued much, becauſe many ſinnes are forgiuen her. *Coloſ. 1. 19. and 2. 9. 9 Chriſt is the moſt plentifull fountaine of all goodneſſe, but then he powred out his giftes moſt bountifully, when as he exhibited and ſhewed himſelfe to the worlde. d That is, grace vpon grace, as a man would ſay, graces heaped one vpon another. 10 The true knowledge of God proceedeth onely from Jeſus Chriſt. *1. Timothie 6. 16. 1 iohn 4. 12. e Who is neereſt to his father, not onely in reſpect of his loue towards him, but by the bonde of nature, and for that vnion or oneneſſe that is betweene them, whereby the Father and the Sonne are one. f Reuealed him and ſhewed him vnto vs, whereas before he was hid vnder the ſhadowes of the Lawe, ſo that the quickeneſſe of the ſight of our mindes was not able to perceiue him: for whoſoeuer ſeeth him, ſeeth the Father alſo. 11 John is neither the Meſſias, nor like to any of the other Prophets, but is the herault of Chriſt who is now preſent. g He did acknowledge him, and ſpake of him plainely and openly. h This rehearſing of one and the ſelfe ſame thing, though in diuers wordes, is vſed much of the Hebrewes, and it hath great force, for they vſe to ſpeake one thing twiſe, to ſet it out more certainely and plainely. *Actes 13. 25.

thou

FIGURE 5.3. Title page of *The Holy Gospel of Iesus Christ according to Iohn*. From *The Bible, that is, the Holy Scriptures contained in the Old and New Testament*. Printed by Robert Barker, 1602. Reproduced with the permission of Azusa Pacific University.

Just like "The Heartie Confession's" ballad confession, the Prayer Book confessions come into performance through a theatrical scene where the glosses, liturgical directions, and ornamentation of the physical text are acted out in symbolic bodily movements, audience responses, and song. Godly ballads invoke the theatrical habits of performed religion by imitating the composite nature of these other texts' physical and performed appearances, but they relocate these habits to the street, alehouse, and home. Each of these venues has its own ritual of sorts, and godly ballads reflect the processes of religious entertainment in such venues. The section breaks and titles in "The Heartie Confession" insinuate pauses in physical action. Its front matter reflects the *in situ* activity of taking the ballad in hand, or perhaps of dining, drinking, praying, or even of hearing a ballad's godly message repeated at home. Ballads like this one are intertheatrical; they conjure the felt authority of other performance types and invoke the attitudes and habits of audience perception established at other performance venues.

Through these citational and imitational characteristics, ballads are able to enact performatively their themes in the moment of their performance. A 1642 ballad entitled "A Song of Syon of the Beauty of Bethell" employs similar copious marginalia and ornamentation, and its visual and theatrical citational strategies fulfill, in a sense, its godly themes (figure 5.4).

Here the ballad is surrounded by a title and spiritualized authorial attribution above the stanzas: "By a CITIZEN of SYON." It also includes the printer's advertisement and Bible verses below, biblical glosses in the margins, and rectangular line boxes and ornamentation dividing the page into sections. This style of design was especially popular among ballads printed in the 1630s and 1640s and, as I have suggested, aesthetically harkens to the godly ballads of previous generations.[42] The design visually encloses the printed verses of the song. We might interpret this nostalgic style as a form of aesthetic self-authorization, especially given that only a few years later the production and sale of ballads would be severely constrained by authorities.[43] It is also noteworthy that this ballad was printed just after Parliament issued the Grand Remonstrance, which criticizes certain ecclesiastical influences in government and, among other things, called for the

FIGURE 5.4. Ballad, "A Song of Syon of the Beauty of Bethell," 1642. Reproduced with the permission of the Huntington Library, Miscellaneous 180158.

controversial removal of bishops from Parliament. Perhaps this context relates to the song's references to the "grave *Porters*" who guard the spiritual house from "Dogs," "Wolves," and "noysom beasts." In this vein, the ballads' demand that ecclesial authorities answer to "*Christ* as only *King*" should be taken with some amount of political invective in addition to spiritual instruction.

Lyrically, the song is an exhortation to flee worldly wealth in favor of spiritual comfort, presented as a description of the kind of charity that exists in the true church. It is fitting that this motif was popular among early modern godly ballads, given that their audiences were of mixed economic status. The poor heard a song about hope and solidarity while the rich heard a warning that implied the possibility of sharing in this same solidarity through acts of charity. The first three verses read:

> One *ᵃthing beleevers hearts* are fixt upon,
>   that thing of *God* they are to *seeke* alone;
> And *seeking seeke they must* till they obtaine,
> ᵇ preferring it before all earthly gaine.
>
> ᶜ That precious thing is, *that they may be blest*,
>   to sit in * *Gods own House, and here to rest*,
> Even all their daies, *in* glory to abide,
> whatever outward want they have beside.
>
> ᵈ *That they may view the beauty of the Lord*,
>   and in his worship ever more accord:
> ᵉ Gods glory is the thing they doe desire,
>   and in his Temple *daily to enquire*.⁴⁴

The initial verses establish an inner-outer distinction between those who seek "*earthly gaine*" and those who "*rest*" "*here*" within "*Gods own House.*" In many ways, this notion could be said to be the theme of a great deal of the most widely circulated religious literature of the late sixteenth and seventeenth centuries. We hear the admonition against preferring worldly gain espoused in sermons, chapbooks, and religious tracts—perhaps even appearing in godly print more often than not. Therefore, to understand this religious message in ballads means attending to those theatrical idioms that position the genre within the context of godly performance and print and also that set this theme apart.

In this manner, the inner-outer distinction in the ballad's lyrics as well as its design emphasizes a common moral message of religious print in ways that stand out specifically in ballad performance. If, as in "The Heartie Confession of a Christian," this ballad is intended as a type of popular "somme" or prescription of piety, then readers, to receive its message and identify with Syon, must move through the ballad's various titles, glosses, epigraphia, and ornaments. When the ballad is read—which would have been the case during most performances of it, by the singer or by auditors, public or private—singers and audience members must weave in and out of italics, between border lines, and with digressions through superscript letters. Entering into the "Temple" of salvation becomes a matter of part-icipating—of piecing together the whole godly broadside in its many visible parts. Thus singing a godly ballad with this style of print design implies a kind of performative literacy, akin to the sermon-going literacy prevalent in Donne's sermons. Isolating the words of the song alone is simple enough, but singers also accepted the responsibility of serving as the mouthpiece for the full referential weight held in its citations, conventional details, and marginal material.

Through the processes of their making and dissemination, ballads possess an "agentized allure" that I argue simultaneously takes the form of a textual tradition and countless improvised communities of auditors and spectators.[45] In short, godly ballads imitate intertheatrical religious forms, and they also imitate themselves, orienting "us towards performance as an autopoietic system directed as much towards a making-possible of future performances as towards a history of given ones."[46] In one way, the idiomatic conventions of the broadside and song—routine allusions, dialogue, ornament, marginalia—employ a citational strategy that seeks to acquire legitimacy as a religious form by imitating and referencing official forms of prayer, scripture reading, liturgy, and conventions of religious print. Yet at the same time, these idiomatic conventions themselves become an aspect of religious expression; that is, conventionality itself acquires the status of a religious habit that audiences come to associate with ballads. And this happens performatively, in the repetition of godly ballads in public and private spaces.

It is worth acknowledging that it may not be intuitive to think of a convention or theatrical habit as a conscious vehicle for belief in the transcendent. Yet conventionality should be understood, as it has been by those who have advanced J. L. Austin's description of ordinary or felicitous performative speech, less as a set of fixed rules and more as a pattern that artificially settles in a performance but that is also held in check by a given conventional usage's effects in other, sometimes less overt, theatrical scenarios.[47] In other words, awareness of a religious truth claim emerges in performance culture in tandem with idiomatic and, indeed, theatrical articulations of it. Through repeated acts of *recognizing* a song as a godly ballad and, reciprocally, through the gradual formation of an identity that *can be recognized* as a godly ballad, religious ballads' imitative strategies become, in performance, a form of theatricality inherent to the ballad genre. Paradoxically, it is through imitation that godly ballads claim a kind of autonomy.

To understand the circularity of this description, it is important to think of ballads comparatively, as part of a larger performance culture where theatricality and religion recurrently influence one another as performative phenomena. Ballads are on a spectrum of theatrical practice that includes commercial plays, jigs, town festival performances such as cycle plays, state and religious ceremonies, and sermons. Just as ceremony, sacrament, and other forms of religious mediation serve as models for these performance types to incorporate theatrical phenomena into their representations of religious and moral instruction, dramatic character, and dramatic action, so do godly ballads ground their religious presence in their theatrical conditions. Ballads are particularly forthright about the human strategy behind their means of production, economics, and imitation of other cultural forms, and this imitative strategy itself becomes a characteristic of ballad religion.

"A Song of Syon" was, of course, written for and disseminated through performance, and it is worth remembering that only the text in the middle of this broadside—not including the superscripts—was heard by audiences, unless balladeers read some marginal notes and epigraphs for the sake of advertising the visual appeal of the ballad sheet. Furthermore, the text as sung in performance spaces was surrounded by the various marginalia of particular environments. Where the printed ballad is hedged in by biblical citations and by authorizing glosses, the sung ballad is hedged in by people and by a sensory atmosphere often conducive to performance and sales. Visually and tangibly, audience members who purchase or hold the ballad as it is being performed lengthen its theatrical reach much as a sermon auditor might hold a note tablet. We can imagine the ballad hawker holding the broadside as a kind of prop. Aurally, the ballad sonically enters a space, is enclosed by its acoustic reach and echo barriers, and combines with local ambient noises collected together to create a distinctive ballad tone. Where the biblical glosses reveal the ballad to be overtly imitative of other religious literary forms—sermons, chapbooks, the Prayer Book, the Bible—in performance this imitation survives only in part. When read, "A Song of Syon" shapes readers' attitudes toward its central text, but when sung, its religious identity appears in a mixed atmosphere and undergoes a perceptual dispersion rather than a centering. Once the song reaches the ears of its auditors, it is reorganized by its audible qualities, especially those that are most recognizable, such as its familiar phrases, tune, and allusions. It becomes bordered by a culture that expects conventionality and by an audience that is familiar with its idioms. Even the authorial attribution to "a CITIZEN of SYON" suggests its essentially imitative status: there is no apparent center to a godly ballad in performance outside of its recognition in the perceptions and minds of its audience—its "citizens."[48]

As in other performance genres, the performative effect of early modern ballads depends on the presence of an audience. Many godly ballads speak from a first-person perspective that imaginatively implies a small audience or even an individual interlocutor—or a composite interlocutor. Even in songs that do not involve dialogue, there is often an implicit audience disposition of dialogue, as it were, contained in the theatrical conditions of exchange, print, imitation, and repetition in customers' homes. In fact, the audience's function as the "recognizer" of the genre is especially crucial to ballads. A seventeenth-century ballad entitled "The Dying Tears of a Penitent Sinner," published as early as the 1620s but in frequent print through the 1670s, is particularly revealing of its dependence on such audience recognition (figure 5.5).[49]

Deathbed ballads were one of the most common types of religious ballads in the seventeenth century. This particular woodcut from the late 1670s was used frequently for this narrative situation—depicting an oversized person speaking to a crowd of seven gathered around his bed, sometimes expounding on the book lying on his lap. The speaker appears less ill than energetic and excited to teach his audience. Like many seventeenth-century ballads, this one is divided into two parts: the left side of the sheet and "The second part, to the same Tune" on the right.[50] As a deathbed ballad, "The Dying Tears of a Penitent Sinner" serves two didactic purposes. It offers advice about

FIGURE 5.5. Woodcut from ballad, "The Dying Tears of a Penitent Sinner," 1678–80. Reproduced with the permission of the British Library, Roxburghe 2.113.

what is most important in life, and it serves as an example of (hopefully) dying well.

However, in terms of moral or theological instruction, the first part of the ballad is quite sparse, really only offering one-and-a-half stanzas that can be described as instructive:

> Thy promise is, good Lord, that when
>   a sinner doth intend
> Quite to forsake his wicked life,
>   wherein he doth offend.
>
> Thou wilt forgive, and pardon grant,
>   for his offences all . . .

As is often the case, the second part of the ballad transitions to a more didactic mode. Though still relatively sparse, the speaker offers several popular expressions of soteriology in the following vein:

> He did indure the punishments
>   which unto us was due:
> Because we should shake off our sins,
>   and learn to live a new.

The second part then provides some lines mentioning details of the Crucifixion narrative—the scourging, the thieves, and the spearing of Jesus's side.

Still, in a godly ballad of twenty-five verses, it is important to ask what the vast majority of verses are saying if they are not instructing. In this case, most of the ballad's content is in the form of general petitions and cries, reflections on these petitions, and articulations of the speaker's position relative to his audience. In short, the predominant effect of the ballad is to frame an audience act of recognition—by creating a speaker perspective and performance situation, harkening the audience, invoking the mode of prayer, and providing clues that signify a religious deathbed ballad. The ballad is full of nondidactic expressions of self-identity and desire, proclaiming its utterly conventional nature through the same techniques it uses to address God. The effect is not instructive but orientational, establishing the relations between God, speaker, ballad singer, deathbed audience, and ballad audience.

To make the matter more complex, the identity of the audience alternates and is sometimes composite. This is another distinctive of godly ballads. Much of the time, the speaker directs his cries toward God, as in the following excerpts:

> O Gracious God, O Father dear,
> > in mercy look on me . . .
>
> To thee; O Lord, I make my moan,
> > to thee I call and cry . . .
>
> And thou O Lord, wilt hear my voice,
> > when on thee I do call.
>
> O Heavenly God, O Father sweet,
> > In mercy look on me . . .

In addition, interspersed throughout are cries directed toward the dying penitent's immediate audience surrounding his deathbed:

> Draw near kind friends and neighbours all,
> > which now are come to see;
> And to bear witness of my death,
> > give ear a while to me . . .
>
> If we consider of his pains,
> > and how his time he spent:
> It well may make our stony heart,
> > to soften and relent.
>
> And now dear Wife and Children all,
> > I bid you all adieu . . .

In performance, the deathbed audience combines with the audience surrounding the balladeer. The result is an intensified first-person voice—intensified not only in language but also in situation, sound, and the immediacy of the crowd surrounding the balladeer. Smith has elaborated on the "residual" memory implied by early modern ballads' reliance on the conventions of their own tradition, arguing that ballads incite memories of "pastness" and feelings of "passion" in the same moment: "With respect to the present they serve as reference points to the past, as gestures towards experiences that the audience, like the protagonist, is presumed already to have had."[51] The intimacy created by a shared experience of memory has everything to do with the ways that godly ballads enact religion.

Like King Henry's ceremony making, godly ballads create a hypothetical memory that demands to be fulfilled, and they call on the audience to fulfill it now. The conflation of speaker and balladeer, as well as narrative addressee and performance audience, is thus integral to ballad religion because it is the rapport built between the balladeer and his audience that allows for the process of recognizing the conventions that constitute a ballad's godliness. In fact, many of the most recognizable ballad lyrical conventions are expressions whose main purpose is to orient the audience toward the ballad singer, as when the speaker in "The Dying Tears" calls out, "Draw near kind friends and neighbours all." This initial performative move is typical: the audience's most direct act of religion in godly ballads coincides with their first response to the theatrical setting, their first act of recognizing a theatrical performance. In this call for audience attention, the speaker engages audiences in recognizing a speech act that is familiar and, thus, in adopting a listener position that in turn projects familiarity onto the performance.

These sorts of supplicatory speech conventions add a multistable dimension to the speaker's identity. There is a kind of flashing between the actor and the character, together co-present in the "exhibition of a specific, individual physicality." Fischer-Lichte comments on the actor-character crossover: "A spectator first perceives a certain movement of an actor in its specific energy, intensity, thrust, direction, and tempo, and then suddenly understands it as a symbolic appeal to or threat of the character."⁵² This is the case, she suggests, especially in performances and scenes that resist audience absorption and that integrate the circumstances of the audience's audition and visuality into the spectacle. I have been arguing that many of the early modern performing arts function this way. In ballads, in particular, not only does the physical presence of the actor's body create a continuity with his symbolic presence as a character and thus resist absorption, but the musicality of the actor's song connects the actor to the character. The transition between the second and third lines of the ballad—"Draw near kind friends and neighbours all, / which now are come to see; / And to bear witness of my death"—has a heightened sense of the spectacular and the *coup de théâtre* of the ballad situation. With the words "my death," auditors discern that it is a deathbed ballad and interpret everything that follows in that light. They know that the singer standing or even dancing before them is fictionally posthumous and yet somehow is also imagined as if he were lying in bed. Moreover, the repetitiveness of the song's tune ("The Faithful friend") over twenty-five verses operates as a bridge between the corporeal and the symbolic. Like the actor's body, the song's tune, the singer's tone, and possibly its accompanying instrumentation function—and continue to function—as an "appeal" to the audience.

The result is that the music shows the audience its own social and spiritual condition and its foundational role in bringing the ballad's representation into the present space. And in ballads, where much more is at stake than dramatic illusion, the music sounds out as an appeal not only to the narrative situation but to the poverty of the hawker, to his reputation as a singer, and, in the performance of a godly ballad like this one, to the spiritual well-being of the audience community at hand.

Yet simply reading the ballad might give the false impression that the author is interested merely in catering to the crowd's expectations: auditors want the sensational experience of hearing a ballad, and its superficial godliness adds the feel-good factor of being morally acceptable, especially as compared to, say, crime and sex ballads. This characterization, as I have been arguing, is incomplete. It *is* the case that closing a deathbed ballad with "And now dear wife and Children all, / I bid you all adieu" is superficial insofar as it lacks authorial originality and even takes the tone of a play epilogue, just as the opening call to hearers appeals to the audience's necessary participation in the narrative and performance situations. Yet especially in godly ballads these aspects of conventionality and disenchantment extend rather than inhibit the emotion and applicability of the ballad's themes. For example, an early seventeenth-century religious ballad entitled "A Most Excellent Ditty, Called Collins Conceit" grounds its dramatic authority in the fact that there are ballads "of sundry sorts" bouncing around the city and purporting godliness.

> In my conceit if men would looke,
>   where sacred virtues dwell.
> And live according to Gods booke,
>   then all things should be well.[53]

The suggestion is that the ballad performance milieu is a sort of movement of cultural reform, one that is especially aware of its generic trends. And godly ballads make this awareness explicit.

By disclosing their own strategies of genre and theatricality, godly ballads create narrative situations that enact a performative *real presence*. The audience of "The Dying Tears," of course, knows that the speaker is not lying on his deathbed, but the combination of the ballad's forthright superficiality and the audience's decision to enter into the relatively intimate (though often public) performance space adds a popular ritual dimension to the performance. Many such godly ballads tie their religious messages to the means of their appearing. Hence, the presence of the speaker's sins and the audience's "stony heart" become more than fictional in the performance event. Moreover, although the appeal to "friends and neighbours all" may be a market gimmick to turn heads, it enacts the deathbed-Crucifixion parallel, compelling a kind of religious observation where the witnesses of Christ's death become the imagined predecessors to the ballad audience at hand. Even the select details used to represent the Crucifixion narrative—whip, thieves, spear—like the conspicuous details of Chester's *The Last Supper*—bread, cup, table—imbue the act of recognizing them with a greater moral weight, somewhat akin to Donne's sermon literacy. And this moral pathos increases through the combination of biblical narrative representation found throughout cheap print and the exposure of ballad theatricality inherent to the genre.

Pausing for Belief

Ballad religion is an activity of a performance community. The key to understanding religion in early modern ballads is realizing that they do not intend to offer theological nuance or even much in the way of religious instruction. As we have seen, most of the instruction that they do offer is already commonplace, and it is the theatrical and practical strategies that frame moral instruction that are more operative in performance. As two of godly ballads' most conspicuous instruments of performance, imitation and conventionality engage ballad audiences in acts of recognition and familiarity and thus constitute a pattern of performative behaviors of Protestant practice specific to the people who performed, sold, heard, bought, and redistributed godly ballads.

I will now look more closely at this act of recognizing the parts of godly ballads: the perceptual and psychological process of attributing wholeness to media and the different ways that godly ballads metatheatrically repurpose this process in performance. As I have argued, godly ballads interact with the broader performance culture and are subject to the interpretation of groups of people rather than to individuals only. I want to proffer one other major aspect of religion in ballad performance and in the process of ballad recognition: the activity—or nonactivity—of pause.

By way of illustration, imagine a spinster, or someone of any common occupation, walking through a market, on her way to hear a sermon, or perhaps passing by the theaters in London's Bankside. Were she to come upon a ballad performance in public, it would have been an unconstrained occasion. Its ambient environment likely would have been loud and unfocused, enclosed perhaps by a monger's stall on one side, a crowd on the other, and whatever structural barriers could be used for sound amplification. The volume and tone of the speaker's voice would have varied in response to swells in ambient noise. Additionally, the ballad's audience would have been amorphous. People such as the spinster might have entered the performance area mid-ballad to listen and might have also departed mid-ballad. This would make the conventionality and repetitiveness of ballad verses useful, as hawkers would have aimed to convince passersby to stop and pause for just a few moments, hopefully long enough to appeal to their tastes. Thus, in the broader early modern culture of performance, where new plays were commissioned and performed weekly, where sermons were delivered daily, and where animal fights and baitings consistently drew crowds, godly ballads provided a unique, if unexpected, experience of pause and rest—a kind of improvised centering of attention in close quarters. As paradoxical as it may sound given the prolific production of early modern ballads and also given their reputation among religiously motivated detractors, this situational pause is at the heart of the religious experience they created.

The notion that godly ballads incited an experience of pause through their performances does not, in fact, conflict with their performative calls to urgent moral action. A consistent characteristic of ballad religion is the rhetorical warning directed at listeners and readers. It is common to hear a balladeer shout phrases like "Awake!" or "Awake, sinners!" several times in a ballad. This is the case, for example, in the late seventeenth-century "Great Brittains Arlarm to Drowsie Sinners in Destress" (figure 5.6), where the opening lines adopt the voice of a street evangelist or a prophetic pamphlet:

> Rouse up dull Sinners all with one accord,
> With prayers & tears now call upon the Lord,
> Security hath lulld us fast asleep,
> When as we have most cause to mourn and weep.[54]

This is a typical opening for godly ballads with prophetic messages, as is its tune, "Aim Not Too High," also known as "Fortune my Foe." Prophecy ballads tend to include an amount of topical allusion to urban-specific vices and to recent national events that some took as omens, such as earthquakes and fires. In this broadside, local vices are illustrated by a prominent woodcut of a steeple-less St. Paul's Cathedral, burned in 1666, prior to this ballad's publication; at the time it would have symbolized the tension between decrepit religion amid disaster and the need for united faith.

This combination of imagery specifically invokes the theatrical identity of sermon-going and shares remarkable affinities with early modern art-of-hearing treatises. The ballad author's and printer's use of St. Paul's Cathedral in a prophecy ballad mirrors the connections Donne draws between rightly interpreting the prophetic signs of the times and profitably bracketing the idiomatic interference of a cathedral sermon-going experience. Such emphases on apocalyptic events and on death have prompted Margaret Spufford to say that popular religious print tended to be negative and anxiety inspiring.[55]

FIGURE 5.6. Ballad woodcut, "Great Brittains Arlarm to Drowsie Sinners in Destress," 1672–96. Reproduced with the permission of the British Library, Roxburghe 2.202–3.

Yet despite the intention to energetically rouse its audiences to action and awareness, godly ballads often do so through an imperative to stop moving and to listen. As in "Great Brittains Arlarm," many prophecy ballads direct their charges specifically toward various social and familial relationships—parents and children, rich and poor, lender and borrower—in an attempt to shake people out of ungodly habits in everyday life. With respect to the event of their performance, godly ballads and particularly prophecy ballads encourage audiences to participate by transforming street performance into an occasion for recognizing one's neighbors and for reflecting on the pace of their day-to-day activities. This follows from the several ballads I examined that accuse audiences of thoughtlessly going through their daily work and recreation without pausing for reflection. Even the poor who cannot afford to gamble or to stroll into church fashionably dressed are exhorted to slow the fast pace of their worrying and to take comfort in God's spiritual provision.

Reinforcing this reflection, the last two verses of "Great Brittains Arlarm" prompt a final moment of corporate pause:

Once more, I say, O sinners now awake,
And all your hanious sins in time forsake:
Who knows but that the Lord will hear our prayer:
And shew us mercy for unfeigned years.

And let each one that reads what here is pend,
Strive night and day their lives for to amend:
That God in mercy all our Souls may save,
When as we fall into the silent Grave.

Godly ballad authors do not perceive their potential readers and auditors to be generally static and restful in life. On the contrary, as we see here, they imagine their songs as exceptional opportunities for audiences to stop and reflect. These are, in fact, spiritual events in the same sense that other performance genres such as ceremonies, festival plays, and sermons are spiritual events; they create a space and time in which audiences can practice faith—with emphasis on the artificiality of the opportunity and the collective consent to its performative efforts. The ballad points to the repentance that will happen later, "in time"; to the future event in which "the Lord will hear our prayer" and the "mercy" he will "shew us . . . for unfeigned years"; and finally to the salvation received "as we fall into the silent Grave." Such intertemporality transforms its audience's awareness of time into a motivation for future repentance.

In this respect ballads functioned like the liturgy: to focus attention and to make congregants aware of their individuality amid their group collectivity. Ballads make audiences *reflective*, in multiple senses of the word, of the immediacy of belief within the immanent experience of the improvised environment. In these two stanzas the speaker intends his ballad to serve as a kind of communal prayer, with its activities of listening, reflecting, and repenting. The speaker (and author) also imagines the ballad as an object "pend" (penned), printed, and read by individual audience members. Even as merely imagined, activities of hearing and reading require that audiences pause and think about the ballad and identify it as a coherent object or statement that prompts response.

There is something physically intrinsic to the pause of hearing a ballad performed that prompts activities of recognition, community affiliation, and the promotion of virtues like temperance. This may be surprising, since ballad performances were by no means sedate events. They were often conducted amid a plethora of city noises—such as other forms of music, hawkers' cries, animals, crowds, and the sounds of outdoor labor. In fact, antiballad polemicists argued that ballads actually added to these noises rather than occasioning quietness. Writers alleged that godly ballads, in particular, dragged religion through the uncontrolled mania of popular media and its commotion. As in art-of-hearing treatises, this complaint highlights the significant nuance of ballads' emphases on focused audience attention, since becoming an audience member of a ballad performance means fighting off distractions. We have seen how the perceptual static and marginalia of the performance environment are even reflected in godly ballads' physical designs. Battling, managing, and repurposing the perceptual and psychological noise of a performance event is a key aspect of the early modern performing arts broadly, and especially insofar as audiences look to these events for religious instruction or practice.

A seventeenth-century ballad called "The Distressed Pilgrim" demonstrates how the audience's simple activity of stopping to hear a ballad creates a space for belief. "The Distressed Pilgrim" plays up the conflation of speaker and singer that occurs in many ballads. He introduces himself as "a Pilgrim poor and bare" who was once rich and generous to his friends and family but is now "exceeding poor."[56] His complaint is that those who were once closest to him now "will not so much as turn aside" to help him but "rather seek to scoff and scorn, / and jeer my Poverty." In addition to the character's invective, this is a potentially alienating public acknowledgement of the economic conditions that have forced the monger into such a stereotypically transient trade. The pilgrim's expressed reason for singing this song is to ask for advice: "Now in the midst of all my Woes, / what shall I do or say?" The ballad audience is challenged with self-identifying as either a good neighbor or a bad neighbor.

> As I do wander up and down
>   in sorrow, I am crost;
> From Place to Place, from Town to Town,
>   My Substance is all lost:
> But yet I think within my self,
>   As I shall tell to ye,
> Though God hath taken all my Wealth,
>   Yet patience works for me.

At this point in the performance, a third speaker entity emerges. Between the actual ballad singer and the distressed pilgrim enters a semi-fictitious traveling ballad monger, a stereotype of the ballad hawker that audiences have come to expect, an aggregate of the conventional speaker voice and the social reputation of balladeers. It is important to remember that the ballad singer in a given performance could just as easily be a tavern patron, a stage player, or any other person who purchased the ballad. Still, even an individual singing this ballad among friends at home would reflect the persona of a stereotypical balladeer in a social and economic situation rooted in the cultural imagination of popular performance—somebody in poverty, out of fortune, and yet generous in his advice. In essence, the speaker identity is created by a singular performance situation among a culture of generically similar performances. And even when the ballad is sung in an alehouse or at Paul's Walk, audiences become complicit in channeling the ethic of neighborliness that is characteristic of the moral ballad tradition and performance idiom.

Printed as early as 1666, the year of the Fire of London and the end of a serious epidemic of bubonic plague, audiences at early performances of "The Distressed Pilgrim" might also see a victim of civic catastrophe—or even a kind of universalized poor worker, representing those who suffered the most from citywide disaster. The last line of the quoted verse repeats what amounts to a one-line burden that changes somewhat throughout the ballad. In slightly different forms, it reads: "Yet patience works for me," or "Let patience work for me," or "For a patient man Ile be." Patience is the primary recurring attribute, expressing in the form of a Christian virtue the audience's physical and psychological activity of pause, their attention to the speaker. The performative speaker-character has been wandering in sorrow and has landed here, in this city, and at this particular performance place. The transient speaker addresses the audience members as transients in their own urban lives; he suggests that although audience members may be at home, they are spiritually homeless. Both parties stop in order to learn and to practice patience together as "co-subjects" of the "common situation" of performance, triggered when the speaker asks the audience, "What shall I do or say?"[57] The audience steps into the performance and theoretically steps out of the society that has impoverished the ballad speaker, while the speaker steps out of his wandering vagrancy and addresses the audience with presumed introspection—"But yet I think within my self." And the two meet together in the performance to create a moral and religious experience that is economically empathetic and momentarily reflective, where godly virtue meets social need. The ballad calls this moment "patience."

Audiences affirm the godly ballad virtue of patience through spectatorship and participation. We might be reminded here of the great contingency that Shakespeare places on patient listening in the final act of his late play *Pericles*, where so much is contingent on Pericles's attention and on Marina's reciprocal perseverance in conversation.

Simply by stopping and listening—in the market, at the tavern, outside a playhouse, or at St. Paul's Cathedral—the audience does what those who "will not so much as turn aside" fail to do. Of course, in one way, the ballad-monger wants to sell ballads, and this is very much a part of the religious community that the performance creates. And as part of the whole godly ballad, economic motives are integrated into the godly performance event. As in "The Distressed Pilgrim," economic activity joins other ballad virtues of temperance, charity, and patience. Audience attention thus transforms the ballad's many commonplace or cliché phrases—"a second Job to be"; "I tast ofs Holy Rod"; "Come Woe or Wealth, come Life or Death"; "He suffered on the Tree"—into a kind of mutual understanding between the poor and the patient. Rather than discrediting the ballad speaker as unoriginal or unprofessional, these commonplaces lend him an ethos that recurs in similar godly ballads. They contribute to his egalitarian authority to present religious advice in a familiar parlance. Oddly though, in this case, the ballad's last verse seems to suggest that the speaker has been on his deathbed and dying the entire time: "And now adieu unto the World," et cetera. However, this too is so patently conventional that it does not distract from the immediate community of balladeer and audience at hand. If anything, the line contributes to a feeling of closure and the end of wandering and busy distraction.

The pauses enacted by performances intend to slow normal life to the down-tempo pace of belief as it is described in ballad texts. Appropriately, then, one of the more frequently occurring religious themes in ballads is the admonition to beware the fleetingness of wealth and good fortune. In a direct way, the activities of pause that I have been describing combat unhealthy attitudes toward ephemerality. Ballad performances purport to take an experience of the familiar and to encircle it in a space of patience and pause. This slowing can be thought of as another kind of imitation or borrowing from more established church performance genres. Only, instead of using the daily structure of bell ringing, the long labor of biblical cycle plays, the repetition of liturgical choreography, and the longevity of sermons, ballads must use the comparatively short and simple material at hand—broadsides, crowds, commerce, drama, and, in particular, music—to create a unique rhythm of pause and reflection.

Recent scholarly insight into the role of music in ballad performances speaks to their intertheatricality. Marsh discusses how ballad tunes fit into the broader culture of early modern music. He distinguishes how audience experience ballad music by a kind of "shuffling": "This was a great age of cultural regurgitation, and in balladry the individual parts occur again and again in patterned but also constantly shifting alliances."[58] Audiences recognized ballad tunes and therefore must have carried previous thematic associations of other tunes into their new ballad settings. This shuffled effect is exacerbated by the recycling of language conventions and woodcuts. Woodcuts were often spliced together from previous ballads and other forms of print and repurposed in new combinations to illustrate new stories. Also, in contrast to the more controlled early modern practice of psalm singing, the musicality of ballads was intended to stimulate the senses and to enhance the mirthful environment. Godly virtues like temperance meant something specific in ballads, and such virtues were performed intrinsically in a ballad event by the singer and audience alike.

Hearing ballad music would have been a recognizably self-referential, mirthful, and "shuffled" experience. Godly ballads, in particular, use music as an apparatus for pause. For example, an early eighteenth-century ballad entitled "The Great Tribunal" metatheatrically criticizes its own musicality but does so with a greater aim in mind:

> With Cherubims of Angels compassed round,
> No murmuring, but a sweet harmonious Sound
> Of Hallelujahs to the King of Kings,
> Under the shadow of his blessed Wings.[59]

The suggestion is that angelic music is beautiful and that ballad tunes are mere "murmuring" in comparison. Nevertheless, heaven's music and ballad performances share the quality of being heard with godly intention, of constituting a community of listeners "compassed round."

The same phenomenon occurs in the performance of "A Wonderful Prophecy" from the 1680s. It tells the story of a saintly girl who dies, resurrects to offer prophecies representative of conventional godly ballad morality, dies once more, and finally serves as a nostalgic memorial to the same ballad community that she represents. It is a variation on the deathbed scenario. One especially noteworthy feature of this ballad is that, at the girl's final passing, the crowd surrounding her deathbed hears heavenly music:

> At her decease, an Harmony
>   Of Musick there was heard to sound,
> Which ravishd all the Standers by,
>   It did with Sweetness so abound.[60]

The fictional "Standers by" and the ballad crowd merge insofar as both exercise the patience of pausing to hear the prophecy of this saintly girl, respectively in story and in person. Moreover, mentioning miraculous music almost certainly incited recognition of the often not-so-perfect singing of the ballad performance, but it could also prompt a kind of pride in association, as if the music of godly ballads participated in a higher musical tradition by virtue of the fact that balladry perpetuated such sacred stories. Godly ballads create scenarios that represent their speakers, in their best moments, as exemplifying these forms of Christian humility and thereby transcending the popular and often unadorned conditions of their performances. In godly ballads in particular, music lends their poor, dying, and prophetic speakers a Lazarus-like appearance of holy destitution, at least rhetorically.

I am suggesting that music contributes to the formation of godly patience by extending the familiarity of ballad conventions and godly tropes, and also by setting the tone of a religious audience community, especially as godly ballads tended to reuse the same tunes. We might think of ballads as having environments that stand in counterdistinction to that of sermons at Paul's Cross. Whereas the outdoor sermon venue sought to disperse God's Word into its extensive space—full of busy-minded socialites hoping to be noticed, and only faintly reaching the ears of the poor standing far off—godly ballads sought to create a mutual and intimate experience of commerce, recognition, song, pause, and patience within a space that might be substituted with any other. Ballads served to pull together—rather than to fill and stretch—their diffuse public environments. Thus, more than in comparable performance types such as sermons, morality drama, psalm-singing, and dances, music in godly ballads harnesses the social circumstances of their performances to reflect the spiritual stakes of the social habits of their audiences. Godly ballad theatricality in this way not only reveals the human strategy behind performances—which is explicit—but also makes visible the practical social conditions that permit and inhibit different aims of human venture and interaction. Hence the determined work that ballads do to orient their speakers, singers, and audiences toward one another.

Godly ballads draw on performance culture to celebrate their own form of theatricality, and as with other early modern performance genres, the implications of this theatricality are heightened when the lyrical content is religious or when ballads are brought into religious contexts, such as antitheatrical polemics. One mid-sixteenth-century ballad by Thomas Brice, the Protestant hero of Queen Mary's reign, entitled "Against Filthy Writing and Such Delighting," does not hold back from confronting religious antiballad polemics that attack ballads' combination of mirth and religion:

We are no foes to Musicke wee, amis your man doth take us
so frendes to thinges corrupt and vile, you all shall neuer make us
If you denie them such to bee, I stand to proue it I[61]

Such confidence in defending religious practice is characteristic of godly ballads. Brice finds himself in a position of having to defend the status of religion in popular songs by condemning those songs that take the popular and vulgar too far. His strategy is in part *pro hominem*—"I stand to proue it I"—a performative move that mirrors the multistable speaker positions of many godly ballads.

Another broadside from the same decade in defense of popular religious music is "A Commendation of Musicke" by the famous sixteenth-century ballad author Nicholas Whight. Whight's argument is similar to Brice's in its defense of godly ballads for their balancing of mirth and restraint. The ballad defends the effects of popular music on the grounds of its natural provenance (as Cavendish also does), its scriptural precedents, and its poetic tradition. Wright even draws on Galenic medical thought to champion ballads' physiological benefits for hearers. Still, it is his final argument, he says, that encapsulates them all: music exhibits "concord." By concord he means an element that unifies and moderates the "good" of one's listening experience.[62] Ballad concord, distinct from other types, is a kind of intermediary situated in the middle of the theatrical extremes of the ballad atmosphere. In its enactment of the virtues of moderation in dramatic form, we might compare this kind of genre-specific concord to the classical unities of dramatic tragedy, where the unity and balance of the performance are thought to allow the audience to respond appropriately.

By its formal qualities—its "harmony," "skyll," and "measure"—music acts as the intermediary, or "mery meane," between its vices. As an influential advocate of godly ballads, Whight conceives of the experience of ballad music as unifying even at the levels of physiology and form. This picture puts a different spin on the shuffled character of ballad music, especially regarding religious ballads. Many of the conventions of godly ballad music that might be viewed as imitative or unoriginal contribute to the unity of the ballad tradition. Even the extreme repetitiveness of the songs—their twenty-odd verses, repeated burdens, predictable melodies, and recycled tunes—engages audiences in an experience of "measure" and "concord," patience and group unity.

It is significant that the physical activity of stopping to hear a performance, combined with the psychological and social activities of recognizing and piecing together ballad parts, always exists in a kind of rhetorical tension with ballads' diffuse environments and audiences' often fragmented listening experience. This is the productive paradox that we have seen in medieval theater, commercial plays, ceremony, and sermons: authors and performers superficially denounce the noise and distraction of their environments and performance conditions, yet they capitalize on the audience's sensitivity to these conditions by incorporating them into their production of meaning, especially in scenes and performances that seek to effect religious awareness and practice. The rhetorical binary of theatricality and religion is a precondition—often performatively thrown off as a false pretext—of performance culture. The way that religion is presented in ballads—in music, imitation, and repetition, and through the active participation of audiences in recognizing and pausing for ballads—is on the one hand distinct to the ballad genre and its performances but on the other hand particularly reliant on the consent of audiences. In fact, the specific virtues of patience, reflection, moderation, and charity that godly ballads promote likely emerged as a generic pattern through cooperation with the response of ballad audiences and with the increasing establishment of identifiable ballad performance venues, reception habits, reputations, and even laws.

In the vocabulary of James Elkins, when an audience stops to hear a godly ballad performed and thus authorizes it, there is a sense in which the godly ballad "stares back" at them.[63] Smith would remind us that even the medium of song "pushes at the boundary between the human body as an autopoietic system and the built environment as an autopoietic system. Through singing, the body projects itself into space and claims that space as its own."[64] Audiences pausing to hear a godly ballad performance present themselves also as objects of perception, like the parishioner at liturgy who in participating in corporate confessional prayers simultaneously presents himself to his neighbor, to the sight of the priest, and to the reflective words of absolution. Godly ballads provoke response, an awareness of the genre's tradition, an awareness of others within the performance space, and a concession that each of the ballad's allusions and imitations is an instance of the ballad looking out at other expressions of religion. Elkins imagines a scenario in which audiences refuse to acknowledge that objects look back at them, suggesting, "If I resist the idea that objects look back at me and that I am tangled in a web of seeing, then I am also resisting the possibility that I may not be the autonomous, independent, stable self I claim I am."[65] Autonomy is not a privilege that ballad audiences enjoy, and it is the misconception that subject autonomy is a necessary prerequisite for "authentic" religious practice—that is, belief that is understood as heartfelt—that has historically neglected godly ballads' contributions to religious culture and practice.

What we might call the practical religion of godly ballads in performance exploits the performative tension between their practice of consolidating their identity internally through conventionality and imitation and their habit of distributing the realization of this religious identity outward into the audience who receives and enacts it. Godly ballads are circular. They do not obtain their religious identity from theological insight or even from original moral instruction, especially since their authors are rarely established religious authorities, if known at all; instead, godly ballads incite belief through use and recycling—when audiences borrow a line of verse as a commonplace, or use their performance to pause for reflection, or when other godly ballads take their woodcuts, epigraphs, *sententiae*, tunes, and narratives for their own ends.

A final example demonstrates this circularity and what we might call the theatrical phenomenology of godly ballads. "Some Fyne Gloues" (figure 5.7) is a unique early godly ballad from the late 1560s whose full title reads: "Some fyne gloues deuised for Newyeres gyftes to teche yonge people to know good from euyll wherby they maye learne the. x. commaundementes at theyr fyngers endes. x. other good lessons be written within the fyngers, the tree of Vertues with her braunches in the right palme and the Route of vyces in the lefte, with a declaration of the other pytures folowinge in meter."[66]

As is clear from its elaborate design, this ballad was created to be held and read in addition to being sung, and it was printed long before the seventeenth-century black-letter layout was regularized. It inhabits a broadside form somewhere between a ballad and a graphic illustration or poster. Nonetheless, "Some Fyne Gloues" exists as a kind of print improvisation and expansion on what was still a predominately oral genre. Surrounded with smaller images and notes, the central figures are two gloves: the left filled with sins, the right with virtues, the fingers with specific New Year's resolutions to behave with godliness, and one of the Ten Commandments hovering above each fingertip. The song lyrics explain the images and captions.

"Some Fyne Gloues" is intended to be a gift. One would purchase the ballad and pass it on (its title suggests, to someone young) as a New Year's gift. The "New Year's Gift" was an early print titular trope. Often, it was a book written for a patron as a gift for the new year, and in the sixteenth century the majority of "New Year's gift" books were religious in theme. In fact, the New Year's trope was a trend for godly print and especially for single-sheet broadsides and songs published in the late 1560s and early 1570s. For example, two other broadsides published within two years of "Some Fyne Gloues" are entitled "A New Yeres Gyft, intituled, A Playne Pathway to Perfect Rest" and "A New Yeres Gift, Intituled, A Christal Glas for All

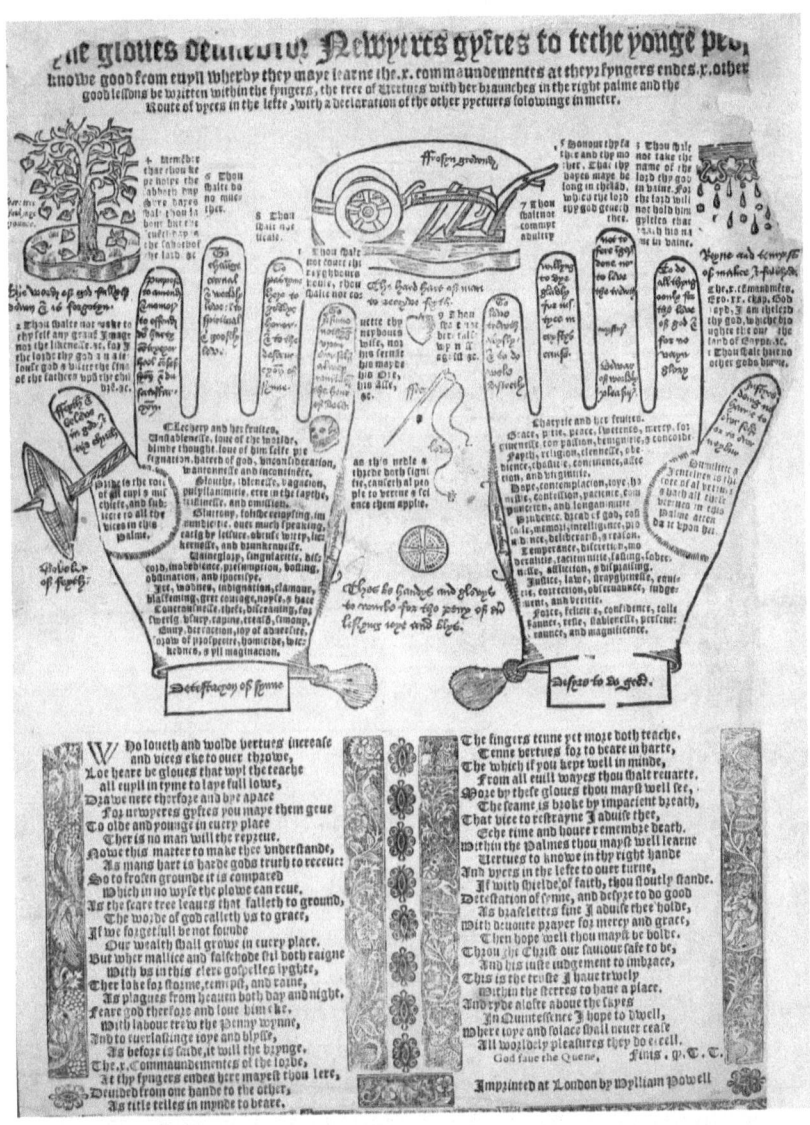

FIGURE 5.7. Ballad, "Some Fyne Gloues," 1560–70. Reproduced with the permission of the Huntington Library, Britwell 18343.

Estates to Looke in wherein They May Plainly See the Iust Rewarde, for Unsaciate and Abhominable Couetousnesse."[67] Representative of the trend, both broadsides are moralistic and warn of vanity and idleness. Like "Some Fyne Gloues," they repurpose the New Year's gift trope as an instrument for practical piety.

The religious appeal of "Some Fyne Gloues" is in its copious inclusion of practical morality and in the experience of fullness and unity among parts that such copiousness triggers. Significantly, that an audience member of this ballad's performance might buy the ballad only to give it away reflects the recycled and circular identity of religion in godly ballads. The gloves depicted on the broadside mirror the writing, printing, selling, holding, reading, purchasing, and gifting that took place by the hands of authors, printers, mongers, audiences, and gift recipients. The gloves also emphasize action and the practical dimension to ballad piety. Thus, taking the broadside as a whole, its diversity of content speaks to the status of religion as it appears in ballad culture. One can almost hear the diverse sensory ballad atmosphere when looking at the busy broadside.

Perhaps because ballad printing was still emergent at this point, "Some Fyne Gloues" captures the moment of diasporic song and spectacle that was lost once it was spoken. "Although sound itself is fleeting," as Ong describes it, "what it conveys at any instant of its duration is not dissected but caught in the actuality of the present, which is rich, manifold, full of diverse action, the only moment when everything is really going on at once."[68] Such a description of the presentness of sound highlights the affective intensities activated by listening to a song in ballad performance environments. The ballad author or printer of "Some Fyne Gloues" was likely motivated not only by religious content but also by the attempt to replicate the composite experience of godly ballads in performance. And there is a feeling of urgency in this desire to capture the activity of hearing—where, as in sermons, hearing a ballad betrays the false myth of passive listening. In the upper left corner of the broadside appears a tree with falling leaves. A description to its left reads, "The seare tree leaues faulynge to the grounde," and the caption below adds, "The word of God fallyth down & is forgotyn." In this context, remembering the word of God—as opposed to forgetting, or perhaps just walking past the ballad in performance—alludes most directly to the "Newyeres" gift itself as a memorial object. The historical suggestion is of a society that is infused with godly emblems and religious knowledge, such as those represented here, but has failed to put this knowledge to practical use.

This ballad extends the pause of audience participation at its performance into the printed artifact of hands. Like many later ballad woodcuts that illustrate a scene from the ballad's narrative, "Some Fyne Gloues" depicts the immanence of the human body in an activity of belief. Godly ballads like this one draw attention to the conditions *at hand* to inspire belief. At one moment the hands represent the ballad's reach toward its audience, and, at the next they are the audience's hands, metonyms for their ears and eyes and for listeners' presence in an audience circle. The song echoes these bodily associations. Note that the gloves are torn at the outside seam. The song explains, "The seame is broke by impacient breath," referring to impatience in frivolous living and in failure to remember that death always waits at the door. Again, we see a godly ballad emphasize the theme of patience. Here, however, patience manifests specifically as remembrance—remembering death, memorizing the Ten Commandments, and memorializing one's New Year's resolutions to live a godly life.

Engaging this ballad's cluttered yet effusive visual and aural environments incorporates audience members into a collective memory of a time past, before the Word of God was "forgotyn"; and it performatively reorients the present moment toward a New Year's future that is in alignment with this past. Remedially, to put on the broadside's gloves is to pause for remembrance and to become complicit in a system of circulation aimed at religious and moral participation, channeling the vertical and sacred experience of time prominent in the religious festivals of the Christmas season that inaugurated the new year.

EARLY MODERN BALLADS share many of the theatrical characteristics of the broader performing arts, including the practice of extending their thematic content into the conditions of their audience reception. To this end, where ballads perhaps differ from other performance types is in their emphasis on godly practice over theology and confessional identity, which makes the notion of authorial or spiritual authenticity problematic, if authenticity is thought to exclude intersubjectivity. Godly ballads demonstrate an alternative form of authenticity—or perhaps correct a false one. In ballad performances, religious psychology exists in a constant process of responding to the ballad by recognizing the virtues that derive from its theatrical culture—consolidating the moment into an activity of pause and reflection and then redistributing religious practice once again into the circulation of balladry in print, song, imitation, hearing, and exchange. Ballad religion is marked by a flexible spiritual attitude that integrates faith, sharing, and the embracing of practical limitations.

In fact, godly ballads depend on the transparency of their various motives and human strategies for making their themes relevant and empowering their narrative and moral voices. For instance, the Nativity ballad relies on clichés, allusions, and ballad commonplaces in order to prompt audiences to acts of recognition that are critical to godly ballad community. Likewise, a moral ballad cannot create an occasion for reflection and pause unless it first threatens to get lost among noise and distraction—a form of performative divestiture. Nor can prophecy or charity ballads promote social generosity without the performer conflating himself with the ballad speaker and making this theatrical process transparent. Religion facilitates the performativity of godly ballads by providing the social and ethical opportunity to actualize belief in the performance event itself and to extend this religious practice into performance culture broadly through ballad circulation, imitation, and conventionality.

In effect, the godliness of the early modern godly ballad is an exposé of its own exposure to both psychological and popular forces—commerce, polemic, propaganda, entertainment, publicness, and intertheatricality. One might protest that these forces or motives cancel the effect of authenticity, but I would suggest the opposite. Performative "authenticity" may be an indefinable and inevitably anachronistic idea, but performative religious practice is not. Like gloves, godly ballads point out toward their popular surroundings and ask that audiences stand within a public yet separate space, patiently recognizing—thereby enacting—and mutually transforming theatrical *and* religious practice through one another.

Chapter Six

THE DEVILS AMONG US

Intertheatricality in Doctor Faustus *and Its Afterlives*

Chapter 2 showed how the Chester Whitsun cycle created dramatic tension by obscuring the divine and through creatively negotiating the pressures on religious performance that began in the Reformation period. By the late Elizabethan period and the earliest productions of Marlowe's *Doctor Faustus*—which, we should remember, were almost contemporaneous with the last productions of the Chester cycle—the theatrical technique of concealing the divine and positioning characters before God's absence had become a regular practice of plays. Dramatists frequently made use of new technologies and genre innovations to integrate religious and theatrical material from moments of tragic reversal to scenes of transcendent wonder in plays like *The Jew of Malta*, *The Winter's Tale*, and *The Virgin Martyr*. In many ways, early modern theater's ability to mix religious themes of judgment and miracle with narrative techniques like dramatic irony is indebted to the nuances of medieval theater. Scholars have explored *Doctor Faustus*'s inclusion of miracle and cycle drama elements, often because of Marlowe's demons, angels, and pageant of vices.

Relatedly, but more specifically, I want to begin this chapter by exploring medieval theater's and Marlovian theater's shared investment in the sensational—that is, in theatricality on display. As in English miracle and biblical drama, *Doctor Faustus* boldly discloses its theatrical strategy and thereby reflects the social and moral importance of the audience's activities of spectatorship in the playhouse. In particular, I suggest that despite his atheistic reputation Marlowe appreciated the profound dramaturgical and emotional capabilities of drama when it takes advantage of the phenomenal intersections of theatricality and religion.

This chapter uses the genre examples of the previous chapters to provide an expansive account of *Faustus*'s intertheatrical world—its God, devils, legends, affects, spaces, and intertheatrical afterlives. I am bringing together aspects of the play in early modern England that have typically been separated from one another or overlooked. To view the performative effects of theatrical presence in commercial drama we must curate scenes of audience response in the playhouse as well as in the larger performance culture. My strategy, therefore, is to study the marginalia of the spectacular performance panorama that Marlowe's play helped create. This chapter will look in detail at several of the companion performances and texts related to *Faustus* and in particular at the many Faustus-themed and Faustus-affiliated ballads sung in England's urban center. I argue that these performances are not mere residuals of various companies' productions of the play; rather, they exist horizontally with Marlowe's play and contribute to a public reputation and larger intertheatrical response to *Doctor Faustus*. I bring these performances alongside the play itself and especially its textual history, which I argue can be read as indicative of early audience reception. Changes in the printed text reveal what audiences enjoyed and how their reception of the play actively shaped it in performance and in print. The same can be said of architectural and stage property changes to *Faustus*'s earliest and most consistent performance venue, Henslowe's Rose Theater, which served as the site of performative competition between Faustus's devils and the playhouse audience.

With each scenario—legend, ballad, text, playhouse—I argue that the theatrical entanglements and perceptual noise of *Faustus*-the-play stretched out into performance culture broadly and that such performative expansion reveals some prospects for the play's interaction with religion at theatrical levels. The intertheatrical identity and audience reception that emerge from this picture reflect the play heritage's social valuation of community and sensitivity to acts of spectatorship, as is consistent throughout early modern performance culture's apperceptions of religion. My conclusion is that, as evident across performance types, *Faustus* audiences felt a special investment in the religious terms of Faustus's fall and responded to this investment by pitting themselves against the play's devils—those medieval and early modern performative embodiments of theatricality gone sour.

EXEUNT ANGELS

Like many performances in early modern England, *Doctor Faustus* exploits the obscurity of God to call attention to the spectator's role in the spectacle—that is, to visuality. As an illustration, I begin by considering a painting of St. Gregory's legendary vision of Christ by the Master of the Holy Kinship (figure 6.1), a painting that combines many of the elements that are prominent in the performances examined in this book—cycle drama, the sacrament, the diffuse atmosphere of liturgy, the density of Christian ceremonialism, and the mixture of institutional and popular perspectives on devotion.

FIGURE 6.1. Master of the Holy Kinship, *Mass of St. Gregory*, 1486. Oil on panel. Reproduced with the permission of the Museum Catharijneconvent, Utrecht.

Many depictions of St. Gregory's Mass surround Christ with instruments of his torture and sometimes with laypeople gazing up at the miracle. In this rendition, painted in 1486, the famous legend of Christ's appearance at Communion is invaded by an unruly crowd of characters harassing the altar. These extra characters are Christ's tormentors. They represent the soldiers and crowds that mock Christ in the biblical accounts, but they also represent those who proverbially mock the Eucharist, such as heretics or perhaps unruly laity. We could note that these marginal figures, especially in contrast to the vested clergy, appear in costume; they are characters holding props and are posed in dramatic gestures. Notice that while the rowdy characters in the vision look directly at Christ, Gregory and his assistants appear not to notice Christ (not uncommon in some depictions of the legend). But the two groups are part of the same spectacle; they converge in a *coup de théâtre* that simultaneously represents a historical scene and acknowledges the beholder's gaze.

From another perspective, the raucous characters behind the Christ vision most directly resemble the medieval players that performed biblical scenes on pageant carriages around England in the fifteenth and sixteenth centuries. I reference this painting and the biblical cycle plays as paratexts that speak not only to *Doctor Faustus*'s interest in spiritual warfare but to the particular demands of the sensational on the phenomenology of a scene. While depictions of Gregory's vision often surround Christ with scenes of his passion and *Arma Christi*, the Master of the Holy Kinship has shifted emphasis onto the supporting characters of the Passion story. The effect is that the painting conveys a distinction between the representation of a miraculous vision and the imagination of that vision as a dramatic scene. On one level, the Christ vision is a symbolic representation of the Eucharist in the field of visual perception, while on another level the represented vision is theatricalized and appears as a moment of dramatic action. This addition raises questions about theatrical distraction, but it is not a wholesale warning against theatricality, since the liturgical attendants and the vision in some ways remain separate. There is no indication that the cast of onlookers surrounding Christ disturb him or that they distract Gregory and his attendants, yet the distinction is somewhat blurred through marginal figures and certain objects such as the missal and the altar ledge. The effect for the viewer is a feeling that the background characters are somewhat too imposing for the altar party to miss, an impression that the artist has taken too great an interest in Christ's tormentors—like the Chester cycle, performatively, I would suggest, transferring some of the responsibility for making the miracle coherent from St. Gregory to the viewer of the painting.

That cycle plays remained a powerful expression of faith despite their characteristically vulgar and comedic presentation is evinced by Protestant bishops' suppression of them for fear of their Catholic influence. Indeed, scholars such as Helen Cooper, John Parker, and Ruth Lunney have shown that Elizabethan drama has more intellectual continuity with late medieval genres than we often assume, if even in the form of nostalgia for unreformed hedonism, as Parker maintains: "The revolution of *Faustus* revolves around a past of unreformed ecstasy."[1] I've argued above that the preeminent dramatic problem of the Chester cycle—one of England's longest-lasting biblical play cycles—is that of immanence and absence: God and the divine vision he represents exit the stage in the first play and are immediately replaced by the potential distraction of Lucifer's immanent beauty. As God vacates his throne on the carriage platform, dramatic conflict takes its place. Just so in the painting of Gregory's vision. With the addition of self-acknowledged theatricality comes the transfer of the scene's moral imperative from the represented characters alone to the audience and their community.

In a similar way, *Doctor Faustus* acknowledges theatricality and applies its moral imperatives to both characters and audience. Revelry and devotional focus converge to this effect in a scene from the 1616 quarto of the play. Faustus has finished pressing his servant-demon Mephistopheles for the secrets of the cosmos but is disappointed that Mephistopheles refuses to discuss the creation of the universe (or, for that matter, to discuss God at all). Sensing for the first time that devotion to Lucifer does not in fact mean unfettered access to knowledge, Faustus charges himself: "Think, Faustus, upon God, that made the world" (2.3.74).[2] Insulted, Mephistopheles vows to "remember this" and exits the stage (75). Meanwhile, in this moment of potential anagnorisis, where Faustus is on the verge of foreswearing his pursuit of forbidden knowledge and entrapment in demonic company, the audience witnesses a series of entrances, exits, angels, demons, and performances on stage. In short, Faustus suffers an onslaught of theatricality. It begins as Faustus curses Mephistopheles:

> *Faustus.* Ay, go, accursèd spirit, to ugly hell!
>   'Tis thou hast damned distressèd Faustus' soul.
>   Is't not too late?
>   *Enter the two* ANGELS
> *Bad Angel.* Too late.
> *Good Angel.* Never too late, if Faustus will repent.
> *Bad Angel.* If thou repent, devils will tear thee in pieces.
> *Good Angel.* Repent, and they shall never raze thy skin.
>   *Exeunt* ANGELS
> *Faustus.* O Christ, my Saviour, my Saviour,
>   Help to save distressèd Faustus' soul!
>   (76–84)

At this, demons flood the stage, and before long the morality dialogue between the two angels is overwhelmed by a full-fledged pageant of vice—both reminders of medieval dramatic forms.

>   *Enter* LUCIFER, BEELZEBUB, *and* MEPHISTOPHELES
> *Lucifer.* Christ cannot save thy soul, for he is just.
>   There's none but I have interest in the same.
> *Faustus.* O, what art thou that look'st so terribly?
> *Lucifer.* I am Lucifer,
>   And this is my companion prince in hell.
> . . . .
> *Beelzebub.* Faustus, we are come from hell in person to show thee some pastime. Sit down, and thou shalt behold the Seven Deadly Sins appear to thee in their own proper shapes and likeness.
> *Faustus.* That sight will be as pleasant to me as paradise was to Adam the first day of his creation.
> *Lucifer.* Talk not of paradise or creation, but mark the show. Go, Mephistopheles, fetch them in.   [*Faustus sits.*]

> [MEPHISTOPHELES *fetches the* SINS.]
> [*Enter the* SEVEN DEADLY SINS.]
> Beelzebub. Now, Faustus, question them of their names and dispositions.
> Faustus. That shall I soon.—What art thou, the first?
> (84f.–89, 100–110)

Faustus watches the show of the Seven Deadly Sins in total enthrallment. The distraction has worked, and Faustus concludes the scene by saluting Lucifer in one direction and escorting Mephistopheles the other: "Farewell, great Lucifer. Come, Mephistopheles. / *Exeunt omnes, several ways*" (174–174f.).

Ornstein summarizes this failure of potential self-discovery and narrative reversal when in 1968 he writes: "Aware at last that he cannot command the elemental forces of nature, [Faustus] would lose himself in them; in ironic peripeteia, his creative impulse becomes a passion for self-annihilation."[3] If we stopped examining the scene here, we might conclude that some kind of evacuation had occurred, that Faustus's momentary cry for repentance had been oversaturated by the pageant of vices. Furthermore, we might observe that this demonic play bears an uncanny metatheatrical resemblance to the Faustus drama itself and to the playhouse where it was being performed in the midst of similar atmospheric distraction. Such a reading, however, is incomplete without also considering the effects of festivity and the religious ways of seeing that the demons introduce into the scene, their very presence perhaps shaping how the audience views itself before the performance.

To account for audience response, imagine Faustus as St. Gregory kneeling before the altar. The Good Angel, the Old Man, or perhaps God himself is the Christ figure—an icon in the balance, subject to the multiple audiences of protagonist, tormenters, and viewers of art. Yet the pageant players are still the pageant players; the tormenters are still the tormenters, demons invading Faustus's perspective, crowding the stage with distraction and conspicuous theatrical charm. Just like viewers of the painting, the playhouse audience must account not only for the miracle but also for the painting's internal audiences and potential detractors. The audience's response is distinct from that of

Faustus (or St. Gregory) in that it accounts for and measures Faustus's response. Faustus plays audience but is also part of the show, and the audience is caught in a more contextual, social, and atmospheric battle for perceptual control, for peace, and perhaps for an experience of dramatic resolution.

Such theatrical tension enters at the levels of audition and vision. Isolating some of Faustus's lines with the cues and stage directions from the 1616 quarto reveals the scene's decisive shifts in visual and auditory scenography:

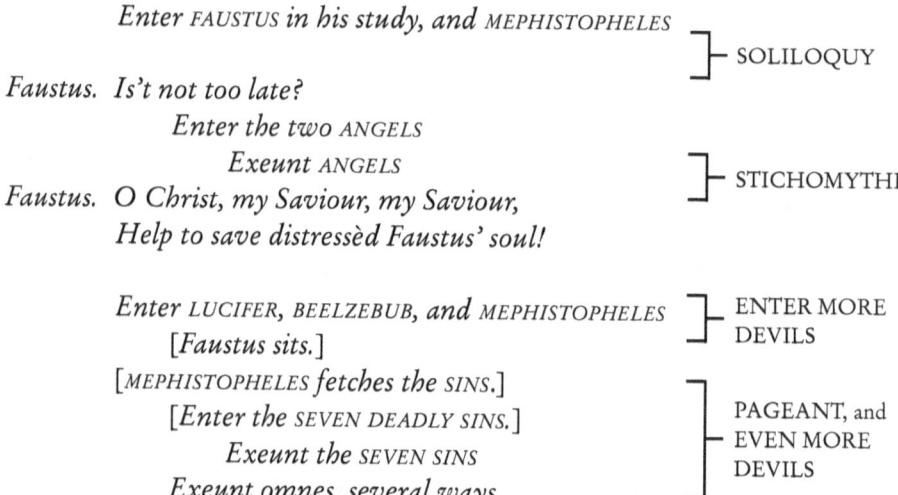

Faustus, the focal character throughout this scene, is like the eye of a storm that begins quietly with a moment of soliloquy and possible repentance and then surges and is closed in by entrances of angels, demons, and demons impersonating vices that consume the theatrical platform. The auditory progression begins with Faustus's vocal dominance—a vocality culturally connotative of the preacher's voice in a sermon at St. Paul's, or the consecration liturgy at a neighborhood parish, or the Expositor of medieval biblical drama, or the Chorus at the end of this play. It then moves to the bifurcated sounds of the good and bad angels' stichomythia—a moral tug-of-war wholly familiar and intelligible to the theater audience. And finally it moves to the sounds of a play-within-a-play where Faustus engages demonic characters in dialogue while they present themselves to music. Here, the comforting sounds of prologue, soliloquy, and intellectual inquiry give way to Faustus's comical groundling-like rebuffs: "Out, envious wretch!" "Choke thyself, Glutton!" (133, 154). Like the bread of Chester's *The Last Supper* and the Prologue in *Henry V*, the vices allude to the theater audience and its environment. Given evidence of drainage problems at the cramped Rose playhouse, Pride's comical complaint carries visceral relevance: "But fie, what a smell is here! I'll not speak a word more for a king's ransom, unless the ground be perfumed and covered with cloth of arras" (2.3.116–18).[4] Similarly, Envy alludes to the social dynamics of early modern theaters where economic status determines who sits in the galleries and who stands in the mud: "But must thou sit and I stand? Come down, with a vengeance," reminding critics that the "spectacle that seduces [Faustus] . . . is the very one that theatre audiences have paid to see" (131–32).[5]

Faustus, Mephistopheles, Lucifer, and—significantly—the playhouse audience watch the show together. From here on, the audience is implicated in Faustus's oscillations between boredom and excitement. Robert Weimann has argued that devils' and vices' intimate engagements of the audience, such as we see here, encourage the audience to identify with them and therefore promote nonconformity with state religion.[6] Alternatively, we might extend V. A. Kolve's argument, originally about cycle drama, to the festiveness of the devils' pageant in *Doctor Faustus*, where the devils' buffoonery may provoke the audience to a form of laughter that functions as ridicule, "a festival equivalent in play of the treatment they [the devils] may expect from God when he comes to judge at the end of time."[7] Similar to what we have seen in the Chester cycle's sense of festivity, Henry's use of ceremony, and godly ballads' use of music, this scene's pageant-within-a-play is a distraction for Faustus, but it also provides a connection to the verticality of Christian festival time. It adds a theatrical layer of memory and repetition, both representing something and bringing it into immanence in the present moment. That is to say, the play is funny and elaborate, but it is also nostalgic and foregrounds its own theatricality as operative beyond the work of representation. In the same moment, the audience can be distracted alongside Faustus and metatheatrically recognizing the missed opportunity to repent.

In other similar instances of devilish spectacle, Marlowe's audiences come to feel that their own activities of attention and dramatic participation are at stake in such an environment where devils constantly appear on stage as utility characters—bringing food, performing plays, tormenting clergy, impersonating historical figures, empowering the hero, and ultimately dragging him to hell. Faustus is tricked into treating theater as mere entertainment instead of as an occasion also for intellectual and spiritual discernment. The suggestion to the play audience is that there is something more to the playgoer's prerogative. As Erika Lin suggests, "Plays-within-plays . . . articulated broader anxieties about interpreting seemingly real sensory experiences, and these epistemological challenges and their moral consequences were not merely thematized within the drama but enacted in performance."[8] At one moment the content of the stage is monologue and conversation, and at the next it is revelry and debauchery. The audience feels the painful hubris of Faustus's immersion into the pageant, and thus he is revealed to be an inept playgoer who "loses himself" in drama. With its metatheatrical pathos for Faustus's folly, the scene creates a desire in the audience for solitude, to once again see Faustus sitting alone in his study. As a result, the audience adopts the performative role of maintaining for Faustus the sense of personal embodiment that he loses—to know oneself and one's surroundings and to attend to the connection between the two.

Doctor Faustus is written with a practiced and flexible audience in mind. Playgoers at early productions would have engaged spectacles like the pageant of the Seven Deadly Sins or the moment of Faustus's incantation through multiple intentions at once. They registered the represented meaning of the scene but also confronted the immanent risk and moral relevance of the scene as simply present—as is suggested by many sensational legends about the play's devils that swirled around play-going society. And as elsewhere in performance culture, there is also a collective intention by which the audience meets the spectacle, a sense that such provocative and religiously laden material at the commercial theater can be interpreted through the community at hand and by the performance society as a whole. A principal cause of this collaborative dimension to visuality in *Doctor*

Faustus is that Faustus himself has become a cautionary symbol of the dangers of solitude and of the need for a community of good scholars, as the play presents it. Yet another performative factor that contributes to the audience's solidarity is the crowded presence of devils in the play. *Doctor Faustus* is a play that mixes devils with the audience and even *in* the audience.

I mean this in the literal theatrical sense in which devils are on stage virtually all the time—primarily in the form of Mephistopheles, less frequently in the form of Lucifer, frequently but less specifically in the form of various devils summoned to perform what Faustus wants, including sexual acts in the guise of Helen of Troy, and perhaps most commonly of all in the many devils that lurk in the background, unrequested by the magician, watching Faustus slowly surrender his soul. In the scene of the pageant of the Seven Deadly Sins, the multiplication of devils on stage impersonating vices is not quite as sudden as we might imagine given that devils could be spotted watching from the background throughout the play. However, like the figures of the *Arma Christi* in the painting of St. Gregory, what is nuanced about these demons in the pageant is their assumption of agency as morality play–like characters, transitioning from onstage bystanders to histrionic personas. In this light, attending to the "devils in the audience" also cues a kind of theatrical bracketing where we can consider ways that the devils themselves influence the audience's perspective toward a legendary hero-villain as well as its access to the kinds of moral censure traditionally associated with the tragic genre. How does a play-within-a-play represent the audience experience of devils in the theater space? And how do plays like *Doctor Faustus* juggle diabolical themes between the hardscape and the softscape of the playhouse—furniture and character, popular conditions and dramatic belief—so that audiences respond not only to the story but also to the space and activity of spectatorship?[9]

Marlowe's dramatic treatment of theatrical spectacle mirrors the ambiguity—I would argue, a productive sort of ambiguity—in critical discourse on the tragic nature of Faustus himself. Few critics come to the play with the assumption that it is exclusively didactic or homiletic. Rather, as Harry Levin states, we expect to meet a bedazzling magician "violating the taboos of medieval orthodoxy" by disastrously pursuing his "Icarian desire for flight."[10] Even if one prioritizes its cautionary tragic arc, *Faustus* still stands out among Elizabethan plays for its exemplary use of stage technology, high-profile props, comic exuberance, and visual spectacle.

Notably, however, this same irreverent theatricality and stage magic is often understood as bolstering Faustus's case against God. Early modern accounts of the play attest to the fact that audiences were awed by its stagecraft and devil-forwardness. John Melton's 1620 report of a performance of *Doctor Faustus* at the Fortune Theatre by Palgrave's Men remembers it as an experience where "a man may behold shagge-hayr'd deuills runne roaring ouer the Stage with Squibs [fireworks] in their mouthes, while Drummers make Thunder in the Tyring-house and the twelue-penny Hirelings make artificiall Lightning in their Heauens."[11] Early editions of the play gradually became more theatrical in their deployment of demon characters, thunder, fireworks, and stage machinery, all reinforcing the impression that the play's staggering popularity resulted largely from its spectacularity and ostentatiousness. Then of course there are the well-known rumors of extra devils appearing on stage and of the playhouse seismically jolting for treading too close to real necromancy.[12]

Such a reputation squares somewhat unevenly with the play's generic unity as a tragedy and specifically with the spiritual edifice that limits and ultimately judges Faustus's intellectual ambition as an elaborate "tumble in confusion" (5.2.137). Outside of explaining this juxtaposition of irreverence and morality as an audience's vicarious experience of sin, in the vein of Stanley Fish reading of Milton's Satan, how can audiences be imagined to adopt the spiritual binaries of the good and bad angels, heaven and hell, contentment and ambition, when Faustus's activities between these poles explode with humor, rhetoric, and stagecraft that in some ways exceed its moral message? This very question has caused Cleanth Brooks to conclude that "Marlowe is scarcely answerable for some of the stuff that was worked into the middle of the play."[13] Add to this that Faustus was performed by one of the Elizabethan period's most exciting actors, Edward Alleyn, who conjured demons onto the stage, boxed the ears of the vulnerable Pope, and slept with Helen, and we might be tempted to suppose that so-called "medieval" moral orthodoxy has been overwhelmed and emptied by theatricality.[14]

Indeed, critical conversation about *Faustus*'s orthodoxy or subversiveness has hinged on the question of theatricality. Anticipating romantic reincarnations, Robert Ornstein suggests in an influential essay that "Marlowe attempts in art the impossible: namely, to translate into specific human terms and effective theater his amorphous, rhapsodic idea of man's transcendent potentialities."[15] Ornstein views the problem of religion in *Faustus* as a failure to "fashion appropriate artistic correlatives for his metaphysical vision," since Elizabethans were easily "awed by a few squibs, or by flights of poetic fancy and seriocomic sorceries." As Levin writes, Marlowe allows too much "incongruity between the monologues and gestures, between the seemingly unlimited possibilities envisioned by Faustus's speeches and their all too concretely vulgar realization in the stage business"—an argument not dissimilar from Stephen Greenblatt's suggestion that the excessiveness of ceremony and repetition undermines the play's spiritual structure.[16]

Such readings interpret the play's dramatic excesses as instruments of secularity. Other interpretations, however, focus on narrative structure rather than on the phenomenology of spectacle and performative religion and thus sometimes find a surprisingly straightforward orthodox message.[17] At the very least, even if theatricality does not entirely undercut the play's Icarian framework, we can acknowledge that it is no mere accident of *Doctor Faustus*. Marlowe's is a play that "explores the danger of its own dazzling theatricality" at the same time that it "celebrates" it.[18]

Far and away, the most conspicuous aspects of Faustian scenography were the many devil characters populating the stage, playhouse, legends, and broadsides in early modern versions of the Faustus story. Later editions of the play added demons and increased their activity—as performance and print production responded positively to how these devils enhanced the sensationalism of the play but also inflamed theatricality itself as a critical theme. Scholars have taken up the topic of devils on the Renaissance stage, often addressing the question of whether early modern audiences would have responded similarly to medieval audiences. The most extensive treatment of stage devils is by

John Cox, who contends with E. K. Chambers and argues that stage devils were not mere insignia of secularized folk tradition but instead formed a connection to the medieval use of devils for "moral and spiritual vitality" in drama.[19] Cox shows how in early modern theater and in Marlowe's work in particular devils continued their medieval practice of competing with God for human souls, as we see with Mephistopheles.[20] The question arises, then, of whether devils on stage and in the playhouse were merely comical and grotesque or actually carried the weight of spiritual reality that we find, say, in the Chester cycle.

From one perspective, a stage devil in *Doctor Faustus* carries with it a structure of binary spiritual powers. These are the metaphysical binaries that John Faustus intellectually opposes, for example, in his rejection of hell. Especially in the beginning of the play, he advocates for a dialectical account of spiritual realities, not settled in a "substance" but forming a "system of oppositions that it established and fulfilled," to borrow from Stuart Clark's description of early modern witchcraft.[21] Thus devils might represent a political ideology that Marlowe wishes to expose by unsettling audiences' equation of demonology and sin. "The audience at the end of *Faustus*," writes Simon Shepherd, "is left with an eminently privileged sharing of the main character's inner life but simultaneously an awareness of watching a show; the unresolvable choice makes a political knowledge in that one response is always conditioned by its opposite."[22] In this way, Marlowe's nuanced disclosure of character interiority and skepticism undermines the orthodoxy of an old spiritual framework.

Yet a reading of *Doctor Faustus* as a touchstone on the path toward theatrical secularism and cultural skepticism does not account for the fact that the dramatic force of early modern culture's reception of the play derived from imaginings of real hell, balladic comparisons to the social destructiveness of notable religious deviants, and, most immediately, the increasing presence of devil characters crowding a relatively small stage platform of ninety-four square feet.[23] Kristen Poole offers the helpful qualification that in the spiritual climate of early modern England and particularly in the world of Faustus, "To study the devil is to study beliefs about nature *and* the nature of belief."[24]

Yet much of the critical discussion of the sensationalism of Faustus inherits an understanding of early modern theatricality that neglects the circumstantial and cultural aspects of performance events in the vein of Barish and, moreover, that defines theatricality almost exclusively by its manifestations in commercial theater, with the occasional exception of considering the vice tradition. Positioning the play's uses of theatricality in comparative performance culture offers new perspectives on Faustus's protagonism, particularly as the play conscripts the audience into the action of the scene. I propose an approach that considers a larger collection of Faustian personnel, including Marlowe, Henslowe, Alleyn and the other players, Birde and Rowley as potential revisers to the text, the various producers and disseminators of legendary Faustus performance rumors, the many authors and redactors of Faustus-affiliated ballads, and, most of all, the audiences of Faustus performances broadly conceived. Viewed together, this cast of actors helps provide a fuller understanding of the play's intertheatricality and performative applications of religion, encouraging a trans-Reformational interpretation that deploys medieval theatrical strategies even as it suspends such sensational theatricality within a Protestant climate somewhat more sensitive to images and spectacle.

In what follows, I speculate about early modern audience reception of *Doctor Faustus* and theorize a phenomenology of the diabolical in performance culture by looking at parallel revisions in text, playhouse, street, alehouse, and reputation. Devils are icons, as it were, of the theatrical conditions on which *Faustus*'s religious reception hinges, and, as I will show, early reception of the play attests to the audience's participation in the conditions—both doctrinal and environmental—that ultimately send Faustus to hell. I contend that audiences may have felt as if they were competing with devils in the playhouse and in intertheatrical contexts. Audiences did not compete against theatricality, however, but *for possession* of theatricality—defined in all its commercial, technological, and environmental fullness. As is corroborated in ballads, early audiences of various versions of Marlowe's story thought of it as an occasion to claim ownership of the grounds of moral, religious, and, indeed, sensationally theatrical entertainment.

Faustus's Afterlives in Ballad Communities

Audience reception of *Doctor Faustus* is complicated by the fact that the story of Faustus existed in many contemporary forms that demanded different kinds of audience response and credulity. We can imagine these various forms to deictically proximate a broader cultural attitude toward the play and the mutually informing relation it builds between theatricality and religion. The different forms of the Faustus story in the sixteenth and seventeenth centuries interacted with one another, and, to a significant extent, so did their audiences. These forms include

- two notably different early versions of the play
- a sequel in the 1590s focusing on Wagner
- a farcical adaptation in the later seventeenth century[25]
- a popular broadside ballad probably first registered in 1589[26]
- numerous other ballads that recycled Faustus ballad woodcuts as well as others that self-identified "To the tune of Doctor Faustus"
- P. F.'s 1592 English translation of the German Faust Book entitled *The Historie of the damnable life, and deserved death of Doctor Iohn Faustus*
- the many friar and devil plays that exploited the success of Marlowe's play
- the widespread anecdotes of spiritual mischief occurring onstage during performances of *Doctor Faustus*

This last cultural form of the Faustus legend may be the most directly indicative of audience reception, but it is also the sparsest. The most elaborate of these rumors are the cracking of the Theatre in Shoreditch at the appearance of devils; Middleton's unaccounted extra devil onstage during the first recorded performance at the Rose in 1594; Prynne's "visible apparition" of the devil; and the rumor that Edward Alleyn wore a large cross around his neck during performance out of anxiety about his role in impersonating a heretic.[27] Even if legendary occurrences like these are apocryphal, they disclose the depth of social and religious anxiety surrounding the diabolical in the early modern performing arts and their theatrical practices.

Ballads, in particular, connect to the play and its reputation in consistent ways that suggest that audiences in the broader performance culture actively contributed to the creation of a moral perspective on the Faustus story. As I have argued, religious ballads integrate their environments and generic conventions into their content and facilitate a performatively interactive, spontaneous, and diversely motivated religious and moral occasion. Thus, beyond the question of whether Faustus-affiliated ballads depict the story as orthodox or subversive, we can search for aspects of the story's general theatricality that particularly flourish in the street ballad form. The answer suggests that audiences may not have received the excessive theatrical conventionality and repetitiveness of *Doctor Faustus* as subversive to the story's moral order, as Greenblatt and others have contended.[28] Rather, the intertheatrical performance history of Faustus is abundant in its role as moral caution. Faustus ballads exhibit a heightened awareness of the story's theatrical distractions, spontaneous audience community, speaker voice, affect, topicality, and performative effect. And perhaps most notably, Faustus-themed and affiliated ballads extend the category of theatrical devils into local and national relevance.

In February of 1589, probably shortly after the initial success of *Doctor Faustus*'s earliest productions, "A ballad of the life and deathe of Doctor Faustus, the great Cunngerer" was registered. No print of a broadside with this specific title survives. Because a relatively large number of similarly titled Faustus ballads do survive, however, it is probable that the "the great Cunngerer" either underwent a small print run or simply changed names. The later ballad is entitled "The Just Judgment of GOD shewd upon Dr. John Faustus." "The Just Judgment," or sometimes simply "The Judgment," went through numerous printings in the seventeenth century, roughly from 1640 to the late 1680s.[29] Extant versions of "The Just Judgment" and "The Judgment" are almost identical, but they do contain several minor and consistent differences.[30] "The Just Judgment" was first registered in 1624, though a manuscript copy of it survives from around 1616.[31] Given these three versions, it is clear that at least one Faustus ballad was in virtually continuous circulation for almost a century following the play's earliest performances.

Still, the world of Faustus balladry extends far beyond simple retellings of the Faustus story. Several woodcuts originating as Faustus illustrations were recycled in other ballads that share thematic elements with "The Just Judgment" and with Marlowe's play. Additionally, the attribution to the "tune of Doctor Faustus" appears in a number of extant ballads, none of which are "The Just Judgment" or "The Judgment." We can think of the field of ballads that constellate these songs, woodcuts, and tunes as involved in a kind of thematic "shuffling" in the ballad genre where commercial factors, authorship, tradition, performance conditions, and audience reception all intermingle in the process of adaptation.[32]

"The Just Judgment" and "The Judgment" are both to the tune "Fortune my Foe"—the same tune as is elsewhere called "the tune of Doctor Faustus." Extant examples of "The Judgment" contain the cut of Faustus in his study with a book and a devil (figure 6.2), and examples of "The Just Judgment" contain a copy of the famous Faustus woodcut (figure 6.3), almost identical to the woodcut on the title page of the 1616 quarto. Some copies of the Faustus ballad have neither of these cuts, and many include an additional cut.[33]

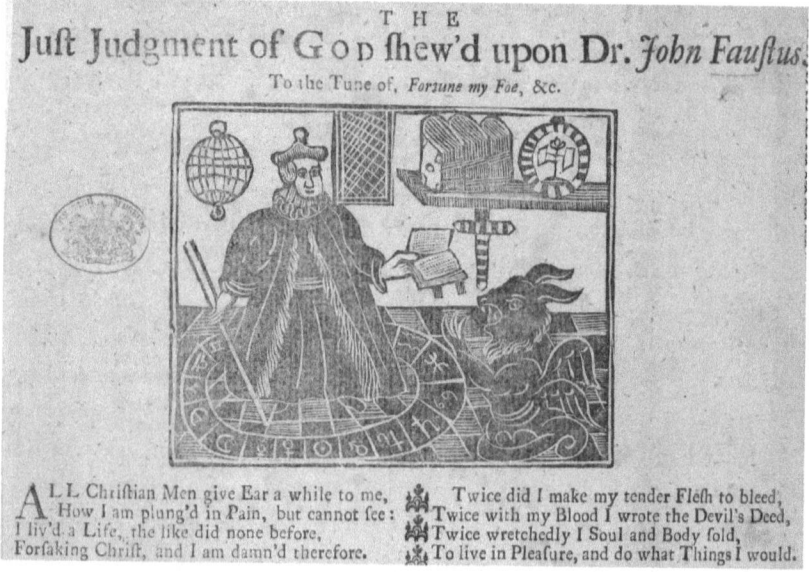

FIGURE 6.2. Ballad woodcut, "The Judgment of God shewed upon one John Faustus," 1686–88. Reproduced with the permission of Magdalene College, Pepys 2.142.

FIGURE 6.3. Detail from ballad, "The Just Judgment of GOD shew'd upon Dr. John Faustus," 1640. Reproduced with the permission of the British Library, Roxburghe 3.28–281.

An example in the Pepys collection under the name "The Judgment" showcases an identifiably Faustian woodcut of a man in his study, pictured perhaps like a theater "discovery" space or gallery. It also includes an illustration of a doctor arguing with colleagues (figure 6.4), intended to depict the play's early scene: the darker interlocutors could be Valdes and Cornelius and the lighter ones in the foreground could be the scholars who try to dissuade Faustus.

FIGURE 6.4. Ballad woodcut, "The Judgment of God shewed upon one John Faustus," 1686–88. Reproduced with the permission of Magdalene College, Pepys 2.142.

The visual appearances of most Faustus broadsides reference the play and are intended to catch one's eye with recognizable imagery, yet they also function intertheatrically and positively contribute—as unique though interconnected performance texts—to the culture of Faustus reception. For instance, the woodcut from "The Just Judgment" (Roxburghe) shows an identifiable conjurer, a devil, occult letters and symbols drawn in a circle of incantation, and a book about necromancy, one assumes. The image is not primarily an illustration of the performance of Marlowe's play, but, like the other Faustus woodcuts it is a constructive text in its own right. Woodcuts' circulation in print gives them a status like that of the stage devil, at once nostalgically meaningful and also practical.

This is generally the case for other conventions of balladry, including their tunes. The tune of "The Just Judgment," "Fortune my Foe," was one of the most popular particularly for godly and moral ballads, and the opening line—"All Christian men give ear a while to me"—announces itself to the passerby as a familiar genre convention particularly for godly ballads, potentially suited for one's home collection or for the wall of a nearby alehouse. Such conventionality is not merely routine; and when conventions reference a play like *Faustus* they are not merely derivative. Ballad conventionality gives audiences a point of access, and, as I have argued, it incites habits of spectatorship and audience participation that contribute to the formation of a ballad community integral to the religious ballad subgenre.

Beyond the tune, title, and woodcut, and even beyond the general story of Faustus's fall, the song of "The Just Judgment" references the play especially by reproducing its emphasis on the physical materials of contract—seals, bonds, signatures, and books.[34] This thematic interest in the contractual framework and accouterments of the Faustus tragedy suggests that the intertheatrical reception of the story reinforced especially the binary nature of Faustus's spiritual predicament: that *the* critical moment is his decision to sign the contract, and that the physical props are there to prove it.

These physical emblems and the strict contractual binary that they embody, moreover, relate in a nuanced way to the materiality of the spiritual realm as represented in the play's treatment of hell. Poole has described this tendency in the play to implant the spiritual in the physical as an "overdetermined materiality."[35] Why should things and places matter so much? And did audiences hear Faustus's overconfident allegation—"I think hell's a fable"—and interpret it as a trustworthy commentary on the binary nature of spiritual realities and therefore of his tragic fall (2.1.130)? In any case, the result is a kind of spatial volatility that prompts questions about who defines and controls spiritual space and, by extension, play space.

Faustus ballads have an interesting way of translating this relation between spatial fixity and the materiality of Faustus's deed. For instance, ballad authors prioritize the accuracy and reliability of their representations of the details of Faustus's deed. If we understand balladry to provide evidence of the reception of the Faustus story in performance culture, then we can think of this preoccupation with material accuracy as an attempt to redistribute the iconic props of *Faustus*'s stage productions. Consider "The Just Judgment's" emphasis on writing and sealing:

> Then I did shun the Holy Bible book,
> Nor on Gods Word would ever after look
> . . . .

Twice with my blood I wrote the Devil a deed
. . . .
And wo unto the Hand that seal'd the Bill
. . . .
[The Devil] did perform as Bond and Seal did bind

Like many first-person voiced ballads, this one constructs a shared past with the audience, and in this case it is the past of *Faustus*'s stage performance and perhaps of the Faust Book, referenced in the objects and events of books, words, blood-ink, the deed, acts of writing and sealing, and the contract. These details serve to authorize the ballad much as godly ballads use allusion, citation, and marginalia. And as in other godly ballads, the practice of authorizing goes both directions: it also contributes to the ballad's identity as imitative and self-affirming.

Importantly, here, such essentials include props and other specifically theatrical objects. Writing about "tableau" images like these objects in the play and ballad, Ruth Lunney suggests that Marlowe's drama marked a change in the theatrical use of the emblem: "[The] traditional allegorical uses [of the emblematic sign in theater] are included in, but now appropriated by and subordinated to, narrative and rhetorical ones. The visual sign loses some of its transparency and becomes increasingly arbitrary in nature, although this change is by no means complete or even consistent."[36] According to this argument, the visual signs of Faustus's infamous books, writing utensils, and conversational dealings with the devil, as are reproduced on the title page, signal Faustus's "escape from the exemplary frame" of "the continuing contest between good and evil" by becoming "detached" from "the old rhetoric of conflict" and attending instead to "the individual moments of his non-representative experience."[37] The question Lunney raises is important because it determines how we understand audience response and because it addresses the relation between theatricality and religion: Do the transparency and exploitations of emblems in commercial drama limit their power as icons? Just the opposite: like *Henry V*'s Prologue, early modern performances frequently extended their thematic reach through the performative move of theatrical exposé. And if the Faustus ballads are any indication, then it seems that the story's reputation advances specifically through the recycling of these emblematic signs. Their effect in the ballad, in fact, is to reinforce an interpretation of the Faustus story within the binary between good and evil rather than to substitute this binary with scenes of "non-representative experience."

The Faustus ballad is also devoted to presenting its credibility about certain details in an imagined authentic narrative. These include, among others, that Faustus is from Wittenberg, raised by his uncle, well educated, and rich (from the *Damnable Life*); that he wants "both Sun and Moon to stay" (that is, to stop); that Faustus's scholar friends "staid" in an adjacent room and "heard a doleful cry" at his demise; that the devil appeared in "Friars weeds"; and the numerical details that Faust cut himself twice to draw blood, lived under contract for twenty-four years, and was reckoned at "Twelve oClock."[38] The early reception history of *Doctor Faustus* thus places high value on specificity and accuracy. This is also true of other early play ballads from the period, such as a ballad entitled "Titus Andronicus Complaint," probably published at the same time as the earliest Faustus ballad. The details in the "The Just Judgment," however, orient uniquely around the tragedy's central moment of transgression in a way that is out of proportion with the more theatrical emphases of the B-text revisions, which I discuss below.[39] This focus reflects the ballad's interpretation of the exactness of Faustus's fault. According to the ballad, it was not so much Faustus's curiosity that damned him as the fact that he signed and read the wrong things—captured, as it were, by the still shots of books, deeds, and contracts. In both the play and ballad, dramatic reconciliation is driven by the audience's reliance on such emblems—as stigmatized props as well as interpretive symbols—rather than by a desire to move past them, and these props became for ballad audiences the preeminent signs for interpreting a play that had caused so much social concern and excitement—theaters cracking and devils appearing.

Especially given the central significance of emblems, allusions, and citations to the construction of performative moral practice in the broader culture of godly balladry, we should take these contractual moments—"Twice with my blood I wrote the Devil a deed"—and detailed allusions especially seriously as nodes of audience reception.

I am not suggesting that early modern interpretations of the Faustus story were uncomplicated but that—despite whatever potential ambiguities of the story these ballads might reproduce—Faustus's intertheatrical reputation decisively maintained the play's traditional heaven-versus-hell binary and the surprisingly unphilosophical manner in which he pledges his soul to Lucifer. Treating ballads as products of theatrical reception requires attending to not only which aspects of the original performance reappear in ballads but, more specifically, which aspects reappear in the most emotionally heightened and performative aspects of ballad performance.

Ballad Speakers and the Faustus Faithful

As I discuss in the previous chapter, another performative component of godly balladry—a component that creates or achieves something beyond what it represents—is speaker voicing. Godly and moral ballads use the speaker's identity and voice to create a specific form of audience awareness centered on the virtues of patience and charity. "The Just Judgment" is sung in the first-person voice of Faustus himself, which affiliates the Faustus story with a common trope in deathbed, gallows, and afterlife ballads where speakers call their audiences to repent and to moralize their own faults. The Chorus is the only speaker who approaches this kind of editorial voice in the play. Surprisingly, of the ballads marked "To the Tune of Doctor Faustus," and also among ballads related to the Faustus ballad but about other famous spiritual deviants such as William Lilly and John Lambe, only ballads of the actual Faustus story are in the first person. Juan Prieto-Pablos notes that Faustus refers to himself in the third person excessively in Marlowe's play, often in his articulations of religious nonconformity. Thus Marlowe's uses of the first person, Prieto-Pablos contends, typically express an emphatic desire to repent—"*I* will renounce this magic and repent" (2.3.11, my italics).[40]

Notably, first-person voicing in the ballad has an opposite effect from the play's usage. Whereas the play uses first person to announce Faustus's personal resolve and intended repentance especially in soliloquy, the ballad's use of the first-person voice is postdictable; it reminds audiences that Faustus is speaking from hell and that his resolve to repent failed tragically.

> You Conjurors and damned Witches all,
> Example take by my unhappy Fall:
> Give not your Souls and Bodies unto Hell,
> See that the smallest Hair you do not sell.

As a result, the ballad audience becomes an extension of the playhouse audience; they must combine their memories of the Faustus story (i.e., that his resolution failed) with their embracing of the profuse conventionality of the ballad form. These conventions include the ballad's publicness and environmental diffusion as well as its references to the ballad tradition. We might read the cry of "The Just Judgment" to "You Conjurors and damned Witches all" as an intertheatrical allusion to the many ballads that share its tunes and woodcuts.

Both the first-person voice and the preoccupation with factual accuracy create an intensified intertheatrical environment, where an audience's "residual" memories are collected in the prominent voice of the speaker addressing them.[41] The identity of the ballad speaker in "The Just Judgment," like the speaker identities in many godly ballads, appears to ballad audiences in multistability—that is, as a figure that inheres representationally and theatrically at once. The didacticism found in the Faustus ballad when, for example, the speaker addresses the audience in such comments as "Forsake the Devil and all his crafty ways, / Imbrace true Faith that never more decays" is of course foreign to Marlowe's play yet completely typical of moral ballads. At the same time, the devil's "crafty ways" are most viscerally experienced in the playhouse performance, amid its theatrics and dancing devils, so the ballad speaker exists simultaneously in reference to the play and within the unique genre integrity of the ballad performance. Both identities acknowledge the audience and respect the story as a theatrical occasion, eventuated across its various forms.

In fact, a predominant characteristic of the Faustus story's intertheatrical reception is the emphasis on the situation of the performance—how Dr. Faustus's fall unfurls in theatrical space and in specific circumstances. At playhouse and ballad performances of the story, audience members would encounter something that threatened their presence but that comforted and directed it at the same time. There would be devils and forbidden books, but also recognizable conventions and the unchanging nature of Faustus's diabolical contract—allowing some degree of familiar understanding and safe emotional distance. Thus, from one perspective, we find complaints directed toward the play's sensationalism, as when William Winstanley in 1687 states that *Faustus*'s popularity was merely due to its appeal to the "vulgar," while, from the opposite perspective, we find others that attribute spiritual power to the play's sensational spectacles, as when William Vaughan in 1600 denounces a trend of curiosity with magic as deceptively dangerous to people's souls—notably mentioning Marlowe by name as an especially prominent "Atheist."[42]

We can expect there to have been a kind of reputation and social memory unique to Faustus's aggregate intertheatrical audience. This audience is also part of the general public of performance culture but specifically takes on a "Faustus" audience role when, for instance, audience members stop to hear "The Just Judgment," when a spontaneous audience forms around the speaker who, in this case, is remembered in the play to be both a legendary deviant and a well-known stage player. The balladeer thus becomes not only Faustus but also an impersonation of the famous Edward Alleyn and possibly also the prominent actor Richard Fowler, who may have played Faustus in the 1620s and 1630s at the Fortune.[43] Effectively, the performance's first-person voice, creation of character, allusion to theater culture, and reliance on recognizable visual cues position the ballad audience in allegiance to the ballad itself and thus incite an attitude of theatrical proprietorship: ballad auditors' confidence in the moral message of the ballad corresponds to their expectations in the morally upright reactions of the play audience.

Speaker multistability, ballad conventions, material emblems, and conspicuous reminders of Faustus's damning contract—such elements of the balladic reception of *Doctor Faustus* describe the performative potentials of Marlowe's theatricality as actualized before an audience and in a community. To be clear, reading Faustus ballads as suggestive of popular reception of the dramatic story is historically indirect and depends on identifying reception patterns in the ballads and connecting them to the ballad author's decision to reference *Doctor Faustus*. One such pattern is that popular religious practice takes the form of group identity when the ballad performance uses environment, convention, and theme to align audiences with a malleable yet still normative social religious identity. Moreover, as we will see, these patterns correlate to the environmental effect of watching a play with devils in the audience. The various ballads that reference the play by using the Faustus tune and woodcuts reinforce this attitude by fashioning their own ballad audiences as local communities of faithful Christians who participate in condemning Faustus-like religious deviance, reframing the Faustus ballad's emphasis on spiritual allegiance around an immediate group, neighborhood, and city.

In Faustus-affiliated ballad performances specifically — ballads that use the Faustus-affiliated tune or woodcuts, or that directly allude to it — audiences performatively participate in expelling religious deviants from their communities. Because they coexist on a horizontal spectrum of Faustus texts, performance types, and stories, Faustus-affiliated ballads form a particularly tight-knit group among other collections of ballad topics and publics. The seventeenth-century ballads "Lilly Lash't with his own ROD" and "The Recantation of a Penitent Proteus" respectively tell the stories of the apothecary William Lilly and the famous dissembler Richard Lee who was forced to deliver a public confession for supporting the execution of Charles I.[44] "Lilly Lash't" expressly places Lilly in the company of "Great Faustus, Bacon and Lamb," and "The Recantation" references Faustus by instructing readers to sing it "*To the Tune of* Doctor Faustus." Both men figure not only as religious deviants but also as threats to state and society.

Moreover, these ballads label their transgressors as ethnic and religious others. For example, in addition to accusing Lilly of "jugling" (trickery) and deceit, the ballad calls him the "Lord of Gypsies" and dwells on his ethnic affiliations with the Scots. Likewise, "The Recantation" labels Lee a "Changling" in his ecclesial misallegiance but also in religious belief, as when in the first-person voice Lee proclaims that he would be willing to put on his *"Friday Face"* were Turks to conquer England and enforce observation of their Sabbath. The ballads thus elaborate on the well-known religious transgressions of these criminals by excluding them from national loyalty; they are outsiders who dangerously found their way into the ballad community, so their religious deviancy is narrated through ethnicity as a way of projecting domestic objects of fear outward onto foreign identities.[45] Marlowe's Faustus, on the other hand, is not particularly disloyal to his normative German heritage. On the contrary, the ostentatious scenes — augmented in the B-text — where Faustus torments the Pope reflect and also create a kind of Protestant nationalism themselves.[46] Faustus, in these scenes, is still under contract with Lucifer, but to some extent audiences concede this deeper sin for the sake of enjoying the humor in his exploitation of popery.

Marlowe's play and its affiliated ballads assemble an audience that self-identifies as a community of the faithful, defined rather specifically through the environmental and intertheatrical conditions and signs of its various performances. The audience is on the religiously and socially acceptable side of the contract that Faustus signs — and the play, legends, texts, and ballads collectively contribute to this "acceptability." They sit and stand as spectators to demonic activity, and they listen from the "living side" of the Faustus ballad to Faustus's posthumous warnings. In this, audiences join together in claiming a kind of patronage of Faustus performances and specifically of their theatrical manifestations. Faustus-affiliated ballads indeed have a distinct identity in performance culture. One sign of this is the fact that ballads like "The Recantation" choose to advertise that they are sung to the "Doctor Faustus" tune when they could just as easily name the tune titles "Fortune my Foe" or "Aim not to High," which had the same melody as "Doctor Faustus" but were far more popular in broadsides. It is also noteworthy that the 1589-registered "A ballad of the life and deathe of Doctor Faustus, the great Cunngerer" was published not long before the publications of two other play-based ballads, retellings of *Titus Andronicus* and *Arden of Feversham*, both of which are to the tune "Fortune my Foe."[47] However, neither the "Titus" nor the "Arden" ballad lends its title as an alternate to tune titles like "Fortune my Foe." Thus to advertise the tune of "Doctor Faustus" is to draw on what we might describe as the subconvention of ballads to invoke the Faustus theme through their tune imprints — the specific musicality of that melody as applied to the themes and performance world of the Faustus story. Something similar could be said of Faustus woodcut shuffling.

In addition to this shuffling of tunes and advertising matter, and in addition to the shared basic theme of religious deviance, the predominant investment that Faustus-affiliated ballads share is in their local specificity and topicality. Ballads that identify to the tune of "Doctor Faustus" and that include Faustus woodcuts — prominent though few in number — frequently reference local and historical details so as to give the ballad audience a feeling of actual time and place. In some ways this is fitting for the broadside ballad genre because ballad performance sites were often ad hoc and constantly changing.

Thus, recasting the Faustus ballad to apply to familiar places and events added a degree of topical permanence and local credibility, implicating local audiences in the condemnation of specific villains' arrests and executions. "Lilly Lash't," for example, includes a printed marginal note explaining that *"Lylly was a Tayler before he pretended Astrologie and Apprentice[d] to Pawlin in the Strand,"* giving geographical specificity to Lilly's biography before his crimes. Similarly, a ballad entitled "Youths Warning-peice," which tells the story of the Faustus-like apothecary William Rogers and identifies "To the Tune of Doctor Faustus," authenticates itself by grounding its factual accuracy in local lore:

> But it is true, and too too lately knowne
>   Twas done, not farre from hence, and cleerely showne
> By men, whose credits are wel knowne ith City,
>   Come then, and listen to my dolefull ditty.[48]

Even more, "Youths Warning-peice" closes with a white-letter endnote providing further popular support for its validity. It reads: "If any desire further information touching the manner of this mans Life, sicknesse, and death, let them read the Sermon Preached at his funeral, which is Printed by Authority." These local details are not dissimilar in strategy to the Faustus ballad's preoccupation with narrative accuracy; both types performatively incite audience solidarity through affirmation of the familiar story and its—at least imagined—historical specificity.

Many of these ballads are devoted to the capture and punishment of their deviants, and just as godly ballad audiences conflate the speaker and singer and adopt social roles in response to the speaker's multidimensional identity, the audiences of Faustus ballads performatively embody the role of social enforcer. For instance, a ballad featuring the 1616 Faustus woodcut called "The Tragedy of Doctor *Lambe*" is about a conjurer who is chased down by a mob and brutally killed. The speaker offers the usual call to attendance—"Your patience for a space, / Whil'st I make his narration"—but then draws on the phenomenality of a crowded, standing ballad audience as well as on local details of time and place to heighten the emotion of the song's angry mob.[49] Interestingly, according to the narrative, Lambe's capture begins in a playhouse "cald Fortune" on the "fourteenth day of June . . . . In the afternoon." Lambe is spotted at the Fortune by a "crew of Sea-men bold" who follow him to a tavern identified as "The Horshoe neere to More-gate, / Where he did carouse." These "Sea-men" conscripted the help of "Some Prentises" that were in the tavern to "kill the English Devill" outside, allowing auditors to visually imagine the exact street space of the murder outside the Horseshoe Tavern as a counterlocality to their own performance site. These details also add specificity to the youth culture of London apprentices and draw on the identity of that subculture, as "Prentices" were known for organizing into unruly mobs.[50]

Remarkably, the shuffling among performance genres here is represented by the physical shuffling of people from the Fortune to a tavern—from a theater to London's favorite public venue for posting and singing ballads. As in the Faustus ballad, there is a significant degree of agency attributed to the audience for enforcing social orthodoxy by their patience, economic support, and buy-in to the emotions of the drama. Ballad audiences thus merge with theater audiences in this ballad and, by extension, repeat and repurpose the emphases on contract, fidelity, and theatrical atmosphere found in Marlowe's play, "The Just Judgment," and the general Faustus lore.

We can imagine spontaneous audiences of these ballads to adopt a mind-set of locality, Protestant community, and familiarity. Whether individual audience members can actually corroborate or picture the specific places of the event is less consequential than how the narrative details work as theatrical icons for the audience. Like Erpingham's cloak in *Henry V*, the factual and topical details of Lily, Lee, and Lambe appear as mere facts and thus gain the ability to point to something more significant—or, more accurately, to assert that thing's significance in their quotidian or material presence. In these Faustus-affiliated ballads, the near-fetishistic interest in the details of criminals and their deaths asserts the significance of the audience and its identity as orthodox and socially upstanding. These are performative attitudes—or, in a sense, ballad virtues—of attendance, and they relate intertheatrically to the activities of Marlowe's own audience in recognizing and resisting the distraction that Faustus experiences during the pageant of the Seven Deadly Sins. Faustus's cautionary tale looms as a sort of umbrella narrative, so the dangers of theatrical spectacle that lead him astray translate in the ballad performance setting as the theatrical vices of impatience, distraction, and individualism that godly ballads generally condemn and against which ballad audiences congregate. In turn, Faustus-affiliated ballads reclaim theatricality not as an inherent distraction but as a tool for combatting the distraction of daily life, as it functioned in broader godly and moral ballad culture.

The godly virtues that audiences identified in and enacted by attending a Faustus ballad performance as well as, I would venture, a performance of Marlowe's play at the Belsavage or Rose theater proceed from the central activity of individuals joining together to expel the "devils" from England by first expelling them from their neighborhoods, taverns, and playhouses. When audiences respond, then, to the balladeer's ubiquitous call—"All Christian men give ear a while to me"—they participate in a mixture of sensationalism, theatricality, and proactive religious intentionality that also characterizes productions of *Doctor Faustus*. Obviously stage devils are not in the audience at ballad performances. They appear in woodcuts, tunes, and verses. Nonetheless, the phenomenon of devil infestation in ballad performance comes primarily in forms of local community and the ways that audiences inhabited an impromptu locality countering the ballads' infamous places of religious crime—such as Faustus's study, the Fortune, the street outside the Horseshoe Tavern in Moregate, and even the tiring-houses of St. Paul's Cathedral and St. Mary's, Cambridge, where the "Penitent Proteus" secretly discloses his duplicity before delivering his false confession. The devils of Faustus-affiliated ballads were real people with larger-than-life reputations.

At productions of *Doctor Faustus* in the 1590s and early 1600s, devils were ubiquitous, and audience response to this can be estimated in part by comparing the strikingly different atmospheres of these ballads. Although the audiences for ballads constituted spontaneous communities of the godly ballad faithful, ballad venues, unlike the venues of plays, were often variable and unrestricted; thus their locations were separate from but in a sense also continuous with the public spaces of notorious religious deviancy. Hence, they often utilized such ballad performance conventions as calls for audience patience, emphasis on recognizable narrative details, moralization, and, in the Faustus ballad, the first-person voice. These ballads exhibit a cultural attitude toward *Doctor Faustus*'s playhouse reputation by creating spontaneous environments that reference the diabolical through allusive details, tunes, and woodcuts and by expelling them through godly ballad performative habits.

Responding to the Theatrical in the B-Text

A comparative analysis of the Faustus story across Faustus-affiliated ballads informs an understanding of character devils on and around the stage in playhouse performances of *Doctor Faustus*. Devils in the forms of character demons, reports of real demons at performance, and diabolical social and religious deviants converge in the personas of devils in the theater. The sensationalism of Mephistopheles and his demons on stage prompted an audience reaction that is reflected thematically in the play and is engaged performatively by the audience. In this section, I want to look more specifically at the period of time beginning with the play's first performances in the late 1580s and ending with the publication of the B-text, the quarto of 1616. Because its main printings in 1604 and 1616 are so different, *Doctor Faustus* provides a unique opportunity to theorize audience attitudes particularly toward its religious themes and toward the play's shifts in theatrical technique. Whereas the 1604 text is succinct and genre oriented, the 1616 text is augmented significantly by stagecraft, comedy, and devils. My contention is that developments in the published play speak to how audiences received the play and its integrations of theatricality and religion.

Given some of the consistencies in its revisions, it is surprising that the so-called B-text of 1616 has not been used more often to estimate audience reception of the play. The play was first printed in 1604 in what is called the A-text, about seventeen years after its first performance. It enjoyed tremendous popularity through the 1590s. According to the *Diary* of Philip Henslowe (whose company owned the play) it was performed at least twenty-three times between the years of 1594 and 1597 alone.[51] Stretch these figures back to 1588 and forward to 1616 when the B-text was printed—a total of twenty-five additional years, minus short stints of theater closures—and we get perspective on why the B-text revisions could register audiences' tastes and habits in theater as well as their religious attitudes toward the play. Just prior to the registration of "A Ballad of the life and deathe of Doctor Faustus the great Cunngerer," the play's earliest recorded performance in 1588 at the Belsavage survives in William Prynne's 1633 tale of an apparition of a devil appearing on stage. Its next recorded performance in 1591 comes from Thomas Middleton's tale of the cracking of the Theatre in Shoreditch. Notably, these two retrospective accounts of supernatural mischief describe the earliest extant records of productions. The year 1594 marks the first contemporaneously recorded performance by the Lord Admiral's Men at the Rose playhouse, and the idiosyncrasies of this performance history continue in 1594 when a fictional account of a performance account called *The Second Report of Dr. John Faustus* is published in London. The Admiral's Men held Marlowe's play through the 1590s; Henslowe merged later in the decade with Pembroke's Men and then in 1603 also with the Earl of Nottingham's Men, both of which performed the play. Moreover, Continental productions of Faustus tragedies occurred in Austria (1608) and in Dresden (1626), and the play was performed by Prince Charles' Men until the theaters were closed.⁵² Of course, the majority of these recordings are made by Henslowe, and there is a good possibility that it was performed by Lord Strange's Men and Pembroke's Men even before the merger, since both companies regularly produced Marlowe's plays.

We can see, then, that the A-text of 1604 comes well after the play's remarkable commercial success, and it is unsurprising that the printed form of the play in the middle of its heyday would be significantly different from the version printed nearer the end of its most popular performance run, especially as more companies began performing it and altering it. The B-text quarto of 1616 omits 36 lines and adds 676 lines to the A-text.⁵³ Most of them are probably due to the revisions made by William Birde and Samuel Rowley in 1602 for which they were paid £4, though the A-text is printed just two years after the payment.⁵⁴ Editions of plays often varied, but, as scholars have long recognized, the B-text differs not only in volume but in narrative emphasis. Critical attention has focused on which of these two texts is the more authoritative—that is, the more Marlovian—and the best evidence seems to land on the earlier A-text.⁵⁵

Yet I want to draw attention back to the B-text for what it might suggest about early audience attitudes toward the play. If certain kinds of scenes and theatrical features were added, then the decisions to add and augment these elements were likely influenced by favorable audience reception of similar elements in recent productions. An alternative explanation is that the B-text might be seen to simply record the changes that were made and eventually established by individual companies and players over time. In either case, textual revision and audience reception go hand in hand.

Three initial categorical themes emerge in the B-text revisions and suggest patterns of audience reception: humor, official and unofficial censorship, and theatricality. In its own way, each revision category contributes to the formation of the audience identity of theatrical engagement and religious and social orthodoxy that we have seen corroborated in Faustus balladry. To say that the B-text is more comical than the A-text is simply to assume that the primary reason for many of the added scenes was entertainment. The two most augmented scenes are of Faustus antagonizing the Pope and foiling the pathetic resistance of the knight Benvolio. A third scene somewhat less enlarged is the finale. Here, the B-text brings back the good and bad angels and gives more lines to the devout scholars. Such additions compensate for the augmented comic scenes by reinforcing the original terms of Faustus's momentous decision in the first act. Still, while the changes to the finale are philosophically and theologically suggestive, the Pope and Benvolio scenes nevertheless constitute the most noticeable changes in the B-text. And while their primary effect is simply to celebrate Faustus's magical antics, we should not confuse this with celebrating Faustus's achievements. In fact, the B-text humor has the opposite effect: the increased comedy actually serves to trivialize Faustus's power by framing it as mere entertainment rather than as commendable ambition.

Consider, for instance, the changes in the scene with Benvolio. Benvolio, who is merely known as the "Knight" in the A-text, elaborates on his rivaling of Faustus in the B-text by scheming to attack Faustus with his posse. The B-text fills out Benvolio's personality, turning him into a drunk and raising the stakes of his clash with Faustus to the point of public insult. Where in the A-text Benvolio's initial opposition to Faustus merely notes his magical demeanor—"I'faith, he looks much like a conjurer"—the B-text has Benvolio more boldly accuse Faustus of deception: "Blood, he speaks terribly. But for all that, I do not greatly believe him. He looks as like a conjurer as the Pope to a costermonger" (A, 4.1.12; B, 4.1.71–73). In short, the B-text pits Benvolio not only against Faustus's particular form of magic but also against the larger theatrical vicinity that Faustus's magic and devils create.

The editors Bevington and Rasmussen take Benvolio's initial reaction in the A-text to be ironic, but a more comprehensive explanation is that the B-text revisers saw fit to position Benvolio not only in opposition to Faustus's trickery but also in opposition to his diabolical status in the playhouse.[56] And this revision may have been made in response to how audiences and performers gradually came to locate Benvolio within the larger theatrical atmosphere of *Faustus* productions. Until he is horned, the A-text Knight treats Faustus as harmless, but from the outset the B-text Benvolio threatens the theatrical magic that made Faustus an instant success on the London stage, even publicly doubting the devils with which the audience has become so familiar. Hence, his second complaint to Faustus pits him against the play's reputation for the sensational: "Well, Master Doctor, an your devils come not away quickly, you shall have me asleep presently. Zounds, I could eat myself for anger to think I have been such an ass all this while, to stand gaping after the devil's governor and can see nothing" (4.1.85–89). Note too that the B-text stages Benvolio "*at the window*" built above the stage where a trumpeter customarily announced the beginnings of plays, as occurs later in the scene at the entrance of Alexander and Darius—a not insignificant scenic detail that perches the knight above the players, the devils, and most of the audience, contesting through spatial rivalry the unfurling of dramatic action and conformity to the play's presentation of spiritual battle (71). Benvolio uses conspicuous stagecraft, replacing the rousing playhouse *sennet* with curses ("Blood," "A plague upon you," and several "Zounds"). Such curses replace and therefore challenge not only Faustus's power but also the spiritual authority of the terms set out by the good and bad angels who debate for Faustus's soul (B, 4.1.71, 87, 128, 138, 150). The B-text revisions to Benvolio do not pit theatricality against God, the Good Angel, and religious orthodoxy but place theatricality itself in the balance, urging the audience through the strategies of comedy and spectacle to claim ownership of it.

Such textual readings and speculations about the early audience reception of the play show continuity with the Faustus ballads' emphases on locality, nationalism, and orthodoxy by framing the theatricality of the scene itself as part of the tragedy's warnings about religious deviance. Remembering that the play begins with Faustus's shockingly clear-cut decision to side with the devil and also with the props and symbols of that definitive contract, the B-text revisions not only make the play funnier but also expand the scope of this binary between orthodoxy and deviance, good and bad, angels and demons, God and Lucifer. Thus, as in ballad performance, these details of textual revision and audience engagement exploit elements of religion to increase audience sensitivity toward the theatrical. In fact, being on "God's side" becomes a strategy for situating and incorporating the performative identity of the audience into the play's action.

We can look more closely at this audience sensitivity toward the theatrical and ask how textual changes like those to the Benvolio scene portray audience attitudes toward the play in the first few decades of its performance. In the first place, it is significant that these changes are not just textual; they are also dramaturgical and scenographical. For instance, they make greater use of the playhouse space and use more props, such as Faustus's false head. They are also theological insofar as Benvolio defies the spiritual beings that haunt the playhouse—and that also reappear in *Faustus*'s ballad afterlives and in marvelous performance legends. Of course, not much can be definitively affirmed about early audience reception, but one reasonable inference is that augmentations in textual and dramaturgical theatricality reflect—and also create—an audience that adopted an attitude of familiarity and even commercial patronage toward the dramatic medium and space. More specifically, in Benvolio the B-text develops an additional category of villain (after Mephistopheles and Lucifer) to the effect of consolidating playgoers' defense of the theater in the face of such a demon-infested play. In other words, the revisions to Benvolio help to converge the play's theatrical and thematic portrayals of Faustus's fate.

This also explains why Benvolio meets such a surprisingly cruel and violent fate. Where the A-text ends the scene with Faustus simply agreeing to "release him," the scene in the B-text ends with Faustus leaving the horns and commanding Mephistopheles to throw Benvolio down "some steepy rock / That, rolling down, may break the villains bones," maiming him and forcing him and his friends to live out their lives in a secluded castle (A, 2.1.88; B, 4.2.89–90). Perhaps with the exception of ordering Mephistopheles to torment the Old Man at the end, Faustus's act of violence here is his darkest exercise of power. It is solely intended for revenge on an irrelevant court knight and excessive beyond the desired theatrical sensationalism of Faustus walking onstage holding his severed head. Yet this startling B-text development suggests that audiences accepted Benvolio's demise—perhaps even in a mood of good humor and as a comic sacrifice. Still, Faustus could enact such violence only on a character who has the kind of metatheatrical identity the play attributes to Benvolio, threatening the magician as well as the theatrical magic of the play. The B-text has turned a comic victim into an enemy of the theater in general—serving him right for defying the show.

The B-text's somewhat decreased emphasis on its comic protagonists, Wagner and Robin, and its substitution of the diminished Dick for Rafe further reinforce the likelihood that audiences took comic scenes as opportunities to champion theatricality and its moral capabilities. Audiences have more overall to laugh at in the B-text, in terms of quantity, but laughter is focused on Benvolio and on the Pope and is thus given a more specific thematic purpose. Hence, the B-text develops the comic role of the Pope in much the same way that it does Benvolio. These changes include some topical details, such as his humiliation of Bruno and the allusion to "the holy council held at Trent," but the most effective change is the Pope's heightened buffoonery (3.1.105). For example, he turns Bruno into a step with which to ascend his throne, with "*A Flourish*," and he indecorously accuses his fellow clergy of being "Villains" and "Lubbers" (97f., 3.2.65, 75). With some license, one could even imagine a bombastic pelvic thrust when, in defense of public chastisement of Bruno's "haughty insolence," the Pope grips his papal belt and brags (3.1.135):

> Behold this silver belt, whereto is fixed
> Seven Golden keys fast sealed with seven seals
> In token of our sevenfold power from heaven,
> To bind or loose, lock fast, condemn, or judge,
> Resign, or seal, or whatso pleaseth us.
>
> (3.1.153–57)

The Pope is embarrassed, of course, when his food is stolen, his ears are boxed, and he learns that Bruno has escaped. His "silver belt" is outperformed, in a sense, by the "power" of Faustus's devilry. Such additions not only indicate that audiences responded to the play's degradation of the Pope but also suggest a felt desire within the *Faustus* play-going public for comic opponents like the Pope who explicitly challenge the protagonist for power. Audiences wanted to see Faustus sized up against other notorious religious figures. As with Benvolio, the audience finds itself applauding the humiliation of a theatrical archvillain—that is, a villain both of the play and of the playhouse, as represented and as theatricalized.

Reflecting the Faustus ballads' ethnic framing of religious deviants, Marlowe's audience adopts a participatory identity of nationalism and Protestant orthodoxy by responding lightheartedly to the play's treatment of Benvolio and the Pope as antagonists to the theater. This is in some ways related to the B-text's revision of curses and profanity. Revisions to the script's uses of profanity and theological language may attest to a circumstance where *Doctor Faustus* becomes both more sensational and also more legally acceptable as its language changes over time. Official censorship explains only some of these changes in language, since many changes in diction likely resulted from multiple disconnected revisers and performers, but even when these are viewed collectively we can note some trends. For instance, while the B-text is more freewheeling with general profanity, it is actually more discriminating with the A-text's most explicit theological language. The result is a revised play whose language is crass overall but also moderate compared to the A-text's less crude version that includes some more pointed moments of religious explicitness. For example, whereas Benvolio and the Pope use more obscene language in the B-text (e.g., "Villains," "Lubbers," "Zounds") than they do in the A-text, the B-text cuts out theologically explicit A-text mentionings of "divinitie" and "trinitie."[57] The 1606 Act of Parliament that restricted profane uses of such words surely also influenced such changes. Another notable example occurs at Faustus's first impression of Lucifer and Beelzebub. The B-text simply has Faustus vow "never to look to heaven," but the A-text elaborates with graphic violent detail: "Faustus vows never to look to heaven, / Never to name God or to pray to him, / To burn his Scriptures, slay his ministers, / And make my spirits pull his churches down" (B, 2.3.96–97; A, 2.3.94–98).

The same theological explicitness even disappears in the critical scene of Faustus's desperate monologue at the eleventh hour. Here, the A-text's theologically evocative "See, see where Christ's blood streams in the firmament! / One drop would save my soul, half a drop. Ah, my Christ!" is diminished in the B-text to "One drop of blood will save me. O, my Christ" (A, 5.2.88–89; B, 5.2.151)! Given that the B-text generally adds rather than subtracts lines from the A-text, these changes where the B-text cuts lines suggest a measure of calculation and intent, specifically regarding the play's reputation as provocative and sensational. Collective self-censorship of this sort can be understood as indicative of audience attitudes, especially when we consider Debora Shuger's reminder that early modern censorship developed from canon law and intended primarily to guard against libel and personal attack. Censorship litigation was, in fact, relatively lax with potentially dangerous ideas.[58] Hence, as Bevington and Rasmussen note, the B-text treads sensitive topical ground by adding Bruno to the Pope episode.[59] The Pope excommunicates Bruno and the Emperor as well as those who ally with the Emperor—"Curse the people that submit to him"—alluding not too subtly to Pope Pius V's excommunication of Queen Elizabeth in 1570 (3.1.128).

In sum, among other signs of audience reception, the B-text suggests that theatricality and religion developed symbiotically in advancing the performative identity of *Doctor Faustus*. The two poles of this identity and its intertheatrical relatives might be, on the one hand, scenes of necromancy, performed by the most famous players, replete with devils, forbidden books, and incantation circles, and, on the other hand, the singularly orthodox transition into balladry. Yet in between is a no-holds-barred theatrical demonstration. The B-text has more explicit stage directions, more stage effects, a bigger cast, and more props than the A-text. For instance, in addition to theatrical property such as Faustus's false head and the devils' fireworks, Henslowe purchased at least five items that were probably used for this play: a "dragon in fostes" or demon costume; a "poopes miter" and "crosers stafe," possibly used in the papal train; a "throne" to descend from "the hevenes"; and a "Hell mought" (mouth), probably staged in the final scene.[60]

We might pause briefly to consider the addition of a "Hell mought" in light of the play's specific theological comments about the nonspatial locality to hell, as in Mephistopheles's explanation: "Why, this is hell, nor am I out of it" (1.3.75). The result of the stage direction *"Hell is discovered"* is somewhat of a muddle: the play makes physical what audiences probably imagined Faustus's descent to hell to look like, despite Mephistopheles's instruction to the contrary. Moreover, such spatial contradictions reinforce rather than challenge the play's undercurrent of binary oppositions—between allegiances, books, counterlocalities—by using aspects of the performance environment to fuel the audience's popular imagination. The "Hell mought" shows the ability of theatrical property and stagecraft to contribute in sophisticated and thought-provoking ways to the moral and religious problems introduced in dramatic dialogue. Together with expansions in comedy and self-censorship, performances probably became more forthrightly theatrical as years went on, assimilating theatricality as an expression of socio-religious solidarity in the context of the various performative phenomena of *Faustus*.

Competing with Devils in the Playhouse

In the background—physically and thematically—of the heightened theatricality of the play's early Stuart-era performances is the audience's competition with devils for atmospheric control of the playhouse. Audiences and devils compete for whose interpretation of the theatrical will win the day. I am referring to stage devils both as actual characters that use performance tricks to distract Faustus and as multistable presences that operate in a similar way to figures in modern performance art. There is no strict distinction between what they represent and what they performatively embody, which is to say that their presence operates as a threat to characters in the drama as well as to the audience at hand.

Fittingly, the B-text has far more devils appear on stage than the A-text. Stage directions in the B-text frequently invite demons on stage merely to watch Faustus conjure and wrestle with his soul. For instance, before Faustus draws his incantation circle, and even before the appearance of Mephistopheles, the B-text stage directions read, "*Thunder. Enter* LUCIFER *and four Devils* [*above*], FAUSTUS *to them with this speech*," while the A-text has Faustus enter alone and unaccompanied, at least according to the stage directions (1.3.0f.). In the B-text, Lucifer and these four devils appear "above" in the same upper space that Benvolio uses—a noteworthy connection—simply to watch Faustus's first experiment in necromancy. This is a rather striking addition because it shows the playhouse to be infested by devils even before we meet Mephistopheles.

Demons are central to the English playhouse and the performance world of Faustus in particular, but they are also perennial rivals to the theatrical scene. They are there the way a nemesis is there in a modern television drama; once the writers kill off Sherlock Holmes's counterpart, Professor Moriarty, new villains fail to live up to as deep a rivalry. The presence of devils is central to early modern theater, but at any given moment they are perceptually marginal, threatening to descend from above and in later performances threatening to enter the play imagination from outside the playhouse—through other devil plays, Faustus-affiliated ballads, and lore in the broader Faustus-affiliated performance culture. So when Mephistopheles appears twenty-five lines later as a "*dragon*"—another detail not found in the A-text—taking advantage of Henslowe's newly purchased costume, the dramaturgical message to the audience is that the devils now have full range of the playhouse. From this point on in the B-text a cast of devils enter and exit the scene at will, sometimes without indication in the stage directions, as is the case when devils enter with Mephistopheles at the beginning of act 5, before Faustus's resurrection of Helen. In this instance, the devils apparently remain on stage until Mephistopheles leaves later, but their activity is unguided. The most probable explanation in terms of staging is that the devils in these scenes stand or sit in the background, perhaps occasionally retreating to the dressing room behind the stage at the Rose and other theaters, and come forward to the main platform and *platea* when their activity is required—to carry dishes of food or to physically torment a character.[61]

The spaces, then, of the Belsavage, the Theatre in Shoreditch, and the Rose playhouse—diabolically infamous in legend—become, through imagination and dramaturgy, macrocosms of the struggle within Faustus's soul. Recognizing that his interiority is dispersed into the playscape helps to clarify the question of the play's celebration of Faustus's independence of thought. It is sometimes supposed that early modern theater's gradual secularization coincides with dramatic advances in character interiority and social nonconformity.[62] According to this perspective, the B-text expansions of Faustus's antics could be understood as tipping the balance away from the dramatic closure instituted by peripeteia and catastrophe and toward the popular entertainment of magic and parody, thus fortifying the idea that by 1616 Faustus's sensational reputation may have outgrown the play's moral framework. Perhaps, according to this line of thought, Faustus's ambition exceeds the bounds of genre.

However, *Doctor Faustus* and especially its B-text incarnation affirm a different account of the relation between advances in theatricality and in religion. In fact, given its theatrical excesses and extensive use of the period's staple dramaturgical tools, the play is the thing that, in fact, might be understood to outgrow the nonconformist spark of Faustus's mind. These staples include aspects borrowed from medieval drama, as in the pageant of the Seven Deadly Sins, as well as the attributes that survive the transition into street balladry, such as props, topical criminality, and a narrative emphasis on Faustus's demonic contract. It is as if the audience engages the phenomenon of the playhouse with an intensity that puts Faustus in his place. The play's primary tools for creating this audience effect are its religious props, treatments of space, and characters. As I have argued, the religious backgrounds of such theatrical elements in ceremony, liturgy, sermon literature, cheap godly print, and cycle theater incite the audience to an increased sensitivity to the performative effects and human strategies of theatrical mediation.

We might ask, then: How can *Doctor Faustus* be seen to celebrate intellectual independence when, even before his first incantation, Faustus is never alone? The play's treatment of space is consistent with audience attitudes toward devils lurking in the background, since even Faustus's famed study is infested with demons. To put it simply, there are two types of space in the play: Faustus's "study" and everywhere else—including Rome, the Emperor's palace, and the rooms adjacent to the study where the other scholars pray in the final scene. As we see in the pageant of the Seven Deadly Sins, Faustus's study is a place of contention. It is the only place where Faustus reflects alone, without theatrical distraction, and thus the place where devils spy in the background. This elucidates the spatial significance of act 4, scene 4, when Faustus sleeps in a chair in his study. Despite the comic scene that ensues, with the horse-courser unwittingly pulling off Faustus's leg, this is the only moment after the opening soliloquy when Faustus is truly undistracted in his study, totally vulnerable and alone in his dreams.

And whether Faustus is alone in his study or accompanied by devils bears on how we understand the phenomenal space where he first practices "cursèd necromancy" (Prologue, 24). As depicted in the title page and broadsides, the stage directions describe his iconic posture: Faustus *"holds a book," "draws a circle," "sprinkles holy water,"* and *"makes a sign of the cross"* (1.3.0f., 7f., 23f.). On this stage-within-a-stage, there is a certain crudeness to Faustus's theatrics. He waits for the "gloomy shadow of the night" and "Orion's drizzling look" before he describes a diagram that can only have impressed audiences as elaborate:

> Within this circle is Jehovah's name
> Forward and backward anagrammatized,
> Th'abbreviated names of holy saints,
> Figures of every adjunct to the heavens,
> And characters of signs and erring stars,
> By which to spirits are enforced to rise.
> (1.3.8–13)

Now no fewer than three borders circumscribe Faustus: his drawn circle, the stage platform, and the larger playhouse structure—and possibly a fourth, if we include the godly ballad audiences devoted to protecting their greater community. Importantly, they all share the same central performative value of a heightened appreciation for the capabilities of theatrical media to be symbolic and yet also really present. There appear in the same objects and movements a prominent display of pragmatic authorial and theatrical craft and an attempt at representing character depth in Faustus's ambition.

Moreover, while spatial analogies between magic and the audience are not as compelling in a merely representational understanding of theater, Crane reminds us that "performing" something in early modern drama meant making and embodying it, so that structural coincidences like these concentric circles are not really coincidences at all but structures that cross the social-theatrical divide. They facilitate the power of an audience's presence to surround Faustus and effectively help him call "spirits" to "rise," like a kind of reverse icon.[63] Similarly, Turner's insight on the pragmatics and geometry of dramatic space depicts the playscape as an icon that moves both directions. "Theatrical iconicity," he writes, "is a *perforated* mode of representation: the (implied) presence of the offstage space always functions as a negatively determining limit, an unrepresentable invisibility behind the wall, the 'blink of the eye' that punctures theatrical representation as the spectator's phenomenological projection."[64] Faustus's circle—voyeurized and therefore made conspicuous by "LUCIFER *and four Devils [above]*"— is "perforated" by its comparability to the stage and playhouse and by the fact that its activities disperse devils beyond the confines of the study. In making imaginatively and dramaturgically conspicuous use of the materials of the stage, Faustus's circle points to what cannot be represented by stagecraft. Only in this case the "unrepresentable invisibility behind the wall" is, in fact, embodied by the devils. These devils are iconically within the wall (as in the title page image), but they exceed their representational status. For outside the incantation circle lies another circle, followed by another beyond that one.

To describe theatrical figures as iconic is not to add an unnecessary layer of abstraction to a medium that was predominantly an endeavor of dramatic craft and entertainment but, on the contrary, simply to insist that the objects, figures, and spaces through which a representation is performed remain present during and after the performance. Thus the process, in a sense, of intertheatrical Faustus-affiliated performances and the process whereby a story is translated into other performance types and back again both contribute to drama. In a word, early modern theatricality merges scene and setting and creates additional meaning from the excess.

As an example, there is practical as well as performative significance to the fact that Henslowe had the Rose built with fourteen sides. The number fourteen was probably chosen primarily because a fourteen-sided polygon could be constructed using the instruments readily available to early modern builders. It is noteworthy, however, as Andrew Gurr and Jon Greenfield have pointed out, that this structural rubric was created by the artist Albrecht Dürer, thus demonstrating the metaphysical fusion of courtly artistic imagination and pragmatic theatrical making. Moreover, despite the Rose's fourteen-sided configuration, excavations have shown it to be remarkably small and even poorly constructed—one example of which were the perennial drainage problems in the yard, resulting in muddy standing room for the groundlings.[65] Still, Marlovian drama's early modern (and premodern) combining of mimesis and pragmatics carries a certain resonance with "th'abbreviated names of holy saints" and the "figures of every adjunct to the heavens," where the overtly symbolized—abbreviated, figured, adjuncted—nature of Faustus's stage magic affirms the same iconicity embodied by its devils. Witmore describes this phenomenon in metaphysical terms: "The unity of theatre is not formal, like the definition of a triangle (a three-sided figure made up of straight lines)." Rather, "The unity of theatrical substance is both immanent and material: it actually resides *in* the physical bodies, sounds, and smells of the theatre, but it emerges *around* the interactions of those elements in a kind of personality or pitch portrait that is necessarily 'played by the picture of Nobody.'"[66]

If the playhouse is viewed as a macrocosm of Faustus's study, its practical constraints reflect audience reception insofar as stage features act performatively as dramatic icons. The texts of Marlowe's play are designed with respect to its performance spaces, so religion, the dominant moral context of the tragic action, also becomes an instrument for stagecraft. Faustus's study was probably staged in the "discovery area" situated between the two stage doors in the wall at the back of the platform. Both the A- and B-texts reveal Faustus *"in his study"* after the Prologue, and it is likely that this revelation involved either drawing back the curtain of a discovery area or coming forward from it. A discovery area was added to the Rose sometime between 1588 and 1592. This means that this cutout at the back of the stage was a new addition when Marlowe wrote *Doctor Faustus* and potentially provided novelty enough to become involved significantly in his play.

As a practical resource for staging Faustus's infamous study, the discovery area provides a spatial interpretive framework for the question of Faustus's independence of mind. We have seen how the Faustus ballad woodcuts incorporate a specific sense of location. Two of the woodcuts reproduced in this chapter show him in his study, and a third shows him at a table—perhaps the table to which Faustus directs Cornelius and Valdes in anticipation of his education in magic: "Then come and dine with me, and after meat / We'll canvass every quiddity thereof, / For ere I sleep I'll try what I can do" (1.1.157–59). Like woodcuts frequently found in deathbed ballads, with which the Faustus ballad shares characteristics of speaker voice, these illustrations communicate a strong impression of being in a room endowed with a specific purpose. For the Faustus-affiliated ballads, locality has a poignant phenomenological impact: audience communities gather and sanction a community of the faithful in opposition to counter-localities of religious deviants. Faustus's study can be seen as a hyperlocality of its own, particularly in light of the contemporaneous addition of the discovery area. I call it a "hyperlocality" because the study analogizes any number of spaces that represent domestic orthodoxy—audience members' homes, the internal life of the mind, or a neighborhood parish. His study even represents Wittenberg as Faustus's homeland, which he explicitly differentiates from the broad world of the East, as he self-identifies in his contract with Lucifer: "I, John Faustus of Wittenberg, Doctor, by these presents, do give both body and soul to Lucifer, Prince of the East" (2.1.105–6). Yet the study is also present beyond its representative status. It is there as a real theatrical space, just as the devils are there and just as the audience is there.

In this way, the emblematic picture of Faustus in his study holding a book, or as depicted in one woodcut, pointing to a deed, portrays the onstage area used for his study as a location of memory, always pointing back to the contract and to the binary spiritual entities that surround and propel the play. The play combines religious themes and theatrical strategy to the end of creating a place of contestation, represented by the study but immanently present in the playhouse itself. From the outset of the play's Prologue, imagery of consumption and swelling, which are physical metaphors for breaking the rules of place, animate the floor, benches, and bay galleries that hold the audience with dramatic purpose. Faustus appears in the confines of his study, and there he first expresses in soliloquy the famous characterization of being "swoll'n with cunning of a self-conceit" and "surfeit[ing] upon cursèd necromancy" (Prologue, 19, 24). To swell with "self-conceit" is, as Levin has described it, to mismeasure one's limits and to "overreach," but the meanings of the Prologue's language extend beyond the psychological. Faustus overindulges in theatrical distraction; he "surfeits" on the intellectual curiosities of his study, defying even the practical theatrical realities of play-going culture—its builders, structures, audiences. He sides with the devils, and the play space swells with their presence. Thus his cognition diffuses throughout the study and playhouse in the form of theological sin as well as mismanaged theater consumption.

The contents of Faustus's swelling are the play's devils. Where *Henry V*'s Prologue empowers the audience's moral and social ownership over "the swelling scene" of "so great an object" as war, Faustus's inhabitation of the play space does just the opposite: it undermines the narrative and physical structure of theater that is needed to drag him to hell and therefore creates a desire in the audience to reclaim the familiar cipher-like quality of dramatic character. It would be better for him, in other words, to be like Henry, "subject to the breath" of the audience to whom he can appeal. But in Marlowe's play, Faustus alienates his proverbial soldiers in the audience.

And it is not just the imaginative space that swells and undergoes change. Several important structural changes to the Rose were made in 1592, and they offer possibilities for considering how audiences may have physically and perceptually rivaled devils in the playhouse. The theater was furnished with decorative pillars between the bay galleries that partially surrounded the back and sides of the stage.[67] These would be natural lurking places for the devils half-hiding in the background, and one can imagine the iconic effect of a dragon hanging serpent-like onto a Corinthian pillar. Moreover, evidence suggests that two of the bay galleries adjacent to the stage were used for audience seating, providing perspective on how the devils in the audience could have literally been *in* the audience.[68]

These devils constitute an alternative and, I would argue, competing audience to the playhouse. They are there in a similar capacity that the theater audience is there—watching, anticipating, and, most importantly, willing the action. The devils' intentionality, as represented by their visible presence and as imagined by the audience, affects the audience's experience of Faustus and his haunting poetry. They complete the circle, in a sense, of the theater-in-the-round when they stand behind the scene and connect one side of galleries to the other. They raise the questions: For whom this spectacle is being performed, and what exactly is the spectacle? Is the main spectacle Faustus's distraction, as it is perhaps for the devils, or is it the play as a whole, taken by the audience in its tragic form to be a cautionary tale promoting moderation, patience, humility, and socially productive Christian living?

Finally, in 1592 the Rose extended its stage into the yard, expanding its surface area and, by consequence, positioning the standing audience around the stage and not merely in front of it. This protruding stage was increasingly popular in the 1590s at playhouses like the second Blackfriars, the Fortune, and the Swan. So we might understand the Rose to simply be keeping up with the trends, but the "trends"—I am contending—are evidence of early audience reception of the most popular plays being performed at the time. Bevington and Rasmussen confirm this approach in reference to the B-text revisions: "Certain [theatrical] features [of the B-text] pointing to an intermittent playhouse influence should not be ignored in an attempt to reconstruct the nature and evolution of printers' copy for the 1616 quarto. A play that had undergone at least one major revision for a revival might well be expected to show some effects of adaptation for practical use in the theatre, and we believe this to be the case with *Doctor Faustus*."[69] How did audiences inhabit the play space, and how might these trends have informed a playwright's imagination? More specifically, if we focus on characters traditionally recognized for their subversion and individuality, what kinds of theatrical conventions grew in popularity at a symbiotic rate with the Faustuses, Tamburlaines, Friar Bacons, and Hamlets of the period?

One answer, given these textual and architectural developments, is that audiences gained a rounder, multiple perspective on dramatic action as plays like Faustus began to implicate the audience in such dramatic contests for the playhouse. Bowsher and Miller note that the new construction caused audience "moshing" or more general crowding among standing audience members near the stage.[70] To summarize these environmental factors: later Elizabethan and early Stuart productions of the play were more crowded than earlier productions; audiences surrounded more of the stage; there were more devils and more theatrics; and the tragic finale used new company properties and technology to reinforce the spiritual binary of heaven and hell. If we take these to be interconnected developments, then the theatricality of *Doctor Faustus* can be understood to expand at a parallel rate to its performative creation of an in-house community of the Protestant faithful.

The audience's physical proximity to the play's devils provides a perpetual interpretive focus on Faustus's experiments in necromancy. Immediately after signing the contract with his blood and "*Giving the deed*," Mephistopheles hands Faustus a kind of instruction manual (2.1.115):

> [*Presenting a book.*]
> Here, take this book and peruse it well.
> The iterating of these lines brings gold;
> The framing of this circle on the ground
> Brings thunder, whirlwinds, storm, and lightning.
> Pronounce this thrice devoutly to thyself,
> And men in harness shall appear to thee,
> Ready to execute what thou command'st.
> *Faustus.* Thanks, Mephistopheles, for this sweet book.
> This will I keep as chary as my life. *Exeunt.*
> (2.1.157f.–166)

Here, recognizable Marlovian props, devils, stagecraft, and religious deviancy all intersect. Stage directions call for thunder four times in the B-text and only once in the A-text. Recall Melton's account of *Doctor Faustus* that "a man may behold shagge-hayr'd deuills runne roaring ouer the Stage with Squibs in their mouthes, while Drummers make Thunder in the Tyring-house and the twelue-penny Hirelings make artificiall Lightning in their Heauens." A similar conflating of theatrical magic with Faustus's witchcraft occurs here when audiences come to associate "this circle on the *ground*" with the practical and intellectual *grounds* of belief in the round theater. Mephistopheles's gifts of "thunder" and "lightning" unsettle the crowds that stand and sit around Faustus's study and likewise heighten the concentric analogies that link the incantation circle, Faustus's study, the stage platform, and the fourteen-sided theater itself. For special diabolical powers to exist *here* within the circle, there must be an implied space out *there* defined by an orthodox theatrical usage.

Theatricality and stagecraft thus are morally directive but not partisan. The religious condemnation of magic in the play is used to heighten the importance and reach of theatricality, not to diffuse it. Hence, devilry is one possible response to theater, while responsible spectatorship is another. At contention in these most emblematic scenes of doubt and resolve—the scenes reproduced in popular adaptations of the story—are the sensory experiences of characters and spectators. Faustus cuts himself, while God scars the words *"Homo, fuge!"* into his arm, prompting in Faustus a momentary vertigo as he loses trust in his own senses: "Whither should I fly? / If unto heaven, he'll throw me down to hell.— / My senses are deceived" (2.1.77–79). Both Faustus and the playhouse audience are caught in a struggle to make their bodies conform to their souls, to align their sensations with the truer spiritual reality. Thus Faustus's first statement of explicit regret is actually a response to astronomy and the beauty of the heavens: "When I behold the heavens, then I repent / And curse thee, wicked Mephistopheles, / Because thou hast deprived me of those joys" (2.3.1–3). These lines take on immediate significance in the theater as they are delivered under the covering over the stage platform, often called the "heavens," newly rebuilt in 1592, from which a throne descended in the final scene using machinery installed in 1595.[71] Audiences would, in fact, look up to the heavens quite often in plays like *Doctor Faustus* that made extensive use of their stage resources, so Faustus's moment of doubt reaches the audience on a familiar visual level.

Yet Mephistopheles and his distractions are too omnipresent for Faustus's regret to last very long. He is interrupted on the verge of repentance by the two angels and then by Mephistopheles's surprisingly unimpressive astronomical knowledge. As discussed above, in 1600 William Vaughan, while mentioning Marlowe by name in his *Goldengroue*, describes the danger of keeping conversation with the devil as a problem of sensory contact: "For the coniurer or magician, it is almost impossible that hee should be conuerted, by reason that the Diuell is always conuersant with him, and is present euen at his very elbow, and will not once permit him to aske forgiuenesse."[72] There is an expressed risk that mere proximity to the devil will inhibit conversion as it does with Faustus, whose most private moments are never actually private and for whom demonic magic is a distraction from angelic warnings. Ramie Targoff has surveyed some of the early modern antitheatrical writings that warn society of the unseen performative transformation that audiences undergo by merely being around theater. According to this logic, habitual play-going might turn an audience member into a social or religious deviant of the exact varieties that Faustus-affiliated ballads dramatize: "The apparent publicness of the theatrical performance serves ultimately to promote only undesirable and hence secretive behavior outside of the theater's walls."[73] Audience members themselves might become the devils of Faustus ballad lore! The structural changes to the Rose Theater in the 1590s as well as revisions to the B-text of *Doctor Faustus* constitute a changing spatial context in which both audiences and stage devils take on increasingly active yet adverse roles in drama.

    I have not been suggesting that Marlowe—possibly *the* famous Elizabethan atheist dramatist—wanted to create an experience that reinforced traditional faith. Rather, I am arguing that he was acutely cognizant of a play-going world in which theatricality and religion were environmentally integrated—a cultural reality also recognized by *Faustus*'s producers, revisers, and adaptors. Marlowe's devils demonstrate some of the remarkable ways that Renaissance theatricality uses its relation to religious practices of mediation and iconicity to performative effect, as it is the audience's solidarity as a community of the faithful that invests them even physically in Faustus's struggle. Audiences create a phenomenal desire for anagnorisis—a moment of self-discovery, removed from theatrical distraction. Such discovery comes too late for Faustus precisely because he does not exercise the independence, or individuality, of thought that critics and Romantic rewritings of his story have celebrated. He may not conform to orthodox Christianity, but he cannot escape conforming to the pleasure-seeking habits of demonic theater.

In fact, it is worth noting how often Faustus is disappointed by the remarkably little knowledge Mephistopheles offers him. Not long after expressing his boredom with the traditional disciplines of philosophy, medicine, law, and divinity, Faustus articulates an abrupt frustration with Mephistopheles's reluctance to discuss heaven and hell: "Learn thou of Faustus manly fortitude, / And scorn those joys thou never shalt possess" (1.3.84–85). He voices similar disappointed in Mephistopheles's ideas on the topic of damnation: "Think'st thou that Faustus is so fond to imagine / That after this life there is any pain? / No, these are trifles and mere old wives' tales" (2.1.36–38). Later, in an especially desperate attempt to use intellectual conversation to distract himself from the spiritual warfare emblematized by the good and bad angels, Faustus sighs in disappointment of Mephistopheles's knowledge of the heavens: "These slender questions Wagner can decide" (2.3.47). Faustus's devilry is actually dissociated from his intellection. Either his soliloquies and doubts are crowded out by onlooking devils and Mephistopheles being "present euen at his very elbow," or the knowledge he does pursue leads to the same feelings of boredom he expresses in the opening soliloquy. Even his final exercise of supernatural power—his rendezvous with Helen of Troy, another devil in disguise—reveals a disjunction between his body and his mind, since this sensual episode follows his reflective response to the Old Man: "O friend, I feel thy words to comfort my distressèd soul. / Leave me a while to ponder on my sins" (5.1.61–62).

The problem of the theatrical in Marlowe's play is one primarily of Faustus's surroundings, and the audience inherits this problem. What one feels, sees, and derives entertainment from is either spiritually edifying or a devil's trick. The same language of caution is found in the Faustus ballads and is applied even more personally to specific neighborhoods and known criminals. Faustus's boredom with divinity, philosophy, and the like, in this way, acts like a warning against the wrong kind of play-going attitude, and the play's prominent use of iconic scenes, props, and stagecraft draws the audience into a crux of interpretation, centering on the ubiquitous books and deeds that signify Faustus's fate. In this way, the play's strategy is much like the theatrical strategy at work in the Chester cycle, *Henry V*, sermons, and godly ballads; props, personnel, spectacle, and spatial elements are foregrounded—sometimes excessively—to the end of forcing the audience to reflect on their own presence at and contribution to the drama. Mephistopheles confesses this strategy of deception through the conspicuous emblems of the play's popular imagination: "When thou took'st the book / To view the Scriptures, then I turned the leaves / And led thine eye" (5.2.99–101).

Alongside the devils on stage, above the stage, and perhaps in galleries, the audience surrounds the play and creates circularly imagined environs that form somewhat unfittingly around the central binary of heaven and hell. One way to describe the performative conflict that results is that there is a battle for the middle. What is in the middle, and who controls it? Such an observation may remind us of Cleanth Brooks's suggestion that *Doctor Faustus*, like the tragedies of *Samson Agonistes* and *Murder in the Cathedral*, lacks a narrative middle, by which he means that nothing within these twenty-four years of revelry seems to influence Faustus's outcome. Faustus makes a decision, plays with his power, and suffers the consequences. Brooks concludes that "the play *does* have a sufficient middle," of sorts. It consists, he suggests, of Faustus's experiential knowledge of the reality of hell, where Faustus learns what it means to be living in hell.[74] This contradicts the view that the bulk of the play is mere "filler": "Hence, one can stuff in comedy and farce more or less *ad libitum*, the taste of the audience and its patience in sitting through the play being the only limiting factors."[75] Yet whereas Brooks intends this last statement sarcastically, I contend that the audience's "tastes" and "patience" are exactly what drives the play's continuing competition between heaven and hell—or audience and devils—despite its profusion of humor.

In some ways, it is the middle of the play that is at stake. Does the play's characteristic theatricality belong to the devils or to the Protestant community present in its playhouse and ballad performances? Historically, do the expansions of this theatricality in the text, playhouse, technology, and properties contribute to the triumph of Faustus's proto-Romantic curiosity and individual will, or, as I have argued, do they attest to a play-going society's largely medieval claim on theatricality as an experience of solidarity and even cultivation of religious community? Furthermore, we can recognize that the middle of the play—its sensationalism, its devils, its theatrical reputation—extends out into performance culture and especially into balladry, where it undergoes the performative transformations unique to godly ballad performance, in turn influencing the play's reputation, its reception, and perhaps also its revisions. In short, Marlowe, his textual revisers, and Faustus's intertextual partners give the middle of the play to the audience members, inviting them to delve into the pleasure of the theatrical and yet charging them to ward off its devils.

POSTLUDE
Ending with a Jig

I have argued that early modern performance culture and lived religion share a network of theatrical strategies and performative interests in enlisting the perceptual content of the audience at hand. Early modern theatricality comprises a set of structures and expectations along a spectrum of performance types, and these types intersect with one another at crossings shaped in part by the nostalgia and change of the Reformation period. One way that the various spheres of theater draw on Christian practice and even occasioned religious activity is in performances' insistence on the thematic and often spiritual relevance of their environments and social situations. In some manner, each of the performances I've discussed makes the performative move of resisting dramatic rapture and then turning its audience's resulting self-awareness into a dramatic act itself. And the performative power of such theatrical exposure and audience response is made possible in part by the trans-Reformational tendency to look back to older religious forms, as early modern performances harness the ambiguities and pressures of Protestant reform to extend their dramatic material intertheatrically and performatively.

Early modern audiences engaged performances in two minds at once—attending to the fiction as well as to their own acts of spectatorship. This dual intentionality is a critical component to the festival and ritual quality of theatricality across the Reformation period. It is a common element in each of the three vignettes I discuss in chapter 1—boy bishop festivities, Elizabeth I's coronation progress, and *Twelfth Night*—and I want to close by adding one final vignette that stretches the limits of the festival phenomenality of the theatrical event even further: the postlude jig.

Judging by contemporary complaints accusing jigs of inciting social disorder and distracting audiences from the dramatically advanced content of the play, early modern jigs might be considered as the farthest removed in performance culture from the expressly religious events of Christmastide and sermon performances. Yet while jigs were part of the new commercial drama, their theatrical ancestry reaches back to modes of integrating drama and religion that predate the Reformation. Thus I want to suggest that their function in this new commercial setting was to reinforce the greater, trans-Reformational religious context of the playhouse and of performance culture as a whole.

Famous stage jig performers like Richard Tarlton were known for bantering with the audience and improvising speeches. Will Kemp of the Chamberlain's Men was known for his dancing and dramatic clown roles and then after 1599, when he left the company, for the "Nine Days Wonder" during which he danced from London to Norwich.[1] Jigging was physical, musical, improvisational, and sometimes even acrobatic. Roger Clegg notes that in this way the jig was atmospherically characteristic of the "rowdy proto-capitalist playhouse" where "music, singing, and dancing mingled with the variously evolving branches of slapstick, sword-play, bawdy, satire and farce, a dramatic heritage more physical than literary."[2] Later in the seventeenth century the term *jig/jigg* would contain a host of related meanings—from music and dance, to dialogue and sex—but in the Elizabethan and early Stuart periods, its home was on the stage.[3] Some early modern writers opposed play companies' uses of jigs at the end of the final act, as when Thomas Dekker memorably judges that the "Sceane after the Epilogue hath beene more blacke (about a nasty bawdy jigge) then the most horrid Sceane in the Play was."[4] Still, as the opening to Marlowe's *Tamburlaine the Great* attests, others embraced the jig's place as an idiom, as it were, of the greater play event: "From iygging vaines of riming mother-wits, / And such conceits as clownage keeps in pay / Weele lead you to the stately tent of War."[5]

Furthermore, according to Philip Massinger's account, jigs were so central to audiences' expectations of the playhouse routine that they even threatened the spirit of the play that preceded it: "If the gravity and height of the subject distaste such as are onely affected with Jigges, and ribaldrie (as I presume it will,) their condemnation of me, and my Poem, can no way offend me: my reason teaching me such malicious, and ignorant detractors deserve rather contempt, then [sic] satisfaction."[6] In some ways dramatic jigs are on the opposite end of the performance culture spectrum from liturgical and sermon events like boy bishop festivities and cycle plays, but in other ways they elaborately cull from the performative nuances afforded by the theatrical milieu of trans-Reformational England. Thus, more than a possible distraction or base entertainment, the jig acts as a kind of theatrical intermediary between these explicitly religious performance types and the play that precedes it.

Descriptions of the jig variously as "ribaldrie" and as "nasty bawdy" notwithstanding, the majority of jigs that survive today are cohesive dramas. Such dramatic jigs are short yet complete stories with characters, plots, and tunes; and the recycling of staple character types and themes among them, as in ballads, suggests that jigs constitute an advanced genre. Dramatic jigs normally take the form of a dialogue between two or more characters. Typical themes include sexual seduction, pranks, and the mixing of social levels. At the end of a play performance, the company clown would reenter the stage, perhaps with one or two more players, and then perform his song. And indeed, the dramatic jig was more a dialogue song than a dance, though dancing frequently accompanied it.

To watch a jig performed after a play may well have had a jarring effect, especially if it followed a tragic catastrophe, but it is worth pointing out that jigs share many of their thematic and theatrical elements with even the bleakest of early modern tragedies—music, dancing, sexuality, rampant wordplay, deception, conspicuous reliance on particular stage properties, thwarted ambition.[7] And this partial list does not account for how the postlude jig reprises the musical and farcical activities that frequently occurred before plays and between acts.

To close the comparative study of *Performance and Religion in Early Modern England* with a jig has a similar effect to ending a play with a jig: it does not terminate the event but expands it. The jig extends the play into the audience, other performance forms, and a common playhouse vocabulary. It extends forward into future plays and, in many cases, into future audiences, since in the Elizabethan period new audience members would enter the playhouse after the play ended in order to see the jig specifically. Postlude jigs even stretched into future performance events, taking form in broadside print and being sung by new performers in alehouses and market stalls—we might imagine, for example, at the entrance to the premiere of a new play. Conversely, early modern jigs were nostalgic and also looked backwards in time. In a sense, jigs were "born old":[8] they made sure that a time past persisted into the time present through their folk characters, music, and wooing dramas, and by invoking May games, Morris dancing, wedding plays, interludes, pastorals, and the role of the medieval Vice.

The intertheatricality of postlude jigs was also intertemporal in that it allowed for audience members to bring attitudes of play-going from previous theatrical and religious eras into the commercial playhouse setting. Consider, for example, one particularly elaborate jig that first appeared in manuscript and was eventually printed as a broadside with the title "Frauncis new Jigge, betweene Frauncis a Gentleman, and Richard a Farmer" (figure 7.1).[9] It was entered in the Stationers' Register on October 14, 1595, and was printed in the early seventeenth century.

The broadside attributes authorship to George Attwell, a member of Strange's Men and possibly also the Queen's Men. This fact along with the complexity of the song's dramatic setting makes it likely that "Frauncis new Jigge" was performed on stage as a postlude, though we cannot know for certain. This jig involves four characters and follows a predictable plot of attempted adultery and reconciliation through disguise. Frauncis petitions Besse, the wife of Richard the Farmer, but she resists. Besse arranges a rendezvous under false pretenses and switches clothes with Mistress Frauncis, who puts on a mask and spends the night with her husband. The next morning Mistress Frauncis unmasks herself, and the drama ends with reconciliation.

The story involves multiple scenes and conversations among two, three, and four characters. Each section is sung to a different tune. The

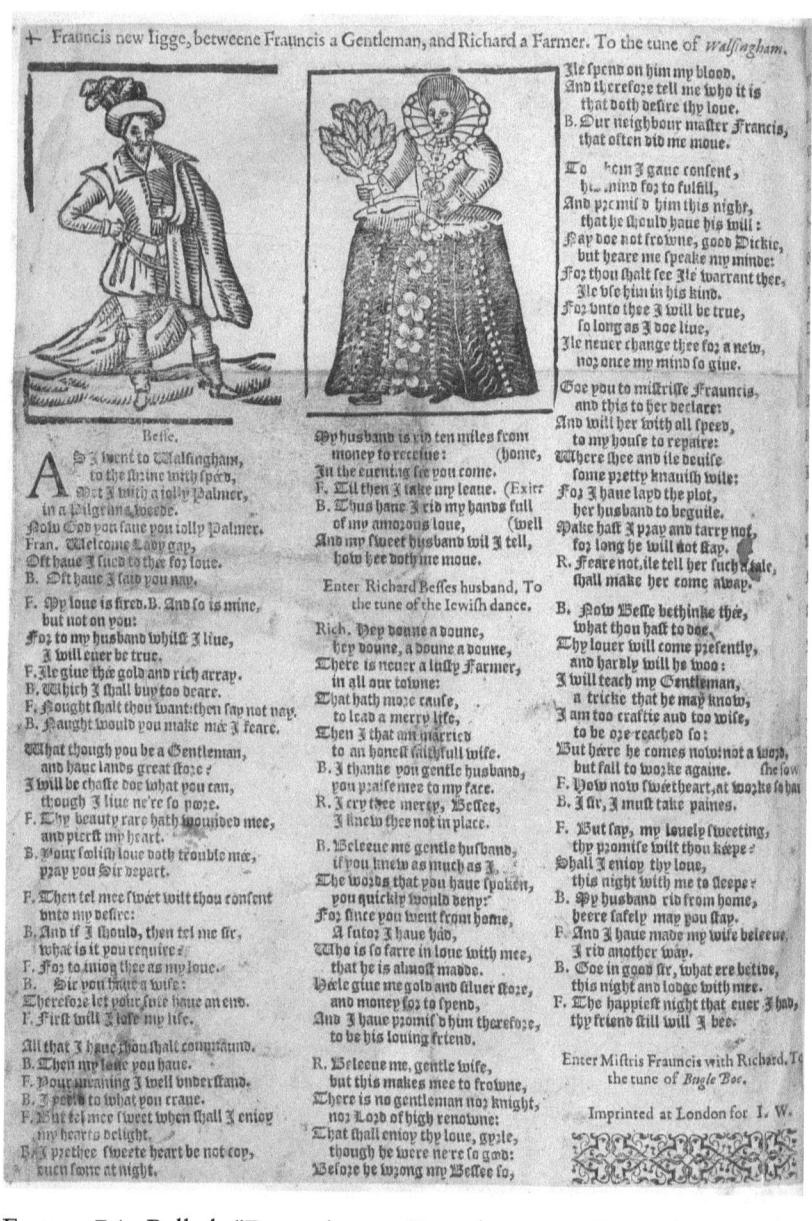

FIGURE 7.1. Ballad, "Frauncis new Iigge, betweene Frauncis a Gentleman, and Richard a Farmer," 1617. Reproduced with the permission of Magdalene College, Pepys 1.226–27.

The Second part of *Attowels* new Iigge. To the tune of as I went to *Walsingham*.

W. I Thanke you neighbour Richard,
    for bringing me this newes:
R. Nay, thanke my wife that loues me so,
    and will not you abuse.
W. But see whereas shee stands,
    and waiteth our returne.
R. You must goe coole your husbands heate,
    that so in loue doth burne.
B. Now Dickie welcome home,
    and Mistris welcome hither:
Grieue not although you finde
    your husband and I together.
For you shall haue your right,
    nor will I wrong you so:
Then change apparrell with me straight,
    and vnto him doe goe.
W. For this your kind goodwill,
    a thousand thankes I giue:
And make account I will requite
    this kindnesse, if I liue.
B. I hope it shall not need,
    Dick will not serue me so:
I know he loues me not so ill,
    a ranging for to goe.
R. No faith, my louely Besse,
    first will I lose my life:
Before Ile breake my wedlock bonds,
    or seeke to wrong my wife.
Now thinks good Master Frauncis,
    he hath thee in his bed:
And makes account he is grafting
    of hornes vpon my head.
But softly stand aside,
    now shall wee know his minde,
And how hee would haue vsed thee,
    if thou hadst beene so kind.

Enter Master Francis with his owne wife,
hauing a maske before her face, supposing
her to be Besse.
    To the tune of goe from my window.

F. Farewell my ioy and hearts delight,
    til next wee meete againe:
Thy kindnes to requite, for lodging me al night,
    heeres ten pound for thy paine:
And more to shew my loue to thee,
    weare this ring for my sake.
W. Without your gold or fee you shal haue more
F. No doubt of that I make. (of mee.
W. Then let your loue continue still.
F. It shall til life doth end.
W. Your wife I greatly feare. F. for her thou
    so I remaine thy freind. (needst not care.
W. But youle suspect me without cause,
    that I am false to you:
And then youle cast mee off, and make mee but a
    since that I proue vntrue. (scoffe,
F. Then neuer trust man for my sake,
    if I proue so vnkind: (borne,
So often haue you sworne, sir, since that you were
    and soone haue changde your minde.

Nor wife nor life, nor goods nor lands,
    shall make me leaue my loue,
Nor any worldly treasure make me forgoe my
    nor once my mind remoue. (pleasure,
W. But soft a while, who is yonder? doe you see
    my husbands out alasse.
F. And yonder is my wife, now shal we haue alife
    how commeth this to passe?
R. Com hither gentle Besse I charge thee do con-
    what makes Master Francis heere. (fesse
B. Good husband pardon me, Ile tel the troth to
R. Then speake and doe not feare. (thee.

F. Nay, neighbour Richard harke to mee,
    Ile tel the troth to you.
W. Nay tell it vnto me, good sir, that I may see,
    what you haue here to doe.
But you can make no scuse to colour this abuse,
    this wrong is to to great.
R. God sir I take great scorne you should profer
W. Now must I cole this heate. (me the horne

F. Say neighbour Richard be content,
    thou hast no wrong at all:
Thy wife hath done thee right, and pleasurde me
F. This frets mee to the gall. (this night.
God wife forgiue me this offence,
    I doe repent mine ill.
W. I thanke you with mine hart, for playing this
    though sore against your will. (kind part,

Say gentle husband frowne not so,
    for you haue made amends:
I thinke it is good gaine, to haue ten pound for
    then let vs both be friends. (my paine:
F. Ashamed I am and know not what to say,
    god wife forgiue this crime:
Masse I doe repent. W. But I could be content,
    to be serued so many a time.

F. God neighbour Richard be content,
    ile woo thy wife no more:
I haue enough of this. W. Then all forgiuen is,
    I thanke thee Dick therefore.
And to thy wife ile giue this gold,
    I hope youle not say no:
Since I haue had the pleasure, let her enioy the
F. God wife let it be so. (treasure.

B. I thank you gentle Mistris. R. Faith & so do I,
    sir, learne your owne wife to know:
And shote not in the darke, for feare you mis the
B. He hath paid for this I trow. (marke.
All women learn of me. F. All men by me take
    how you a woman trust. (heed
W. Say women trust no men. F. And if they do:
W. Ther's few of them proue iust. (how then?
Farewell neighbour Richard, farewell honest
    I hope wee are all friends. (Besse
W. And if you stay at home, and vse not thus to
    heere all our quarrell ends. (rome

    FINIS.   George Attowell.

At London Printed for I. W.

jig begins "To the tune of Walsingham," then transitions "To the tune of the Jewish dance" when Richard enters. The second part of the song opens "To the tune of Bugle Boe" and closes with the revelation scene "To the tune of goe from my window." The entire jig is sung, and every line is in dialogue except for Besse's short prologue:

> AS I went to Walsingham,
>   to the shrine with speed,
> Met I with a jolly Palmer,
>   in a Pilgrims weede.

The frame narrative is a conventional pilgrimage diversion, which was signaled by the tune of Walsingham, the title of which invoked other songs of pilgrimage in popular imagination. Although this particular tune and place-oriented subject matter took many individual song forms, Sir Walter Raleigh is credited with writing one of Walsingham's most famous iterations, which begins with the line, "As you came from the holy land of Walsingham," and proceeds with a similar romantic diversion.[10] The tune is referenced in Fletcher's *Honest Man's Fortune* and in Dryden's play *Limberham*; both instances allude only to the tune as whistled rather than sung. Alternatively, verses from the song, but not its tune, are quoted in Beaumont's *The Knight of the Burning Pestle*, in the last scene of *Hans Beerpont, his invisible Comedy*, and in *The Weakest Goeth to the Wall*, the earliest of the three, printed in 1600.[11] The ballad was also known to Shakespeare, as Ophelia sings a line from the second stanza—"How should I your true love know"—in act 4, scene 5 of *Hamlet*.[12]

The cultural associations of the tune of "Frauncis new Jigge" attune us to a rich intertheatrical habitat for what might otherwise seem to be a merely derivative and bawdy story. Walsingham held a priory and the shrine of Our Lady of Walsingham until its dissolution in 1538 and played host to thousands of pilgrims in the earlier decades of the sixteenth century.[13] The family of Walsingham songs thus carried strong associations to the specific and, to many, endeared phenomenon of the shrine as a pilgrimage destination, so it is fitting that its most elaborate setting was composed by William Byrd, a conspicuous Catholic presence in Elizabeth I's chapel. A manuscript ballad by Philip, the Earl of Arundel, a Catholic executed during Elizabeth I's reign, is entitled "A Lament for Walsingham" and expresses the Catholic nostalgia that these other ballad references channel with more subtlety. Referring to the shrine, its final stanza reads:

> Sin is where Our Lady sat,
> Heaven turned is to hell;
> Satan sits where Our Lord did sway:
> Walsingham, Oh farewell![14]

The style of the lament is echoed in Richard Corbett's ballad "The Fairies' Farewell," which similarly locates the detrimental effects of Protestant reform on land and the loss of enchantment, "lamenting the passing of a time when divine beneficence had been communicated through the agency of popular customs":[15]

> Lament, lament, old Abbeys,
>   The Fairies' lost command!
> They did but change Priests' babies,
>   But some have changed your land.[16]

As dean of Christchurch, Oxford, for a time, Corbett was reputed to have sung ballads in disguise as parishioners entered the church for a sermon. The motif of combining disguises and singing continues as John Aubrey records a related anecdote of Corbett putting on a ballad hawker's "leathern jacket" and singing his songs in an alehouse in order to help him sell broadsides.[17]

Each of these various tunes and verses intersects with the specific performance circle of "Fraunics New Jigge" at distinct points, and, as I have argued of ballad tunes generally, the musicality of such tunes operates within a sense of vertical time. That ballad tunes were commonly derived from older pastimes and were also recycled in intentional relation to their specific themes demonstrates their capacity for performatively summoning the festival tradition of the past while also invoking a time future when events including individual song and jig performances are experienced within the associative context of the Christian liturgical seasons. To indicate a tune like "Walsingham," moreover, would have exaggerated this intertemporal effect.

These factors of tune recycling, intertextuality, and intertemporality show the tune assignment of Walsingham in "Francis New Jigge" to be loaded with old-religion nostalgia but, more importantly, also to beckon toward an early modern performance culture that unreservedly circulated material and that owned a certain kind of collective autonomy—to state it paradoxically—especially regarding its inculcations of religious practice, new and old, into dramatic forms. "Walsingham" is one of many items of popular religious *and* theatrical knowledge that refuses to fit neatly into a confessional movement but instead gains a unique theatrical-religious identity through its many rewritings and repurposings in poems, plays, ballads, jigs, and sermons—as later Protestant sermons attacked the shrine as a symbol of idolatry.[18]

The ballad's and its tune's play on the cultural memory of a time past, I suggest, is characteristic of the performative effects of postlude jigs in the playhouse. On stage, "Frauncis New Jigge" may have been performed as a singular drama after the final act of the play, but given the reputations of clowns for engaging in audience banter, acrobatics, tricks, and dancing, sung dramas like this one also probably appeared among a collection of postlude entertainments and thus may have been received not simply as farcical diversions but also as brief escapes into organized dialogue drama. Because of their notable uses of dialogue, plot, and elements of song and dance, and despite their reputation for sidetracking the emotional resolution of the play that preceded them, it is not a stretch to say that jigs may have struck the majority of audience members as of a piece with the play, as both were surrounded by inter-act amusements, games, and songs.

There is a way in which the pilgrimage framing device in "Frauncis New Jigge" reflects the perceptual attitude with which audiences watched it. With the first line, the pilgrimage creates a scene of festival, liberty, and desire not unlike that which *Twelfth Night* introduces with its title and the early performance occasion as recorded by Manningham. And as with Viola, it is only through an identity trick that relational fidelity can be restored.

FRAUNCIS. But tel mee sweet when shall I enjoy
    my hearts delight.
BESSE. I prethee sweete heart be not coy,
    even soone at night.
    My husband is rid ten miles from home,
    money to receive:
    In the evening see you come.
FRAUNCIS. Til then I take my leave. EXIT:
BESSE. Thus have I rid my hands full well
    of my amorous love,
    And my sweet husband wil I tell,
    how hee doth me move.[19]

Frauncis and Besse meet when they cross paths to and from the shrine. The religious pastime context introduces elements of pastoral and saturnalia through which Frauncis is emboldened to importune Besse, and Besse, for her part, instead of simply turning him away, takes the opportunity—perhaps the saturnalian occasion—to facilitate a bed trick replete with disguises and a mask. If we imagine this jig being performed after plays, for example, *Twelfth Night* or even *Doctor Faustus*, with its male player disguised as a demon and then further disguised as the female Helen, then its bawdiness and popular setting appear to come in stride, particularly at the provocative moment when Besse and Mistress Frauncis swap articles of clothing.

In a significant way the jig's performative strategies draw on the trans-Reformational underpinnings of early modern theatricality. Jig clowning, for instance, evolves from the Vice tradition. Its dance and musicality, combined with the free-speaking commentary of fool characters, correspond in a way with the chorus role. To understand the jig's intermediary function, a helpful comparison can be drawn between the performative roles of the Elizabethan clown and the ancient chorus. In Attic theater, *choreutai* served a ritual function. In tragedies performed at the Festival of Dionysus, the chorus performed in the orchestra between the main platform and the audience, and their lines were sung and pantomimed. Its music and mimetic movements integrated the play into the greater religious festival, which was structured around songs, symbolic bodily movement, and processions. In this way tragic choruses were intertemporal in depicting the fiction and the ritual occasion at once.[20] Thus, while the Greek chorus warned characters about the fickleness of Fortune and encouraged moderate action, it also formed a continuum with the broader occasion and with its dominant perceptual registers in music and collective movement.[21] It may seem asymmetrical to compare the choruses of Aeschylus and Euripides to the jigs that followed plays by playwrights like Shakespeare at least until 1600, but I posit that the performative capabilities of intermediary characters like the clown serve a function that accompanies drama through many periods and places, especially when performances feature in larger festival events. While Renaissance dramatic choruses do not seem to have engaged in ode singing and pantomime, they share a theatrical identity in the playhouse with many other acts of music and clowning, including mummings, pantomime, dumb shows, intra-act entertainment, ballads sung during the action, fools, and, most of all, jigs. These predominantly musical and clownish forms adopted a ritual, or performative, function in the early modern playhouse as intermediaries between the genre forms that playwrights adapted and the medieval religious world of festival endemic to England.

The jig thus reminds us that the greater atmosphere and history of the early modern playhouse is that of religious festival—and also ritual, when viewed through the comparison to choruses—and it incites the kind of audience collectivity and perceptual self-awareness in which events like the boy bishop festivities, Elizabeth's coronation, and the Chester cycle ground their spiritual and political action. Writing about tragedy, David Wiles states, "Clown and tragic hero remained in some measure descendants from the allegorical interlude, and each represented different fragments of the experience of a single mankind."[22] We can think of the jig, like the Greek chorus, the medieval Vice, and the early modern Lord of Misrule, as pulling the audience away from scenes of isolation that risk tragic downfall—scenes like Henry V's desperate soliloquy and Faustus's self-musings in his study—as well as from scenes of immobile solitude in comedy—such as Olivia in mourning and the lovesick ramblings of Orsino. In turn, the jig repositions the audience before scenes of revelry, transgressive pleasure, and pastoral mirth that imbue laughter and quotidian domestic friendship with a feeling of transcendence that the drama theatrically invokes by harkening to its history in liturgy, seasonal festivals, wedding celebrations, and, though at some distance, the sacramental underpinnings of miracle drama.

Postlude jigs remind audiences that even tragic plays exist in a greater context of comedy, understood in the sense of *commedia*, structured around a whole view of Christian history, where the "experience of the participants is transition from guilt to innocence, from separation to communion."[23] We can see this deference to the larger festival setting especially in jigs' scenes of resolution. For instance, "Frauncis new Jigge" closes with a stanza of interwoven dialogue between four characters who pledge to forget one another's grievances in the spirit of community:

BESSE. I thank you gentle Mistris. RICHARD. Faith & so do I.
    sir, learne your owne wife to know:
  And shoote not in the darke, for feare you mis the marke.
BESSE. He hath paid for this I trow.
  All women learn of me. FRANCIS. All men by me take heed
    how you a woman trust.
WIFE. Nay women trust no men. FRANCIS. And if they do:
    how then?
WIFE. Ther's few of them proove just.
  Farewell neighbour Richard, farewell honest Besse
    I hope wee are all friends.
WIFE. And if you stay at home, and use not thus to rome
    heere all our quarrell ends.

The last lines are allotted to the Wife, the only nameless character, who asserts one final contingency, that Francis "stay at home, and use not thus to rome." Were this scene to be performed at the end of a play or especially following a tragic catastrophe it might stand out, first, for its commitment to the domestic and, second, for the emotional flexibility demonstrated by its characters, who accept an exchange of confession and forgiveness by simply appearing before one another.

It is key to understand scenes of reconciliation like this one within the phenomenality of their appearing in the playhouse, and especially with regard to the clown's distinct capacity to inhabit two intentional positions at once—what I have been calling performative multistability.[24] The clown is always character and player simultaneously, and while this dual identity exists in the jig, it is present with even stronger duality during the play that precedes it, where with each of the clown's appearances the audience anticipates the recognizable player breaking character and stepping in between—as he frequently does. Thus the clown puts the audience in mind of the paradoxes and framing drama of festival: hierarchy and subversion, feasting and fasting, seasonal change—"Our stern alarums changed to merry meetings," "All things that we ordained festival / Turn from their office to black funeral."[25] And the jig, where the clown is allowed to orchestrate a performance of his own, rebinds the play that preceded it to the intergeneric performance culture from which it came by drawing the audience's attention to the performance in the here and now, giving it over to the capacious mirth of the playhouse event.

On the one hand, we might attribute the ease with which Frauncis, his Wife, Besse, and Richard resolve a problem—a problem that in a full-fledged play might have proved detrimental to their community—to the narrative derivativeness that we come to expect from jigs and ballads, but in the inter- and intratheatrical context of the playhouse event this conventionality is a function of the jig's ritual capacity to hold multiple times and multiple identities at once. "Frauncis new Jigge" is intertemporal in that the characters' reconciliation exists in the vertical time of festival, where social upheaval is understood holistically as a condition of the same human waywardness that empowers the drama of events like the Chester cycle and King Henry's Crispin's Day speech. Likewise, the jig is multistable in that the characters, like the clown and the chorus, simultaneously represent a fictional identity and embody the society immediately present at the playhouse. Or put another way, Frauncis, his Wife, Besse, and Richard embody the kind of society that the jig wants to *project onto* the audience. In contrast with the isolationism that produces suffering in plays, these jig characters specify an attitude characterized by circumspection and by performative mobility—the ability to move through performance types and to adapt to the audience identities that they incite.

IN ATTUNING ITS audiences to the larger picture of the playhouse event, the postlude jig magnifies the theatricality and human strategies of the play that precedes it. In this way, the jig is exemplary of early modern performance culture as a whole. Like the jig, the other performance events I have examined in this book grasp the theatrical nuance of their historical connections to festival occasions and redistribute these theatrical Christian contexts through situational forms such as ceremony, acoustical echoes, and stage devils. And they present these intermediary forms as constructive problems that demand complex involvement from the audience. Early modern performances forthrightly expose their audiences to the processes of theatrical becoming in order to reflect human strategy, and they do so predominantly without discriminating between past and present, content and frame, representation and ritual. Performance culture owes the capaciousness of its objects, bodies, spaces, and illocutions as well as its audiences' dexterous viewing habits to the trans-Reformational energies that persisted in theater itself. To end with a jig, then, is to turn audience members toward one another; to emphasize the collectivity of emotion, interpretation, and devotion; and to organize the theatrical event not around individual genre types but around the fluent and creative audiences through which we discover innovative—though, often *old*—points of felicitous contact.

NOTES

Prelude

1. Cummings, *Mortal Thoughts*, 159.
2. Weimann and Bruster, *Shakespeare*, 1.
3. Beckwith, *Signifying God*; Clopper, *Drama, Play, and Game*; Cooper, *Shakespeare*; Schreyer, *Shakespeare's Medieval Craft*.
4. Schreyer, *Shakespeare's Medieval Craft*, 7.
5. Groves, *Texts and Traditions*, 59.
6. Clopper, *Drama, Play, and Game*, 3–4.
7. Targoff, *Common Prayer*; Sterrett, *Unheard Prayer*; Swift, *Shakespeare's Common Prayers*; Rosendale, *Liturgy and Literature*.
8. Knapp, *Shakespeare's Tribe*.
9. Marsh, *Music and Society*; B. Smith, *Acoustic World*; Fumerton, *Ballads, Performance*. See also Smith and Lupton, "Ballads+."
10. Gurr, *Shakespeare Company*; Stern, *Making Shakespeare* and *Documents of Performance*; Wiles, *Shakespeare's Clown*; Weimann and Bruster, *Shakespeare*.
11. Waldron, *Reformations of the Body*; Owens, *Stages of Dismemberment*; Maus, *Inwardness and Theater*; Craik and Pollard, *Shakespearean Sensations*; Jackson, *Image Ethics*; Zysk, *Shadow and Substance*. I regret not to have interacted more with Zysk's trans-Reformational study, as it was published after my book was completed.
12. O'Connell, *Idolatrous Eye*; Williamson, *Materiality of Religion*; Degenhardt and Williamson, *Religion and Drama*; Poole, *Supernatural Environments*; Lin, *Shakespeare*. See also the essays in Mardock and McPherson, *Stages of Engagement*.
13. B. Smith, "Premodern Sexualities," 325. A collection of historical phenomenological approaches to Shakespeare is found in Curran and Kinney's special issue of *Criticism* entitled "Shakespeare and Phenomenology."
14. M. Smith, "Describing the Sense," 151.
15. K. Jackson and Marotti, "Turn to Religion," 176.

Chapter One
EARLY MODERN THEATRICALITY ACROSS THE REFORMATION

1. Find this liturgy detailed in Leach, *Schools of Medieval England*, 148–50. Practices varied even in dioceses within England, with some boy officiant practices occurring on St. Nicholas's Day. An overview of the boy bishop tradition in England in the years after the Reformation can be found in DeMolen, "*Pueri Christi Imitatio*," 17–28.

2. See Nichols, "Two Sermons," 1–29.

3. Chambers, *Mediaeval Stage*, 1:347; Leach, *Schools of Medieval England*, 152.

4. Chambers, *Mediaeval Stage*, 1:361.

5. Massingberd, *English Reformation*, 88.

6. Nichols, "Two Sermons," 14.

7. Ibid., 19.

8. Ibid., 20.

9. Opinion about the received efficacy of the progress varies, but the event's mastery of the theatrical is usually recognized. For example, Richard McCoy argues that Elizabeth's "considerable theatrical skills diverted attention from the problematic religious ritual to secular civic pageant"; McCoy, "'Wonderful Spectacle,'" 217–18. Alice Hunt writes that while we may "never know what Elizabeth I or contemporary witnesses really understood about her coronation, . . . it is clear that it cannot be dismissed as an empty form, as just 'idle' ceremony, or indeed as simply the abominable 'idol' of Catholic ceremony"; Alice Hunt, *Drama of Coronation*, 173.

10. Alice Hunt, *Drama of Coronation*, 4.

11. Leahy, "Propaganda or a Record," 3.1–20.

12. Alice Hunt, *Drama of Coronation*, 173.

13. Warkentin, *Queen's Majesty's Passage*, 75.

14. A December 7, 1558, document from *London: Corporation City of London, Court of Aldermen*, Repertories, XIV, 1558–1561, fols. 97r–98r, in Warkentin, *Queen's Majesty's Passage*, 117.

15. Alice Hunt, *Drama of Coronation*, 66; and Kinney, *Renaissance Drama*, 19.

16. Warkentin, *Queen's Majesty's Passage*, 79.

17. Ibid., 86.

18. Ibid., 80.

19. Ibid., 79–80. Elizabeth also instructed a messenger to precede her train on the procession route and to order the crowds to be quiet enough for the queen to hear the speeches. About the cacophony at James I's similar progress, Bruce Smith notes that "the narrator of James's entry adds to the murmur of the Masses the tolling of bells in the towers of 123 parish churches and the clamor of drinkers taking advantage of the wine flowing in the conduits, and the aura of aural chaos threatens to overcome the best-laid plans of the devisers"; "Sounding Shakespeare's London," paper presented at "Urbanmusics" Conference, Barcelona, September 24–26, 2015.

20. Translations are from Kinney, *Renaissance Drama*, 24.

21. "quietness, n.," *OED Online*, 3rd ed.

22. Merleau-Ponty, *Phenomenology of Perception*, 421.

23. Matt. 2:1, Authorized Version.

24. Two extended arguments supporting the view that Shakespeare wrote the play specifically for performance at Middle Temple are Gras, "*Twelfth Night*," 545–64, and Arlidge, *Shakespeare*.

25. Martin, *Minutes of Parliament*, 1:318.

26. Marston, *What You Will*, sig. A2r, Av3.

27. Ibid., sig., A3r.

28. Martin, *Minutes of Parliament*, 418.

29. James P. Bednarz, quoting the play itself, comments that Marston's title "is accommodating and obliging rather than the work of an author who rails against 'squinting *Critickes*, drunken *Censure*, splay-footed *Opinion*'"; Bednarz, "John Marston's Induction," 300. In a productive exchange, Bednarz is responding to Rebecca Yearling's critique of his treatment of the Induction's invective on Ben Jonson. Bednarz argues that Marston's play demonstrates a greater respect for his audience, which I find to be commensurate with the perspective of comedy in festival culture: "In *What You Will*, Marston at Paul's refused to duplicate Jonson's superior attitude toward his audience at Blackfriars and emphasized instead his own unfitness for the task at hand" (301). See Yearling, "John Marston's *What You Will*," 109–23, and Yearling, "*What You Will*," 2:308–13.

30. See Wiles, *Shakespeare's Clown*, 1–10.

31. Ibid., x.

32. Barber, *Shakespeare's Festive Comedy*, 4–5.

33. See Colie, *Resources of Kind*. References to *Twelfth Night* are from Shakespeare, *Twelfth Night*, ed. Elam.

34. Masten, "Editing Boys," 119.

35. W. Slights, "'Maid and Man,'" 327–48.

36. Jane Taylor explores some of the early modern complexities of performative sincerity in "'Why Do You Tear Me,'" 19–43. See also Smith, "w/Sincerity."
37. Jenkins, "Shakespeare's *Twelfth Night*," 177.
38. Fischer-Lichte, *Transformative Power of Performance*, 88–89.
39. Witmore, "Eventuality," 386–401.
40. West, "Intertheatricality," 154–55.
41. B. Smith, *Acoustic World*, 136.
42. George Wither mentions "base fellows" who "bring forth a rhime, / A curtain jig, a libel, or a ballet / For fidlers, or some rogues with staff and wallet / To sing at doors." "Satire III: Of Weakness," in *Poems*, 1:283.
43. Postlewait, "Theatricality and Antitheatricality," 97; Barish, *Antitheatrical Prejudice*, 132.
44. Howard, *Stage and Social Struggle*, 48.
45. Knapp, *Shakespeare's Tribe*, 9; Donne, *Sermons*, 10:132.
46. O'Connell, *Idolatrous Eye*, 17.
47. Turner, "Generalization," 4. Turner's collection *Early Modern Theatricality* includes studies of interiority, sources, stages, occasion, mobility, and reading, among many other topics. His editorial argument revises Barish's notion of "equivocal" theater by insisting on the audience's complicity in conducting the theatrical; theatricality purportedly offers "a new account of the specific and plural modes of being that ideas assume, of how we live with them and of how they often live parasitically through us" (21).
48. Michael Jackson, "Introduction," 6.
49. Crane, "What Was Performance?" 170.
50. Julia Lupton summarizes, "Drama and phenomenology are thus closely linked, since each makes the company of others into a condition of action." Lupton, *Thinking with Shakespeare*, 15. Kearney and Curran add that Renaissance explanations of "feeling and sensing," like many other instances of affect, "resist objectification because they are always, in part, inside us, even as they also depend upon social and material environments to occur": Curran and Kearney, "Introduction," 354. As Witmore states, Shakespeare "used the specific resources of the theatre—that is, its physical limitations; its reliance on sound, speech, and gesture; its indebtedness in performance to the passage of chronological time—to say equally specific things about the relatedness of beings in the world and their mutual participation in some larger, constantly changing whole"; *Shakespearean Metaphysics*, 6. Similarly, Smith has suggested that "peculiarly important to

historical phenomenology are the stories that THWS [the historical William Shakespeare] and his contemporaries told themselves about perception, about what was happening to their bodies and brains when they looked, listened, read, and loved"; B. Smith, *Phenomenal Shakespeare*, 34.

51. Husserl, *Ideas*, 201.

52. I have explored literary critical "description" as a form of imaginative variance in M. Smith, "Sense of Confession."

53. Merleau-Ponty, *Phenomenology of Perception*, 159.

54. Ibid., 421.

55. I am inspired here by Lupton's stress on the preposition *with* in *Thinking with Shakespeare*.

56. Fischer-Lichte, *Transformative Power of Performance*, 16.

57. Consider, for example, that an aspect of performance takes on a referential function when its primary purpose is external to the action, as when a character reports offstage events already known to the characters but told for the sake of the audience. The referential overlaps with the phatic (the creation of context and mutual understanding of idiom) as the representation overlaps with its theatrical frame: both the referential and representational defer meaning, while the phatic and the theatrical provide the means to grasp it. Pfister, *Theory and Analysis*, 106–7.

58. Austin, *How to Do Things*, 22.

59. Fish, "How to Do Things," 1003. See also Fish's more recent article, "There Is No Textualist Position," 629–50.

60. A. Parker and Sedgwick, *Performativity and Performance*, 13.

61. Josette Feral describes performativity as a modality of the theatrical: "In integrating performativity within itself, theatricality sees it as one of its fundamental modalities, giving theatricality its power and meaning. In fact, such an approach allows us to better understand any spectacle, which is an interplay of both performativity and theatricality." From the foreword to "Theatricality," special issue, *SubStance*, 5.

62. "What's so surprising, in a thinker otherwise strongly resistant to moralism, is to discover the pervasiveness with which the excluded theatrical is hereby linked with the perverted, the artificial, the unnatural, the abnormal, the decadent, the effete, the diseased. We seem, with Austinian 'etiolation,' to be transported not just to the horticultural laboratory, but back to a very different scene: the Gay 1890s of Oscar Wilde." A. Parker and Sedgwick, *Performativity and Performance*, 5.

63. Ibid., 2.

64. Weber, *Theatricality as Medium*, 8; my italics.
65. Ibid., 10.
66. Crane, "What Was Performance," 184.
67. Fried, *Absorption and Theatricality*, 95.
68. Ibid., 95–96.
69. Lin, "Festivity," 227. She writes also that festivity "permeated the generic conventions and semiotic practices of theatrical performance and profoundly shaped the affective experiences and interpretive modes of early modern audience members" (213).
70. Husserl, "Pure Phenomenology," 12.
71. Shakespeare, *King Henry V*, Prologue 28.
72. Donne, *Sermons*, 9:123.
73. An abbreviated list of publications on early modern English Catholicism includes Bossy, *English Catholic Community*; Haigh, *Reformation and Resistance*; Walsham, *Church Papists*; Duffy, *Stripping of the Altars*; and Questier, *Catholicism and Community*.
74. Greenblatt, *Shakespearean Negotiations*, 109. Some scholars have continued to advance a similar thesis about the mutual exclusivity of religious belief and theatrical representation. In Dollimore's account, theatrical representation, by virtue of its patent artificiality, reveals the ideology of cultural practices. Dollimore, *Radical Tragedy*, 11–13. In essence, these readings view theater itself as critiquing the performative functions of religion, gender, the state, or whatever cultural institution is being theatrically represented. Thus the ways that theatricality works upon human psychology and social habits are at the center of the turn to religion in early modern drama studies. If we take this approach to its extreme, as Anthony Dawson does, we might consider whether the nature of theatrical representation is psychologically exclusive from religious activity, that "theatrical belief replaces religious faith" in drama; Dawson, "Shakespeare and Secular Performance," 97. Or, in John Parker's opinion, Christianity's influence on Renaissance theatricality may amount merely to a "specific brand of feigning that pretends to repudiate whatever mimetic practice it most depends on"; J. Parker, *Aesthetics of the Antichrist*, 16–17.
75. As Jean Howard says: "Theater's representations of religious content do not simply effect 'the straightforward promulgation of dogma' or its opposite but, at the very least, present audiences with the raw 'ideological contestation' that representation brings to light—contestations, for instance, between mysteries that are sustained and others that are debunked"; *Stage and Social Struggle*, 7. See also White, *Theatre and Reformation*.

76. Diehl, *Staging Reform*, 5.
77. K. Jackson and Marotti, "Turn to Religion," 177.
78. Waldron, *Reformations of the Body*, 56.
79. Beckwith, *Shakespeare*, 172.
80. Schwartz, *Sacramental Poetics*, 7; Coleman, *Drama and the Sacraments*, 60–90. Though it focuses on early modern lyric poetry rather than drama, Kimberly Johnson's recent book also addresses the void of sacramental reform by drawing attention to audience response and to related semiotic troubles in sacramental theology; Johnson, *Made Flesh*.
81. Bishop, *Shakespeare*, 87.
82. Kastan, *Will to Believe*; McCoy, *Faith in Shakespeare*. For an earlier version of the sacramental theater argument, see Barber, "Family in Shakespeare's Development," 188–202.
83. Elsewhere, I discuss the "ritual poetics" of sacramentally laden texts and performances. Such works are sacramentally remarkable, I argue, precisely because they are devoid of God's presence and are encountered as "disincarnate"; M. Smith, "Disincarnate Text."
84. Groves, *Texts and Traditions*, 26–59.
85. Cooper, *Shakespeare*, 43–44.
86. Paul Whitfield White offers the important reminder that there were many professing puritans in early modern England who did not lump the theaters in with the religious ceremonialism they attacked, and that in fact some had "a personal investment in playing—sponsors, playwrights, and players"; White, "Theater and Religious Culture," 134.
87. Perkins, *Reformed Catholike*, 1598, 295–96.
88. Ibid., 297.
89. Perkins, *Treatise*, 35.
90. Hooker, *Of the Laws*, 2:244.
91. Ibid., 2:245; italics added.
92. Ibid., 2:236, 37.
93. Cummings, *Mortal Thoughts*, 173.
94. Schalkwyk, *Speech and Performance*, 106.
95. One compelling argument that Shakespeare did, in fact, have sacramental theology in mind when writing *Hamlet* is Zysk, "In the Name."
96. Augustine, *Confessions*, 4.
97. Poole, *Supernatural Environments*, 6.
98. Augustine, *Confessions*, 5.
99. Ibid., 201.
100. Hall, introduction to Hall, *Lived Religion in America*, viii.
101. Orsi, *Madonna of 115th Street*, xxiii–xxiv.

Chapter Two
THE REAL PRESENCE/ABSENCE OF GOD IN THE CHESTER CYCLE PLAYS

1. The last recorded performance of the Chester cycle was in 1575, while cycle plays at Doncaster and Durham appear to have been produced up to 1576, and another in Coventry in 1579. Guilds continued to produce plays in Lancaster and Kendall into the seventeenth century; see George, *Lancashire*, xliii, 29.

2. Schreyer, *Shakespeare's Medieval Craft*; Groves, *Texts and Traditions*; Clopper, *Drama, Play, and Game*.

3. Clopper, *Drama, Play, and Game*, 138.

4. Davidson, "Tretise of miraclis pleyinge," 2:243–47, 216–19.

5. Lerud, *Memory, Images*, 6.

6. Rogerson, "Affective Piety," 93.

7. James, "Drama and Social Body," 3–29; Scherb, *Staging Faith*; Gibson, *Theater of Devotion*; Coleman, *Drama and the Sacraments*; Wickham, *Early English Stages*.

8. Beckwith, *Signifying God*.

9. *Sarum Missal*, trans. Warren, 362. Except when noted, I use this edition for translations of the Sarum rite. It is translated from the folio edition of 1526 and takes some license in order to grasp the theological and symbolic intent of the Latin song. On occasion, I will provide my own more literal translation.

10. Mills, *Chester Mystery Cycle*, 1.136f. Citations from the plays are from this edition and will appear in the text (play number. line numbers) unless otherwise noted.

11. For the letter of suppression to Wakefield, see Cawley, *Wakefield Pageants*, 125. For the troupe's visit to York, see Johnston and Rogerson, *York*, i.

12. See especially Johnston, "Feast of Corpus Christi." In addition to well-cited introductions to individual play cycles, several books outline early references to festivals, processions, and plays, including Kolve, *Play Called Corpus Christi*; Rubin, *Corpus Christi*; and Walters, Corrigan, and Ricketts, *Feast of Corpus Christi*.

13. Mills, *Recycling the Cycle*, 146.

14. Salter, "Banns [pt. 2]," 139, 145.

15. Schreyer suggests that the "booke" refers to the "White Book of Pentice"; *Shakespeare's Medieval Craft*, 65.

16. Ibid., 64, 67.
17. Salter, "Banns [pt. 2]," 142–43.
18. Clopper, *Drama, Play, and Game*, 23.
19. Goodman, *Christopher Goodman's Letter-book*, 119. For an in-depth discussion of Goodman's book, see Mills, *Recycling the Cycle*, 146.
20. Goodman, *Christopher Goodman's Letter-book*, 119, quoted in Mills, *Recycling the Cycle*, 147.
21. Davidson, "Tretise," 2.369–61.
22. See Clopper, *Drama, Play, and Game*, 106.
23. Lumiansky and Mills, *Chester Mystery Cycle: Essays*, 266.
24. Waldron, *Reformations of the Body*, 77.
25. James, "Drama and Social Body," 98. Following John Bossy's article "Mass as Social Institution," historians have explored how the Eucharist in general served to unify social groups (34–35).
26. E. Baldwin, Clopper, and Mills, *Cheshire*, xxvi.
27. Rice and Pappano, *Civic Cycles*, 43.
28. Mills, *Recycling the Cycle*, 117. Mills is reluctant, however, to say that the body of Christ as a symbol contributes in any deliberate way to this integration.
29. Rice and Pappano, *Civic Cycles*, 4.
30. A good example of one approach to this problem is Beckwith's use of ritual theory in Bourdieu and Merleau-Ponty to argue that medieval drama enacts—rather than merely represent—social relations; Beckwith, *Signifying God*, 28–41.
31. E. Baldwin, Clopper, and Mills, *Cheshire*, 71–72.
32. Witmore's discussion of immanence is especially helpful for its combining of dramaturgy and metaphysics. He focuses specifically on the metaphysical thought of Whitehead, Bergson, and Spinoza for contextualizing Shakespeare historically among philosophers. Witmore, *Shakespearean Metaphysics*, 3.
33. Husserl, *Idea of Phenomenology*, 24.
34. States, "Phenomenological Attitude," 371.
35. Berger, *Sacred Canopy*, 112.
36. Gregory, *Unintended Reformation*.
37. C. Taylor, *Secular Age*, 15.
38. Ibid.
39. Miri Rubin calls the Eucharist the "raison d'etre" of the feast/procession. *Corpus Christi*, 245.
40. Ibid., 34.

41. Rancière, *Politics of Aesthetics*. See especially 7–14.
42. Augustine, *Confessions*, 4.
43. Beckwith, *Signifying God*, 66.
44. Davidson, *York Corpus Christi Plays*, 35.253–58.
45. I have considered the theatrical frames of real presence as a kind of "ritual poetics" in an essay included in a special issue of *Christianity and Literature* on sacramentality and literary studies; M. Smith, "Disincarnate Text."
46. Fischer-Lichte, *Transformative Power of Performance*, 27.
47. Rancière, *Politics of Aesthetics*, 8.
48. Lerud argues at length for cycle drama's various inheritances from Aristotle's *De anima*, and this influence largely explains the "living picture" characterization: *Memory, Images*. Note that Rancière too briefly discusses this difference between accounting for aesthetic change between painting and drama as "living" rather than as three-dimensional; Rancière, *Politics of Aesthetics*, 10–11.
49. Salter, "Banns [pt. 2]," 146.
50. Yates, *Error, Misuse, Failure*, xvii.
51. Marion, "They Recognized Him," 150.
52. Kelly, "Doubt and Religious Drama," 55.
53. Hall, *Lived Religion in America*, 7.
54. While the Carpenters are mentioned in only one source for the Whitsun plays, there is evidence to suggest that later sources' labels of "wrights" refer to the carpenters. See Lumniansky and Mills, *Chester Mystery Cycle: Essays*, 170.
55. Salter, "Banns [pt. 1]," 9.
56. Lumiansky and Mills, *Chester Mystery Cycle: Essays*, 206.
57. Ibid., 191.
58. Purkess, "Crammed with Distressful Bread?," 12.
59. Lupton, *Thinking with Shakespeare*, 64.
60. *Sarum Missal*, 361. The Latin version of the noted passage reads, "Oculi omnium in te sperant, Domine, et tu das illis escam in tempore opportuno; Aperis tu manum tuam: et imples omne animal benedictione," Here and subsequently, the Latin edition used is *Missale ad Usum Insignis Ecclesiae Sarum*, sig. O6v–O7r. I have expounded abbreviated words.
61. *Sarum Missal*, 42. "Te igitur clementissime pater per ihisem christum filium tuum dominum nostrum supplices rogamus ac petimus uti accepta habeas et benedictas. Hec + dona. Hec + munera. Hec + sancta sacrificial illibata. . . . que tibi offerimus."

62. Weber, *Theatricality as Medium*, 10.
63. Salter, "Banns [pt. 2]," 142.
64. Seel, *Aesthetics of Appearance*, 56.
65. Ong, *Presence of the Word*, 6.
66. Milton, *Complete Prose Works*, 6:553. Many have written on this topic. A good overview can be found in Macy, "Of Mice and Manna," 157–66.
67. Harris, *Untimely Matter*, 4.
68. Schreyer, *Shakespeare's Medieval Craft*, 73–103.
69. See my discussion of Austin and performativity in chapter 1.
70. Arendt, *Human Condition*, 53, quoted in Lupton, *Thinking with Shakespeare*, 12.
71. Lupton, *Thinking with Shakespeare*, 12.
72. M. Morton, "Making Space," 7–8.
73. The central panel of Dieric Bouts the Elder's triptych *The Last Supper* (1464–47) and Domenico Ghirlandaio's fresco *The Last Supper* (1480), both fifteenth century, are two additional examples of "pav-ed floors and windows bright."
74. Mills, *Recycling the Cycle*, 153.
75. *Sarum Missal*, 361. Latin: "Caro mea vere est cibus: et sanguis meus vere est potus." *Cibus* is translated as "meat" rather than "food."
76. *Sarum Missal*, 362. Latin: "panis vivus et vitalis / hodie proponitur."
77. "Quem in sacrae mensa coenae, / turbae fratrum duodenae / datum non ambigutur."
78. *Sarum Missal*, 362. Latin: "In hac mensa novi regis / novum Pascha novae legis / phase vetus terminat. / Vetustatem novitas, / umbram fugat veritas, / noctem lux illuminat."
79. *Sarum Missal*, 363; italics added. Latin: "Dogma datur Christianis, / quod in carnem transit panis, / et vinum in sanguinem. / Quod non capis, quod non vides, / animosa firmat fides, / praeter rerum ordinem. / Sub diversis speciebus, / signis tantum et non rebus, / latent res eximiae: / Caro cibus, sanguis potus; / manet tamen Christus totus / Sub utraque specie."
80. *Sarum Missal*, trans. Pearson, xxii.
81. Salter, "Banns [pt. 2]," 146.
82. Wickham, *Early English Stages*, 27.
83. Coleman, *Drama and the Sacraments*, 33.
84. Lerud, *Memory, Images*; Scherb, *Staging Faith*.
85. Beckwith, *Signifying God*, 60.

86. Gibson, *Theater of Devotion*, 8.

87. Groves, *Texts and Traditions*, 59, 52.

88. As Mills summarizes, "The repeated use of prophecy in the cycle becomes a form of internal cross-reference, giving added coherence to the structure, and also confirmation that historical events move to God's controlling will." *Recycling the Cycle*, 161. See also Harty, "Unity and Structure," 137–58.

89. Salter, "Banns [pt. 2]," 142.

90. Bruce Smith writes at length about this phenomenon in *Acoustic World*. See also my treatment of Claudius's "O" and its interaction with the perceptual lines of early modern round theater in M. Smith, "Describing the Sense."

91. John 16:25 (Authorized Version).

92. Matt. 28:9, 2 (Geneva Bible).

93. Lupton, *Thinking with Shakespeare*, 64.

94. Levinas, *Totality and Infinity*, 79. For the nuances to Levinas's *désincarné*, I am indebted to conversations with Kent Lehnhof. See his essay "Theology, Phenomenology, and the Divine in *King Lear*." I have explored the "disincarnate" as a way of talking about the performativity of so-called sacramental poetics in M. Smith, "Disincarnate Text."

95. "*Désincarné*" is Levinas's term; *Totalité et infini*, 77.

96. M. Smith, "Disincarnate Text."

97. Bishop, *Shakespeare*, 3.

98. Defoe, *Political History*, 55.

99. Salter, "Banns [pt. 2]," 137. David Mills suggests that the actors were probably gilded, based on the angels' description as "gayer than gold"; *Chester Mystery Cycle*, 14.

100. Salter, "Banns [pt. 2]," 142.

101. Rice and Pappano, *Civic Cycles*, 66.

102. Richard Rastall observes that late medieval audiences would have recognized the conventional precedence of heaven being a place of music. In his essay on music in the cycle, Rastall follows John Stevens in framing the function of music in the plays as "representational." In heaven, for instance, music often represents "Divine Order." See Rastall, "Music in the Cycle," 116.

103. Davidson, *York Corpus Christi Plays*, 1.49.

104. Ibid., 1.129–30.

105. Lumiansky and Mills, *Chester Mystery Cycle: A Reduced Facsimile*.

Chapter Three
HENRY V AND THE CEREMONIES OF THEATER

1. B. Smith, *Acoustic World*, 14.
2. Henslowe, *Henslowe's Diary*, 200–201. I've modernized *v*'s and *u*'s.
3. Benson, *Sermon Preached at Paules Cross*, 81; H. Smith, *Sermons*, 645.
4. Prynne, *Histrio-Mastix*, 158.
5. Shakespeare, *Hamlet*, 2.2.491–93.
6. A fuller explanation of the "ceremonialism controversy" of English reform, especially as it relates to literature, can be found in Guibbory, *Ceremony and Community*, 1–43.
7. Gosson, *Playes Confuted*, sig. A8v.
8. Shakespeare, *Shakespeare's Poems*, 305; "cipher, cypher, *n*." and "cipher, cypher, *v*." *OED Online*, 2nd ed.
9. B. Smith, *Acoustic World*, 14.
10. Womersley, *Divinity and State*, 332. With Womersley's, the three most comprehensive studies of *Henry V* and ceremony are chap. 1 of Zeeveld, *Temper of Shakespeare's Thought*; chap. 4 of Hardin, *Civil Idolatry*; and chap. 4 of Knapp, *Shakespeare's Tribe*. Of these four, only Zeeveld argues that Henry fully embraces his ceremonial role. Contrariwise, Hardin and Womersley read Henry as an ideal Protestant king and an iconoclast of sorts, while Knapp lands somewhere in between but emphasizes Henry's antimaterialism in a Protestant vein. A short but insightful study of the iconoclastic elements of *Henry V* and its attention to staging and imagination is Siemon, *Shakespearean Iconoclasm*, 76–113.
11. Other claims that Henry undergoes a conversion/transformation include M. Hunt, *Shakespeare's Religious Allusiveness*; Jordan, "Henry V," 108–19; La Guardia, "Ceremony and History," 68–88; McCoy, "'Thou Idol Ceremony,'" 240–66; Rosendale, "Sacral and Sacramental Kingship," 121–40; C. Slights, "Conscience of the King," 37–55; C. Clegg, "Feared and Loved," 179–207.
12. Sams, *Real Shakespeare*, 11.
13. Although *Henry V* was probably written in 1599, the year that the Globe opened, its original place of performance is unknown. However, the title page of the First Quarto edition of the play says that it was played "sundry times," a good indication that it was performed at some time in the Globe. Creede, *Cronicle History*.

14. Gosson, *Schoole of Abuse*, sig. A2v. Thomas Platter visited both the Globe and a local cockpit in his 1599 trip to London and observed that the cockpit was "built like a theater"; *Platter's Travels in England*, 167–68.

15. For a brief definition of the categorical intention in phenomenology, see Sokolowski, *Introduction to Phenomenology*, 88–90.

16. Merleau-Ponty, *Phenomenology of Perception*, 421.

17. Weber, *Theatricality as Medium*, 14–15.

18. See Craik's introduction to his edition of *King Henry V*, 17–18.

19. The 1600 Quarto includes another fascinating use of *pardon*: "With pardon vnto both your mightines. / . . . / What rub or bar hath thus far hindred you, / To keepe you from the gentle speech of peace?" (5.2.23–67). Among *bar*'s many meanings, the notable repetition of "pardon" here is a reminder of the physical bars that separate the audience from the "gentle speech" of the stage.

20. The First Quarto begins this scene with Pistol immediately addressing the disguised Henry and thus cuts out Henry's request of Erpingham: "Lend me thy cloak, Sir Thomas."

21. "Scenery comes into existence in order to deny that it exists," from States, "Phenomenological Attitude," 372.

22. Sedgwick, *Touching Feeling*, 17.

23. Seigworth and Gregg, "Inventory of Shimmers," 1.

24. Rayner, *Ghosts*, 74, 81.

25. Fischer-Lichte, *Transformative Power of Performance*, 8.

26. M. Hunt, *Shakespeare's Religious Allusiveness*, 35; Knapp, *Shakespeare's Tribe*, 131–32.

27. States, "Phenomenological Attitude," 373.

28. Foucault, *Archaeology of Knowledge*, 7.

29. Shakespeare, *King Lear*, 1.2.86–87, my italics.

30. Nashe, *Pleasant Comedie*, sig. H2v.

31. Womersley points out that Henry's insistence on individual culpability was common in contemporary Protestant discourse, but instead of reading Henry's wavering as a counterpoint to this Protestant vein, Womersley excuses it as "Imperfect sanctification." *Divinity and State*, 335.

32. Shakespeare, *Troilus and Cressida*, 1.3.209–10.

33. Cummings, *Mortal Thoughts*, 170.

34. De Grazia, *"Hamlet" without Hamlet*, 186.

35. Preiss, "Interiority," 48.

36. Admittedly, the meaning of this last "all" is the cause of critical disagreement. There are three main critical options. The first is that "all" means *all sin*, especially the sin of Henry's father. This is the generally accepted

reading. A second option reads "all" as referring to "all that I can do," meaning Henry's Catholic-minded works of penitence, and the third interprets "all" as all that Henry has gained. For commentary on the three possibilities that I consider, see Appendix B to Shakespeare, *Henry V*, ed. Gary Taylor, 295–301.

37. Alan Sinfield and Jonathan Dollimore describe Henry's disguised response to Bates and Williams as "spiritual counsel," "the high point of Henry's priestly function." Sinfield with Dollimore, "History and Ideology," 122.

38. This wording is that of Morris, *Sense of Space*, 33.

39. Shakespeare, *King Henry IV, Part 2*, 5.2.44–45.

40. On iconophobia, see Collinson, *From Iconoclasm to Iconophobia*.

41. Morris, *Sense of Space*, 37.

42. Ibid., 25.

43. Ibid.

44. Constance Slights, in "Conscience of the King," argues that Henry's confidence at the Battle of Agincourt is the culmination of his Protestant conclusion at the end of the soliloquy — "Imploring pardon" — of the representative struggle to Protestant theology. Jonathan Baldo, in "Wars of Memory," makes the connection between the secular and sacred readings explicit when he reads Henry's forswearing of ceremony as a strategy for nationalizing ceremonial authority in St. Crispin's Day. Eric La Guardia makes a similar argument in "Ceremony and History" but puts it in terms of history and ceremony, with Henry choosing history over ceremony — ceremony holding religious connotations.

45. Hardin, *Civil Idolatry*, 126; Rabkin, "Rabbits, Ducks," 287.

46. Hardin, *Civil Idolatry*, 126.

47. M. Hunt, *Shakespeare's Religious Allusiveness*, 36. Additionally, David Womersley insightfully observes that the speech depicts a vision of apocalyptic unity that foils the anxieties earlier expressed by Williams; Womersley, *Divinity and State*, 331–32.

48. Rayner, *Ghosts*, 76, my italics.

49. Marlowe, *Complete Works*, 460.

50. Roy C. Strong's "Popular Celebration" is an informative article on this festival.

51. For further discussion of monarch veneration and alleged idolatry in Elizabethan England, see Montrose, "Idols of the Queen," 108–61.

52. Strong, "Popular Celebration," 100.

53. Ibid., 99.

54. Ibid., 98.

55. More, *Utopia*, 237–39.
56. Hooker, *Of the Laws*, 2:118.
57. Kinney, *Renaissance Drama*, 20.
58. Smuts, "Public Ceremony," 67.
59. Cavendish, *Life of William Cavendish*, 329, my italics. Following the suggestion of the editor, I have amended "maskers" to "masters."
60. "distance, *n*." *OED Online*, 2nd ed.
61. While not exploring its nuances as a ceremony, Joel Altman observes what he describes as a "sacramental" communion between the audience and King Harry in this speech, joining "past to present, audience to soldiery, in an honorable fellowship transcending time and space." Altman, "'Vile Participation,'" 16.
62. Holinshed, *Chronicles*, 79. *J*'s, *u*'s, and *v*'s have been modernized.
63. Witmore, *Shakespearean Metaphysics*, 23–24. Italics have been removed.
64. David Mills, *Chester Mystery Cycle*, 15.77.
65. See Cressy, "God's Time," 394.
66. The link between Hal's soliloquy and the St. Crispin's speech is also made by M. Hunt, *Shakespeare's Religious Allusiveness*, 24–38.
67. Shakespeare, *King Henry IV, Part 1*, 1.2.185, 194.
68. Holinshed, *Chronicles*, 79.
69. Gosson, *Schoole of Abuse*, sig. D3v.
70. Ibid., sig. B6v.
71. Ibid., sig. B7r.
72. Heywood, *Apology for Actors*, sig. F2r.
73. Gardiner, *Letters*, 485.
74. Heywood, *Apology for Actors*, sig., F2r. I have modernized *v*'s and *u*'s.
75. Byrd, *Gratification*.
76. "unsensible, *a*." *OED Online*, 2nd ed.; Bray, *Documents*, 275.
77. Löwith, *Meaning in History*, 186. With a view toward the entire liturgical yearly calendar, vertical time is also cyclical time. In this way, Henry appears in a similar manner to that described by Erika Lin in connection to *The Shoemaker's Holiday*: "The actual historical personage represented by the fictional King becomes less important than the ritual embodiment of a festive monarch." Lin, "Festivity," 224.
78. Alison Chapman has surveyed several depictions of the "shoemaker's holiday" in Renaissance drama. Whereas shoemakers are elsewhere accredited with the creation of the holiday, Chapman argues that in *Henry V* the prerogative for creating St. Crispin's is taken by the king,

which represents a larger shift from popular craftsmen and society to the state for control of the liturgical calendar. Chapman, "Whose Saint Crispin's Day?"

79. Trudell, "Occasion," 233.
80. Ibid., 236, my italics.
81. Lin, "Festivity," 226.
82. Rancière, *Politics of Aesthetics*, 8.
83. Merleau-Ponty, *Primacy of Perception*, 8.
84. Ibid., my italics.
85. Hooker, *Of the Laws*, 2:236, 37.
86. Ibid., 2:351.
87. Ibid., 2:352, my italics.
88. For discussion of this phenomenon, see Freedberg, *Power of Images*; Kibbey, *Interpretation of Material Shapes*, 42; Koerner, *Reformation of the Image*, 107–8.

Chapter Four
GOD'S IDIOMS

1. Donne, *Sermons*, 8:292. Hereafter, all citations of the sermons are to this edition by Potter and Simpson and are given parenthetically in the text by volume and page number.
2. "idiom, n." *OED Online*, 3rd ed.
3. O'Connell, *Idolatrous Eye*, 90.
4. For details about the specific sermon attendees and the allowance of children, I am indebted to Peter McCullough and Mary Morrissey. See City of London, *Order of my Lord Maior*, and Bruce, *Calendar of State Papers*, 300.
5. Wall, "'That Holy Roome,'" 67–70.
6. Crankshaw, "Community, City and Nation," 53–54. For the specific state of singing at St. Paul's, see Wall, "'That Holy Roome,'" 61–84.
7. Quoted in Lamb and Lamb, *Works*, 4:527.
8. B. Smith, *Acoustic World*, 61.
9. Earle, *Microcosmographie*, sig. K1v–K2v.
10. Chamberlain, *Letters Written*, 162.
11. Dekker, *Dead Tearme*, 51.
12. I examine these possibilities in a review of the *Virtual Paul's Cross Project*; M. Smith, "Meeting John Donne."
13. Perkins, *Commentary on Galatians*, 140.

14. Younge, *People's Impartiall and Compassionate Monitor*, 8.

15. The most comprehensive study of these treatises is Arnold Hunt, *Art of Hearing*.

16. Roberts, *Day of Hearing*; Mason, *Hearing and Doing*; Egerton, *Boring of the Ear*; Harrison, *Difference of Hearers*; Burkitt, *Poor Man's Help*. For a list of hearing treatises, see Appendix A to Sullivan's excellent introduction to the art-of-hearing genre, "Art of Listening."

17. Zepper, *Art or Skil*, sig. B1.

18. Williams, *Right Way*, 154.

19. Church of England, *Booke of common praier*, sig. M8, N1.

20. For instance, after one sermon in 1659, Andrew Hay went to his "familie exercise" and "first prayed and then did read the sermones prettie exactlie." Hay, *Diary*, 72–81.

21. T. Morton, *Ecology without Nature*, 48. See also Derrida, *Dissemination*, 20, 106.

22. Fiennes, *Journeys*, 6.

23. Brathwaite, *Essay Upon the Five Sences*, sig. B4v.

24. O'Connell, *Idolatrous Eye*, 36–62.

25. Marion, *Visible and the Revealed*, 9–10. In this discussion Marion is building on the work of the philosopher Rudolf Bultmann.

26. Orsi, "Everyday Miracles," 10.

27. See the anamorphic analogy of the cork in chapter 3.

28. "Archbishop Laud's Visitation of Salisbury in 1634," 122.

29. Shepard, *Subjection to Christ*, sig. N8v.

30. Granger, *Paul's Crown of Rejoycing*, sig. F4.

31. Craig, "Psalms, Groans, and Dogwhippers," 104–23.

32. Mason, *Hearing and Doing*, 667–68, 685.

33. Harrison, *Difference of Hearers*, sig. C8.

34. See Patrick, *Discourse of Profiting*, sig. G1v.

35. Mason, *Hearing and Doing*, 622.

36. Ong, *Presence of the Word*, 128. In Ong's text, the entire passage is italicized.

37. Egerton, *Boring of the Ear*, sig. E1v.

38. Connor, "Ear Room."

39. See M. Smith, "Disincarnate Text."

40. In the first circumstance, see Robert Burton's instruction that fear of God's wrath is often a sign of salvation: God causes anxiety "in some," he writes, "to make a way for his mercy that they repent and be saved, to heal them, to try them, exercise their patience, and make them call upon him, to confess their sins and pray unto him. . . . So that this, which they

take to be such an insupportable plague, is an evident sign of God's mercy and justice, of His love and goodness." Burton, *Anatomy of Melancholy*, 734. For discussion of staging faith, see Scherb, *Staging Faith*. Stephen Greenblatt discusses "regenerative violence" in *Renaissance Self-Fashioning*, 188. Other works that explore Renaissance drama's sacramental functions include Bishop, *Shakespeare*; Knapp, *Shakespeare's Tribe*; Schwartz, *Sacramental Poetics*; Beckwith, *Signifying God* and *Shakespeare*; and Johnson, *Made Flesh*.

41. Schwartz, *Sacramental Poetics*, 13–14.

42. As opposed to a straightforward substitute of drama/poetry for sacrament, Johnson's *Made Flesh* shows how early modern poets reflect the contentions and confusions among an array of theological opinions on the sacraments.

43. For a version of this critique, see Aers, "Whisper in the Ear," 177–202.

44. Granger, *Paul's Crown of Rejoycing*, sig. B1.

45. See also Jeanne Shami's discussion on the Word preached as "efficacious" in *John Donne and Conformity*, 142.

46. M. Smith, "Disincarnate Text."

47. Church of England, *Booke of common praier*, sig. N1v.

48. On the importance of the words of institution in Donne's time, see Richard Hooker's discussion in *Of the Laws*, 2:322–23.

49. Donne, *Devotions upon Emergent Occasions*, 119.

Chapter Five
PERFORMING RELIGION IN EARLY MODERN BALLADS

1. Kahn, *Future of Illusion*, 7. I refer to Kahn's gloss on the "secular" because of its focus on agency and creativity.

2. Chettle, *Kind-harts Dream*, sig. C1r.

3. Samuel Gardiner, *Constitutional Documents*, 139.

4. W. Baldwin, *Canticles*, sig. A3v.

5. Sternhold and Hopkins, *Whole Book of Psalmes*.

6. Nashe, *Pierce Pennilesss's Supplication*, 42.

7. Orsi, *Madonna of 115th Street*, xiii.

8. Ibid., xliv.

9. Gerould, *Ballad of Tradition*, 11.

10. Fumerton, "Why the Broadside Ballad."

11. Atkinson, *English Traditional Ballad*, 11.

12. I borrow the terminology of "ballad publics" from Patricia Fumerton. It's a concept she explores at length in the book *Moving Media, Tactical Publics*. See especially the introduction and chaps. 3, 5, and 6.

13. Fumerton, "Why the Broadside Ballad."

14. Watt, *Cheap Print*, 44–51.

15. "Story of David and Berseba." For this and the majority of the ballads I discuss, I am indebted to the English Broadside Ballad Archive, at the University of California, Santa Barbara, https://ebba.english.ucsb.edu.

16. Watt, *Cheap Print*, 108–9, 95–96.

17. Green, *Print and Protestantism*, 445.

18. Ibid., 470.

19. Ibid., 471.

20. Würzbach, *Rise of the English Street Ballad*, 237.

21. Peter Lake, for example, has studied the case of early modern murder pamphlets to argue for a more sophisticated and creative characterization of "popular" religious practice in England, particularly as it plays out in print, literacy, and "popular taste"; Lake, "Deeds against Nature," 257–84, esp. 258. An additional problem with these criticisms is that they fail to account for the general diversity of recognized forms of orthodoxy in early modern England, brought to light by recent scholarship on recusant and aberrant religious affiliation. I am thinking of the many arguments for Catholic continuity after the Reformation. See especially Duffy, *Stripping of the Altars*; Haigh, *English Reformations*; Walsham, *Church Papists*; and A. Milton, *Catholic and Reformed*.

22. A small sample of such work would include Lin, *Shakespeare*; Schreyer, *Shakespeare's Medieval Craft*; Degenhardt and Williamson, *Religion and Drama*; Williamson, *Materiality of Religion*; Kearney, *Incarnate Text*; and K. Jackson and Marotti, *Shakespeare and Religion*.

23. Pound, "English Ballads," 186.

24. B. Smith, "Putting the 'Ball' Back."

25. B. Smith, *Acoustic World*, 173. In ballad performances the "human body," he writes, is "the site where *objects* becomes *subjects*." B. Smith, afterword, 323.

26. Marsh, *Music and Society*.

27. "Ballad of Anne Askew" [1624].

28. See, for instance, "An Askew"; "Ann Askew"; and "Ballad of Anne Askew" [1688–1709].

29. Orsi, "Everyday Miracles," 9. Orsi's example is of the modern-day veneration of New York City water in a memorial grotto whose devotees

admit the water's municipal origins but cherish the water as if it carried the power of the miraculous.

30. Jonson, *Bartholomew Fair*, 3.5.17–18.

31. This breakdown of Husserl's complicated psychology of perception is taken from Zahavi, *Husserl's Phenomenology*, 36.

32. Atkinson, *English Traditional Ballad*, 12.

33. "Most Excellent Ballad."

34. "Angel Gabriel."

35. Green, *Print and Protestantism*, 458. I am applying Green's analysis to this ballad in particular.

36. Stanyhurst, "From the Translation," 141; Webbe, "Discourse of English Poesie," 1:246.

37. See M. Smith and Lupton, "Ballads+."

38. "Heartie Confession." I have modernized letters but not spelling.

39. Cavendish, *Sociable Letters*, 217.

40. Ibid., 218.

41. Church of England, *Boke of Common Praier*, sig. P8r; also, *The New Testament of Our Lord Iesus Christ*, 577.

42. "Song of Syon."

43. I am referring to the restrictions created on September 20, 1647. See Firth and Rait, *Acts and Ordinances*, 1021–23.

44. I've converted the ballad's in-text marginal flags into superscripts for clarification. In the original, as can be seen in the reproduced image, the italicized scripts are just slightly smaller than normal.

45. Jeremy Chow describes ballads as agents of "solicitation" in "Ballad as Body."

46. West, "Intertheatricality," 157.

47. See my discussion of Austin's "performativity" in theatrical contexts in chapter 1.

48. See my discussion in chapter 6 of the religious influence of topicality and localness in balladry.

49. Tessa Watt uses this ballad, as well as "Ann Askew," as an illustration of the argument that the "broadside ballad was not an appropriate medium for doctrinal or emotional complexity, if it was to be performed by travelling singers intent on catching the attention of the audience" (*Cheap Print*, 126), whereas ballads like this were indeed appropriate for "Protestant propaganda." Part of my contention is that the "complexity" lost with the ballad verse medium is largely reclaimed by the performance, where audience participation, even at the level of comfort and recognition, involved a degree of complexity specific to popular religious performance.

50. "Dying Tears."
51. B. Smith, "Shakespeare's Residuals," 196.
52. Fischer-Lichte, *Transformative Power of Performance*, 88.
53. "Most Excellent Ditty."
54. "Great Brittains Arlarm."
55. Spufford, *Small Books*, 207.
56. "Distressed Pilgrim."
57. Fischer-Lichte, *Transformative Power of Performance*, 17.
58. Christopher Marsh, "Balladry."
59. "Great Tribunal."
60. "Wonderful Prophecy."
61. Brice, "Against Filthy Writing."
62. Whight, "Commendation of Musicke."
63. James Elkins, *Object Stares Back*.
64. B. Smith, *Acoustic World*, 180.
65. Elkins, *Object Stares Back*, 74.
66. "Some Fyne Gloues."
67. "New Yeres Gyft."
68. Ong, *Presence of the Word*, 129.

Chapter Six
THE DEVILS AMONG US

1. Among many examples are Lunney, *Marlowe*; J. Parker, *Aesthetics of the Antichrist*; Cooper, *Shakespeare*; Morse, Cooper, and Holland, *Medieval Shakespeare*.
2. Given the prominence of textual criticism about this play, I have clarified in every quotation which version of the *Faustus* play I am using. Both A- and B-text quotations from *Doctor Faustus* come from the following edition: Marlowe, *Doctor Faustus: A- and B-Texts (1604, 1616)*. Unspecified in-text citations are from the B-text in the same edition. For comparisons I have also relied heavily on Greg, *Marlowe's Doctor Faustus*.
3. Ornstein, "Marlowe and God," 1380.
4. The stage sloped down toward the yard and caused runoff problems. Greenfield and Gurr, "Rose Theatre, London," 336.
5. Lin, *Shakespeare*, 123.
6. Weimann, *Shakespeare*, 32–33.
7. Kolve, *Play Called Corpus Christi*, 144.
8. Lin, *Shakespeare*, 73.

9. I borrow this distinction between theatrical "softscape" and "hardscape" from Lupton, "Shakespearean Softscapes," 144.

10. Levin, *Overreacher*, 26, 161.

11. Melton, *Astrologaster*, 31.

12. Prynne mentions "the *visible apparition of the Devill on the stage at the Belsavage Play-house, in Queene* Elizabeths *dayes, (to the great amazement both of the Actors and Spectators) whiles they were there prophanely playing the History of* Faustus"; Prynne, *Histrio-Mastix*, 556. Middleton writes in allusion to *Faustus* that "hee had a head of hayre like one of my Diuells in Doctor Faustus, when the olde Theatre crackt and frighted the Audience"; Middleton, *Blacke Booke*, sig. B4r. And E. K. Chambers quotes a manuscript report of one-devil-too-many: "Certaine Players at Exeter, acting upon the stage the tragicall storie of Dr. Faustus the Conjurer; as a certain number of Devels kept everie one his circle there, and as Faustus was busie in his magicall invocations, on a sudden they were all dasht, every one harkning other in the eare, for they were all perswaded, there was one devell too many amongst them"; *Elizabethan Stage*, 424.

13. Brooks, "Unity," 372.

14. John Parker, in "Faustus, Confession," examines the question of emptying religion in *Doctor Faustus*, arguing that the play reflects the loss of auricular confession in England.

15. Ornstein, "Marlowe and God," 1379.

16. Levin, *Overreacher*, 120; Greenblatt, *Renaissance Self-Fashioning*, 193–221.

17. To 1991, David Bevington provides a summary of orthodox readings of *Doctor Faustus* in "Marlowe and God." More recent studies have not taken a hard line on the question but often find some middle ground between skepticism and the spiritual reality of the play by attending more to performance conditions and the intersecting of dramaturgy with intellectual atmosphere. A selection includes Banerjee, "I, Mephastophilis"; Hamlin, "Casting Doubt"; Lunney, *Marlowe*; Gates, "Unpardonable Sins"; Jeffrey, "Communion"; Duxfield, "'Resolve Me'"; J. Parker, *Aesthetics of the Antichrist*; Anderson, "Theater of the Damned." See also Pinciss, "*Dr. Faustus*."

18. Diehl, "Dazzling Theater," 235.

19. Cox, *Devil and the Sacred*, 107. See also Chambers, *Mediaeval Stage*, 2:68–105, and Weimann, *Shakespeare*.

20. Moreover, Cox shows that Marlowe's onstage devils computed ambiguously as instances of theatricalized religion, noting that such drama-

tized "ritual" is adjudged "blasphemous" by Faustus and his demonic crew but also embodies a "potent reality" insofar as spiritual ritual results in supernatural activity. *Devil and the Sacred*, 125.

21. Clark, *Thinking with Demons*, 9.
22. Shepherd, *Marlowe*, 107–8.
23. Henslowe, *Henslowe's Papers*, 2.
24. Poole, *Supernatural Environments*, 57. To the same point that the devil represented a stage presence in many ways unassailable by mere skepticism, Cox writes: "The play's ritual, too, is hell, nor are we out of it, but hell is a potent reality, which equivocates . . . to the inevitable destruction of those who palter with it." *Devil and the Sacred*, 126. Andrew Sofer would go as far as speculating that black magic and theatrical magic share the quality of using performative speech acts, so "*Doctor Faustus* equates conjuring with the dangerous verbal magic of performativity itself." Sofer, "How to Do Things," 2.
25. The sequel is called *The Second Report of Doctor John Faustus, containing his appearances and the deeds of Wagner*. The seventeenth-century adaptation is Mountfort's *The Life and Death of Doctor Faustus, made into a Farce*.
26. The relation between plays and broadside ballad versions of play narratives is still predominantly unexplored. In a recent essay from a valuable collection on ballad performance, Lori Newcomb writes: "We hypothesize that some narratives originated as ballad, then were rewritten as a play (*Titus Andronicus*, according to some theories of the play's origins); we know that several plays were rewritten as ballads (if the *Titus* ballad in fact derived from the play, and as *Midsummer Night's Dream*, *Merchant of Venice* and *Winter's Tale* were anthologized during the Interregnum). I like to think of these more substantive overlaps—plays and ballads on common themes—as cognates, a common idea in different material 'dialects.'" Newcomb et al., "Shakespeare in Snippets."
27. "Themselues for spirits arme, / The Gull gets on a surplis, / With a crosse upon his breast, / Like *Allen* playing *Faustus*, / In that manner he was drest." From Rowlands, *Knave of Clubs*, sig. D3r.
28. Greenblatt, *Renaissance Self-Fashioning*, 193–221.
29. "The Just Judgment of GOD shew'd upon Dr. John Faustus"; "The Judgment of God shewed upon one John Faustus."
30. See Goldstein, "Account."
31. MacD. P. Jackson, in "Three Old Ballads," reviews the earliest records of the Faustus ballad, including the manuscript, and argues that

there is good reason to assume the 1589 ballad is the same as that which circulated in the seventeenth century.

32. Marsh, "Balladry."

33. The patterns and variations are reviewed by Goldstein in "Account."

34. For consistency, when referencing the verse text of the ballad I will use "The Just Judgment of GOD shew'd upon Dr. John Faustus," from ca. 1640, British Library, Roxburghe, 280–81. It includes one woodcut, similar to the 1616 quarto of the play.

35. Poole, *Supernatural Environments*, 43, 49.

36. Lunney, *Marlowe*, 51, 54.

37. Ibid., 138–39.

38. It is not clear exactly how much the extant Faustus ballad is based on Marlowe's play because some details in it were not in the 1588 production, or at least not as far as we can tell. For example, in the finale of the ballad the devil dismembers Faustus; in the B-text he is also dismembered, but in the A-text he is simply dragged to hell. This may evince the ballad's reliance on the translated 1587 Faust Book, where he is also dismembered, but it is impossible to know, since we cannot compare the ballad licensed in 1588.

39. "Titus Andronicus Complaint."

40. Prieto-Pablos, "What Art Thou Faustus?"

41. I invoke the definition of *residuals* from B. Smith, "Shakespeare's Residuals," 196.

42. Winstanley, *Lives*, 134. Winstanley borrows the wording of his account of Faustus's cultural reputation from Edward Phillips ten years earlier in *Theatrum Poetarum*, 2.24–25. Vaughan, *Golden-groue*, sig. Y8v.

43. Fowler is described as "the man . . . [who] plaid the devil in Doctor *Faustus*" at the Fortune, when he had an altercation with an audience member who threw a pipe at him. The "devil" could refer to Lucifer or Mephistopheles, but it probably more likely refers to Faustus, as Fowler was the preeminent actor at the Fortune at the time. [John Tatham], *Knavery in All Trades*, sig. D4v–E1r.

44. "Lilly Lash't with his own ROD"; "Recantation of a Penitent Proteus."

45. D'Amico discusses this function of ethnicity in relation to Moors in *Moor*, 343.

46. That *Faustus*'s popular effect is nationalistic runs contrary to some critical opinion; see, for instance, Marcus, *Unediting the Renaissance*, 57–58.

47. In "Three Old Ballads," MacD. Jackson discusses at length the relation between these two ballads and the 1589 Faustus ballad, arguing persuasively that the versions of these ballads registered in the sixteenth century are the same as the versions extant from the seventeenth century. Seventeenth-century examples of these ballads are "Titus Andronicus Complaint" and "Complaint and lamentation."

48. "Youths Warning-peice."

49. "Tragedy of Doctor *Lambe.*"

50. I am grateful to a paper given by Donald Heverin that elaborates on the subculture of London apprentices: "Apprentice Counterpublics."

51. Henslowe, *Henslowe's Diary*, 21–60.

52. Summaries of the early performance history of *Doctor Faustus* can be found in Healy, *"Doctor Faustus,"* 79–81, and also Bevington and Rasmussen's introduction to Marlowe, *Doctor Faustus*, 48–50.

53. These figures are from Bevington and Rasmussen's introduction to Marlowe, *Doctor Faustus*, 63.

54. Bevington and Rasmussen (ibid., 62–64) discuss the complexities of this general consensus that many of the Birde and Rowley additions appear in the B-text and not the A-text.

55. I find the following studies especially convincing: Rasmussen, *Textual Companion*; Rasmussen, "Rehabilitating the A-Text," 221–38; and Kuriyama, "Doctor Greg," 171–97.

56. Bevington and Rasmussen's commentary to Marlowe, *Doctor Faustus*, 172.

57. It is not included in the B-text, but the A-Text has Faustus proclaim that "divinitie is the basest of the three" disciplines with "law" and "physic" (1.1.109–10). And where the A-text has Mephistopheles say, "The shortest cut for conjuring / Is stoutly to abjure the Trinity" (1.3.53–54), the B-text reads ". . . Is stoutly to abjure all godliness" (1.3.51).

58. Shuger, *Censorship and Cultural Sensibility.*

59. Bevington and Rasmussen's commentary to Marlowe, *Doctor Faustus*, 238n129.

60. Henslowe, *Henslowe's Diary*, 320, 7, 319.

61. For staging, see Wickham, *"'Exeunt to the Cave,'"* 186.

62. I am thinking particularly of Cavell, *Disowning Knowledge*; Maus, *Inwardness and Theater*; Bell, *Shakespeare's Tragic Skepticism*; Bertram, *Time is Out of Joint*; Hamlin, *Tragedy and Scepticism*. *Hamlet* has been the focus of much of this work. Brian Cummings has recently contended with scholars' connections of soliloquy and secularization, protesting that "it is

only modernity's obsession with the idea of the birth of secular consciousness that has made us make this confusion"; *Mortal Thoughts*, 175.

63. Crane, "What Was Performance?" 172–74.
64. Turner, *English Renaissance Stage*, 29.
65. Greenfield and Gurr, "Rose Theatre, London," 336.
66. Witmore, *Shakespearean Metaphysics*, 101.
67. For a survey of the Rose's reconstructions, see Bowsher and Miller, *Rose and the Globe*, 120–30.
68. Ibid.
69. Bevington and Rasmussen's introduction to Marlowe, *Doctor Faustus*, 75.
70. Bowsher, "Encounters between Actors," 49, 136.
71. Bowsher and Miller, *Rose and the Globe*, 168.
72. Vaughan, *Golden-groue*, sig. Y8v.
73. Targoff, "Performance of Prayer," 54.
74. Brooks, "Unity," 377; my italics.
75. Ibid., 368.

Postlude

1. While the Globe and other playhouses south of the city predominantly stopped staging jigs, theaters like the Curtain, the Fortune, and the Red Bull continued the practice and garnered even more raucous reputations for it, prompting in 1612 an *Order for suppressinge of Jigges att the ende of Playes* by the Middlesex Magistrates. Yet while postlude jigs waned in some areas of London, postlude songs continued, especially in the form of in-act epilogues. The two most extensive accounts of the early modern jig are Baskerville, *Elizabethan Jig*, and R. Clegg and Skeaping, *Singing Simpkin*.
2. R. Clegg, with Thomson, "'He's for a Jig,'" 68.
3. West, "When Is the Jig Up," 204–7.
4. Dekker, *Strange Horse-Race*, sig. C4v.
5. Marlowe, *Tamburlaine the Great*, sig. A3r.
6. Massinger, *Roman Actor*, sig. A2v.
7. For a discussion of the shared theatrical characteristics of jigs and tragedies, and *Romeo and Juliet* specifically, see M. Smith and Lupton, "Ballads+."
8. West, "When Is the Jig Up," 205.

9. The most dramatically elaborate extant forms of jigs are jig ballads. These are ballads that either have a titular reference to the "Jig" or exhibit formal jig characteristics, including dialogue and recognizable jig music with short-long steps in duple or triple lines.

10. Alison Chapman discusses the network of Walsingham songs and ballads in "Met I with an Old Bald Mare," 217–31.

11. These references are recorded in Chappell, *Popular Music*, 1: 121–22.

12. See Thompson's note in Shakespeare, *Hamlet*, 4.5.23.

13. This reputation made the shrine at Walsingham the target of anti-Catholic agitation. See Waller, "Ralegh's 'As You Came.'"

14. Transcription taken from Chappell, *Popular Music*, 1:122.

15. Marcus, *Politics of Mirth*, 17.

16. Corbett, *Poems*, 49–52.

17. Aubrey, *Aubrey's "Brief Lives,"* 184–85.

18. For an overview of the Walsingham tune in the early modern imagination, see Waller, *Walsingham*, 91–114.

19. The broadside includes only the first initial of each name. I have spelled them out.

20. Christiane Sourvinou-Inwood writes, "Such an explanation in terms of the chorus' ritual importance would coincide with the ritual importance of choruses in Greek festivals in general. But were tragic choruses really also perceived as choruses in honor of Dionysos in the here and now? I believe that they were." *Tragedy and Athenian Religion*, 50.

21. "Whatever its deep cause, the special communicative power of the tragic ode is grounded in its ability to freely link and combine, to serve as a direct intermediary between various levels of reference, and incorporate all strands into the rest of the choral narrative and the whole of the play"; Gagné and Hopman, *Choral Mediations*, 2.

22. Wiles, *Shakespeare's Clown*, 59–60.

23. Hardison, *Christian Rite*, 284. For a discussion of the coexistence of *commedia* and tragedy in Corpus Christi drama, see Elliott, "Sacrifice of Isaac." Naomi Conn Liebler, in *Shakespeare's Festive Tragedy*, discusses how the medieval festive heritage influenced the genre of tragedy differently than it did comedy, but with equal impact.

24. Borrowed from Fischer-Lichte, *Transformative Power of Performance*. Although relatively little has been written in recent years on the early modern jig, one consistent observation is of the jig's and its clown's ability to face the audience and face fellow characters simultaneously. See

Wiles, *Shakespeare's Clown*, x; Weimann and Bruster, *Shakespeare*, 4–6, 101; Ford, "Kemp, Shakespeare," 169.

25. Shakespeare, *King Richard III*, 1.1.7; Shakespeare, *Romeo and Juliet*, 4.5.84–85. Leah Marcus, writing about masques and their festival occasion, recalls the importance of the immediacy of the event as an intermediary to more transcendent allegorical registers: "We will experience such [festival] art as entombing its occasion (and perhaps us hapless readers as well) only if we fail to dig ourselves out of its mire of topicality, to move beyond the 'voice' to the 'sense' of the masque, its articulation of 'more removed mysteries'"; *Politics of Mirth*, 22.

BIBLIOGRAPHY

The following are abbreviations used in the Bibliography:

EBBA English Broadside Ballad Archive [EBBA], University of California, Santa Barbara, https://ebba.english.ucsb.edu.

REED Records of Early English Drama

Primary Sources

"An Askew, Intituled, I am a Woman Poor and Blind." 1695. British Library, Roxburghe 1.8. EBBA 30013.
"The Angel Gabriel, his Salutation to the Virgin Mary." 1685. Magdalene College, Pepys 2.30. EBBA 20653.
"Ann Askew, intituled, I am a VVoman Poor and Blind." 1684–86. Magdalene College, Pepys 2.24. EBBA 20648.
"Archbishop Laud's Visitation of Salisbury in 1634." *Wiltshire Notes and Queries* 1 (1893): 10–23.
Aubrey, John. *Aubrey's "Brief Lives."* Vol. 1. Edited by Andrew Clark. London: Henry Frowde, 1898.
Augustine. *Confessions*. Translated by Henry Chadwick. Oxford: Oxford University Press, 2009.
"A Ballad of *Anne Askew*, intituled: *I am a Woman poore and blind*." 1624. Manchester Central Library 853.5. EBBA 36045.
"A Ballad of *Anne Askew*, intituled: *I am a Woman poore and blind*." 1688–1709. National Library of Scotland, Crawford 558. EBBA 32991.
Baldwin, Elizabeth, Lawrence M. Clopper, and David Mills, eds. *Cheshire: Including Chester*. REED. Toronto: University of Toronto Press, 2007.
Baldwin, William. *The Canticles or Balades of Solomon*. London, 1549.
Benson, George. *A Sermon Preached at Paules Crosse the Seauenth of May, M.DC.IX*. London, 1609.

The Bible, that is, the Holy Scriptures contained in the Old and New Testament: translated according to the Ebrew and Greeke, and conferred with the best translations in divers languages: with most profitable annotations upon all the hard places, and other things of great importance. London: Robert Barker, 1602.

Brathwaite, John. *Essay Upon the Five Sences.* London, 1625.

Bray, Gerald Lewis, ed. *Documents of the English Reformation.* Cambridge: James Clark, 2004.

Brice, Thomas. "Against Filthy Writing and Such Delighting." 1562. Huntington Library, Britwell 18274. EBBA 32093.

Bruce, John, ed. *Calendar of State Papers, Domestic Series, of the Reign of Charles I: 1631–1633.* London, 1862.

Burkitt, William. *The Poor Man's Help . . . Hearing of the Word Preached.* London, 1694.

Burton, Robert. *The Anatomy of Melancholy.* London, 1883.

Byrd, William. *A Gratification vnto Master John Case, for his Learned Booke, lately made in the Praise of Musicke.* London, 1586.

Cavendish, Margaret, Duchess of Newcastle. *The Life of William Cavendish, Duke of Newcastle.* Edited by C. H. Firth. London: John C. Nimmo, 1886.

———. *Sociable Letters.* Edited by James Fitzmaurice. New York: Garland, 1997.

Chamberlain, John. *Letters Written by John Chamberlain during the Reign of Queen Elizabeth.* Edited by Sarah Williams. Westminster: J. H. Nichols and Sons, 1861.

Chettle, Henry. *Kind-harts Dream.* London, 1593.

Church of England. *The boke of common praier, and administration of the sacramentes.* 1573.

———. *The Booke of common praier, and administration of the Sacramentes, and other rites and ceremonies in the Churche of Englande.* 1559.

City of London, Court of Aldermen. *The order of my Lord Maior, the Aldermen, and the Sheriffs, for their meetings, and wearing of their Apparell throughout the yeere.* London, 1621.

"[The] complaint and lamentation of Mistresse Arden of [Fev]ersham in Kent." 1610–38. British Library, Roxburghe 3.156–157. EBBA 30458.

Creede, Thomas, ed. *The Cronicle History of Henry the Fift.* London, 1600.

Davidson, Clifford, ed. *A tretise of miraclis pleyinge.* Washington, DC: University Press of America, 1981.

———, ed. *The York Corpus Christi Plays.* TEAMS Middle English Texts Series. Kalamazoo, MI: Medieval Institute Publications, 2011.

Defoe, Daniel. *The Political History of the Devil*. Edited by Irving N. Rothman and R. Michael Bowerman. New York: AMS, 2003.

Dekker, Thomas. *The Dead Tearme*. In *The Non-dramatic Works of Thomas Dekker*, edited by Alexander B.Grosart, 4:1–84. New York: Russell and Russell, 1963.

———. *A Strange Horse-Race*. London, 1613.

"The Distressed Pilgrim." 1678–88. British Library, Roxburghe 3.40–41, EBBA 30392.

Donne, John. *Devotions upon Emergent Occasions*. Edited by Anthony Raspa. Oxford: Oxford University Press, 1987.

———. *The Sermons of John Donne*. Edited by George R. Potter and Evelyn M. Simpson. 10 vols. Berkeley: University of California Press, 1953–62.

"The Dying Tears of a Penitent Sinner." 1678–80. British Library, Roxburghe 2.113. EBBA 30599.

Earle, John. *Micro-cosmographie*. London, 1629.

Egerton, Stephen. *The Boring of the Ear*. 1623.

Fiennes, Celia. *The Journeys of Celia Fiennes*. Edited by Christopher Morris. London: Cresset, 1947.

Firth, C. H., and R. S. Rait, eds. *Acts and Ordinances of the Interregnum, 1642–1660*. London: Wyman and Sons, 1911.

"Frauncis new Iigge, betweene Frauncis a Gentleman, and Richard a Farmer." 1617. Magdalene College, Pepys 1.226–227. EBBA 20102.

Gardiner, Samuel Rawson, ed. *The Constitutional Documents of the Puritan Revolution, 1625–1660*. 3rd ed. Oxford: Clarendon, 1906.

Gardiner, Stephen. *The Letters of Stephen Gardiner*. Edited by James A. Muller. Cambridge: Cambridge University Press, 1970.

George, David, ed. *Lancashire*. REED. Toronto: University of Toronto Press, 1991.

Goodman, Christopher. *Christopher Goodman's Letter-book* (c 1539–1601). Plas Power MSS, DD/PP/839.

Gosson, Stephen. *Playes Confuted in Five Actions*. London, 1582.

———. *The Schoole of Abuse Conteining a Pleasunt Inuectiue against Poets, Pipers, Plaiers, Iesters, and Such like Caterpillers of a Comonwelth*. London, 1579.

Granger, Thomas. *Paul's Crown of Rejoycing. How to Heare the Word with Profit*. London, 1616.

"Great Brittains Arlarm to Drowsie Sinners in Destress." 1672–96. British Library, Roxburghe 2.202–3. EBBA 30669.

"The Great Tribunal." 1700. British Library, Roxburghe 3.469. EBBA 31169.

Harrison, William. *The Difference of Hearers.* London, 1614.

Hay, Andrew. *The Diary of Andrew Hay of Craignethan, 1659–1660.* Edited by Alexander George Reid. Edinburgh: Edinburgh University Press, 1901.

"The Heartie Confession of a Christian." 1593. Huntington Library, Britwell 18278. EBBA 32097.

Henslowe, Philip. *Henslowe's Diary.* Edited by R. A. Foakes. 2nd ed. Cambridge: Cambridge University Press, 2002.

———. *Henslowe's Papers: Being Documents Supplementary to Henslowe's Diary.* Edited by Walter W. Greg. London: A. H. Bullen, 1907.

Heywood, Thomas. *An Apology for Actors Containing Three Briefe Treatises.* London, 1612.

Holinshed, Raphael. *Chronicles of England, Scotland, and Ireland.* Vol. 3. London, 1808.

Hooker, Richard. *Of the Laws of Ecclesiastical Polity.* 2 vols. Edited by Christopher Morris. London: J. M. Dent, 1907.

Johnston, Alexandra F., and Margaret Rogerson. *York.* REED. Manchester: Manchester University Press, 1979.

Jonson, Ben. *Bartholomew Fair.* In *The Selected Plays of Ben Jonson,* vol. 2, edited by Martin Butler. Cambridge: Cambridge University Press, 1989.

"The Judgment of God shewed upon one John Faustus." 1686–88. Magdalene College, Pepys 2.142. EBBA 20760.

"The Just Judgment of GOD shew'd upon Dr. John Faustus." 1640. British Library, Roxburghe 3.28–281. EBBA 30993.

Kinney, Arthur F., ed. *Renaissance Drama: An Anthology of Plays and Entertainments.* 2nd ed. Oxford: Wiley-Blackwell, 2005.

"Lilly Lash't with his own ROD." 1660. Huntington Library, Miscellaneous 613179. EBBA 32582.

Lumiansky, R. M., and David Mills, eds. *The Chester Mystery Cycle: A Reduced Facsimile of Huntington Library MS 2.* San Marino, CA: Huntington Library Press, 1980.

Marlowe, Christopher. *The Complete Works of Christopher Marlowe,* Vol. 2. Edited by Fredson Bowers. 2nd ed. Cambridge: Cambridge University Press, 1981.

———. *Doctor Faustus: A- and B-Texts (1604, 1616).* Edited by David Bevington and Eric Rasmussen. Manchester: Manchester University Press, 1993.

———. *Marlowe's Doctor Faustus, 1604–1616. Parallel Texts*. Edited by W. W. Greg. Oxford: Clarendon, 1950.

———. *Tamburlaine the Great*. London, 1590.

Marston, John. *What You Will*. London, 1607.

Martin, Charles Trice, ed. and trans. *Minutes of Parliament of the Middle Temple*. 3 vols. London: Butterworth, 1904.

Mason, Henry. *Hearing and Doing*. London, 1635.

Massinger, Philip. *The Roman Actor. A Tragaedie*. London, 1629.

Melton, John. *Astrologaster, or, The Figure-caster*. London, 1620.

Middleton, Thomas. *The Blacke Booke*. London, 1604.

Mills, David, ed. *The Chester Mystery Cycle: A New Edition with Modernised Spelling*. East Lansing, MI: Colleagues Press, 1992.

Milton, John. *Complete Prose Works of John Milton*. Edited by Don M. Wolfe et al. 8 vols. New Haven, CT: Yale University Press, 1953–82.

Missale ad Usum Insignis Ecclesiae Sarum. London, 1527.

Missale ad Vsum Insignis Ecclesie Sarisburiensis. Paris: Guillelmum Merlin, 1555.

More, Sir Thomas. *Utopia: Latin Text and English Translation*. Edited by George M. Logan, Robert M. Adams, and Clarence H. Miller. Cambridge: Cambridge University Press, 1995.

"A most Excellent Ballad of Ioseph the Carpenter." 1678–80. Magdalene College, Pepys 2.27. EBBA 20650.

"A Most Excellent Ditty, called Collin's Conceit." 1624. Magdalene College, Pepys 1.455. EBBA 20030.

Mountfort, W. *The Life and Death of Doctor Faustus, made into a Farce*. London, 1684.

Nashe, Thomas. *Pierce Penniless's Supplication to the Devil*. Edited by J. Payne Collier. London, 1842.

———. *A Pleasant Comedie, called Summers Last Will and Testament*. London, 1600.

The New Testament of Our Lord Iesus Christ. London, 1575.

"A New Yeres Gyft, Intituled, A Christal Glas." 1571. Huntington Library, Britwell 18347. EBBA 32587.

Nichols, John Gough, ed. "Two Sermons Preached by the Boy Bishop." In *The Camden Miscellany*, vol. 7. Westminster: J. B. Nichols, 1875.

Ordinary of the Company of Bakers in the city of York. 1600. British Library, MS 34605.

Patrick, Simon. *A Discourse of Profiting by Sermons*. London, 1684.

Perkins, William. *A Commentary on Galatians*. Edited by Gerald T. Sheppard. New York: Pilgrim, 1989.

———. *A reformed Catholike: or, A declaration shewing how neere we may come to the present Church of Rome in sundrie points of religion: and vvherein we must for euer depart from them with an advertisment to all fauourers of the Romane religion, shewing that the said religion is against the Catholike principles and grounds of the catechisme.* Cambridge: Printer to the University of Cambridge, 1598.

———. *A treatise tending vnto a declaration whether a man be in the estate of damnation or in the estate of grace.* London, 1590.

Phillips, Edward. *Theatrum Poetarum.* 2 vols. London, 1675.

Platter, Thomas. *Thomas Platter's Travels in England.* Edited by Claire Williams. London: Jonathan Cape, 1937.

Prynne, William. *Histrio-Mastix: The players scourge, or, actors tragaedie.* London, 1633.

"The Recantation of a Penitent Proteus Or the Changeling." London, 1663.

Roberts, Hugh. *The Day of Hearing.* Oxford, 1600.

Rowlands, Samuel. *The Knave of Clubs.* London, 1609.

The Sarum Missal in English. Translated by A. H. Pearson. London: Church Press, 1868.

The Sarum Missal in English. 2 vols. Translated by Frederick E. Warren. London: De La More, 1911.

The Second Report of Doctor John Faustus, containing his appearances and the deeds of Wagner. London, 1594. 2nd ed., 1580.

Shakespeare, William. *Hamlet.* Edited by Neil Taylor and Ann Thompson. London: Arden Shakespeare, 2006.

———. *Henry V.* Edited by Gary Taylor. Oxford: Oxford University Press, 2008.

———. *King Henry IV, Part 1.* Edited by David Scott Kastan. London: Arden Shakespeare, 2002.

———. *King Henry IV, Part 2.* Edited by A. R. Humphreys. London: Arden Shakespeare, 1967.

———. *King Henry V.* Edited by T. W. Craik. London: Arden Shakespeare, 1995.

———. *King Lear.* Edited by R. A. Foakes. London: Arden Shakespeare, 1997.

———. *King Richard III.* Edited by James R. Siemon. London: Arden Shakespeare, 2009.

———. *Romeo and Juliet.* Edited by René Weis. London: Arden Shakespeare, 2012.

———. *Shakespeare's Poems.* Edited by Katherine Duncan-Jones and H. R. Woudhuysen. London: Arden Shakespeare, 2007.

———. *Troilus and Cressida*. Edited by David Bevington. London: Arden Shakespeare, 1998.

———. *Twelfth Night*. Edited by Keir Elam. London: Arden Shakespeare, 2008.

Shepard, Thomas. *Subjection to Christ in all his ordinances . . . ineffectual hearing of the word*. London, 1652.

Smith, Gregory, ed. *Elizabethan Critical Essays*. Vol. 1. Oxford: Clarendon, 1904.

Smith, Henry. *The sermons of Maister Henrie Smith Gathered into One Volume*. London, 1593.

"Some Fyne Gloues." 1560–70. Huntington Library, Britwell 18343. EBBA 32523.

"A Song of Syon of the Beauty of Bethell." 1642. Huntington Library, Miscellaneous 180158. EBBA 32377.

Speculum Humanae Salvationis. 1375–1400. Morgan Library, MS M.766.

Stanyhurst, Richard. "From the Translation of the *Aneid*." In G. Smith, *Elizabethan Critical Essays*, vol. 1.

Sternhold, Thomas, and John Hopkins. *The Whole Booke of Psalmes, Collected into Englysh Metre*. London: John Day, 1562.

"The Story of David and Berseba." 1602–46. British Library, Roxburghe 1.88–89. EBBA 30061.

[Tatham, John]. *Knavery in All Trades: or, The Coffee-House. A Comedy*. London, 1664.

"Titus Andronicus Complaint." 1624. Magdalene College, Pepys 1.86. EBBA 20040.

"The Tragedy of Doctor *Lambe*, The great suposed Conjurer." 1628. Magdalene College, Pepys 1.134–35. EBBA 20059.

Vaughan, William. *The Golden-groue, moralized in three Bookes*. London, 1600.

Warkentin, Germaine, ed. *The Queen's Majesty's Passage and Related Documents*. Toronto: Centre for Reformation and Renaissance Studies, 2004.

Webbe, William. "A Discourse of English Poesie." In G. Smith, *Elizabethan Critical Essays*, vol. 1.

Whight, Nicholas. "A Commendation of Musicke." 1563. Huntington Library, Britwell 18346. EBBA 32586.

Williams, Gryffith. *The Right Way To The Best Religion; Wherein Is Largely Explained The Summe & Principal Heads Of The Gospel. In Certaine Sermons & Treatises*. London, 1636.

Winstanley, William. *The Lives of the Most Famous English Poets*. London, 1687.
Wither, George. *Poems*. 4 vols. London, 1839.
"A Wonderful Prophecy." 1725–69. British Library, Roxburghe 3.664–665. EBBA 31351.
Younge, Richard. *The People's Impartiall and Compassionate Monitor; About Hearing of Sermons*. London, 1657.
"Youths Warning-peice." 1636. British Library, Roxburghe 1.434–435. EBBA 30294.
Zepper, Wilhelm. *The Art or Skil Well or Fruitfullie to Heare the Holy Sermons of the Church*. Translated by Thomas Wilcox. London, 1599.

Secondary Sources

Aers, David. "A Whisper in the Ear of Early Modernists; or, Reflections on Literary Critics Writing the 'History of the Subject.'" In *Culture and History, 1350–1600: Essays on English Communities, Identities and Writing*, edited by David Aers, 177–202. Detroit, MI: Wayne State University Press, 1992.
Altman, Joel B. "'Vile Participation': The Amplification of Violence in the Theater of *Henry V*." *Shakespeare Quarterly* 42, no. 1 (Spring 1991): 1–32.
Anderson, David K. "The Theater of the Damned: Religion and the Audience in the Tragedy of Christopher Marlowe." *Texas Studies in Literature and Language* 54, no. 1 (2012): 79–109.
Arendt, Hannah. *The Human Condition*. Chicago: University of Chicago Press, 1998.
Arlidge, Anthony. *Shakespeare and the Prince of Love: The Feast of Misrule in the Middle Temple*. London: Giles de la Mare, 2000.
Atkinson, David. *The English Traditional Ballad: Theory, Method, and Practice*. Burlington, VT: Ashgate, 2002.
Austin, J. L. *How to Do Things with Words*. 2nd ed. Cambridge, MA: Harvard University Press, 1975.
Baldo, Jonathan. "Wars of Memory in *Henry V*." *Shakespeare Quarterly* 47, no. 2 (Summer 1996): 132–59.
Banerjee, Pampa. "I, Mephastophilis: Self, Other, and Demonic Parody in Marlowe's *Doctor Faustus*." *Christianity and Literature* 42 (1993): 221–41.

Barber, C. L. "The Family in Shakespeare's Development: Tragedy and Sacredness." In *Representing Shakespeare: New Psychoanalytic Essays*, edited by Murray M. Schwartz and Coppélia Kahn, 188–202. Baltimore: Johns Hopkins University Press, 1980.
———. *Shakespeare's Festive Comedy: A Study of Dramatic Form and Its Relation to Social Custom*. Princeton, NJ: Princeton University Press, 1959.
Barish, Jonas. *The Antitheatrical Prejudice*. Berkeley: University of California Press, 1981.
Baskerville, Charles. *The Elizabethan Jig and Related Song Drama*. Chicago: Chicago University Press, 1929. Reprint, New York: Dover, 1965.
Beckwith, Sarah. *Shakespeare and the Grammar of Forgiveness*. Ithaca, NY: Cornell University Press, 2011.
———. *Signifying God: Social Relation and Symbolic Act in the York Corpus Christi Plays*. Chicago: University of Chicago Press, 2003.
Bednarz, James P. "John Marston's Induction to *What You Will*: A Reexamination." *Ben Jonson Journal* 17, no. 2 (2010): 293–308.
Bell, Millicent. *Shakespeare's Tragic Skepticism*. New Haven, CT: Yale University Press, 2002.
Berger, Peter L. *The Sacred Canopy: Elements of a Sociological Theory of Religion*. New York: Anchor Books, 1967.
Bertram, Benjamin. *The Time Is Out of Joint: Skepticism in Shakespeare's England*. Newark: University of Delaware Press, 2004.
Bevington, David. "Marlowe and God." *Explorations in Renaissance Culture* 17, no. 1 (1991): 1–38.
Bishop, T. G. *Shakespeare and the Theatre of Wonder*. Cambridge: Cambridge University Press, 1996.
Bossy, John. *The English Catholic Community, 1570–1850*. New York: Oxford University Press, 1976.
———. "The Mass as Social Institution, 1200–1700." *Past and Present* 100 (1983): 29–61.
Bowsher, Julian. "Encounters between Actors, Audience and Archaeologists at the Rose Theatre, 1587–1989." In *Contemporary and Historical Archaeology in Theory*, edited by L. McAtackney, M. Palus, and A. Piccini, Studies in Historical and Contemporary Archaeology 4, 63–66. Oxford: Archaeopress, 2007.
Bowsher, Julian, and Pat Miller. *The Rose and the Globe: Playhouses of Shakespeare's Bankside, Southwark, Excavations, 1988–90*. London: Museum of London Archaeology, 2009.

Brooks, Cleanth. "The Unity of Marlowe's *Doctor Faustus*." In *A Shaping Joy: Studies in the Writer's Craft*, 367–80. New York: Harcourt Brace Jovanovich, 1971.
Cavell, Stanley. *Disowning Knowledge in Six Plays of Shakespeare*. Cambridge: Cambridge University Press, 1987.
Cawley, A. C., ed. *The Wakefield Pageants in the Towneley Cycle*. Manchester: Manchester University Press, 1958.
Chambers, E. K. *The Elizabethan Stage*. Vol. 1. Oxford: Oxford University Press, 1923.
———. *The Mediaeval Stage*. Vol. 1. Oxford: Clarendon, 1903.
Chapman, Alison. "'Met I with an Old Bald Mare': Lust, Misogyny, and the Early Modern Walsingham Ballads." In *Walsingham in Literature and Culture from the Middle Ages to Modernity*, edited by Dominic Janes and Gary Waller, 217–31. Farnham: Ashgate, 2010.
———. "Whose Saint Crispin's Day Is It? Shoemaking, Holiday Making, and the Politics of Memory in Early Modern England." *Renaissance Quarterly* 54, no. 4 (2001): 1467–94.
Chappell, W. *Popular Music of the Olden Time*. 2 vols. London: Chappell, 1859.
Cheney, Patrick, ed. *The Cambridge Companion to Christopher Marlowe*. Cambridge: Cambridge University Press, 2004.
Chow, Jeremy. "Ballad as Body." In Fumerton, *Making of a Broadside Ballad*.
Clark, Stuart. *Thinking with Demons: The Idea of Witchcraft in Early Modern Europe*. Oxford: Oxford University Press, 1999.
Clegg, Cyndia Susan. "Feared and Loved: *Henry V* and Machiavelli's Use of History." *Ben Jonson Journal* 10 (2003): 179–207.
Clegg, Roger, and Lucie Skeaping. *Singing Simpkin and Other Bawdy Jigs: Musical Comedy on the Shakespearean Stage: Scripts, Music and Context*. Exeter: University of Exeter Press, 2014.
Clegg, Roger, with Peter Thomson. "'He's for a Jig or a Tale of Bawdry—': Notes on the English Dramatic Jig." *Studies in Theatre and Performance* 29, no. 1 (2009): 67–83.
Clopper, Lawrence. *Drama, Play, and Game: English Festive Culture in the Medieval and Early Modern Period*. Chicago: University of Chicago Press, 2001.
Coleman, David. *Drama and the Sacraments in Sixteenth-Century England: Indelible Characters*. New York: Palgrave Macmillan, 2007.
Colie, Rosalie. *The Resources of Kind: Genre Theory in the Renaissance*. Berkeley: University of California Press, 1973.

Collinson, Patrick. "*From Iconoclasm to Iconophobia: The Cultural Impact of the Second English Reformation.*" Stenton Lecture for 1985. Reading: University of Reading, 1986.

Connor, Steven. "Ear Room." Audio Forensics Symposium, Image-Music-Text Gallery. Lecture, London, November 30, 2008.

Cooper, Helen. *Shakespeare and the Medieval World.* London: Arden Shakespeare, 2012.

Corbett, Richard. *The Poems of Richard Corbett.* Edited by J. A. W. Bennett and H. R. Trevor-Roper. Oxford: Clarendon, 1955.

Cox, John. *The Devil and the Sacred in English Drama, 1350–1642.* Cambridge: Cambridge University Press, 2000.

Craig, John. "Psalms, Groans, and Dogwhippers: The Soundscape of Worship in the English Parish Church, 1547–1642." In *Sacred Space in Early Modern Europe*, edited by Will Coster and Andrew Spicer, 104–23. Cambridge: Cambridge University Press, 2005.

Craik, Katharine, and Tanya Pollard, eds. *Shakespearean Sensations: Experiencing Literature in Early Modern England.* Cambridge: Cambridge University Press, 2013.

Crane, Mary Thomas. "What Was Performance?" *Criticism* 43, no. 2 (2001): 168–87.

Crankshaw, David J. "Community, City and Nation, 1540–1714." In *St. Paul's: The Cathedral Church of London, 604–2004*, edited by Derek Keene, Arthur Burns, and Andrew Saint, 45–70. New Haven, CT: Yale University Press, 2004.

Cressy, David. "God's Time, Rome's Time, and the Calendar of the English Protestant Regime." *Viator* 34 (2003): 392–406.

Cummings, Brian. *Mortal Thoughts: Religion, Secularity, and Identity in Shakespeare and Early Modern Culture.* Oxford: Oxford University Press, 2013.

Curran, Kevin, and James Kearney. Introduction to "Shakespeare and Phenomenology," special issue, *Criticism* 54, no. 3 (2012): 353–64.

D'Amico, Jack. *The Moor in English Renaissance Drama.* Gainesville: University Press of Florida, 1991.

Dawson, Anthony. "Shakespeare and Secular Performance." In *Shakespeare and Cultures of Performance*, edited by Paul Yachnin and Patricia Badir, 83–97. Aldershot: Ashgate, 2008.

Degenhardt, Jane Hwang, and Elizabeth Williamson, eds. *Religion and Drama in Early Modern England: The Performance of Religion on the Renaissance Stage.* Burlington, VT: Ashgate, 2011.

De Grazia, Margreta. *"Hamlet" without Hamlet*. Cambridge: Cambridge University Press, 2008.

DeMolen, Richard L. "*Pueri Christi Imitatio*: The Festival of the Boy-Bishop in Tudor England." *Moreana* 45 (1975): 17–29.

Derrida, Jacques. *Dissemination*. Translated by Barbara Johnson. London: Continuum, 2004.

Diehl, Huston. "Dazzling Theater: Renaissance Drama in the Age of Reform." *Journal of Medieval and Renaissance Studies* 22 (1992): 221–35.

———. *Staging Reform, Reforming the Stage: Protestantism and Popular Theater in Early Modern England*. Ithaca, NY: Cornell University Press, 1997.

Dollimore, Jonathan. *Radical Tragedy: Religion, Ideology and Power in the Drama of Shakespeare and His Contemporaries*. 3rd ed. Durham, NC: Duke University Press, 2004.

Duffy, Eamon. *The Stripping of the Altars: Traditional Religion in England, 1400–1580*. New Haven, CT: Yale University Press, 1992.

Duxfield, Andrew. "'Resolve Me of All Ambiguities': *Doctor Faustus* and the Failure to Unify." *Early Modern Literary Studies* 16 (2007): art. 7.

Elkins, James. *The Object Stares Back: On the Nature of Seeing*. Boston: Houghton Mifflin Harcourt, 1997.

Elliott, John R., Jr. "The Sacrifice of Isaac as Comedy and Tragedy." *Studies in Philology* 66, no. 1 (1969): 36–59.

Feral, Josette. Foreword to "Theatricality," edited by Josette Feral, special issue, *SubStance* 31, nos. 2–3 (2002): 3–13.

Fischer-Lichte, Erika. *The Transformative Power of Performance: A New Aesthetics*. New York: Routledge, 2008.

Fish, Stanley E. "How to Do Things with Austin and Searle: Speech Act Theory and Literary Criticism." *Modern Language Notes* 91, no. 5 (1976): 983–1025.

———. "There Is No Textualist Position." *San Diego Law Review* 42, no. 2 (2005): 629–50.

Ford, Elizabeth. "Kemp, Shakespeare, and the Composition of *Romeo and Juliet*." *Early Theatre* 13, no. 2 (2010): 162–75.

Foucault, Michel. *The Archaeology of Knowledge and The Discourse on Language*. Translated by A. M. Sheridan Smith. New York: Pantheon Books, 1972.

Freedberg, David. *The Power of Images: Studies in the History and Theory of Response*. Chicago: University of Chicago Press, 1991.

Fried, Michael. *Absorption and Theatricality: Painting and Beholder in the Age of Diderot*. Chicago: University of Chicago Press, 1980.
Fumerton, Patricia, ed. *Ballads and Performance: The Multimodal Stage in Early Modern England*. Early Modern Center Imprint, University of California, Santa Barbara, forthcoming.
——, ed. *The Making of a Broadside Ballad*. Early Modern Center Imprint, University of California, Santa Barbara, 2015. http://press.emcimprint.english.ucsb.edu/the-making-of-a-broadside-ballad/index.
——. *Moving Media, Tactical Publics: The Broadside Ballad in Early Modern England*. Philadelphia: University of Pennsylvania Press, forthcoming.
——. "Why the Broadside Ballad." In Fumerton, *Making of a Broadside Ballad*.
Gagné, Renaud, and Marianne Govers Hopman. *Choral Mediations in Greek Tragedy*. Cambridge: Cambridge University Press, 2013.
Gates, Daniel. "Unpardonable Sins: The Hazards of Performative Language in the Tragic Cases of Francesco Spiera and *Doctor Faustus*." *Comparative Drama* 38, no. 1 (2004): 59–81.
Gerould, Gordon Hall. *The Ballad of Tradition*. New York: Oxford University Press, 1957.
Gibson, Gail McMurray. *Theater of Devotion: East Anglia Drama and Society in the Late Middle Ages*. Chicago: University of Chicago Press, 1994.
Gillespie, Stuart, and Neil Rhodes, eds. *Shakespeare and Elizabethan Popular Culture*. London: Arden Shakespeare, 2006.
Goldstein, Leba M. "An Account of the Faustus Ballad." *Library* 16, no. 3 (1961): 176–89.
Gras, Henk. "*Twelfth Night, Every Man Out of His Humour*, and the Middle Temple Revels of 1597–98." *Modern Language Review* 84 (1989): 545–64.
Green, Ian. *Print and Protestantism in Early Modern England*. Oxford: Oxford University Press, 2000.
Greenblatt, Stephen. *Renaissance Self-Fashioning: From More to Shakespeare*. 2nd ed. Chicago: University of Chicago Press, 1980.
——. *Shakespearean Negotiations: The Circulation of Social Energy in Renaissance England*. Berkeley: University of California Press, 1989.
Greenfield, John, and Andrew Gurr. "The Rose Theatre, London: The State of Knowledge and What We Still Need to Know." *Antiquity* 78, no. 300 (2004): 330–40.

Gregory, Brad S. *The Unintended Reformation: How a Religious Revolution Secularized Society*. Cambridge, MA: Harvard University Press, 2012.
Groves, Beatrice. *Texts and Traditions: Religion in Shakespeare, 1592–1604*. Oxford: Clarendon, 2007.
Guibbory, Achsah. *Ceremony and Community from Herbert to Milton: Literature, Religion, and Cultural Conflict in Seventeenth-Century England*. Cambridge: Cambridge University Press, 1998.
Gurr, Andrew. *The Shakespeare Company, 1594–1642*. Cambridge: Cambridge University Press, 2010.
Haigh, Christopher. *English Reformations and the Making of the Anglican Church*. Perth: St. George's Cathedral, 2007.
———. *Reformation and Resistance in Tudor Lancashire*. Cambridge: Cambridge University Press, 1975.
Hall, David D. Introduction to Hall, *Lived Religion in America*, vi–xiii.
———, ed. *Lived Religion in America: Toward a History of Practice*. Princeton, NJ: Princeton University Press, 1997.
Hamlin, William M. "Casting Doubt in Marlowe's *Doctor Faustus*." *Studies in English Literature* 41, no. 2 (2001): 257–75.
———. *Tragedy and Scepticism in Shakespeare's England*. New York: Palgrave Macmillan, 2005.
Hardin, Richard F. *Civil Idolatry: Desacralizing and Monarchy in Spenser, Shakespeare, and Milton*. Newark: University of Delaware Press, 1992.
Hardison, O. B., Jr. *Christian Rite and Christian Drama in the Middle Ages: Essays on the Origin and Early History of Modern Drama*. Baltimore: Johns Hopkins University Press, 1965.
Harris, Jonathan Gil. *Untimely Matter in the Time of Shakespeare*. Philadelphia: University of Pennsylvania Press, 2009.
Harty, Kevin J. "The Unity and Structure of *The Chester Mystery Cycle*." *Medievalia* 2 (1976): 137–58.
Healy, Thomas. "*Doctor Faustus*." In *The Cambridge Companion to Christopher Marlowe*, edited by Patrick Cheney, 174–92. Cambridge: Cambridge University Press, 2004.
Heverin, Donald. "Apprentice Counterpublics: Heywood's Four Prentices and the Development of a Youth Movement." Paper delivered at the annual meeting of the Renaissance Society of America, San Diego, CA, 2013.
Howard, Jean Elizabeth. *The Stage and Social Struggle in Early Modern England*. New York: Routledge, 1994.

Hunt, Alice. *The Drama of Coronation: Medieval Ceremony in Early Modern England*. Cambridge: Cambridge University Press, 2008.
Hunt, Arnold. *The Art of Hearing: English Preachers and Their Audiences, 1590–1640*. Cambridge: Cambridge University Press, 2010.
Hunt, Maurice. *Shakespeare's Religious Allusiveness: Its Play and Tolerance*. Aldershot: Ashgate, 2003.
Husserl, Edmund. *The Idea of Phenomenology*. Translated by Lee Hardy. Dordrecht: Kluwer, 1999.
———. *Ideas: General Introduction to Pure Phenomenology*. Translated by W. R. Boyce Gibson. London: Gorge Allen and Unwin, 1931.
———. "Pure Phenomenology, Its Method, and Its Field of Investigation." In *Husserl: Shorter Works*, edited by Peter McCormick and Frederick A. Elliston, translated by R. W. Jordan. Notre Dame, IN: University of Notre Dame Press, 1981.
Jackson, Ken. *Image Ethics in Spenser and Shakespeare*. Basingstoke: Palgrave Macmillan, 2010.
Jackson, Ken, and Arthur Marotti, eds. *Shakespeare and Religion: Early Modern and Postmodern Perspectives*. Notre Dame, IN: University of Notre Dame Press, 2011.
———. "The Turn to Religion in Early Modern English Studies." *Criticism* 46, no. 1 (2004): 167–90.
Jackson, MacD. P. "Three Old Ballads and the Date of 'Doctor Faustus.'" *AUMLA: Journal of the Australasian Universities Modern Language Association* 36 (1971): 187–200.
Jackson, Michael. "Introduction: Phenomenology, Radical Empiricism, and Anthropological Critique." In *Things as They Are: New Directions in Phenomenological Anthropology*, edited by Michael Jackson, 1–50. Bloomington: Indiana University Press, 1996.
James, Mervyn. "Drama and Social Body in the Late Medieval English Town." *Past and Present* 98, no. 1 (1983): 3–29.
Jeffrey, David Lyle. "Communion, Community, and Our Common Book: Or, Can Faustus Be Saved?" *Christianity and Literature* 53 (2004): 233–46.
Jenkins, Harold. "Shakespeare's *Twelfth Night*." In *Twelfth Night: Critical Essays*, edited by Stanley Wells. Abingdon: Routledge, 1986.
Johnson, Kimberly. *Made Flesh: Sacrament and Poetics in Post-Reformation England*. Philadelphia: University of Pennsylvania Press, 2014.
Johnston, Alexandra F. "The Feast of Corpus Christi in the West Country." *Early Theatre* 6, no. 1 (2003): 15–34.

Jordan, Constance. "*Henry V* and the Tudor Monarchy." In *Early Modern English Drama: A Critical Companion*, edited by Garret A. Sullivan, 108–19. New York: Oxford University Press, 2006.

Kahn, Victoria. *The Future of Illusion: Political Theology and Early Modern Texts*. Chicago: University of Chicago Press, 2014.

Kastan, David Scott. *A Will to Believe: Shakespeare and Religion*. Oxford: Oxford University Press, 2013.

Kearney, James. *The Incarnate Text: Imagining the Book in Reformation England*. Philadelphia: University of Pennsylvania Press, 2009.

Kelly, Erin E. "Doubt and Religious Drama across Sixteenth-Century England, or Did the Middle Ages Believe in Their Plays?" In *The Chester Cycle in Context, 1555–1575: Religion, Drama, and the Impact of Change*, edited by Jessica Dell, David Klausner, and Helen Ostovich, 47–64. Surrey: Ashgate, 2012.

Kibbey, Ann. *The Interpretation of Material Shapes in Puritanism: A Study of Rhetoric, Prejudice, and Violence*. Cambridge: Cambridge University Press, 1986.

Knapp, Jeffrey. *Shakespeare's Tribe: Church, Nation, and Theater in Renaissance England*. Chicago: University of Chicago Press, 2002.

Koerner, Joseph Leo. *The Reformation of the Image*. Chicago: University of Chicago Press, 2004.

Kolve, V. A. *The Play Called Corpus Christi*. Stanford, CA: Stanford University Press, 1966.

Kuriyama, Constance Brown. "Doctor Greg and *Doctor Faustus*: The Supposed Originality of the 1616 Text." *English Literary Renaissance* 5 (1975): 171–97.

La Guardia, Eric. "Ceremony and History: The Problem of Symbol from *Richard II* to *Henry V*." In *Pacific Coast Studies in Shakespeare*, edited by Waldo McNeir and Thelma N. Greenfield, 66–88. Eugene: University of Oregon Press, 1966.

Lake, Peter. "Deeds against Nature." In *Culture and Politics in Early Stuart England*, edited by Kevin Sharp and Peter Lake, 257–84. Stanford, CA: Stanford University Press, 2003.

Lamb, Charles, and Mary Lamb. *The Works of Charles and Mary Lamb: Dramatic Specimens and the Garrick Plays*. Edited by Edward Verrall Lucas. New York: G. P. Putnam, 1904.

Leach, Arthur Francis. *The Schools of Medieval England*. New York: Macmillan, 1915.

Leahy, William. "Propaganda or a Record of Events? Richard Mulcaster's *The Passage Of Our Most Drad Soveraigne Lady Quene Elyzabeth*

Through The Citie Of London Westminster The Daye Before Her Coronacion." Early Modern Literary Studies 9, no. 1 (2003): art. 3.

Lehnhof, Kent. "Theology, Phenomenology, and the Divine in *King Lear*." In *Of Levinas and Shakespeare: "To See Another Thus,"* edited by Moshe Gold and Sandor Goodhart, with Kent Lehnhof, 107–22. West Lafayette, IN: Purdue University Press, 2018.

Lerud, Theodore. *Memory, Images, and the English Corpus Chrsti Drama.* New York: Palgrave Macmillan, 2008.

Levin, Harry. *The Overreacher: A Study of Christopher Marlowe.* Cambridge, MA: Harvard University Press, 1952.

Levinas, Emmanuel. *Totalité et infini: Essai sur l'extériorité.* Paris: Livre de Poche, 1991.

———. *Totality and Infinity.* Translated by Alphonso Lingis. Dordrecht: Kluwer, 1991.

Liebler, Naomi Conn. *Shakespeare's Festive Tragedy: The Ritual Foundations of Genre.* New York: Routledge, 1995.

Lin, Erika T. "Festivity." In Turner, *Early Modern Theatricality*, 212–29.

———. *Shakespeare and the Materiality of Performance.* New York: Palgrave Macmillan, 2012.

Löwith, Karl. *Meaning in History: The Theological Implications of the Philosophy of History.* Chicago: University of Chicago Press, 1949.

Lumiansky, R. M., and David Mills, eds. *The Chester Mystery Cycle: Essays and Documents.* Chapel Hill: University of North Carolina Press, 1983.

Lunney, Ruth. *Marlowe and the Popular Tradition: Innovation in the English Drama before 1595.* Manchester: Manchester University Press, 2002.

Lupton, Julia Reinhard. "Shakespearean Softscapes: Hospitality, Phenomenology, Design." In *The Return of Theory in Early Modern English Studies*, vol. 2, edited by Paul Cefalu, Gary Kuchar, and Bryan Reynolds, 143–64. New York: Palgrave, 2014.

———. *Thinking with Shakespeare: Essays on Politics and Life.* Chicago: University of Chicago Press, 2011.

Macy, G. "Of Mice and Manna: *Quid mus summit* as a Pastoral Question." *Recherches Théologie Ancienne et Médiévale* 58 (1991): 157–66.

Marcus, Leah. *The Politics of Mirth: Jonson, Herrick, Milton, Marvell, and the Defense of Old Holiday Pastimes.* Chicago: University of Chicago Press, 1978.

———. *Unediting the Renaissance: Shakespeare, Marlowe, Milton.* New York: Routledge, 1996.

Mardock, James D., and Kathryn R. McPherson, eds. *Stages of Engagement: Drama and Religion in Post-Reformation England.* Pittsburgh, PA: Duquesne University Press, 2014.

Marion, Jean-Luc. "They Recognized Him; and He Became Invisible to Them." *Modern Theology* 18, no. 2 (2002): 145–52.

———. *The Visible and the Revealed.* Translated by Christina M. Gschwandtner. New York: Fordham University Press, 2008.

Marsh, Christopher. "Balladry as a Multi-Media Matrix: Best-Selling Songs and Their Significance in Seventeenth-Century England." Paper presented at the conference "Performing the Book: Multi-media Histories of Early Modern Britain," Rutgers University, British Studies Center, February 2011.

———. *Music and Society in Early Modern England.* Cambridge: Cambridge University Press, 2010.

Massingberd, Francis Charles. *The English Reformation.* London: James Burns, 1842.

Masten, Jeffrey. "Editing Boys: The Performance of Genders in Print." In *From Performance to Print in Shakespeare's England*, edited by Peter Holland and Stephen Orgel, 113–34. New York: Palgrave Macmillan, 2006.

Maus, Katharine Eisaman. *Inwardness and Theater in the English Renaissance.* Chicago: University of Chicago Press, 1995.

McCoy, Richard C. *Faith in Shakespeare.* Oxford: Oxford University Press, 2013.

———. "'Thou Idol Ceremony': Elizabeth I, the Henriad, and the Rites of the English Monarchy." In *Urban Life in the Renaissance*, edited by Susan Zimmerman and Ronald Weissman, 240–66. Newark: University of Delaware Press, 1989.

———. "'The Wonderful Spectacle': The Civic Progress of Elizabeth I and the Troublesome Coronation." In *Coronations: Medieval and Early Modern*, edited by János M. Bak, 217–27. Berkeley: University of California Press, 1990.

Merleau-Ponty, Maurice. *Phenomenology of Perception.* Translated by Colin Smith. New York: Routledge, 2002.

Mills, David. *Recycling the Cycle: The City of Chester and Its Whitsun Plays.* Toronto: University of Toronto Press, 1998.

Milton, Anthony. *Catholic and Reformed: The Roman and Protestant Churches in English Protestant Thought, 1600–1640.* Cambridge: Cambridge University Press, 2002.

Montrose, Louis A. "Idols of the Queen: Policy, Gender, and the Picturing of Elizabeth I." *Representations* 68 (1999): 108–61.
Morris, David. *The Sense of Space*. Albany: State University of New York Press, 2004.
Morse, Ruth, Helen Cooper, and Peter Holland, eds. *Medieval Shakespeare: Pasts and Presents*. Cambridge: Cambridge University Press, 2013.
Morton, Mark. "Making Space." *Gastronomica* 12, no. 1 (2012): 7–8.
Morton, Timothy. *Ecology without Nature: Rethinking Environmental Aesthetics*. Cambridge, MA: Harvard University Press, 2009.
Newcomb, Lori Humphrey, et al. "Shakespeare in Snippets: Ballads, Plays, and Performances of Remediation." In Fumerton, *Ballads and Performance*.
O'Connell, Michael. *The Idolatrous Eye: Iconoclasm and Theater in Early-Modern England*. Oxford: Oxford University Press, 2000.
Ong, Walter. *The Presence of the Word: Some Prolegomena for Cultural and Religious History*. New Haven, CT: Yale University Press, 1967.
Ornstein, Robert. "Marlowe and God: The Tragic Theology of *Doctor Faustus*." *PMLA* 83, no. 5 (1968): 1378–85.
Orsi, Robert. "Everyday Miracles: The Study of Lived Religion." In Hall, *Lived Religion in America*, 3–21.
———. *The Madonna of 115th Street: Faith and Community in Italian Harlem*. 2nd ed. New Haven, CT: Yale University Press, 2002.
Owens, Margaret. *Stages of Dismemberment: The Fragmented Body in Medieval and Early Modern Drama*. Newark: University of Delaware Press, 2005.
Parker, Andrew, and Eve Kosofsky Sedgwick, eds. *Performativity and Performance*. New York: Routledge, 1995.
Parker, John. *The Aesthetics of the Antichrist: From Christian Drama to Christopher Marlowe*. Ithaca, NY: Cornell University Press, 2007.
———. "Faustus, Confession, and the Sins of Omission." *English Literary History* 80, no. 1 (2013): 29–59.
Pfister, Manfred. *The Theory and Analysis of Drama*. Translated by John Halliday. Cambridge: Cambridge University Press, 1991.
Pinciss, Gerald M. "*Dr. Faustus* and the Religious Controversy." In *Forbidden Matter: Religion in the Drama of Shakespeare and His Contemporaries*. Newark: University of Delaware Press, 2000.
Poole, Kristen. *Supernatural Environments in Shakespeare's England: Spaces of Demonism, Divinity, and Drama*. Cambridge: Cambridge University Press, 2011.

Postlewait, David. "Theatricality and Antitheatricality in Renaissance London." In *Theatricality*, edited by Tracy C. Davis and Thomas Postlewait, 90–126. Cambridge: Cambridge University Press, 2003.

Pound, Louise. "The English Ballads and the Church." *PMLA* 35, no. 2 (1920): 161–88.

Preiss, Richard. "Interiority." In Turner, *Early Modern Theatricality*, 47–70.

Prieto-Pablos, Juan. "What Art Thou Faustus? Self-Reference and Strategies of Identification in Marlowe's *Doctor Faustus*." *English Studies* 74, no. 1 (1993): 66–83.

Purkess, Diane. "Crammed with Distressful Bread? Bakers and the Poor in Early Modern England." In *Renaissance Food from Rabelais to Shakespeare: Culinary Readings and Culinary Histories*, edited by Joan Fitzpatrick, 11–23. Surrey: Ashgate, 2010.

Questier, Michael. *Catholicism and Community in Early Modern England: Politics, Aristocratic Patronage and Religion, c.1550–1640*. Cambridge: Cambridge University Press, 2006.

Rabkin, Norman. "Rabbits, Ducks, and *Henry V*." *Shakespeare Quarterly* 28, no. 3 (1977): 279–96.

Rancière, Jacques. *The Politics of Aesthetics*. Translated by Grabriel Rockhill. London: Bloomsbury, 2004.

Rasmussen, Eric. "Rehabilitating the A-Text of Marlowe's *Doctor Faustus*." *Studies in Bibliography* 46 (1993): 221–38.

———. *A Textual Companion to "Doctor Faustus."* Manchester: Manchester University Press, 1993.

Rastall, Richard. "Music in the Cycle." In *The Chester Mystery Cycle: Essays and Documents*, edited by R. M. Lumiansky and David Mills, 111–64. Chapel Hill: University of North Carolina Press, 1983.

Rayner, Alice. *Ghosts: Death's Double and the Phenomena of Theatre*. Minneapolis: University of Minnesota Press, 2006.

Rice, Nicole R., and Margaret Aziza Pappano. *The Civic Cycles: Artisan Drama and Identity in Premodern England*. Notre Dame, IN: University of Notre Dame Press, 2015.

Rogerson, Margaret. "Affective Piety: A 'Method' for Medieval Actors in the Chester Cycle." In *The Chester Cycle in Context, 1555–1575: Religion, Drama, and the Impact of Change*, edited by Jessica Dell, David Klausner, and Helen Ostovich, 93–107. Surrey: Ashgate, 2012.

Rosendale, Timothy. *Liturgy and Literature in the Making of Protestant England*. Cambridge: Cambridge University Press, 2007.

———. "Sacral and Sacramental Kingship in Shakespeare's Lancastrian Tetralogy." In *Shakespeare and the Culture of Christianity in Early*

Modern England, edited by Dennis Taylor and David N. Beauregard, 121–40. New York: Fordham University Press, 2004.

Rubin, Miri. *Corpus Christi: The Eucharist in Late Medieval Culture*. Cambridge: Cambridge University Press, 1991.

Salter, F. M. "The Banns of the Chester Plays [pt. 1]." *Review of English Studies* 16, no. 61 (1940): 1–17.

———. "The Banns of the Chester Plays [pt. 2]." *Review of English Studies* 16, no. 62 (1940): 137–48.

Sams, Eric. *The Real Shakespeare: Retrieving the Early Years, 1564–1594*. New Haven, CT: Yale University Press, 1997.

Schalkwyk, David. *Speech and Performance in Shakespeare's Sonnets and Plays*. Cambridge: Cambridge University Press, 2002.

Scherb, Victor. *Staging Faith: East Anglian Drama in the Later Middle Ages*. Madison, WI: Fairleigh Dickinson University Press, 2001.

Schreyer, Kurt A. *Shakespeare's Medieval Craft: Remnants of the Mysteries on the London Stage*. Ithaca, NY: Cornell University Press, 2014.

Schwartz, Regina. *Sacramental Poetics: When God Left the World*. Stanford, CA: Stanford University Press, 2008.

Sedgwick, Eve Kosofsky. *Touching Feeling: Affect, Pedagogy, Performativity*. Durham, NC: Duke University Press, 2003.

Seel, Martin. *Aesthetics of Appearance*. Translated by John Farrell. Stanford, CA: Stanford University Press, 2005.

Seigworth, Gregory, and Melissa Gregg. "An Inventory of Shimmers." In *The Affect Theory Reader*, edited by Melissa Gregg and Gregory Seigworth, 1–27. Durham, NC: Duke University Press, 2010.

Shami, Jeanne. *John Donne and Conformity in Crisis in the Late Jacobean Pulpit*. Cambridge: Cambridge University Press, 2003.

Shepherd, Simon. *Marlowe and the Politics of Elizabethan Theatre*. New York: St. Martin's, 1986.

Shuger, Debora. *Censorship and Cultural Sensibility: The Regulation of Language in Tudor-Stuart England*. Philadelphia: University of Pennsylvania Press, 2006.

Siemon, James R. *Shakespearean Iconoclasm*. Berkeley: University of California Press, 1985.

Sinfield, Alan, with John Dollimore. "History and Ideology, Masculinity and Miscegenation." In *Faultlines: Cultural Materialism and the Politics of Dissident Reading*, 109–42. Berkeley: University of California Press, 1992.

Slights, Camille Wells. "The Conscience of the King: *Henry V* and the Reformed Conscience." *Philological Quarterly* 80, no. 1 (2001): 37–55.

Slights, William W. E. "'Maid' and 'Man' in *Twelfth Night*." *Journal of English and Germanic Philology* 80, no. 3 (1981): 327–48.

Smith, Bruce R. *The Acoustic World of Early Modern England: Attending to the O-Factor*. Chicago: University of Chicago Press, 1999.

———. "Afterword: Ballad Futures." In *Ballads and Broadsides in Britain, 1500–1800*, edited by Patricia Fumerton and Anita Guerrini, 317–23. Burlington, VT: Ashgate, 2010.

———. *Phenomenal Shakespeare*. Oxford: Wiley-Blackwell, 2010.

———. "Premodern Sexualities." *PMLA* 115, no. 3 (2000): 318–29.

———. "Putting the 'Ball' Back in Ballads." *Huntington Library Quarterly* 79, no. 2 (2016): 323–38.

———. "Shakespeare's Residuals: The Circulation of Ballads in Cultural Memory." In *Shakespeare and Elizabethan Popular Culture*, edited by Stuart Gillespie and Neil Rhodes, 193–218. London: Arden Shakespeare, 2006.

———. "Sounding Shakespeare's London." Paper presented at "Urbanmusics" Conference, Barcelona, September 24–26, 2015.

Smith, Matthew J. "Describing the Sense of Confession in *Hamlet*." In *The Return of Theory in Early Modern English Studies*, vol. 2, edited by Paul Cefalu, Gary Kuchar, and Bryan Reynolds, 165–84. Basingstoke: Palgrave Macmillan, 2014.

———. "The Disincarnate Text: Ritual Poetics in Herbert, Paul, Williams, and Levinas." *Christianity and Literature* 66, no. 3 (June 2017): 363–84.

———. "Meeting John Donne: The Virtual Paul's Cross Project." *Spenser Review* 44, no. 2 (Fall 2014). www.english.cam.ac.uk/spenseronline/review/volume-44/442/digital-projects/meeting-john-donne-the-virtual-pauls-cross-project/.

———. "W/Sincerity, Part 1: The Drama of the Will from Augustine to Milton." *Christianity and Literature* 67, no. 1 (2017): 8–33.

Smith, Matthew J., and Julia Reinhard Lupton. "Ballads+: The Tragedy of *Romeo and Juliet* and Its Afterpiece Jig." In Fumerton, *Ballads and Performance*.

Smuts, Malcolm R. "Public Ceremony and Royal Charisma: The English Royal Entry in London, 1485–1642." In *The First Modern Society: Essays in English History in Honour of Lawrence Stone*, edited by A. L. Beier and David Cannadine, 65–93. Cambridge: Cambridge University Press, 1989.

Sofer, Andrew. "How to Do Things with Demons: Conjuring Performatives in *Doctor Faustus*." *Theatre Journal* 61, no. 1 (2009): 1–21.

Sokolowski, Robert. *Introduction to Phenomenology*. Cambridge: Cambridge University Press, 2000.
Sourvinou-Inwood, Christiane. *Tragedy and Athenian Religion*. Lanham, MD: Lexington, 2003.
Spufford, Margaret. *Small Books and Pleasant Histories: Popular Fiction and Its Readership in Seventeenth-Century England*. Cambridge: Cambridge University Press, 1985.
States, Bert O. "The Phenomenological Attitude." In *Critical Theory and Performance*, edited by Janelle G. Reinelt and Joseph R. Roach, 369–79. Ann Arbor: University of Michigan Press, 1992.
Stern, Tiffany. *Documents of Performance in Early Modern England*. Cambridge: Cambridge University Press, 2009.
———. *Making Shakespeare: From Stage to Page*. London: Routledge, 2004.
Sterrett, Joseph. *The Unheard Prayer: Religious Toleration in Shakespeare's Drama*. Leiden: Brill, 2002.
Strong, Sir Roy. "The Popular Celebration of the Accession Day of Queen Elizabeth I." *Journal of the Warburg and Courtauld Institutes* 21, no. 1 (1958): 86–103.
Sullivan, Ceri. "The Art of Listening in the Seventeenth Century." *Modern Philology* 104, no. 1 (2006): 34–71.
Swift, Daniel. *Shakespeare's Common Prayers: The Book of Common Prayer in the Elizabethan Age*. Oxford: Oxford University Press, 2012.
Targoff, Ramie. *Common Prayer: The Language of Public Devotion in Early Modern England*. Chicago: University of Chicago Press, 2001.
Taylor, Charles. *A Secular Age*. Cambridge, MA: Harvard University Press, 2009.
Taylor, Jane. "'Why Do You Tear Me from Myself?': Torture, Truth, and the Arts of the Counter-Reformation." In *The Rhetoric of Sincerity*, edited by Ernst Van Alphen, Mieke Bal, and Carel Smith, 19–43. Stanford, CA: Stanford University Press, 2009.
Trudell, Scott. "Occasion." In Turner, *Early Modern Theatricality*, 230–49.
Turner, Henry, ed. *Early Modern Theatricality*. Oxford: Oxford University Press, 2013.
———. *The English Renaissance Stage: Geometry, Poetics, and the Practical Spatial Arts, 1580–1630*. Oxford: Oxford University Press, 2006.
———. "Generalization." In *Early Modern Theatricality*, 1–23.
Waldron, Jennifer. *Reformations of the Body: Idolatry, Sacrifice, and Early Modern Theater*. New York: Palgrave Macmillan, 2013.

Wall, John N. "'That Holy Roome': John Donne and the Conduct of Worship at St. Paul's Cathedral." In *Renaissance Papers 2005*, edited by Christopher Cobb and M. Thomas Hester, 61–84. Rochester, NY: Camden House, 2005.

———. *The Virtual Paul's Cross Project*. North Carolina State University. http://vpcp.chass.ncsu.edu.

Waller, Gary. "Ralegh's 'As You Came from the Holy Land' and the Rival Virgin Queens of Late Sixteenth-Century England." In *Literary and Visual Ralegh*, edited by Christopher M. Armitage, 284–301. Manchester: Manchester University Press, 2013.

———. *Walsingham and the English Imagination*. London: Routledge, 2011.

Walsham, Alexandra. *Church Papists: Catholicism, Conformity, and Confessional Polemic in Early Modern England*. Woodbridge: Boydell, 1993.

Walters, Barbara, Vincent Corrigan, and Peter Ricketts, eds. *The Feast of Corpus Christi*. University Park: Pennsylvania State University Press, 2006.

Watt, Tessa. *Cheap Print and Popular Piety, 1550–1640*. Cambridge: Cambridge University Press, 1991.

Weber, Samuel. *Theatricality as Medium*. New York: Fordham University Press, 2004.

Weimann, Robert. *Shakespeare and the Popular Tradition in the Theater: Studies in the Social Dimension of Dramatic Form and Function*. Edited by Robert Schwartz. Baltimore: Johns Hopkins University Press, 1978.

Weimann, Robert, and Douglas Bruster. *Shakespeare and the Power of Performance: Stage and Page in the Elizabethan Theatre*. Cambridge: Cambridge University Press, 2010.

West, William N. "Intertheatricality." In Turner, *Early Modern Theatricality*, 151–72.

———. "When Is the Jig Up—And What Is It Up To?" In *Locating the Queen's Men, 1583–1603: Material Practices and Conditions of Playing*, edited by Helen Ostovich, Holger Schott Syme, and Andrew Griffin, 201–16. Burlington, VT: Ashgate, 2009.

White, Paul Whitfield. "Theater and Religious Culture." In *A New History of Early English Drama*, edited by John D. Cox and David Scott Kastan, 133–51. New York: Columbia University Press, 1997.

———. *Theatre and Reformation: Protestantism, Patronage, and Playing in Tudor England*. Cambridge: Cambridge University Press, 1993.

Wickham, Glynne. *Early English Stages, 1300 to 1600.* Vol. 3. *Plays and Their Makers to 1576.* London: Routledge and Kegan Paul, 1981.

———. "'*Exeunt to the Cave*': Notes on the Staging of Marlowe's Plays." *Tulane Drama Review* 8, no. 4 (1964): 184–94.

Wiles, David. *Shakespeare's Clown: Actor and Text in the Elizabethan Playhouse.* Cambridge: Cambridge University Press, 1987.

Williamson, Elizabeth. *The Materiality of Religion in Early Modern English Drama.* Burlington, VT: Ashgate, 2009.

Witmore, Michael. "Eventuality." In Turner, *Early Modern Theatricality*, 386–401.

———. *Shakespearean Metaphysics.* London: Continuum, 2008.

Womersley, David. *Divinity and State.* Oxford: Oxford University Press, 2010.

Würzbach, Natascha. *The Rise of the English Street Ballad, 1550–1650.* Cambridge: Cambridge University Press, 1990.

Yates, Julian. *Error, Misuse, Failure: Object Lessons from the English Renaissance.* Minneapolis: University of Minnesota Press, 2003.

Yearling, Rebecca. "John Marston's *What You Will* and the War of the Theaters." *Ben Jonson Journal* 13, no. 1 (2006): 109–23.

———. "*What You Will*: A Response to James Bednarz." *Ben Jonson Journal* 17, no. 2 (2010): 308–13.

Zahavi, Dan. *Husserl's Phenomenology.* Stanford, CA: Stanford University Press, 2003.

Zeeveld, W. Gordon. *The Temper of Shakespeare's Thought.* New Haven, CT: Yale University Press, 1974.

Zysk, Jay. "In the Name of the Father: Revenge and Unsacramental Death in *Hamlet.*" *Christianity and Literature* 66, no. 3 (2017): 422–43.

———. *Shadow and Substance: Eucharistic Controversy and English Drama across the Reformation Divide.* Notre Dame, IN: University of Notre Dame Press, 2017.

INDEX

absorption, in spectacle, 121
Accession Day, 141
acoustics, 161, 162, 164
Act of Parliament of 1606, 291
Act of Uniformity, 81
Aeschylus, 318
affect, 124
Alleyn, Edward, 264, 267, 268, 278
altar, 85
Altman, Joel, 337n61
anamorphism, 22, 27, 36, 118, 137
  in sermons, 179
angels, 109
antitheatricalism, 4, 32, 47, 54,
  60–61
  in medieval drama, 11
Apology for Actors, An
  (Heywood), 148
apprentices, early modern, 282
Arendt, Hannah, 86
Aristotle, 33
Arma Christi, 256
Armine, Robert, 26
art-of-hearing treatises, 172–82, 237
Askew, Anne, 205
Atkinson, David, 197–98, 208–9
Attic theater, 317
Attwell, George, 311
Aubrey, John, 315
audience interaction, 84, 119
  in ballads, 206, 223, 225, 226,
    235–52

imitation, 93
response to stage devils, 262
audience reception, 40
  and *Doctor Faustus*, 275
  and playhouse architecture, 301
Augustine, 49, 112
  Confessions, 67
Austin, J. L., 36, 40, 85, 227
authenticity, 48, 325n36
  in ballads, 203, 206, 215, 247, 252
  the Faustus story, 275
  Henry V, 121–22, 127–28, 137,
    151
  and religion, 201–3
  Twelfth Night, 24, 28–29

Baldwin, William, 194
ballad authors, 202
  Richard Stanyhurst, 212
ballad broadside design, 217–19,
  223–26, 248
ballad conventions, 209–35
ballad genre
  Christmas ballads, 211
  deathbed ballads, 201, 229
  martyr ballads, 201, 204–6
  prophecy ballads, 236
ballad performance, 196, 204
  cry, 231
  distractions, 239
  environment, 228, 235, 239, 245,
    246

376

Index

Faustus ballads, 272
　reflecting broadside design, 223
　style, 217
ballad reception, 223
ballads, 5, 9
　anticeremonialism, 193
　appearing in plays, 32
　as audience reception, 7, 207
　the Bible, 212
　and the body, 251
　broadside distribution, 194
　definitions, 196
　dialogue, 214
　in *Doctor Faustus*, 273
　Faustus-affiliated ballads, 279–84
　Faustus play ballads, 269, 273–76, 280, 345–46
　folk tradition, 197
　godly ballad criticism, 194
　godly ballad printing, 199, 202–3
　jig ballads, 349
　marginalia, 218
　memory, 232
　morality, 201
　multimedia, 207
　orality, 198
　play ballads, 280, 345n26
　before plays, 32
　and popular piety in print, 202
　popular religion, 342n49
　production, 198
　recycling, 201
　rhyme, 210
　and sermons, 193
　superficial religion, 193
　theme of charity, 242
　theme of patience, 240, 241–42
　topicality, 281

ballads cited
　"Against Filthy Writing and Such Delighting," 245
　"The Angel Gabriel, his Salutation to the Virgin Mary," 211
　"A Ballad of Anne Askew," 204–6
　"A Commendation of Musicke," 245–46
　"[The] complaint and lamentation of Mistresse Arden of [Fev]ersham in Kent," 347
　"The Distressed Pilgrim," 240–42
　"The Dying Tears of a Penitent Sinner," 228–34
　"Frauncis new Jigge," 311–20
　"Great Brittains Arlarm," 236–38
　"The Great Tribunal," 243
　"The Heartie Confession of a Christian," 214–23
　"The Judgment of God shewed upon one John Faustus," 269–73, 276–77, 282–83
　"The Just Judgment of GOD shew'd upon Dr. John Faustus," 273, 277–78
　"Lilly Lash't with his own ROD," 279–81
　"A most Excellent Ballad of Ioseph the Carpenter," 209–10
　"A New Yeres Gyft, intituled, A Playne Pathway to Perfect Rest," 248
　"A New Yeres Gyft, Intituled, A Christal Glas," 248–49
　"The Recantation of a Penitent Proteus Or the Changeling," 280
　"Some Fyne Gloues," 248–51

ballads cited (*cont.*)
  "A Song of Syon of the Beauty of Bethell," 223
  "The Story of David and Berseba," 200–201
  "Titus Andronicus Complaint," 275
  "The Tragedy of Doctor *Lambe*," 282–83
  "A Wonderful Prophecy," 243–44
  "Youths Warning-peice," 281
ballad singers, 206, 240
  popular reputation, 194
  poverty, 233
ballad speakers, 276–77
ballad tunes, 200
  "Aim Not Too High," 236, 280
  "Fortune my Foe," 201, 236, 270, 280
  recycling, 243, 315
  "the tune of Bugle Boe," 314
  "the tune of Doctor Faustus," 270–73, 276, 279, 280, 284
  "the tune of goe from my window," 314
  "the tune of the Jewish dance," 314
  "the tune of Walsingham," 314
ballad woodcuts, 229
  Faustus ballad, 270–73, 282
  recycling, 243, 270
banns of the Chester Whitsun cycle, 58–62, 71, 81, 93, 97, 105
baptism, 46
Barber, C. L., 26–27
Barish, Jonas, 194
Bartholomew Fair, 206–7
Battle of Agincourt, 139, 336n44
bear-baiting, 119

Beaumont, Francis, 314
Beckwith, Sarah, 43, 55, 68, 95, 330n30
bed trick, 317
Belsavage, the, 283, 285, 294, 344n12
benediction, 112
Benson, George, 158
Berger, Peter, 65
Bevington, David, 287
Bible, the
  Geneva, 20, 219
  Gospel of John, 97
  Gospel of Matthew, 16, 100
  the Great Bible, 20, 16
  marginalia, 169
  vernacular, 20–21, 61–62
  vernacular performance, 103–5
Birde, William, 267, 286
Bishop, T. G., 102
Blackfriars, the, 301
Boleyn, Anne, 20, 143
Book of Common Prayer, 81, 149, 219
  marginalia, 16
Bossy, John, 330n25
boy bishop, 8, 14–17, 36, 185
  Feast of the Holy Innocents, 14–15
  liturgy, 14–15
  prayer, 16
  sermons, 15
  theatre, 15
Brathwaite, John, 177
Breviary of Chester History (Rogers), 62
Brice, Thomas, 245
Brooks, Cleanth, 264, 306
Butler, Judith, 37
Byrd, William, 149, 314

Calvin, John, 43
Candlemas, 24
Case, John, 149
Catholicism, 133
Cavendish, William, 144
censorship, 291–92
ceremony
  affect, 130
  anticeremonialism at St. Paul's, 159
  audience perception, 135
  of the body, 138
  Catholic, 19
  ceremonialism, 8
  ceremonialism controversy, 45, 115
  distance, 122, 144
  goddess, 141
  Mass of St. Gregory, 255
  of monarchy, 115
  religious devotion, 150, 152
Chambers, E. K., 266, 344n12
Chapman, Alison, 337n78, 349n10
Chapman, George, 140
character exteriority, 127
character interiority, 121, 124, 132
  in Faustus stories, 266, 294–95
character phenomenon, 123, 126, 144
charity, 93
Charles I, 279
Chester Whitsun cycle, 253
  The Annunciation and the Nativity, 56, 75
  The Ascension, 73
  economics, 63
  Emmaus, 96
  The Fall of Lucifer, 8, 34, 56, 103–13
  The Harrowing of Hell, 96

The Healing of the Blind Man, 97, 110
The Last Judgement, 103
The Last Supper, 8, 71, 74–94
The Resurrection, 96, 100
suppression of, 54–55
Chettle, Henry, 193
children, 17, 21, 26
choristers, 5
Christ Church, 161
Christmas season, 15, 18, 24, 166
church architecture, 82
church calendar, 19, 147, 337n77
church literacy, 170–71
ciphers, 114–17, 120
Clark, Stuart, 266
Clegg, Roger, 309
Clopper, Lawrence, 4, 54, 60
clown, 7, 26, 28, 318, 349n24
cockpits, 119
Coleman, David, 94
commercial theater, 29, 57, 261
communion, preparation for, 173
confession, 43, 49, 215, 219
Connor, Steven, 182
conversion, 9, 125
Cooper, Helen, 44, 257
copperplate map (1559), 161, 163
co-presence, 94
Corbett, Richard, 315
Corpus Christi Mass, 55, 90–94, 105
  Sequence, 90–92
coup de théâtre, 30, 40, 41, 69, 120, 157, 233
  in the *Mass of St. Gregory*, 255
Cox, John, 42, 266, 345n24
craft guilds, 52, 63, 70, 93, 108, 329n1
  Bakers, the, 93

craft guilds (*cont.*)
  Glovers, the, 97
  Tanners, the, 104, 107
Craig, John, 180
Crane, Mary, 34, 296
cross-dressing, 15, 27–28
Croxton *Play of the Sacrament*, 134
Cummings, Brian, 47, 132
Curran, Kevin, 325n50
Curtain, the, 119, 348n1
cycle theater, suppression of, 53–54, 329n11

da Vinci, Leonardo, 86
Dawson, Anthony, 327n74
Defoe, Daniel, 103
De Grazia, Margreta, 132
Dekker, Thomas, 163, 309
Derrida, Jacques, 37, 175
Descartes, Rene, 46
devils
  audience response, 259
  in *Doctor Faustus* print history, 284
  in *The Fall of Lucifer*, 112
  in Faustus ballads, 283–84
  laughter, 261
  in the play audience, 263
  stage devils in *Doctor Faustus*, 10, 293
  as utility characters, 262
Diehl, Huston, 42
disguise, 121–23
disincarnation, 55, 101, 113, 186
Doctor Faustus
  comic elements, 290
  cultural reception, 268–69, 278–84
  cycle drama, 256

genre, 295
reception, 285–93
religion, 299, 303–5
religion and textual revision, 288
stage devils and textual history, 293–94
textual history, 284–93, 347
Dollimore, Jonathan, 327n74
Donne, John, 33, 41
  art of hearing, 172, 176
  Christmas sermon of 1628, 166, 183
  Devotions, 191
  human body, 191
  1640 sermon folio, 155
doubt, 74
  in *Doctor Faustus*, 303
  Mary and Martha, 96, 99–102
  self-doubt, 110
dramatic irony, 129
Dryden, John, 314
Duchess of Newcastle, 217
Dürer, Albrecht, 86–87, 298

Earle, Bishop John, 160
Earl of Nottingham's Men, 285
echo, 175–76
Edward VI, 18, 147
Egerton, Stephen, 181–82
ekphrasis, 75
elevation of the host, 80, 83, 84, 255–57
Elizabeth I, 38, 141
  coronation of, 8, 18–23, 143–49
  "The Uniting of the Two Houses of Lancaster and York," 20, 26
Elkins, James, 247
emotions, 2
enchantment, 43

epiplexis, 156
Erasmus, 15
ethnicity, 279–80
Eucharist, 55
   impersonation of, 73
   liturgy, 188
   semiotics of, 79
   See also sacrament
Euripides, 318
evil, origin of, 103

face-to-face, 86
"Fairies' Farewell, The" (Corbett), 315
faith, 2
   epistemology of, 45
   godly ballads, 252
   open show, 102
   open speech, 99–100
   perception, 65
   as revelation, 74
   sermon belief, 156, 166, 178, 182–83
   in theatre, 57, 92
Feast of Corpus Christi, 8, 20, 58
   illustrations, 87–88
   mass, 78
   procession, 75
   social identity, 62–63
Feast of Ss. Crispin and Crispian, 141–42, 145
Feast of St. John the Evangelist, 15
Feast of St. Stephen, 15
Feast of the Circumcision, 15
Feast of the Epiphany, 24
Feral, Josette, 326n61
festival, 3
   in *Doctor Faustus*, 261
   and drama, 72
   dual intentionality, 308

saturnalia, 27
Whitsuntide, 107
Fischer-Lichte, Erika, 30, 70, 125, 232
Fish, Stanley, 37, 264
Fletcher, John, 314
food, 76–77, 81–84
fools, 131
fortune, 318
Fortune, the, 282, 301, 346n43, 348n1
Foucault, Michel, 127
Fowler, Richard, 278, 346n43
Foxe, John, 204
Fried, Michael, 87
Fumerton, Patricia, 198, 341n12

Gardiner, Stephen, 149
Gerould, Gordon Hall, 197
Gibson, Gail McMurray, 95
Gipkyn, John, 167
Globe, the, 114, 119, 335n14, 348n1
God's Word
   accidents and substance, 175
   sermon culture, 158
   in sermon environments, 173
   the Word preached, 158, 187
Goodman, Christopher, 60
Gosson, Stephen, 116, 148
Grand Remonstrance, 223
"Great Brittains Arlarm," 236
Green, Ian, 196, 202, 212
Greenblatt, Stephen, 185, 265, 269, 327n74, 339–40n40
Greenfield, Jon, 298
Gregory, Brad, 65, 330n36
Grindal, Archbishop Edmund, 60
Groves, Beatrice, 3, 42, 44, 95
Guibbory, Achsah, 334n6

Gunpowder Plot, 171
Gurr, Andrew, 298

Hall, David, 50
Hardin, Richard, 139
Hardison, O. B., Jr., 319, 349n23
Harris, Jonathan Gil, 84
Hay, Andrew, 339n20
hell, 266
Henry VIII, 147
Henslowe, Philip, 114, 254, 267
Henslowe's Diary, 285
heretics, 46, 256
Historie of the damnable life, and deserved death of Doctor Iohn Faustus, The, 268
Holbein, Hans, 20
Holinshed, Raphael, 146
Holmes II, Randle, 59
Hooker, Richard, 46, 143, 152, 170
hospitality, 78, 84, 93
Howard, Jean, 327n75
hubris, 262
human body, 2–3
Hunt, Alice, 323n9
Hunt, Maurice, 126, 139
Husserl, Edmund, 35, 40, 82
  The Idea of Phenomenology, 64
hyperlocality, 299

idolatry, 142
imaginative variance, 82
immanence, 9, 39, 64–66, 80
  of God, 107
  in preaching, 178
  and transcendence, 98
impersonating God, 104
intersubjectivity, 117, 128–29, 137
intertheatricality, 14
  ballads, 214, 219, 226
  in *Doctor Faustus*, 254, 267
  Faustus ballads, 277
  in festival, 79
  intratheatricality, 5
  of jigs, 311
  performative, 39
  poetic, 28
  religious and political, 154
  in *Twelfth Night*, 23
Iscariot, Judas, 83, 88

Jackson, Ken, 6
Jackson, MacD. P., 345n31, 347n47
Jackson, Michael, 33
James, Mervyn, 62
James I, coronation of, 324n19
jigs, 4, 7, 10
  comedy, 319
  criticism of, 309
  definitions, 309–10
  festival pastimes, 311
  jig ballads, 214
  multimedia, 320
  music, 32
  postlude, 26
  suppression, 348n1
  trans-Reformational, 309
Johnson, Kimberly, 328n80, 340n42
Johnston, Alexandra, 58
Jonson, Ben, 16, 324n29
Juliana of Liège, 58

Kahn, Victoria, 192, 340n1
Kastan, David Scott, 43
Kearney, James, 325n50
Kemp, Will, 309
Knapp, Jeffrey, 5, 126
Knox, John, 60
Kolve, V. A., 261

Index

labor
  of ballads, 208
  of theater, 73, 80, 84
Lake, Peter, 341n21
Lambe, John, 276
"A Lament for Walsingham,"
  (Philip, the Earl of Arundel),
  315
Last Supper, the, 86–87
Lee, John, 179–80
Lee, Richard, 279
Lehnhof, Kent, 333n94
Lent, 97
Lerud, Theodore, 95, 331n48
Levin, Harry, 263–64
Levinas, Emmanuel, 101
licentia, 105–6
Lilly, William, 276, 279
Lin, Erika, 262, 337n77
liturgical furniture, 86
  as stage props, 101
liturgy, 81
  and the *Mass of St. Gregory*,
  255
lived religion, 50, 178, 195, 206,
  308
London fire of 1561, 159
Lonekin, Philonax, 159
Lord Admiral's Men, 285
Lord Chamberlain's Men, 24,
  309
Lord Strange's Men, 311
Löwith, Karl, 150
Lunney, Ruth, 257
Lupton, Julia Reinhard, 78, 86,
  325n50

Machiavelli, the figure of, 116
Manningham, John, 24, 38
Marcus, Leah, 350n25

Marion, Jean-Luc, 178
Marlowe, Christopher, 140
  Doctor Faustus, 10
  The Jew of Malta, 253
  Tamburlaine the Great, 309
Marsh, Christopher, 204, 243
Marston, John, 25, 38, 324n29
Mary I, 18, 20
Mary Magdalene, 100–102
Mason, Henry, 180
Mass books, 87
Massingberd, Francis, 15
Massinger, Philip, 310
  The Virgin Martyr, 253
Mass of St. Gregory, 255–57
Maundy Thursday, 78, 92
McCoy, Richard, 43, 323n9
Melton, John, 302
Merleau-Ponty, Maurice, 36, 119,
  151
Merlin, William, 87
Middle Temple, 24–25
Middleton, Thomas, 268, 285
Midsummer festival, 79
Mills, David, 63, 71, 88
Milton, John, 83
  Paradise Lost, 103
  Satan, 264
mimesis, 94
miracle, 3, 99
misrule, 15, 24, 318
monument, in theater, 127–28
morality drama, 19
More, Sir Thomas, 142
Morris, David, 136
Morton, Timothy, 175
Mulcaster, Richard, 18, 144
multistability, 30, 68, 84, 91, 94,
  125, 167, 320
  ballad speakers, 232, 240–41

multitemporality, 17, 53, 84, 150, 316
  godly ballads, 200
Murder in the Cathedral (Eliot), 306
music
  ambient, 32
  Chester Whitsun cycle, 104
  Elizabeth I's coronation procession, 20
  godly ballads, 200–201, 204, 243–45
  liturgy, 90, 104
  in plays, 32
  Romeo and Juliet, 32
  The Tempest, 32

Nashe, Thomas, 130
Newgate Market, 161
nostalgia
  Catholic nostalgia, 315
  jigs, 311
  for medieval theater, 257, 261

O'Connell, Michael, 42
Of the Laws of Ecclesiastical Polity (Hooker), 47
Ong, Walter, 82, 181
original sin, 108
Ornstein, Robert, 259, 265
Orsi, Robert, 50, 178, 195, 206

Parker, John, 257
Parrat, Sir John, 20–21
passion narrative, 93, 96, 256
Passover, 89, 92
pathos, 262
Paul's Cross, 161, 167, 244
Paul's Walk, 160–61, 179
Pavey, Salathiel, 16

Pembroke's Men, 285
Pepys, Samuel, 194
perception, in liturgy, 92
performance culture, 118, 120, 157, 245, 269
performativity
  audience interaction, 306
  audience response, 16, 51
  ballads, 226–27, 230–31
  categorical intentions, 119–20
  ceremony, 139
  cultural studies, 37
  in the demonstrative, 153
  gender, 37
  imitation in ballads, 209–10, 214, 218
  intentional, 37
  objects, 85, 92
  ordinary speech, 36–37
  repetition, 156, 175, 218
  ritual, 70
  as self-consciousness, 74
  sermons, 185
  social, 62
  of theater, 38, 125, 296
  theatrical divesting, 11, 14, 17, 22–23, 27–29, 75–76, 121, 146
  visual art, 257
Perkins, William, 45, 170
Pfister, Manfred, 326n57
phenomenology
  of character, 30, 121–22
  givenness, 110–11
  in godly ballads, 248
  of hearing, 177
  historical phenomenology, 6–7, 34, 325–26
  imaginative variance, 136
  reflection, 35, 56
  of religion, 42, 86, 207

of the scene, 256
of theatre, 6
pilgrimage, 316
plain speech, 23, 99, 170
Poole, Kristen, 49, 266
Postlewait, David, 32
Pound, Louise, 203
prayer, 4
   in ballads, 230–31, 238–39
   Henry V, 132
Preiss, Richard, 132
present participle, 137
Prince Charles' Men, 286
"proclamacion" (William Newhall), 63
profanity, 288, 291
prophecy, 96, 107, 171, 200
props, 256
   Doctor Faustus, 289, 292, 303
   Faustus ballads, 273
Protestantism
   hearing and seeing, 177–79
   and spectacle, 267
Protestant nationalism, 291, 346n46
Prynne, William, 115, 116, 268, 285
Puritanism, 26, 32, 47, 177

Queen's Majesty's Passage, The (Mulcaster), 20–21
Queen's Men, the, 311

Rainolds, William, 142
Raleigh, Sir Walter, 314
Rancière, Jacques, 67–68, 151
Rasmussen, Eric, 287
Rastall, Richard, 333n102
Rayner, Alice, 140
real presence, 68, 82, 126, 158
   in ballads, 234

sermons, 183
See also sacrament
reception of *Doctor Faustus*, 254
recognition, 48, 96, 257, 304
Red Bull, the, 348n1
Reformation, 2
   aesthetics, 67
   anticeremonialism, 115
   Catholic and Protestant, 19
   northern reform, 60
   rise of secularism, 65
   sacraments, 44
   the senses, 125
   sola fide, 133
   of worship, 160
religion
   ballad music, 244
   Catholicism, 71
   conventional religion, 202–3
   critical turn to, 42
   disappearance of God, 56–57, 108–11, 257
   in Faustus-affiliated ballads, 283–84
   and the human body, 5, 17, 61–64, 184
   as imitation, 226
   materialism, 42, 82
   materiality of, 5
   media of devotion, 31, 67
   nostalgia, 23, 31, 118, 150, 218
   obfuscation of God, 100, 102
   popular improvisation, 195
   popular religion, 206
   popular theater, 254
   practice versus doctrine, 50
   and the senses, 6, 8, 43, 61–62, 82, 177
   sermon devotion, 172–74
   spectacle, 29

religion (*cont.*)
  stagecraft, 298
  street devotion, 10
  superstition, 59
  in theater, 96
  versus theater, 327n74
  the Word, 23
  word and image, 12, 62
religious tolerance, 126
ritual, 9
  of godly ballads, 242
  jigs, 318
  of theater, 86, 118–22, 186
ritual poetics, 101
Rogers, William, 281
Rogerson, Margaret, 54–55
Root and Branch petition, 193
Rose, the, 254, 283, 285, 294
  architecture, 297–98, 300–301
  structure, 261
Rosendale, Timothy, 4
Rowley, Samuel, 267, 286
Rubin, Miri, 330n39

sacrament, 8
  aesthetics, 68–71, 185
  drama, 43–44, 55
  imagery in the St. Crispin's Day
    speech, 139–40
  Mass of St. Gregory, 255
  as performative, 44
  ritual, 69
  sacramental drama, 94–95
  sermons, 187
  in theater, 86, 92
  theology, 45–47
Samson Agonistes, 306
Sarum Missal, 56, 81, 87
Schalkwyk, David, 47
Scherb, Victor, 95

Schreyer, Kurt, 84
Schwartz, Regina, 185
*Second Report of Dr. John Faustus,
  The*, 285
secularism, 3, 32, 51
  ballads, 192, 202–3
  and character interiority, 294–95,
    347–48
  and *Doctor Faustus*, 265–66
  sacraments, 95
  secularization theory, 65
Sedgwick, Eve Kosofsky, 37, 124
Seel, Martin, 81
sententiae, 20
sermons, 5, 7
  accidents and substance, 171,
    185–86
  acoustical space, 161–62
  ciphers, 115
  distractions, 159, 179–81
  harkening, 184
  hearing, 169
  liturgy, 173
  note-taking, 176
  politics, 176
  repetition, 173
  rhetoric, 174
  theater, 174
  theatricality, 157, 158–66
  vision, 181–82
  the Word, 40
Serres, Michel, 84
Shakespeare, 4
  medieval, 3
  props, 84–85
  religion, 43
Shakespeare's plays
  Hamlet, 47–48, 115, 314
  1 Henry IV, 147
  2 Henry IV, 135

Henry V, 9, 40, 114–54, 175
Julius Caesar, 130
King Lear, 129
Pericles, 241–42
Richard III, 320
Romeo and Juliet, 320
Troilus and Cressida, 131
Twelfth Night, 8, 23–31, 121, 316
Winter's Tale, The, 97, 253
Shuger, Debora, 42
skepticism, 266
Smith, Bruce, 117, 160, 204, 333n90
Smuts, Malcolm, 143
Sofer, Andrew, 345n24
soliloquy, 47
　in *Doctor Faustus*, 260, 305
　Henry V, 123, 128, 131–34
　theatricality, 131–33
Sourvinou-Inwood, Christiane, 349n20
spiritual despair, 339–40n40
Spufford, Margaret, 237
stage furniture, 85, 104, 119, 292
stage props, 121–24
　table as altar, 85–86, 90
St. Crispin's Day speech (*Henry V*), 138–53
Sternhold, Thomas, 194
stichomythia, 260
States, Bert, 65, 121, 126
St. Nicholas, 15
　Feast of, 323
St. Paul, 187
St. Paul's Cathedral, 9, 157, 236, 260
　architecture, 159
　liturgy 159–60
Strong, Roy, 142

Stubs, John, 16
Sullivan, Ceri, 339n16
Swan, the, 301

Targoff, Ramie, 42
Tarlton, Richard, 309
Taylor, Charles, 65
technology, 73, 98
　in *Doctor Faustus*, 264
Theatre in Shoreditch, 268, 285, 294
theatrical environment, 122
theatricality, 2, 4–6, 308
　ambience, 179
　artificiality, 106
　distraction, 256, 261
　early modern, 31–41
　environment, 9, 246, 259
　event, 31–32, 39
　exposure of, 28, 68–69, 185, 208, 252, 253
　givenness, 62–66
　as moral attitude, 283
　occasion, 30, 38–39, 58, 151
　place, 295
　of the sensational, 253
　the senses, 76
　sermons, 179
　spectacle, 62, 64, 99, 302
　theatricality and representation, 23, 34–36, 62, 70, 112, 262
　of thought, 48
things indifferent, in religion, 168–69
Thomas Aquinas, 58, 90, 186
Tower of Babel, the, 163
tragedy, 92, 263–64
trans-Reformational, 11–12, 41–42, 47, 308–10
　and ceremonialism, 152

trans-Reformational (*cont.*)
  in the Chester Whitsun cycle, 67–70
  in godly ballads, 199
  in *Henry V*, 117, 152–54
  iconoclasm, 60
  in jigs, 317
  perception, 42
  in *Twelfth Night*, 29
transubstantiation, 43, 56, 83
"tretise of miraclis pleyinge, A" 54, 61–62
Trudell, Scott, 151
trust, 21–22
Turner, Henry, 33, 297
Twelfth Night festival, 18
typology, 91, 96, 107

Vaughan, William, 278, 304
vernacular theatre, 61
vice, 26, 317
  pageant of, 258
visuality, 40, 56, 92, 101
  in ballads, 208
  the Master of the Holy Kinship, 255
  and spectacle, 255

Wakefield plays, 57
Waldron, Jennifer, 42, 62
Walsingham, 314–15

Watt, Tessa, 199, 342n49
Weber, Samuel, 38, 80, 120
Weimann, Robert, 2–3, 261
West, William, 31, 225, 309
Westminster, 19
Whight, Nicholas, 244
White, Paul Whitfield, 42, 328n86
Whitehall Palace, 18, 19, 176
Whole Booke of Psalmes, The
  (Sternhold and Hopkins), 194
Wiles, David, 318
Williams, Gryffith, 172
Winstanley, William, 278
Witmore, Michael, 31, 64, 298
Womersley, David, 117, 335n31, 336n47
wonder, 91, 102, 120
words of institution, the, 72, 80–81, 88, 188
Wright, Robert, 142
Würzbach, Natascha, 196
Wycliffism, 54, 61

Yates, Julian, 73
York cycle, 55, 69
  The Fall of the Angels, 111
  Play of the Crucifixion, 68
Younge, Richard, 170

Zepper, Wilhelm, 172
Zysk, Jay, 328n95

MATTHEW J. SMITH is associate professor of English at Azusa Pacific University.

www.ingramcontent.com/pod-product-compliance
Lightning Source LLC
Chambersburg PA
CBHW051249300426
44114CB00011B/946